Women, Birth, and Death in Jewish Law and Practice

Brandeis Series on Jewish Women

Shulamit Reinharz, General Editor
Joyce Antler, Associate Editor
Sylvia Barack Fishman, Associate Editor

The Brandeis Series on Jewish Women is an innovative book series created by the Hadassah-Brandeis Institute. BSJW publishes a wide range of books by and about Jewish women in diverse contexts and time periods, of interest to scholars, and for the educated public. The series fills a major gap in Jewish learning by focusing on the lives of Jewish women and Jewish gender studies.

Marjorie Agosín, *Uncertain Travelers: Conversations with Jewish Women Immigrants to America,* 1999

Rahel R. Wasserfall, *Women and Water: Menstruation in Jewish Life and Law,* 1999

Susan Starr Sered, *What Makes Women Sick: Militarism, Maternity, and Modesty in Israeli Society,* 2000

Pamela S. Nadell and Jonathan D. Sarna, editors, *Women and American Judaism: Historical Perspectives,* 2001

Ludmilla Shtern, *Leaving Leningrad: The True Adventures of a Soviet Émigré,* 2001

Jael Silliman, *Jewish Portraits, Indian Frames: Women's Narratives from a Diaspora of Hope,* 2001

Judith R. Baskin, *Midrashic Women,* 2002

ChaeRan Y. Freeze, *Jewish Marriage and Divorce in Imperial Russia,* 2002

Mark A. Raider and Miriam B. Raider-Roth, *The Plough Woman: Records of the Pioneer Women of Palestine,* 2002

Elizabeth Wyner Mark, editor, *The Covenant of Circumcision: New Perspectives on an Ancient Jewish Rite,* 2003

Kalpana Misra and Melanie S. Rich, *Jewish Feminism in Israel: Some Contemporary Perspectives,* 2003

Farideh Goldin, *Wedding Song: Memories of an Iranian Jewish Woman,* 2003

Rochelle L. Millen, *Women, Birth, and Death in Jewish Law and Practice,* 2003

Women, Birth, and Death in Jewish Law and Practice

Rochelle L. Millen

Brandeis University Press
Published by University Press of New England
Hanover and London

Brandeis University Press

Published by University Press of New England, 37 Lafayette St., Lebanon, NH 03766

Printed in United States of America

5 4 3 2 1

Library of Congress Cataloging-in-Publication Data
Millen, Rochelle L., 1943–
Women, birth, and death in Jewish law and practice / Rochelle L. Millen.— 1st ed.
    p. cm.—(Brandeis series on Jewish women)
Includes bibliographical references and index.
ISBN 1–58465–340–X (cloth : alk. paper) — ISBN 1–58465–365–5 (pbk. : alk. paper)
1. Women in Judaism. 2. Jewish women—Religious life. 3. Women—Religious
aspects—Judaism. 4. Rabbinical literature—History and criticism. I. Title.
II. Series.
BM729.W6M53 2004
296.4'43—dc22   2003021958

This book was published with the generous support of the Lucius N. Littauer Foundation, Inc.

In Memory of

Betty Toni Egert Landesman
ביילא טויבא
Most Beloved Mother
1909–1982

Rosalie Ethel Landesman Katchen
שושנה רייזל
Dearly Beloved Sister
1946–2000

Elaine Beryl Davidson Nemzer, M.D.
חיה בתיה
Special Friend
1952–2000

שֶׁעֲשִׂיתָנִי אִשָּׁה וְלֹא אִישׁ

"... that you have made me a woman and not a man ..."

From a Siddur published in Italy, 1471. Courtesy of The Library of
The Jewish Theological Seminary of America.

Contents

Preface

In the late 1970s, my husband and I decided I would recite *hamotzi* (the bless-ing over bread) at the Shabbat table and that sometimes I would say *kiddush* (the blessing over wine) and he *hamotzi*. Our three teenaged children, students in a modern Orthodox day school, were unnerved; being different from one's peer is always a challenge, never more so than in adolescence. Why did they have to have parents, especially a mother, with such peculiar—indeed, even bi-zarre—ideas? "All right, *Ema* [mother]," they conceded, "but please don't do it when we have friends over!" Thus reluctant and restricted permission was granted. Our middle child, then a tenth grader, expressed her frustration in some detail late one Friday night as she and I sat at the dining-room table long after the others had sought Shabbat (Sabbath) serenity in studying the *parsha* (Torah portion of the week), reading, or crawling under the covers. "*Ema*," she declared after a lengthy and low-keyed discussion, "the problem is that you want to be a man!" "No," I countered, "I am a woman whose love of Shabbat and family need to be expressed through active participation." Indeed, it is that activism of both the intellectual and experiential that has led me on the journey that this volume articulates: an exploration of how Judaism perceives and deals with the rituals surrounding birth and death, particularly as they pertain to women's development.

Over the years, our children have traveled their own paths through the tradi-tion. Each, within the broad parameters tradition designates, has carved out a way leading toward where each needs to go—in terms of Jewish history, gen-eral sociology, and personal trajectory. Now they are parents, living the com-plex adventure of transmitting Judaism, with all its challenges, confusions, longings, and depths of meaning. They have come to understand my journey, which has influenced theirs. My recitations of *hamotzi* and *kiddush* are taken for granted, and are de rigueur for their children. They are familiar with prefer-ences which used to be regarded as quirks. Sensitized to sexist assumptions and language, they can sometimes predict my responses.

I am a Jew, a female, a professional—a tripartite identity that often seems not to cohere.[1] It is true that in the past religious women worked within delim-ited boundaries and nonetheless achieved extraordinary things—in practical as well as spiritual matters.[2] Today's women, however, seek wider ways and greater freedom. Fully cognizant of the ambiguity pervasive in all aspects of life, modern Jewish feminists desire a path that offers satisfaction while they search for an ever-greater coherence of the strands of identity. "The center can-not hold," the poet Yeats proclaimed; at times these aspects of the self can be in conflict: disparate, disconnected, discontinuous. But Judaism as the central prism illuminates the ongoing journey.

This volume explores the identity of Jewish women—Orthodox, Conservative, and Reform—in relation to the life cycle events of birth and death. For me, it is the outcome of years of learning and living.

R.L.M.

Acknowledgments

I am about twelve years old, sitting on the hunter green cover trimmed with flowered fabric that was my bedspread. Absorbed in the vivid writing of Margaret Mitchell's *Gone With the Wind,* I am oblivious to my mother's calls to come into the kitchen and set the table for dinner.

The absorption in texts of all kinds has been part of me for as long as I can remember. This volume is animated by an exploration of my own identity as a reader through an analysis of traditional and contemporary Jewish texts. While its writing has occupied me for several years, it is the result of reflections extending over much of my adult life. All readers, including those of sacred texts, are framed by specific contexts, both personal and historical. My personal context traverses not only the second half of the twentieth century and the beginnings of the twenty-first, not only a particular family and tradition and education, but also a special group of people. It is therefore my pleasure to thank the many whose expertise, friendship, and support have contributed to this project.

My thanks to the Works-in-Progress Group at Wittenberg University, whose members carefully read and commented upon several drafts of the introduction—their suggestions and insights helped clarify my thinking; to Joseph (Yossi) Galron-Goldschlaeger, head of the Hebraica and Jewish Studies Library at the Ohio State University Oxley Thompson Memorial Library, sleuth *par excellence,* whose personal interest in facilitating my research was of inestimable assistance; to Suzanne Smailes, Technical Services Librarian at Thomas Library of Wittenberg University, for her astute comments, warmth, and professionalism; to Bill Young of the Ohio State University Library and to Sally Brown, librarian at Congregation Tifereth Israel in Columbus, Ohio, for their ready help; to Jessie Zawacki, Wittenberg senior, for her careful compilation of the bibliography; to Lauren Proll and Eric Schramm, for their editing expertise. Tina Zians and Cathie Dollinger helped in typing drafts of this work, while to Rosemarie Burley I am especially indebted, not only for her meticulous attention to technical aspects of the final manuscript, but also for her persistent good humor and friendship. Discussions with Kevin D. Arnold, Barbara Kaiser, Eliyahu M. Millen, Donald Reed, and Estelle Schecter helped refine certain ideas.

Phyllis D. Deutsch, senior editor at University Press of New England, has been exemplary in her encouragement of this project, as well as in her careful reading of the various drafts. Susan M. Kahn and Rela Mintz Geffen made valuable comments as the manuscript took final form.

Research support provided by grants from the Hadassah International Research Institute on Jewish Women, the Lucius N. Littauer Foundation, and

Wittenberg University is gratefully acknowledged and helped bring this work to completion.

Family and friends offered moral support, encouragement, and laughter as the process of researching and writing consumed many hours, weeks, and months. This volume is dedicated in memory of three unique women, each of whom, in different ways, influenced me deeply and powerfully, inspired and challenged me. Henoch—life partner, lover, and constant presence—nurtured this work both practically and intellectually. To him, my love and thanks.

Women, Birth, and Death in Jewish Law and Practice

Introduction

The literature on Judaism and feminism is a constantly developing one, encompassing anthropological, sociological, and theological perspectives. Some of the most recent studies have viewed aspects of ritual as they relate to the feminine within a religious context;[1] read rabbinic sources through feminist glasses;[2] and formulated a Jewish theology with mutuality rather than acquisition as its basis.[3] There are those who have argued that Judaism almost by definition is a cultural magnet, influenced within its circumscribed boundaries by historical circumstance;[4] others have described the tradition as in some sense metahistorical.[5] Feminism, in its multitude of nuanced meanings, has been seen as the culprit in the increase of assimilation in the Jewish community and the larger number of divorces over the years.[6] Especially (but not only) in the right-wing communities, increased power for women in the world outside the Jewish community is often seen as a threat to the more subordinate position of women within traditional Jewish society.[7] At the same time, however, there has been a heightened interest in that which is uniquely female, the life experiences that help define the identity of a woman qua female.[8] The uniquely female aspect of human development takes on special significance when put in the context of the Jewish life cycle and the underlying issues of feminism that have an impact upon it.

This volume will examine how the various denominations within Judaism deal with critical aspects of the Jewish life cycle, birth and death, as they pertain specifically to women's development. Underlying this descriptive approach will be an analysis of the conceptual matrices that feed into and to a large extent help determine the legal reasoning, practical recommendations, and accepted rituals by which diverse Jews live. The examination and analysis will proceed both horizontally and vertically. In linear fashion, the description will begin with the rabbinic framework, taking full cognizance of the variety of opinions expressed within it and the different guidelines given to diverse communities and individuals within distinct historical periods. That is, an overview of the halakhic (Jewish legal) literature on each relevant issue will be given. This will lead to the continuum on the horizontal line by concluding the discussion of the rabbinic framework with what may be called "centrist" or "modern" Orthodoxy. This designation refers to the groups within traditional Judaism that accept and advocate the encounter of Judaism with modernity, affirming the infeasibility—and detrimental consequences—of a more isolationist approach. The exploration of the impact of rabbinic sources will continue with how Conservative, and then Reform, Judaism have dealt with the life-cycle issues of birth and death.

The vertical lines are constituted by a series of ambiguous polarities upon which many of the controversies and practical questions regarding feminism and Judaism hinge; they serve as a heuristic device to illuminate the discussion. The first is the understanding of gender itself, which will be interwoven into the discussions of rabbinic sources and the various denominations. Halakhah seems to operate on an essentialist view of sex in which the division of the world into genders is in the nature of the world itself; sex and gender are intrinsic aspects of reality.[9] The opposite viewpoint is that of postmodernism, according to which all knowledge is contextual.[10] Gender, then, becomes a construct created by societies in order to understand reality. In this view, gender is not biological, but rather the way we divide the spectrum of human and historical realities; it is culturally rooted. According to a contemporary historian, the history of cultural and political processes can only be written if it is recognized "that 'man' and 'woman' are at once empty and overflowing categories: empty because they have no ultimate, transcendent meaning; overflowing because even when they appear to be fixed, they still contain within them alternative, denied, or suppressed definitions."[11]

Gender—the various and contradictory social meanings ascribed to sexual difference—is an important conceptual matrix for examining life-cycle events as a central aspect of Judaism, and of Judaism and feminism. The term "gender" suggests that relations between the sexes are a significant aspect of social organization, that masculine and feminine identities are largely determined by cultural elements, and that hierarchical structures of society both determine and are determined by certain differences between the sexes. "Gender" is thus both a descriptive term, mapping out how individual and cultural interactions function, as well as a causal notion, reflecting certain past and present behaviors and social patterns. Gender refers to the socially and hierarchically constructed division of the sexes. To put it somewhat differently, "Gender is the social organization of sexual differences . . . gender is the knowledge that establishes meanings for bodily differences."[12] These meanings are diverse, varying across cultures and historical eras. Thus gender, as a flexible tool of analysis, must be relativized and historicized.[13]

Gender is also a significant means by which power is indicated, providing an instrument with which to unravel complex meanings of human interaction in terms of both society and the individual. In her chapter "Gender," the historian Joan Wallach Scott offers a series of examples from European history that underscore her contention that gender "is a primary means of signifying relationships of power. Attention to gender is often not explicit, but it is nonetheless a crucial part of the organization of equality or inequality."[14] In addition, it is important to take note of the close connections among language usage, gender, and power. One example is the use of the masculine plural—also the generic plural—in Hebrew, which was understood as referring only to males when a reason existed to exclude females. Thus *banim,* meaning "sons" or "children" or "progeny," is interpreted as the generic in *b'nei Yisrael,* the "children of Israel," but as masculine in "And you shall teach them [the commandments] to your children *[banekha]*" (Deut. 11:19). *Banekha* is interpreted by the Sifre to mean "your sons and not your daughters."[15] This becomes the basis of women's exclusion from the obligation to study Torah. Similarly, as indicated by Joan Wallach Scott, theories of language and epistemology provide a tool through which to understand "the construction of social and political meaning." Language, that is, creates "meaning through differentiation."[16] This process is clearly demonstrated in the above instance.[17]

Contemporary thinkers—psychologists, anthropologists, literary figures, and scientists—have debated and analyzed the vortex of issues surrounding the notion of gender. One's conclusion, amorphous and unsatisfactory as it may be, must be that gender has both biological components as well as deeply ingrained social aspects. The debate—or at least one side of it—is wonderfully encapsulated in a short story by Lois Gould. The narrative of "X: A Fabulous Child's Story," begins:

> Once upon a time, a baby named X was born. This baby was named X so that nobody could tell whether it was a boy or a girl. Its parents could tell, of course, but they couldn't tell anybody else. They couldn't even tell Baby X at first.
>
> You see, it was all part of a very important Secret Scientific Xperiment, known officially as Project Baby X. . . .

Baby X plays with tea sets and loves construction toys. Child X likes both the vacuum cleaner and the lawn mower. When other parents declare Child X a misfit, X undergoes extensive tests. The psychiatrist reports in astonishment that these tests prove that not only does X not have an identity problem, but X is also ". . . the *least* mixed up child" the psychiatrist ever examined.[18]

The fictional case of "X" notwithstanding, the issue of the determinants of gender is one of great complexity, involving as it does almost every academic discipline.[19] Some scholars have argued that men and women have intrinsically different ways of thinking about moral issues and that the female moral voice manifests a distinct preference for the ethics of care over the ethics of justice.[20] Various studies have chapters with such titles as "Hormones and Aggression: An Explanation of Power?" "Of Genes and Gender," and "Nature, Culture, and Gender: A Critique."[21] Carolyn Heilbrun has written articulately about women and freedom from gendered thought patterns. Calling to mind Plato's wish for old age in order to be free from sexual drive and passion, Heilbrun suggests that many women do not attain true spiritual, emotional, and intellectual free- dom until menopause, when they are freed, more or less, from the sexist pre- suppositions of our time. At that time, according to Heilbrun, women function as androgynous beings.[22] Psychologists[23] and scientists have meticulously ana- lyzed various aspects of the formation of biologically linked sex.[24] Feminist historians have examined the impact of gender on both history and historiogra- phy.[25] Gender, with all its interdisciplinary nuances, is an important lens through which to understand how Judaism, in its various forms, deals with women's life-cycle events.

There is an underlying assumption made in using gender to elucidate issues regarding women and the life-cycle events of birth and death in Judaism. De- spite the references to Judaism as such, the tradition derives from a masculine framework.[26] The texts, however, are presented as if they were gender neutral, with women viewed as separate, an added—if integral—part of the community. The masculine perspective of the transmitter is normative.[27] However, the rab- binic tradition articulated by the Talmud represents a "contextualized femi- nism," also termed a "benevolent patriarchy."[28] It is not possible to eliminate the patriarchal perspective from the Talmud, to remove it from the social-historical context from which it emerged. But the Talmud, time and again, ameliorates those aspects of the status quo that contravene the ethical sensibilities of its au- thors.[29] Thus, determining the impact of notions of gender in rabbinic sources and their influence upon interpretations of the Jewish tradition is significant.[30] The view through the lens of gender will be articulated in the forthcoming chap- ters in the discussions of rabbinic sources and the various denominations. The influence of gender as a concept, a prism, is pervasive and will be commented upon as it illuminates the issues under consideration.

Public and private constitute a second polarity on the vertical array. One as- pect of this notion is related to the essentialist concept of gender; women as a group are considered in some sources as characterized by an inner sense, an intrinsic quality of privacy that makes them suitable for the domestic and child-rearing functions in society and unsuited for the more public roles through which general culture is developed, transformed, and transmitted. In this view, women represent stasis and the maintenance of the status quo as the preservers of everyday life and necessary creature comforts. This role for women enables men to function in the public arena, in which history moves and is moved forward. This argument may be based on theological premises, such as interpretations of Genesis, chapter 3,[31] or on an amplification of and reading into verses from other biblical books. The most noted of these is the verse from Psalms 45:15, *"kol kevodah bat melekh penimah,"* "the honor of the daughter of the king is inward" (or "lies on the inside"). This is taken to mean that woman is enjoined to develop this trait of personality (i.e., modesty, or the inner, private dimensions of one's personality) to the highest degree; that "the female role" is characterized by its "private nature."[32] Feminists regard this reasoning as a strategy to withhold from women equal roles in the public arena and thus justify a particular political and social aim, the dominance of men in public life. A different viewpoint, however, is seen in the affirmation of the private as higher than the public.[33] While it is the case that spiritual priority is given to private or inner development in Judaism (in contrast to the public concept of fame that dominated Greek thinking and today dominates Western society), the idea that women are considered to possess an intrinsic talent for this set of qualities is clearly suspect. The political and social consequences of emphasizing the presumably more private female nature are the limitation of opportunities for women in the public arena and the reserving of approval for "appropriate" female activities. It is also possible that the converse is the case. As women generally were not as involved in public life as men (a description of dominant social patterns in talmudic times), intellectual explanation/justification was needed; description became prescription.

An example of this would be access to the study of Torah. The mitzvah (commandment) of *limud Torah,* or the study of Torah,[34] which could have been comprehended as inclusive, was interpreted as an exclusive male obligation. Women could study Torah, but were not obligated to do so. Yet text study is the very foundation of Jewish tradition; Torah here means not only the Pentateuch, or written text, but also the (originally) oral discussions edited into what came to be known as the Mishnah and Gemarah, together designated as the Talmud. Women's participation in cultural and intellectual activities—here defined as religious duty—may have been constrained by domestic responsibilities and/or other aspects of societal parameters.[35] But the context of women's lives in rabbinic times, the way women actually lived, clearly was a factor—if not the overriding determinant—of how Jewish society was structured in a legal and political framework.

The public/private polarity has affected women throughout the centuries, not only in terms of religious law and ritual, but also with regard to work in specific occupations and access to advanced education.[36] In certain historical periods in Jewish history, the impact of this division on women's public roles outside the religious sphere was considerably less than at other times. Some read the mishnaic exemption of women from time-specific commandments as resulting from the androcentrism of the taanaim, the authors of the Mishnah.[37] These interpreters view the encouragement of women's private domestic role as a means of denying access to communal ritual and/or leadership. "But whatever the motive [no reason for the exemption is given in the Mishnah], any rule that exempts women from a religious duty incumbent on men *ipso facto* diminishes women's status," argues one.[38] Another contemporary interpreter views women's exemption from the main ritual acts of Judaism as promulgated "in order to restrict their [these acts] performance to men, to heads of household; only people of the highest social standing . . . does God consider most fit to honor or worship Him in this way. This hierarchical arrangement is reminiscent of Temple protocol."[39] A third sees the arrangement in political/sociological terms, providing the space necessary for a role centered almost exclusively in the home. The domestic role, while not mandated, is given preferred status by legal means. This preferred status, however, comes with a commensurate loss of rights.[40] That is, one definition of equality in Jewish law is equal obligation. If one has a lesser obligation, one does not have the same rights as one with a higher level of obligation. An example is communal prayer. Since a man's obligation to participate is mandatory while a woman's is voluntary, a man has the right to lead the prayers (in traditional halakhah) and the woman does not. Jewish law focuses upon obligations, while American jurisprudence emphasizes rights. But obligations and rights are complementary concepts.

The exemption from time-specific commandments is the stratagem used in rabbinic law to assure women of the care and protection they need as those who give birth and nurse infants; to create a societal structure with a family life made more secure by women's taking on the more private, domestic role; to establish and maintain a hierarchy in which those with the more public functions, men, are seen in some ways as having higher social standing.[41]

In Eastern European Ashkenazi society of the early modern period, the woman usually had more secular learning: she spoke the local languages and did the accounting work for small or larger business enterprises. Her husband, in contrast, was immersed in fulfilling his obligation to study Torah. Clearly, although in no society—even that of Plato's *Republic*—could all the males become philosopher-kings, in Jewish society becoming a scholar of Torah was seen as an ideal. Since the woman did not have the same level of obligation to study Torah,[42] she often supported the family through her business acumen and entrepreneurial resourcefulness. Surely Glückel of Hameln represents one of the most well-known examples of this phenomenon.[43]

Women in Western society were increasingly restrained from marketplace activities by the notion that they had to be models of domesticity; men, however, whose wives provided income by working outside the home were viewed as failing in their family obligations. The substantial waves of Jewish immigrants to the United States in the late nineteenth and early twentieth centuries included a cadre of talented women with well-developed skills in various types of businesses. In Eastern Europe, while the domestic woman was accorded prestige, the marketplace activities of women were especially highly esteemed, as they freed husbands for the pursuit of sacred study. In the golden land of America, however, by the turn of the century, this value system was completely reversed. The man who devoted himself to scholarship and left his wife to earn the family income was considered neglectful of his responsibilities, and married women came to do more and more piecework at home, becoming less a part of outside business activity.

A wonderful example of this transformation is described in Anzia Yezierska's novel *Bread Givers,* which depicts the Jewish immigrant experience in the early decades of the twentieth century from a woman's perspective. Anzia's father, Reb Smolinsky, was a highly regarded Torah scholar in Russia, a role he attempts to maintain in the tenements of the Lower East Side of New York. But even the combined wages of his four daughters working in the sweatshops are barely enough to sustain the family. He tries to preserve his patriarchal stance in the family; he is given the best parts of the soup, for instance, although he does not contribute to the sparse family income. He passes judgment on the young men whom his daughters date, paradoxically wanting them to be good providers. When Anzia decides at age eighteen to leave her unhappy home and make her own way, he bellows, "No girl can live without a father or a husband to look out for her. It says in the Torah, only through a man has a woman an existence." Retorts Anzia, "I'm smart enough to look out for myself. It's a new life now. In America, women don't need men to boss them."[44]

As late-nineteenth-century bourgeois attitudes increasingly influenced American values, they tended to buttress rabbinic notions of expressing through legal means a clear preference for women to use their considerable energy and talents primarily in the domestic sphere.[45] It is important to note, however, that the reality of women working outside the home was for long historical periods seen as consonant with the view of women in rabbinic sources. One may be cynical and see this as highly developed only because it was beneficial to men to have women earn family income. But such cynicism undercuts the genuine flexibility in the halakhic system, which in fact did offer a variety of possibilities to women. These possibilities, however, rarely extended to participation in the public arenas of Jewish observance and ritual. This important aspect of the tradition, as it played itself out in the life-cycle events of birth and death, will be discussed on a case-by-case basis in the following chapters.

It is possible to see the public/private line as having developed with a specific goal in mind: the dividing up of the tasks of society in order for the political and social structures to function smoothly.[46] In this view, individual desires may be subsumed under communal needs, which are generally seen to take priority (this will be analyzed further on as the polarity of autonomy and community). But the gendered division of society as a facilitator toward stability and continuity is not the sole factor determining the public/private opposition. The conceptual framework of public/private is also determined by the realities of and assumptions about sexual polarity: the male/female attraction.

One can look at the corpus of halakhah—indeed, at many cultural and legal norms of the Western world—and detect as determining factors, both covertly and overtly, the spectrum of attitudes toward human sexuality. Should the attraction of men to women lead to restrictions upon women? Don't men have the obligation of self-control? And aren't women attracted to men? Whether one looks in I Corinthians in the Greek Bible and reads Paul's interdiction of females speaking in church[47] or delves into the development of the notion in Judaism that a woman's voice is *ervah,*[48] or a kind of erotic stimulus men should avoid;[49] whether one peruses the rabbinic texts that describe the nuances of such issues as in which situations and how much of a married woman's hair must be covered lest men other than her husband find her attractive,[50] or analyzes the reasons given for women not appearing as witnesses in court[51] or being discouraged from reciting kaddish:[52] woman as sexual object is the primary determining factor in all these legal recommendations and requirements. The notion of women as sexual objects in the discussions that follow refers primarily to women in heterosexual relationships. Lesbian partnerships are referred to in classical rabbinic sources, but will not be explored here.[53]

Centuries before Freud, early Israelite tradition dealt with a fundamental fact of society—sexual attraction and desire—and the parameters necessary to both meet individual needs and create communal stability. The complex rabbinic literature regarding sexuality, including views of male and female nature, both celebrate and channel sexuality. Modern-day feminists are often surprised at the subtlety of thinking and psychological nuance present in some rabbinic discussions relating to sex and sexuality. The unambiguous view of the body as "good"[54] has the effect in rabbinic law of creating a society that in many ways protects and respects women and celebrates sexuality within the accepted channels. But at the same time, typologies have been created that speak disparagingly about feminine abilities and innate proclivities. These are based on an essentialist view of femaleness. While sexuality is a good, some sources nonetheless view women as a source of danger or temptation in general, especially in the public arena, so long dominated by men. The issues surrounding sexual polarity thus greatly influence the discussions of the suitability—or lack thereof—of women in the public domain. Debates about women's participation in public religious ritual nearly always have two foci: domestic and child-care responsibilities, and sexuality. In stating this, it must be kept in mind that the authors of rabbinic texts—indeed, the formulators of the tradition itself—were all men; that they functioned historically in periods when women's lives were often far more constrained, due to the lack of birth control and to the dominance of men in Western culture; that the polarity of public/private has within it significant aspects relating to power and the use of power. ("Power" here indicates intellectual, cultural, socioeconomic, and political power, as well as sexual power or the perception of sexual power.)

The gender asymmetry of the nonsexual kinds of power may be founded on male fear of female sexual power, representing fear of male sexual desire. How else to understand all that is projected upon femaleness in rabbinic sources? Men, who perceive themselves as representing "culture"—Torah learning and interpretation, amplification of judicial principles, and development of new concepts—view women as mired in "nature." Women menstruate, grow big with child, bring new life into the world amidst a sea of blood, and nurture new life through lactation. Surely women biologically seem more enmeshed in the processes of nature. The task of culture in human society is to conquer and transcend nature, to harness natural materials and forces toward the realization of human and/or divine purposes. Thus every culture at some level creates a hierarchy of value, an axiology, in which culture affirms itself to be not only distinct from but also superior to nature. Cultures in general regard women as active participants within them, yet women are also viewed as closer to, more rooted in and intertwined with, nature. This perspective allows the male projection of sexuality onto women; women embody not only their own sexual desires, but come to represent male sexuality as well.

While women, except for birthing, are not any closer to or further from nature than men, the perspectives in which femaleness has been construed—and the social implications of these views—have been conflated to place woman in a lower status. To define femaleness as "private" rather than "public" is to affirm this hierarchy. The apologetic claim that asserts great value for the "private" is a way of justifying male dominance in the public arena while creating a reverse axiological hierarchy. This leads to the question of whether any such hierarchy is desirable in a social group that claims equal value of male and female.[55]

Particularly distressing is the use of this view (of woman as closer to nature) in some aspects of rabbinic law that directly affect women's lives. This is evident in the use of the phrase *"tav lemetav tan du milemetav armelu,"* which appears five times in the Talmud[56] and translates as "better to dwell as two than to dwell alone." While this aphorism might be seen as a statement about general existential loneliness, the context makes it clear that it refers to women having a compelling desire for marriage. So strong is this desire presumed to be that it is thought a woman might consider marrying a man otherwise deemed unacceptable rather than remain alone. Whatever the arguments of contemporary scholars about the current relevance of this principle,[57] one aspect of its underlying grid of determinants is the strength of female sexuality. While the principle presumes that female sexual needs, closer to nature, need attending to, practical reasons for this principle might include women's traditional lack of economic independence as well as the greater availability of partners for men outside of marriage. Various interpretations of this principle notwithstanding, the way in which sexuality is conceptualized constitutes the third vertical axis to be considered.

Community/autonomy is the fourth and final organizing line in the discussions that follow. As with gender, public/private spheres, and sexuality, the issues are intricate, complex, and interrelated. This line derives most directly from conflicts in the history of political theory: is the individual a free entity who relinquishes aspects of sovereignty to live in a societal framework, or is the individual endowed with certain rights by virtue of being born into the community? Individualism and collectivism, at least in theory, seem definitely at odds.[58] With regard to women, however, the theoretical questions spin out another layer, an additional formulation related to the earlier three vertical axes. While varying views of the concept of the Jewish community abound, the concern here is with the notion of women's finding greater fulfillment in response to needs of the community—both within and outside their families.[59] Woman is seen as person,[60] with both entitlements and obligations, but as possessing autonomous status primarily when no male claim on her biological function exists. As part of a family unit, her individual identity—what in our society might be designated as self-fulfillment—is viewed primarily as enabler and facilitator of the development and needs of others. Thus her growth derives from focusing outward, into the family and community, while male growth is much more viewed as development of the self. This latter is not to be construed as a narcissistic aim, but as one more independent of the webs of interconnectedness from which community is constructed, an identity not determined by its context, but both of and above its substratum.

In the methodology of this volume, the analysis of gender will be interwoven throughout the text. The other three vertical polarities—public/private spheres, sexuality, and community/autonomy—will be examined in each chapter following the elaboration of the appropriate literature relating to rabbinic sources, and Orthodox, Conservative, and Reform Judaism. (Although Reconstructionism as a denomination of Judaism is over twenty-five years old, its theology and legal rulings will not be discussed in this work.) Through the methodology of these explorations, the understanding of the effect upon Jewish women of birth and death as life events will be enhanced. Visually, the methodological approach looks like the schematic diagram below.

	The Lens of Gender	Public/Private Spheres	Community/ Sexuality	Autonomy
Orthodox				
Conservative				
Reform				

Part I, "Issues Surrounding Birth," includes chapters 1 through 4, dealing respectively with birth, contraception and birth control, fertility, and celebration on the birth of a daughter *(Simhat Bat)*.

Part II, "Death and Mourning," in chapter 5 will reflect upon Kaddish (the memorial prayer for the dead) and the funeral. Chapter 6 is the epilogue.

This volume brings together reflections from several disciplines in order to describe more fully not only the Jewish rites of birth and death—their components and traditional meanings—but also and especially the impact upon, meanings of, and new forms of celebration, remembrance, and commemoration for the contemporary Jewish woman.

I

Birth

Chapter 1

Beginnings

Zion is in labor—and she will bear her children.
                                                    Isaiah 66:7

In the waters of the mother
comes the voyage.
Down canals to the ocean
deep in the maternal sea
Home to the sea
in me.
                                    Quoted in
                            Tikva Frymer-Kensky,
                                Motherprayer

. . . was not the world created specifically for the sake of procreation . . .
                            Mishnah Gittin 4.5 and Eduyot 1.13

Birth stands at the center of the mystery of human existence. Both intensely physical and thoroughly spiritual, it reminds us that though mired in flesh and blood, which ultimately decay and die, we carry the capacity to create, bring forth, and nurture new life. The intermingling of our physicality and mortality with the intimations of transcendence present in a new life is a paradigm of the human paradox that we embody both nature and culture, flesh and spirit, the material and the divine. This paradox presents itself in the very first chapter of Genesis, where God gives the command to procreate.

Part I, "Birth," will deal with several aspects of the halakhic (Jewish legal) perspective on procreation and contraception, fertility, and *simhat bat,* or the celebration on the birth of a daughter. My analyses will focus on the views of woman indicated by the relevant rabbinic texts and the impact of derived legal rulings upon the lives of women. Implicit in the texts and the analyses to follow are controversies regarding fundamental questions of feminist theory: Are maleness and femaleness innate, the results of biological determinants, or are they social constructs, the outcome of deeply ingrained societal attitudes?[1] To what extent—and with what practical implications—does the notion of woman as Other[2] pervade the halakhic texts? Does the construction of gender in rabbinic sources follow the nature/culture dichotomy articulated by anthropologist Sherry Ortner,[3] and if so, what does this mean for Judaism as a whole, for Jewish ethics, for how women celebrate life-cycle events? In what ways are the ideologies of feminism compatible or incompatible with those of Judaism and what can thus be concluded about each; to what extent is the notion of hierarchy[4] a sine qua non of patriarchal cultures? Can Judaism retain its wholeness without hierarchy and what would this mean? While the aim of this volume is to focus upon the life-cycle events of birth and death in Jewish tradition from the viewpoint of their gender perspective and impact, the analyses of practical ritual will be framed within the context of the above theoretical questions.

In dealing with birth—and to a lesser extent with contraception—the core issue is the sex difference itself upon which the distillation of its gendered meanings are based. Birthing is "woman's work" in the purest sense, rooted as it is in female biology. It is from the presence or absence of the biological capacity of birthing that notions of gender emerge. Social culture and political power have developed elaborate, interwoven conceptual constructs that define roles and activities deemed appropriate for each sex. As Simone de Beauvoir has noted, the female is "more enslaved to the species than the male, her animality is more manifest."[5] This is compounded by her natural association with the domestic context, deriving from lactation and the as-yet unsocialized nature of small children. Yet woman's other functions within this very context "show her to be a powerful agent of the cultural process, constantly transforming raw natural resources into cultural products."[6] By virtue of her social locus, then, woman can be seen as intermediate between nature and culture, implying both "middle status" and a "mediating" role; the evolution of woman's secondary or inferior status with regard to culture and transcendence is therefore clear. Although the notions of gender and class are closely allied,[7] only gender will be considered here.

References to birth in the corpus of the Talmud, aside from the numerous technical concerns of birth and *niddah,* or ritual impurity,[8] actually are sparse. Perhaps this is not surprising in a text written and edited exclusively by men. While the centrality of the birth experience in the life of a woman, and its value to the community as a whole, is assumed, the Talmud says little about its meaning. The meaning of birth—so central to religious, political, economic, and personal life—was so obvious as to need no abstract explication; its import was so well understood that a theoretical framework was unnecessary. Possibly the lack of explication provides openings for each generation to find its own meanings. The emphasis on action and deed in the tradition implies philosophical underpinnings that are sometimes left unexplored. There is the negative comment that women die in childbirth because of three transgressions: they are not diligent in observing the commandments of *niddah,* the taking of *challah,* and the lighting of the Shabbat (Sabbath) candles.[9] In this text, female biology is intermingled in a punitive and threatening way with the three commandments for which women are primarily responsible. If women fail to be meticulous in the observance of these three commandments for which husbands and children depend upon them, the consequence will be death in childbirth.

This is a text which has always disturbed me. Its theology seems simplistic—sin will cause evil consequence—and it presumes to punish women in a uniquely womanly fashion, fanning the flames of fear in a time when the dangers of childbirth were far more present than in our age. It offers a view that would cause a woman to be seen as a transgressor after her death in the throes of childbirth, a stigma her family would have to suffer forever. And it is based on the view that threats of such magnitude would lead to punctiliousness in carrying out these three commandments. Surely the contemporary attitude would be in a positive way to encourage devotion to carrying out the commandments. A positive approach presumes women are motivated by devotion to the tradition and wish to express their spirituality through proper observance and care in the home. However, it must be said that the Talmud does at times see a cause-effect relationship between sin and the presence of evil in the world.[10] When one examines the spectrum of comments in the texts, the various statements about the relation between sin and evil seem not simple minded, but rather a loosely structured way of dealing with the conundrum of theodicy. Nonetheless, this statement about death in childbirth can perhaps only be seen in a negative light.

Indeed, the comments of the Palestinian Talmud on this text are overtly negative. The Palestinian (or Jerusalem) Talmud brings an haggadic, or homiletic, elucidation associated with the Mishnah: "The First Adam was the blood of the world . . . and Eve caused him death; therefore the commandment of menstrual separation was given to the woman. Adam was the first pure dough-offering of the world . . . and Eve caused his death; therefore she was given the commandment of the dough-offering. Adam was the candle of the world, for it says 'the soul of Adam is the candle of God,' and Eve caused him death; therefore the commandment of lighting the candle was given to the woman."[11] In this text, the biblical designation "Adam" refers only to the man (male), a problematic reading even in classical rabbinic exegesis. Although this tradition is punitive, even misogynistic, in holding Eve responsible for the entire sin and the mortality that follows, it is important to note that the test[12] does not regard female sexuality[13] as the cause of Eve's disobedience.

The reading of the Babylonian Talmud, in contrast, completely undermines the antiwoman tone of the haggadah, or homiletical narrative, in the version of the Palestinian Talmud.

As a certain Galilean interpreted: I have put into you a portion of blood; therefore I have given you a commandment having to do with blood. I called you the "firstling"; therefore I have given you a commandment having to do with the first [dough]. The soul which I have given you is called a candle; therefore I have given you a commandment having to do with candles. If you keep them, well and good; but if not, I will take away your soul.[14]

Thus the three commandments for which the Mishnah states "women die in childbirth" are understood, on a basic level, as connected to the Jewish people as a whole, both men and women. Why then are women specified and why in childbirth? In rabbinic culture, the spheres of body, nature, and domesticity belong almost entirely to the woman. Indeed, the Talmud itself asks the question, "Why then at the time of giving birth?" and responds that times of risk and danger[15] serve as a test for righteousness. If women are tested in childbirth, when are men tested? Men are at risk when they cross bridges. Clearly "crossing bridges," in the world outside the home, is viewed primarily as a masculine activity. In the pages that follow this statement, the Talmud lists several commandments incumbent upon both men and women and likely to have negative consequences if not performed. Thus the text about women dying in childbirth can be viewed within a larger theological framework that connects commandments, times of danger, and possible effects.

Some talmudic discussions focus upon the nature of sexual intercourse and its impact upon the gender of the fetus.[16] It is clear from these sources that the birth of boys is preferable. Perhaps the texts serve as a kind of manual as to how to actualize such an outcome. It is interesting that the greater the concern of the husband for the sexual satisfaction of his wife, the stronger the likelihood the resulting baby would be a boy. That is, if the woman reaches orgasm first, the fetus—should indeed a fetus result—would be a boy. The expressed preference given to the male infant is a clear sign of patriarchal culture; the devaluation of the female begins, so it seems, even in utero. Perhaps it might also be seen as a way to encourage men to be concerned for the sexual satisfaction of their wives.[17]

The broad perspective, however, indicates the high value placed on the parenting of both females and males. The Talmud gives high praise to those who raise an adopted child, considering the adoptive parents as if they were also biological parents.[18] That is, the level of care and nurture determines parenthood, not only biological factors. The text also indicates the uniqueness of birth by including it among the three activities in the world to which only God, without any subsidiary messengers, so to speak, attends.

R. Yohanan said: Three keys are in the hand of the Holy One Blessed be He which are not in the hands of a messenger. They are: the key of rain, the key of life *[hayah]*, and the key of the resurrection of the dead. (T.B. Taanit 2a)[19]

R. Yohanan's statement indicates that God is directly responsible for the fertility of the earth, the physical world, through provision of adequate rainfall; for the bringing forth of human life; and for the ultimate redemption. It is in each of these areas human beings can feel most powerless. R. Yohanan offers reassurance of God's direct providential care in regard to sustenance, life itself (conception and birth), and life after death, i.e., resurrection. His words echo the text of the Talmud (B.T. Kiddushin 30b), which proclaims the partnership of wife, husband, and God in the creation of every human being; man and woman provide the material aspects (egg, sperm, genetic imprint) while God provides the soul, the breath of life. R. Yohanan's statement also indicates that redemption requires a partnership between the physical universe and human endeavor, through which history is realized and the moral struggle plays itself out.

With regard to rabbinic comments about birth, the text of the Talmud presents a paradox. The biblical injunctions to seek justice, pursue ethical behavior,[20] act with moral sensitivity, and reach toward holiness—both individually and as a society—must reconcile themselves with historical context, social realities, the diversities of human culture. While surely it is accurate to view the pursuit of justice as an undertaking directed against the dominant social forces of a particular historical period, those very forces create a limiting factor beyond which one cannot go; one could not have argued the notion of women's suffrage in the England of 1700, nor the idea of women becoming scholars of mathematics or Bible or rabbinic texts. The embeddedness of patriarchal culture[21] was a glass ceiling beyond which the understanding of justice could not extend.

That women become pregnant with child, bring new life into the world, and are biologically equipped to sustain that new life was understood in rabbinic literature from within a framework that was androcentric[22] almost despite itself. Within the biblical text itself, the reader is confronted with the persistent theme of continuity through childbirth and the views of both male and female biblical characters that focus upon the meaning of birth. This chapter will examine the centrality of procreation in Judaism, the obligation to procreate, the fulfillment of that obligation, and issues regarding contraception.

In Judaism, birth is seen as a blessing. This is consonant with the text of Genesis 1:28: "Be fertile and increase, fill the earth and master it. . . ." Sexuality functions as the bridge between the transcendent and the natural, enabling humans to work within the framework of the world created by God toward its proximate as well as ultimate transformation. The text views sexual desire as intrinsically good, of benefit for both the individual and society. This is evident in the use of the word "good" to describe all of creation in the first chapter of Genesis, as well as in the indirect theology of the aggadic and midrashic literature. One text, for instance, states:

Nahman . . . said: [The Torah says] "Behold it was very good." This refers to the good inclination *[yetzer tov]*. [The Torah also says] "And behold it was very good." The "and" refers to the evil inclination *[yetzer ra]*. This is because the evil inclination is "very good." But [to say] this is astounding! However, without the evil inclination, a person would not build a home, get married, have children, or do business.[23]

The noun *yetzer* can be translated as instinct, inclination, impulse, nature, drive, or passion, even imagination. In verb form it means to generate, produce, manufacture, fashion, or form. Freudians might define *yetzer* as libido, the basic life force. A central task is channeling this fundamental instinct toward the good; sexuality and creative energy can be used for good or evil purposes. What is called the "evil inclination" thus has both constructive and destructive elements. Sexuality cannot free itself from its possible negative aspects, but at the same time it is viewed as a complex and significant good.[24]

The marriage relationship, regarded as the ideal expression of sexuality, is not only a manifestation of the ultimate completeness and completion of the individual, but also the vehicle through which human history continues. The very first mitzvah (commandment) in the Torah,[25] to "be fertile and increase" (Gen. 1:28), seems clearly given both to man and woman. Yet the rabbinic sources understand the mitzvah of procreation as devolving only upon men, a most strange reading of the text. This chapter will examine the various opinions regarding procreation and contraception in light of the rabbinic disputes regarding this first mitzvah.

Procreation is mentioned in only one mishnah, and it is this text, contrary to the plain reading of Genesis 1:28, that ascribes only to men the positive mitzvah to "be fertile and increase." In keeping with rabbinic methodology, the dissenting viewpoint is also articulated. The Mishnah states:

A man is commanded concerning the duty of propagation but not a woman. R. Johanan ben Beroka, however, said: Concerning both of them—it is said, "And God blessed them; and God said unto them: 'Be fruitful, and multiply.'" (Mishnah Yevamot 6:6)

The opinion of the Mishnah is puzzling. What could be more natural than to place the commandment to procreate upon both man and woman, especially since Genesis 1:28 explicitly offers the primordial blessing to male and female? The grammar of the verse is clear: both male and female are the recipients of God's blessing of fertility. In fact, as shall be shown, the authors of the Mishnah and Gemara go to some length to reinterpret the obvious meaning of the verse in a way that places the obligation to procreate solely on the male. How is this accomplished and, further, what does this rereading of the text mean? Why was this important in the rabbinic system, in the legal universe of halakhah? What objectives of Jewish society were attained by explaining the text in this way?

The discussion of this Mishnah in the Talmud offers two readings of the verse to justify the interpretation that the obligation to procreate falls only on the male. The text states:

Whence is this deduced? R. Ile'a replied in the name of R. Eleazar, son of R. Simeon: Scripture stated: "And replenish the earth and subdue it"; it is the nature of a man to subdue but it is not the nature of a woman to subdue. On the contrary! "And subdue it" implies two! R. Nahman ben Isaac replied: It is written, "And thou subdue it." R. Joseph said: Deduction is made from the following: "I am God Almighty, be fertile and increase," and it is not stated, "Be fertile and increase." Now, what is the decision? (T.B. Yevamot 656)

The arguments here are derived from variant readings of the word *vekivshu-hah,* "and subdue [conquer] it." R. Ile'a, in the first analysis, offers a sociological interpretation. Even though the grammar of the verse includes both male and female as the recipients of the blessing, R. Ile'a states what would now be termed an essentialist argument to alter the obvious meaning of the text. "It is the way *[derekh]* of the man to subdue, but it is not the way of the woman to subdue," he says. Intrinsic to observable male behavior or personality, according to this view, is the inclination to pursue, conquer, subdue; the object of male pursuit is not only the intellectual and practical worlds, but also a mate. In contrast—this gendered reading of the text implies—is the "female way," which leads the woman to wait to *be* pursued. The male is active and aggressive, the female passive and compliant. One way to understand this statement is that it describes innate qualities in human nature. But this essentialist reading is undermined by the word *derekh,* meaning "way" or "path." The use of this term catapults what seems to be a clear-cut affirmation of essentialism into a sociological generalization.[26] It was customary for the male to pursue the female at the time that R. Ile'a was writing. But social custom is not necessarily based on innate behavioral proclivities, should we assume that such exist. Rather, social custom may change and social patterns be transformed.[27]

A second reading of R. Ile'a's statement is based on male-female physiology. Perhaps he is alluding to the fact that heterosexual sexuality is defined as the male entering the female; i.e., she is "conquered" or "subdued." While these terms connote a sense of dominance that is unpalatable in Judaism's view of marriage as partnership, they may be a way of indirectly indicating the physiological reality. Either basis of R. Ile'a's proclamation leads to the conclusion that the command to "Be fertile and increase and replenish the earth and subdue it" can be interpreted to apply to males only, despite the grammatical indications otherwise. A sociological insight or physiological fact is used to subvert the plain meaning of the text.

A peculiar aspect of the vocalization of the text, however, provides support for the seeming distortion of the obvious. The word meaning "subdue" or "conquer" is the three-letter root *k-v-sh*. In keeping with the grammatical forms of Genesis 1:28, "And God blessed *them* and said to *them:* Be fertile [plural] and increase [plural] and replenish [plural] the earth and subdue [plural] it," (emphasis mine), the verbs appear to be second person plural. However, the last verb in the sentence is made into plural form through what is called *ketiv haser,* or "defective" spelling, and not *ketiv maleh* or "full" spelling. The shortened spelling means the word could be read in two ways: *vekivshuhah,* which is second person plural; or *vekivshah,* which is second person masculine singular. One reading of the latter may be to infer from the last verb that all five verbs in the verse thus refer only to the male,[28] although this is quite a stretch. Another is to understand the object of the last verb ("subdue" or "conquer") as referring to the woman. In this second option, the verb's "defective" spelling means not only that the subject of the verb is masculine singular, but the object can be either the "earth" in Genesis 1:28 or the woman. Grammatically, both are possible, thus providing support for the mitzvah of procreation being incumbent only upon the male.

R. Joseph attempts to resolve the ambiguity in the text by using a rule of rabbinic reasoning. The meaning of a word or phrase in the Torah can be clarified by locating other places in the text where the same word or phrase appears.[29] In this case R. Joseph indicates that the phrase "Be fertile and increase" is found in Genesis 35:11, where it clearly is addressed only to one person, a male, the patriarch Jacob. He deduces from this use that the ambivalence in Genesis 1:28 can be resolved as similarly referring only to a male.[30]

That the grammatical and linguistic arguments are nonetheless deemed inconclusive is supported by the next passage in the Gemara, of which only the first sentence is quoted above. "Now," the text queries, "what is the decision?" Were the supporting proofs convincing beyond a doubt, there would be no need to seek further validation. The Gemara responds to the question by bringing several cases of practical jurisprudence. That is, when specific cases involving procreation were brought to rabbinic courts, what were the judicial decisions and on what bases were they rendered? The cases related by the Gemara indicate that the mitzvah to "be fertile and increase" is obligatory only on the man, while procreation is what might be termed a "human right" of the woman.

The Talmud refers to two additional biblical verses to illuminate further the issue of procreation. The first is Isaiah 45:18, which reads: "For thus said the Lord / The Creator of heaven who alone is God / who formed the earth and made it / He did not create it a waste, but formed it for habitation" (Tanakh, JPS translation). The phrase "for habitation" *(shevet)* is considered an obligation of all humankind.[31] *Shevet,* or civilized human habitation, is the very purpose of God's creation. The second biblical verse, Ecclesiastes 11:6, says,

"Sow your seed in the morning and don't hold back in the evening, since you do not know which is going to succeed, the one or the other, or if both are equally good" (Tanakh, JPS translation). Some rabbinic arguments use these verses to encourage having more than two children, the minimum number needed to fulfill the mitzvah of procreation. That is, even after having two children, there is a continued obligation (although not a mitzvah) to contribute to human habitation. Interestingly, according to some it is this more general obligation that falls upon the woman.[32] Others, however, maintain that while she is *part* of *shevet,* the woman is not mandated.[33] The growth of societies and cultures through increased population obviously includes women, whose role in this growth is essential. There is no prescription, however, that requires her participation.

Why did case precedent in the tradition use the assumption that women are not obligated to procreate? Why does the Talmud go to such lengths to construct an argument that goes against the plain meaning of the biblical text? Five possible explanations may be posited. First, childbirth is one of the occasions after which one is required to recite a special blessing called *birkhat hagomel* (or prayer of Thanksgiving). Halakhah obligates a person to recite this blessing following a situation regarded as in some way dangerous. Childbirth is considered within the parameters of possible danger to one's person.[34] One reason women may be exempted from the obligation to procreate is that the tradition would not consider requiring a woman to put herself in a situation of possible risk. She may, however, voluntarily choose to put herself in circumstances regarded as perilous.

A second explanation may be found in the rabbinic assumption that the state of marriage and family is more "natural" for a woman; she does not need the force of law to impel her to marry and have children. The woman's desire to have children is self-evident. There are two aspects to this second explanation. One is derived from the talmudic dictum *"tav lemetav tan du milemetav armelu,"*[35] roughly translated as "Better for two to dwell together than for each to dwell alone." While the phrase clearly refers both to man and woman, Resh Lakish in the Talmud interprets it as an unarticulated adult female preference to be in a marriage relationship rather than to be single. This may be seen as determined by the general status of women in talmudic times. Only rarely was a woman economically independent and the lack of birth control made intimacy outside of marriage problematic. In addition, rabbinic authorities wished to maintain in some way the connection between sexuality and family responsibility.[36] A second way to understand this explanation concerns rabbinic assumptions as to the different nature of male and female sexual drives. While the Talmud recognizes the intensity of female sexuality as equal to or even greater than the male sex drive,[37] the female sex drive is also considered more hidden, more passive.[38] This may be seen as a male-gendered description of intercourse and its physiology. The male sex drive is viewed as active and aggressive and capable of running out of control. Perhaps because the woman both literally and figuratively carries the responsibility[39] of any resulting child, she is considered less likely to engage in sexual relations outside the established structure. It is also possible for men to attain sexual pleasure in a more mechanical fashion than it is for women.[40] In the rabbinic view, these factors make it more likely that men would seek sexual satisfaction beyond the accepted social parameters. While from a practical standpoint the significant element is limited birth control in rabbinic times, the texts view this as a conceptual difference in male and female sexuality. Thus it might be said that obligating men in the mitzvah of procreation harnesses male sexual desire toward the social goals of individual growth through investment in a committed relationship, continuity of the social fabric through nurturing a family, and perpetuation of the faith community of the Jewish people.

The third and fourth reasons for woman's exemption, while more technical and less immediately psychological, nonetheless have significant implications for the understanding of birth within the life cycle. They are especially important in view of the dissenting opinion expressed in the Mishnah by R. Johanan ben Beroka, who obligates both man and woman.[41] The redactor of the Mishnah saw as desirable the legal consequences of woman's non-obligation in procreation. Her exemption meant that after ten years of marriage without children, a woman could not compel a divorce, as could her husband if he so wished. In addition, if she married someone who already had children, she could not demand that he have more children with her; his obligation was already fulfilled[42] and she had none. The third explanation is thus that the woman's exemption precluded her initiating a divorce in order possibly to have children with another man. However, a series of three tales in the Babylonian Talmud suggests precisely the opposite: the woman should be allowed to divorce in order to have the opportunity to bear children. This is understood both on an existential and practical level. Having a child fulfills a deep human need at the same time that it provides an older, childless woman with someone to look after her as she ages.[43] Thus the implication of a woman's exemption from the command to procreate—that her husband may divorce a barren wife to marry another (or take a second wife)—is made reciprocal.

The fourth implication of relieving a woman of the responsibility to procreate is that it leaves her free to use contraception if she has not yet had any children and wishes to avoid pregnancy.[44] A fifth, less subtle explanation is implied in the reality of patriarchal society. It simply made sense, in David Feldman's words, "is in the nature of things,"[45] that the man, deemed the more aggressive, be made responsible for carrying out the mitzvah.[46] At least theoretically, society permitted polygyny (although not polyandry). This meant a childless woman might not feel compelled to leave her husband if the husband's duty of procreation could be fulfilled through another wife. Intertwined with notions of individual identity, family, community, and continuity, birth remains a private activity with vast public ramifications. How Judaism construes issues of birth control and contraception is the next focus.

Chapter 2

Birth Control and Contraception

The union of a man and his wife is a mystery of the Creation of the world and its population, for in it humanity becomes a partner of the Holy Blessed One in the works of Creation.

Iggeret Hakadosh
(Anonymous thirteenth-century Jewish mystical work)

"Give me children or else I die!" (Genesis 30:1) So moans Rachel to Jacob, envying her sister Leah's fecundity and lamenting her own barrenness. Biblical interpreters over the centuries have commented not only upon Rachel's deep sorrow, but also upon Jacob's unfeeling response: "Jacob's anger was kindled against Rachel and he said, 'Can I take the place of God who has denied you the fruit of the womb?'" (Gen. 30:2)[1] The interpretation of Isaac Arama's, a fifteenth century Spanish exegete,[2] is surprisingly contemporary. His words allude to the creation of woman in Genesis.

The two names "woman" *(isha)* and "Eve" indicate two purposes. The first teaches that woman was taken from man, stressing that like him you may understand and advance in the intellectual and moral field just as did the matriarchs and many righteous women and prophetesses and as the literal meaning of Proverbs 31 about "the woman of worth" *(eshet hayil)* indicates. The second alludes to the power of childbearing and rearing children, as is indicated by the name Eve—mother of all living. A woman deprived of the power of childbearing will be deprived of the secondary purpose and be left with the ability to do evil or good like the man who is barren. . . . Jacob was therefore angry with Rachel when she said "Give me children or else I die," in order to reprimand her and make her understand this all important principle, that she was not dead as far as their joint purpose in life because she was childless, just the same as it would be, in his case, if he would have been childless.[3]

Jacob was angry lest Rachel view herself—her value, her personhood, her identity—solely in terms of her reproductive capacity. Becoming a mother,

Arama states, is ancillary to Rachel's elemental and intrinsic humanity. Arama's explanation reflects the theme of this chapter.

Judaism views marriage as having two purposes: procreation and companionship. These parallel the two creation stories of Genesis, to which Arama alludes, in which reproduction of the species is given as a blessing and the alleviation of existential loneliness is seen as a sine qua non of the relationship.[4] The dialectic between these joint aims forms the basis for the various discussions regarding contraception.

Rabbinic Sources

The primary text to which all subsequent discourse relating to contraception refers is a passage that appears five times in the Talmud[5] and states:

R. Bebai recited before Rabbi Nahman: Three women use the *mokh* [tampon (cotton and wool pad)] in their marital intercourse: a minor, a pregnant woman and a nursing woman. The minor, because she might become pregnant and as a result might die. The pregnant woman, because she might cause her fetus to become a *sandal* [flat]. The nursing woman, because she might have to wean her child prematurely and that would result in his death. And what age is the minor? From the age of eleven years and one day until the age of twelve years and one day. One who is under or over this age carries on her intercourse in the usual manner. This is the opinion of R. Meir. The Sages, however, say: The one as well as the other carries on her marital intercourse in the usual way and mercy will be vouchsafed from heaven, as it is said [in Psalms 116:6]: "The Lord preserves the simple." (T.B. Yevamot 12b)

That contraception was used in Jewish law is clear from this passage. The volumes of responsa literature that explicate this text are concerned with the parameters of that use. The prohibition against or permissibility of birth control, however, is only a small, if significant, part of Jewish attitudes toward contraception.[6] Marriage is considered a necessity for human happiness; a solitary person is viewed as incomplete.[7] The creation of a family is one of the bases upon which marriage is founded. In addition, as will be discussed, the marriage relationship involves the duty of sexual responsibility of the husband toward his wife,[8] which exists apart from the possibility of conception. Marital sex is viewed as integral to *shalom bayit,* or the peace and stability of the home, the deepening of the companionship between husband and wife. Against these essential factors are weighed circumstances relating to the health of the woman and *hash-hatat zera,* destruction or improper emission of seed. Under what conditions may birth control be used? In some circumstances must it be used? What is the status of "wasting of seed"[9] in the discussion and in determining the preferable types of contraceptives? These questions determine the specific framework of the discussion.

The text from T.B. Yevamot 12b reports the minority opinion of R. Meir in detail and the majority view of the Rabbis in a broad statement at the end. R. Meir has the view that three types of women use a *mokh* in intercourse in order to prevent conception and that they do so because pregnancy would pose a risk for them. The text is not explicit as to how the *mokh* is used: is it precoital, inserted before intercourse, or is it postcoital? The ambiguity of the text leads to extended discussions in the subsequent literature. The three women are paradigms of possibly dangerous situations for a woman carrying a fetus. The first example is that of the minor. In Jewish legal sources, this means she is between the ages of eleven and twelve. Why would a girl be married at such a tender age? The Talmud deals with this question in several places.[10] The marriage of a minor, i.e., a young woman under the age of twelve years and one day, was generally frowned upon,[11] even in earlier eras when marriages took place at younger ages. It was, however, a legally valid procedure and at times construed as a social necessity due to the often unstable social and political conditions under which Jews generally lived. Both R. Meir and the Sages interpret such a union as posing a physical danger to the girl/woman. This issue seems to be not a matter of her specific age as much as her age related to the onset of puberty.[12] Prior to that time, pregnancy would not occur, and after that, based on the presumptions of the Talmud, it would not constitute a physical or emotional hazard.[13] Rabbi Meir seems to require the use of a *mokh* during this one-year period, while the Sages do not. Perhaps the entire discussion is a way of expressing through the legal literature hesitation, caution, and even disapproval of marriage of so young a girl.

The second case is that of the pregnant wife. Sexual intimacy itself during pregnancy is not an issue in Judaism, as intercourse need not have the possibility of conception. The aims of affection, love, companionship, and emotional closeness are, as has been indicated, legitimate purposes of marital sexuality.[14] The concern for the pregnant woman is not actually for a risk to her person but rather is a possible danger to the fetus she is carrying. The concern seems to be that a second pregnancy might superimpose itself upon the already existing one, namely, make it flat as a *sandal* (sandal); but the Talmud in another place asserts, "A woman cannot conceive while already pregnant."[15] So what is the fear? Perhaps the sperm itself was considered injurious to the developing fetus. It is interesting that while the text under discussion speaks of contraception during pregnancy without distinction as to the progression of the pregnancy, another passage views intercourse in the first trimester as injurious both to the woman and the fetus; during the second trimester injurious to the mother but beneficial to the fetus; and in the last trimester of benefit to both.[16] Commentators on this passage over the centuries have attempted to explain its basis, which clearly expresses a concern for the safe development of the fetus as well as the emotional and physical needs of the couple. Interestingly, another passage speaks—without reference to a distinction of trimesters—of the husband's mitzvah of bringing joy to his wife during pregnancy through regular conjugal relations.[17]

The presence of these passages in the talmudic corpus indicates the concern and fear some felt for the health of both the embryo and the pregnant woman. While some of the conclusions and medical assumptions have clearly been superseded by the development of modern gynecology and obstetrics, the ethical, emotional, and psychological aspects of the passages are universally relevant. Some contemporary research on sexuality affirms the observations of the Sages. For example, Masters and Johnson describe heightened sexual interest toward the end of pregnancy and assert that possible risk to the fetus or the onset of premature labor are so small as to negate the general advice to avoid intimacy during the final trimester.[18]

The nursing mother may or must use the *mokh* primarily in order to protect an already existing child. She is considered at risk in that a second pregnancy might affect lactation and compel the weaning of her infant. While the text of course refers to a time when breast feeding was the sole means of nutrition for an infant, the responsa literature analyzes various permutations of similar and related circumstances. Taking into account the well-known fact that pregnancy during lactation was indeed a fairly common occurrence, responsa over the centuries express concern as well for the health of a woman who would be pregnant twice in quick succession. Thus the reference in the text to a nursing mother is interpreted as applicable in ways in which danger might result either for her or for her infant.

These, then, are the three women who are considered at risk and who serve as conceptual models for all the subsequent discussions of contraception. The interpretation of the text leads to the various responsa as to when birth control is understood to be legitimate and which kinds of contraception are preferable. The first question in interpreting the text is whether the language is descriptive, prescriptive, or proscriptive. Is the initial statement saying, "Three women *must* use the *mokh*" or "Three women *may* use the *mokh*"? As a legal text, the Mishnah is concerned with ascertaining permitted and prohibited behaviors. While sociological description is an integral part of legal discourse, its inclusion is for the purpose of reaching a legal decision: is X permitted or prohibited and under what circumstances?

The text states that R. Meir's opinion is a minority opinion, as the Sages disagree with him. The precise meaning of the disagreement can only be clarified once Rabbi Meir's statement is understood. If Rabbi Meir meant that the three women *may* use the *mokh,* the Sages' view would be that they *may not* use the *mokh*. If, however, R. Meir's intention was that the women *must* use the *mokh,* the Sages' contrary argument would be that they *may* but are not required to use it. The talmudic commentator Rashi understood Rabbi Meir's statement as descriptive: the three women in fact use — and may use — the *mokh*. The Sages' contrary view would then be that they may not. The implication of Rashi's view is that contraception is prohibited according to the majority opinion. In contrast, the Tosafot commentary on the text disagrees with Rashi's reading, understanding Rabbi Meir to be maintaining that the women must use a *mokh,* in which case the Sages' opinion is that the women are not required to do so. Another way of saying this is that according to Tosafot, the Sages *permit* the use of contraception, while Rabbi Meir *requires* it. The implication then is that in the opinion of the Sages the women may do as they wish. This seems to be the position of Tosafot.

Interpretation of the minority view of Rabbi Meir's provides one set of guidelines for deciphering the rabbinic understanding of contraception. Another is based upon the issue of whether the *mokh* is to be used pre- or post-coitus. Rashi's opinion gives no specific directive as to the timing of the use of the *mokh,* although his language leans toward insertion prior to intercourse. Tosafot, in contrast, presumes the text refers to a postcoital device. Deriving from the Hebrew root *m-v-k-h,* which means to sink, crush, or soften, the term *mokh* indicates a cotton tampon. Prior to intercourse it would block the cervix, forming a barrier to the sperm, while postcoitus it would absorb the semen already present. The opinion of Tosafot that the use of a *mokh* must be after intercourse accords with the view that its precoital use entails the violation of the law prohibiting wasteful emission of sperm or "wasting of seed." As noted earlier,[19] this phrase, from Genesis 38, refers to the act of Onan, who "cast his seed upon the ground."

The history of the halakhic literature with regard to actual legal precedent on the use of birth control spans the spectrum from the restrictive, based on Rashi's interpretations of the text, to the lenient, following the analysis of Tosafot. The rishonim, the early authorities writing before the *Shulhan Arukh* was published in 1565, generally follow the more lenient reading. That is, while the three women *must* use contraception, all other women *may,* if they wish. One reason for the overriding rejection by the rishonim of Rashi's position is its logical conclusion: if Rabbi Meir means *may,* the Sages mean *may not.* But how can the Sages proscribe the use of precautions in order to avoid danger? Surely this goes against the priority of *pikuah nefesh,* the setting aside of the entire Torah to save life, in all halakhic decisions.[20] Interestingly, that all other women may use contraception is considered "a little too lenient for practical ruling."[21]

A majority of the aharonim, the post-sixteenth-century authorities, follow the readings of the rishonim who follow Tosafot. However, some seem concerned to avoid the open-ended implication or permission to "other women" to use the *mokh,* at least after intercourse. What they do, then, is accept Rashi's interpretation as operative and then proceed to carve out areas of permissibility and limitations of the stricter implications. A survey of the various analyses indicates both a reluctance to offer carte blanche in terms of contraception and a deep concern for the health of the woman. Clearly what is in question here are not the natural risks implicit in pregnancy and childbirth, but danger(s) in addition to those shared by all pregnant women. Thus contraception is indicated at least in circumstances of possible risk.[22]

The opinions of the aharonim may be divided into those which are more permissive and those which are more restrictive. An example of the permissive group is to be found in the work of Rabbi Solomon Luria, author of *Yam shel Shlomo.*[23] R. Luria agrees with Rashi's interpretation that the text on the three women assumes precoital use of the *mokh* and that is why the Sages do not permit the *mokh,* since it would constitute "wasting of the seed," or *hash-hatat zera.* The Sages are not, therefore, objecting to postcoital use of the *mokh.* Luria concurs with Rashi's view that the talmudic text involves disagreement over precoital use of the *mokh,* but demurs in the view that intercourse in such circumstances is improper. Were that to be the case, he argues, intercourse with a barren or pregnant wife would be proscribed. The halakhah, however, encourages sexual intimacy even when procreation is not possible, because of the mitzvah of *onah*[24] or cohabitation, but also in the broader meaning of furthering the happiness within the marriage relationship. R. Luria concludes that while the Sages do not require the three women to use the *mokh* prior to intercourse, they surely neither object to the use of contraception nor prohibit other women from its use. Luria states "That any woman may use the *mokh* is the correct inference."[25] R. Luria's permissive ruling even with regard to sterilization *(kos shel ikarin)* indicates that he views birth control as generally open to all women who wish to prevent further pregnancies. In his view a woman may certainly use a *mokh* prior to intercourse; her desire to do so may be due not only to palpable risk and pain, but also to concern over the emotional, moral, and physical care of the existing children. This is a ruling with broad implications, taking account of both subjective and objective realities.

The restrictive group of aharonim is well represented by R. Akiva Eger, a nineteenth-century talmudist from Posen in Prussia.[26] In discussing this group, it is important to note that contemporary scholarship indicates none of its members seems to have had access to R. Luria's responsum; their analyses contain no references to it.[27] The conclusion of R. Akiva Eger's argumentation, culled from several responsa, is to ban even postcoital birth control in cases of difficult, perhaps hazardous, childbirth. Later interpreters argue with this reading, claiming he could not have been writing about a situation of physical danger, but was referring instead to a woman of "troubled spirit."[28] The reasoning is that in the case of actual physical risk, R. Eger would be lenient; according to this comment, he should be equally lenient in regarding a "troubled spirit" as a risk equivalent to physical endangerment. While R. Eger is the most extreme of the strict interpreters from the period of the aharonim, it is interesting to note that his son-in-law, R. Moses Sofer of Pressburg (d. 1839), also took a restrictive perspective. He added the point that the husband's knowledge and permission should be part of the woman's decision, indicating perhaps that sometimes the husband had not been consulted. R. Eger and R. Sofer excluded (at least) the use of the precoital *mokh* and set the tone for contemporary responsa that reach restrictive decisions. On the one hand, one wonders, however, how these restrictive opinions might have been different had the more lenient view of R. Luria been available as precedent. On the other, it is noteworthy that no other legal authority manifested the bent of mind and kind of analysis expressed by R. Luria.

R. Luria's ruling on the *mokh* reclassified it as a device which does not involve "wasted seed." But it was not until the middle of the nineteenth century that his responsum began to be known.[29] Both in the interim and subsequent to awareness of R. Luria's lenient reading, the development of new (and revisions of old) methods of contraception came into use. Use of the cervical cap or diaphragm was generally accepted as free of the conceptual complications of the *mokh,* since it did not destroy the sperm, but rather prevented sperm from entering the uterus. Normal coitus is maintained. This is not the case with the use of a condom, which some legal decisors regarded as interfering with the sex act: the sperm does not even enter the woman (which of course is the purpose of the condom). In addition, some considered the condom as interfering with the pleasure of the act. However, halakhic decisors recognize that the condom in some cases may be the only device available and may be used in the absence of a preferable alternative. Others claim that since what has been termed "unnatural"[30] coitus is surely permitted within a heterosexual relationship, condoms can certainly be used. R. Luria's opinion cited the talmudic phrase *"guf nehenh min haguf"*[31] to indicate the principle of mutual physical pleasure intrinsic to the marital act, a pleasure somewhat diminished by condoms. While circumstances—especially the contemporary spread of AIDS—may at times warrant the use of condoms, condoms generally are not a preferred method of birth control. Contemporary halakhic decisors accept the use of spermicides and other chemical methods of contraception, while oral contraceptives have the approval even of those who are most restrictive. This is especially so in light of the fine-tuning of birth control pills over the years, as more information on the effect of the pill has become available to pharmacologists and physicians.

Oral contraceptives have a different basis in the talmudic literature than the text about the three women and the *mokh*. Known primarily as *kos shel ikarin,*[32] the cup of roots or herbs, this mixture is considered efficacious as an oral contraceptive in the talmudic literature and the subsequent responsa. While it would be fascinating from a medical point of view to be able to ascertain precisely what this mixture contained, this is not known. Some conjecture that perhaps a placebo effect was operative. Twentieth-century responsa are unaware of the constitutive pharmacological elements; the *kos shel ikarin* seems to have functioned as a folk remedy which did, at times, succeed. When discussed in the responsa, the sterilizing potion is generally assumed to have a permanent effect upon fertility; it also, of course, does not involve wasting of the seed. The oral contraceptive indicated in the Talmud, whatever forms it may have taken in later centuries, is considered to be nearly free of the legal problems involving the *mokh*.[33] In contemporary terms, this means that the pill, certainly in its much safer revised forms,[34] is regarded as the most preferable method of contraception. Given the lack of halakhic impediments to its use, the pill surely revolutionized the pattern of Jewish family life. The use of the birth control pill, however, is always seen as weighed against both the mitzvah to "be fertile and increase" and the deep human desire to create a family.[35]

This brief survey of the rabbinic sources regarding contraception provides the background for exploring what the current literature of Orthodox, Conservative, and Reform Judaism states with regard to contraception. A fuller picture of the current status of this issue requires an examination of both responsa and sociological descriptions of behavior within each group. Thus the assessment will derive from a theoretical framework (the responsa) as well as the parameters of lived experience (everyday life as manifested in sociological descriptions).

Orthodox Perspectives

Orthodox analyses of contraception and responsa, in general, tend to espouse a strict perspective in terms of birth control use. But as a noted author indicates, "'Permitted' or 'forbidden' in the final judgement of Jewish law codes tells only a small part of the story of Judaism's attitude towards birth control."[36] As has been seen, the legal decisions emerge from a complex conceptual matrix expressing a philosophy of human nature, marriage, and sexuality. The legal literature emanating from traditional or Orthodox sources tends to interpret the sources in a way that maximizes the childbearing possibilities for the woman, and of course for her husband and family as well. Some responsa justify their strict stance on purely legal principles. But all legal arguments by definition are grounded in social, political, and historical assumptions.[37]

The noted Orthodox bioethicist, Dr. Fred Rosner, provides an example of the traditional viewpoint.[38] The tone of Rosner's discussion is set at the beginning when he places the question in a moral framework. He is arguing against the view that "preventing the natural process of conception by contraception and preventing the natural process of obesity by diet or pills"[39] are analogous.

That there exist standards of right and wrong as part of a Divine scheme leads to the notion of a moral dimension in considering the use of birth control. Since "be fertile and increase" is a mitzvah, a commandment from the Torah, the use of contraceptives cannot be indiscriminate or completely self-determined, as might the use of diet aids to control weight gain. Rosner states that certain arguments used to justify contraception are "immoral."[40] One is the economic argument, which states that parents should have children according to how many they can adequately support. Rather than turn to contraception as a solution for economic limitations, society should equalize the distribution of wealth and other resources. While recognizing that certain medical conditions preclude pregnancy, Rosner states that "to masquerade behind a medical condition, particularly psychiatric illness[,] is certainly immoral."[41] The same is said of what Rosner terms "reasons of convenience";[42] these include the stability of the marriage, the desire of the wife to pursue professional goals, and the reluctance "to give up an active social life."[43] Rosner concludes that the Jewish attitude toward birth control by any method "is a non-permissive one if no medical or psychiatric threat to the mother or child exists."[44] In cases where danger is present during pregnancy, rabbinic authorities must be consulted in order for birth control to be sanctioned. At that point the hierarchy of acceptability of various methods of contraception comes into play, oral contraceptives being the most preferred.

A volume indicating the views of the Chief Rabbi of Great Britain offers a second Orthodox opinion.[45] "Contraception is therefore prohibited, except when overridden by considerations of the mother's health."[46] A third source proclaims: "Where the reasons for the request to use contraceptives are based on considerations other than medical (i.e., convenience, economic considerations, good looks, interference with career, profession, life-style, etc.), the Rabbis have generally not permitted such use."[47]

At this point it is useful to examine some of the responsa regarding birth control of the great Orthodox *posek*, or halakhic decisor, R. Moses Feinstein. Although born and educated in Eastern Europe, he lived in the United States from 1937 until his death and was regarded as a pivotal figure in the strengthening of the American Orthodox community after World War II. The eight volumes of his *Iggerot Moshe*, based on the halakhic queries sent to him, bear testimony to the high esteem in which he was held by the Orthodox laity, as well as other rabbis and lesser scholars. Encyclopedic halakhic knowledge, coupled with an astute grasp of the nuances of life in American society, made R. Feinstein a much-sought-after decisor in religious and ethical matters.

A responsum from 1979[48] relates the situation of a woman suffering from depression. Feinstein considers this condition to be a danger to the woman and permits the use of a diaphragm. Given the time frame, it is interesting that Feinstein also writes about oral contraceptives and the IUD, but does not recommend use of either due to the frequent breakthrough bleeding they can cause. In later years the strength of hormones in the pill was considerably lowered, eliminating the problem and making this method of contraception overall much safer. Harmful side effects of the IUD led to its discontinuance. As noted, from a halakhic standpoint oral contraceptives are the preferred method, but in 1979 they were not yet perfected. A 1978 responsum describes a family situation in which stress has led both parents, at times, to resort to physical violence with their children. R. Feinstein describes the mother as ill from the many strains of caring for small children (we are not told how many) and says to use a diaphragm for a period of two years.[49] Clearly he sees repeated hitting of children as the outcome of an emotional disorder. At the conclusion of these responsa, Feinstein wishes each person a speedy recovery in language commensurate with the individual situation of the writer. Encapsulating social, historical, personal, and halakhic information, the *teshuvah* or responsa literature as evidenced in R. Feinstein's volumes is a rich and nuanced genre.

In traditional circles the pressure to have children can be very powerful. A young woman I know, still a college student when she got married, was queried six months after the wedding by a young male friend from her hometown: "What!" he exclaimed after looking her up and down, "not pregnant yet?"[50] An ultra-Orthodox woman with five healthy children underwent extensive infertility treatments, including hormone injections and surgery; the stated reason was that everyone else in her neighborhood had at least eight children.[51] Interestingly, the pressure to reproduce is seen as characteristic not only of Orthodox Jews, but also of Israeli society as a whole. As recent research indicates, reproductive technology is underwritten by the Israeli socialized medical system, while contraceptives "are generally not part of the basic basket of medical services covered by Israeli health insurance."[52]

While these experiences and data indicate widespread restrictive interpretations of the various opinions regarding contraception found in the halakhic literature or their summaries, sociological descriptions of the actual behavior of women who identify themselves as Orthodox imply a more complex picture. Statistically, the use of birth control is almost universal among American Jewish women as a group; this includes modern Orthodox, Conservative, Reform, and unaffiliated Jewish women.[53] Even women who are part of right-wing or ultra-Orthodox communities are not immune to the influence of readily available, generally safe contraception. Field work in these communities indicates that over 70 percent of ultra-Orthodox women report using birth control after having at least one child. Interestingly, many stated they had not told their husbands they were using birth control. Others who used contraception said the reason was "health" rather than "personal."[54]

Conservative Perspectives

The Conservative stance on contraception is discussed in a responsum by R. Ben Zion Bokser.[55] As in Dr. Rosner's analysis, Bokser puts the issue in a moral context. He begins his statement expressing concern for the world population explosion, and then narrows the focus: "The moral aspect of birth control faces us . . . in the immediacy of the individual family."[56] In describing this moral aspect, Bokser refers immediately both to economic and health concerns and proceeds to review briefly the rabbinic literature regarding the mitzvah of "be fertile and increase." He notes that the bringing forth of children is a primary way in which human beings partner with God in creation, continuing the weaving of the tapestry of human history.[57] Although the mitzvah of procreation is fulfilled with the birth of a daughter and a son, the Sages advocated larger families, primarily, in Bokser's view, to benefit the parents. Despite urging large families, there was recognition that in some situations it was "morally right" to limit pregnancy.[58] Of greatest concern was the health of the mother, in which case, depending on the individual set of circumstances, birth control was not only permitted, but mandated. According to Bokser's responsum, such would be the case if the fetus had a fatal disease or a mental abnormality. The physician would be the one to assess the condition of the mother and/or the fetus and decide on the appropriate course of action. Although Bokser does not specify, the assumption is that the medical expertise of the physician would inform the ethical/moral decision of the rabbi.

Another reason justifying use of birth control, according to Bokser, is "perilous conditions confronting the community."[59] World overpopulation, however, does not come under this category. As regards the Jewish community, the tragic losses during the Holocaust preclude "overpopulation" as a reason to prevent pregnancy. Among other nations and in other parts of the world, overpopulation cannot precisely be ascertained; should it develop, however, each country, and especially the wealthier nations, would have to deal with its impact. Bokser does not see the concept of world overpopulation as justifying limitation of Jewish births. On the contrary, "The duty to raise a family is indeed of paramount sanctity in Judaism."[60] When it conflicts with the preservation of life, however, the latter is always the higher obligation.[61]

Bokser concludes his analysis by stating that the application of the general guidelines governing birth control necessitate thoughtful and lengthy consideration. But cognizance of its justifiability under certain circumstances means open access to medical information. "The law" (and here Bokser means general law, not halakhah) must guard against the abuse of contraception, but not curtail the dissemination of information.

This responsum carefully traces the arguments in rabbinic sources. It differs from the Orthodox discussions in two ways: economic hardship is recognized as a possible legitimate warrant for the use of contraception and there is a palpable difference in tone. The more brusque tone of Dr. Rosner's analysis may be a result of style, personality, and/or moral stance. While the actual content of the Orthodox and Conservative views as expressed here is very similar,[62] Baker's tone implies greater flexibility and adaptability.

A Conservative rabbi of great stature, R. Isaac Klein published many responsa over the years.[63] In writing about birth control, he states that contraception is forbidden not because it is an unnatural or immoral act, but only when it prevents the fulfillment of the commandment to "be fertile and increase." In some cases, as has been shown, birth control is indeed prescribed. Klein also brings the opinion that one is forbidden to have children at a time of famine.[64] The central concern expressed regards the "evils" of overpopulation; Klein permits use of birth control in order to prevent the population explosion.[65] Other halakhic decisors do not agree; the loss of six million is considered reason enough to bring more Jews into the world. This is the case with Orthodox *poskim* (decisors), as well as the Reform author of many responsa, R. Solomon B. Freehof. Freehof writes: "[A]s far as the Jewish people is concerned, the situation is . . . different than with the world population as a whole. . . . we have lost, through mass murder, six million. . . . To us, every child is doubly precious."[66] In a further discussion of family planning,[67] Klein brings an array of halakhic sources to support his conclusion that despite the high value placed on parenthood in Judaism, in some circumstances it is not only "morally right," but even obligatory to avoid pregnancy,[68] the preferred method being the pill.[69]

Contrary to concerns expressed in both Rosner's and Bokser's analyses, sociological research indicates that among career women in general, Jewish career women are more committed to having children than any other group.[70] However, as within the larger group of white, middle-class American women, Jewish career women tend to postpone childbearing until they attain desired professional achievement and/or economic stability. This creates a problem not yet clearly understood by medical authorities: many women for whom conception and gestation occur readily while in their twenties encounter problems later on. The issue of birth control is grounded in the view that women have the right to protect themselves from unwanted pregnancies—a notion supported, in different ways, both in halakhah and in American law. However, while this protection can be legislated, there is no commensurate "right" to bear children at will. Feminism emphasizes the right to control one's destiny, including one's reproductive destiny. But the moral issues are more complex than the notion of "control" indicates. Assuming the value of having children, it may be that in order to avoid primary or secondary infertility, family needs to be a goal prior to—or parallel with—economic viability and professional accomplishment. Ultimately this entails a rethinking of goals not only by husbands and wives, but also by Jewish communal institutions and society at large.

Women affiliated with the Conservative movement are among the large group of Jewish women who use birth control "as a matter of course."[71] To what extent are the halakhic discussions of Conservative rabbis and scholars part of the decision-making process of Conservative Jews? This is to ask a question different from that which might be asked when describing Orthodoxy. By definition, Orthodox Judaism, from its most right-wing manifestations to its left-wing advocates, is deeply intertwined with halakhah as a central determining force in the theoretical and practical theology of Judaism.[72] The issue of the role of halakhah in the Conservative movement in Judaism is more complex. Committed to the ideological premise "that Judaism is normative yet has a strong developmental dimension," the contemporary Conservative movement has been weakened by a general disregard for and lack of knowledge about the legal traditions of Judaism among its laity.[73] Scholars committed to Conservative ideology have urged that every effort be extended "to make *halakhah* a living reality in the Conservative Movement,"[74] to define better the norms of the movement.

Reform Perspectives

The responsa of the Reform movement operate within parameters different from those of Orthodox and Conservative Judaism. Halakhah, both the norms and the legal process used to arrive at the norms, serve as guidelines to behavior; they are not viewed as binding. Halakhah may recommend, but may not mandate. Thus it would seem unlikely that the Reform movement would develop a substantial corpus of responsa literature. Nonetheless, from its inception in the late eighteenth century, certain issues were argued on halakhic grounds. By the mid-nineteenth century, however, very few responsa were written, although gatherings of Reform rabbis included vigorous and sometimes acrimonious debate with regard to halakhic opinions.

One of the outstanding early proponents of Reform Judaism in the United States, R. Jacob Z. Lauterbach, stressed the continuity of Reform Judaism with rabbinic traditions. Written up until his death in 1942, his responsa attempted to demonstrate that Reform Jews can look to the halakhah for guidance, perspective, and enrichment, even without regarding halakhic formulations as obligatory. Although the responsum on contraception was written in 1927, several decades before the development of the pill and during the time of vigorous advocacy for widely available birth control in the United States,[75] it provides a direction that is helpful in dealing with contraception even now, over three-quarters of a century later. Lauterbach shows how halakhic reasoning can untangle moral conundra and lead to decisions—often even to clarity—regarding issues that are morally complex and ambiguous. The extent to which Reform lay people facing ethical and moral dilemmas consult the responsa literature, however, is small. As one source of ethical guidance among many, the halakhah is given some priority, but is not necessarily decisive.

Lauterbach[76] begins his responsum by differentiating between the authority of aggadah, or homiletics, and halakhah in the Talmud. He uses talmudic sources to argue that questions of religious practice, issues of "what is forbidden or permitted by the law,"[77] cannot be decided according to aggadic sources, but only on the authority of halakhah. This, of course, is to accord authority to halakhah beyond mere recommendation. Lauterbach in this responsum makes clear, based on rabbinic principles, that halakhah carries much greater weight in Jewish legal decisions than haggadah. But this is not to give halakhah the final word.[78] The frame of Lauterbach's argument is to decry as invalid the claim in some responsa[79] that all contraception (except abstinence) comes under the category of "the spilling of seed," or "wasting of semen," comparable to masturbation. These responsa, according to Lauterbach, cite aggadic sources which inveigh against masturbation and apply these sources in a way leading[80] to the conclusion that just as masturbation (Lauterbach also calls it "self-abuse") is prohibited,[81] birth control is proscribed. Lauterbach then proceeds to reformulate the question under consideration. He asks: "Does the Talmudic-rabbinic law permit cohabitation between husband and wife in such a manner or under such conditions as would make conception impossible; and if so, what are the conditions under which such cohabitation is permitted?"[82]

The first part of the question, based on the sources already examined above, is answered in the affirmative. It is clear from rabbinic sources that a husband is not only permitted but even obligated to have sexual intercourse with his wife if she is sterile or has undergone menopause. In such cases, although conception is not possible, ejaculation through intercourse is not considered a "wasteful discharge of semen" *(hash-hatat zera levatalah)*. This is because it results from legitimate gratification of a normal and natural desire—satisfying sexual passion and the expression of love between husband and wife.

Lauterbach then asks if the view that sexual intimacy may take place when procreation is biologically impossible can be applied to a young couple capable of having children. Is it permissible for them to gratify normal sexual desire through intimacy "in a manner not resulting in procreation"?[83] A lengthy analysis of rabbinic sources follows, which concludes that intercourse may take place in any manner even if the specific preference of the couple (as to sexual position, etc.) would prohibit the possibility of conception. Lauterbach's comments with regard to what he terms "coitus abruptus" are especially interesting.[84]

Lauterbach then examines the *baraita* text of the three women and the *mokh,* reviewing the various interpretations, including the more lenient reading of R. Solomon Luria.[85] Lauterbach's elucidation of this pivotal text leads him to the following conclusion: "The rule indicated by the baraita would . . . teach us that, according to the opinion of all the teachers, it is not forbidden to use a contraceptive in cases where conception would bring harm either to the mother or to the child born or unborn."[86] How is the "bringing of harm" to be understood? Here Lauterbach's reading is innovative and creative. Using the text, or *baraita,* as the basis of argument, he says he cannot "see any difference between protecting a child from the danger of being deprived of the nourishment of its mother's milk and protecting the already born children of the family from the harm which might come to them due to the competition [in care and comfort] of a larger number of sisters and brothers."[87] This is directly stated in the reference to "the child born or unborn."

Luria gives permission to a woman who has morally corrupt children—and fears having more like them—to sterilize herself.[88] He bases this upon the text in T.B. Yevamot 65b, in which R. Hiyya's wife drinks a potion to render herself sterile due to extremely painful deliveries. Lauterbach extends this permission to the case of hereditary disease carried by either spouse which "might" be passed to the fetus.[89]

A man may practice total abstinence (although it is not recommended) and then is guilty of not fulfilling the mitzvah of procreation. Similarly, Lauterbach argues, a couple may use birth control, the result of which is also the man's not fulfilling the mitzvah. It is permitted for a man to have intercourse with his wife if conception will not result. The only objection could be that the husband has not as yet fulfilled the mitzvah. If, however, the couple already has two children[90] and is no longer legally obligated to have additional progeny,[91] "there can be no objection at all to the practice of birth control"; a man may not consider additional children a blessing, depending on the particular circumstances of his family.[92]

Lauterbach also brings the opinion that despite his legal obligation to procreate, rabbinic law allows a man to delay marriage and children—indeed, even to remain unmarried all his life. While this view is found in the classic rabbinic literature,[93] Lauterbach proceeds to affirm the primacy of marriage in rabbinic teaching. The Torah asserts, "It is not good for the human being *[adam]* to be alone; I will make a helpmeet opposite him [i.e., Adam]" (Genesis 2:18). It does not state, "I will make a spouse for Adam in order that they have children." The companionship, partnership, affection, and love aspects of the marital relationship are deemed of inestimable value. Nonetheless, a man could be exempted from the religious duty of procreation when such duty would detract from another religious obligation, the study of Torah. Lauterbach indirectly extends the mitzvah of *limud Torah,* or the study of Torah, to "any other moral religious activities which might be interfered with by . . . having children."[94]

Further, Lauterbach criticizes the rabbinic authorities of the eighteenth and nineteenth centuries, those who constitute what Feldman termed the restrictive or "non-permissive school."[95] He sees them as having been unduly influenced by the aggadic and mystical literature, their arguments based upon erroneous interpretations of the relevant texts, which ignored the "correct" interpretations and "sound reasoning" of Solomon Luria.[96] Feldman, writing decades later, showed that what Lauterbach maintained was excessive influence of aggadic texts was also caused by the unavailability of Luria's responsum to the more strict decisors.[97]

Included in the summation of Lauterbach's opinion is not only practical jurisprudence, but also the philosophy of law that undergirds his view of the relationship of rabbinic law to modern Judaism.[98] The summary of Lauterbach's opinion, based upon the "correct" understanding of the relevant texts, the medieval rabbinic authorities, and Luria, reads as follows:

1. "Talmudic-rabbinic law"[99] does not view the use of contraception as immoral. It does not prohibit birth control, but does prohibit "birth suppression."

2. Every "Jew" is required to have at least two children in fulfillment of the biblical command to procreate, which is obligatory for "every man." Lauterbach's careful language implies that while the mitzvah is legally incumbent upon the man, women have an obligation as well.

3. Three conditions exist, however, under which a man may be exempt from this obligation: when engaged in the study of Torah and concerned that family responsibilities will hinder him; when married to a woman unable to have children; and when considerations of health and safety of the woman make childbearing dangerous. In this case, the woman may use contraceptives and is even permitted to sterilize herself.

4. Once the mitzvah is fulfilled through the birth of two children, the man's obligation has been met. The woman may use contraception. Lauterbach offers the following caveat:

5. "Of course," he states, "the use of any contraceptive device 'is allowed' only when both wife and husband consent."[100]

The philosophy of halakhah expounded by Lauterbach expresses a perspective that is not specifically "Reform" nor particularly "Conservative" in its approach. Rather, he articulates the conceptual bases upon which *p'sak halakhah,* legal adjudication of a halakhic issue, has always occurred. One carefully examines the primary sources, i.e., the relevant passages in the Talmud. Then one consults the commentaries of the rishonim, or early (pre-sixteenth century) authorities, and the aharonim, or later (post-sixteenth century) authorities. Next one gathers current information, including historical, scientific, and personal, and scrutinizes the most recent legal analyses relating to the question at hand.

One accepts some opinions and does not accept others. Finally, one formulates one's own response to the issue. "[W]e need not expect absolute agreement on questions of rabbinic law," Lauterbach affirms, but "must be content to have good and reliable authority for our decisions, even though other authorities may differ."[101] The methodology of adjudication described here is that of the classic rabbinic responsa.[102] Even the give and take of traditional halakhic argumentation includes the notion of ascribing lesser value to aggadic statements in arguing halakhic case law.[103]

What, then, makes this responsum representative of the Reform movement?[104] The primary reason is that it was written by a scholar affiliated with the movement. In disregarding the aggadic literature that advocates many children, in following Luria's more lenient reading, and in acknowledging the conflicts intrinsic to all legal rulings, Lauterbach insists on basing his conclusion on firm halakhic ground. Indeed, this is different from many aspects of thinking in the Reform movement, in which halakhah is seen as suggestive or advisory but not binding in any way. The individual takes note of the rabbinic view as one factor in making her/his decision. In this strategy, autonomous ethical thinking takes priority over rabbinic mandate.

Perhaps the perspective of Reform Judaism as exemplified in Lauterbach's responsum is best explained by referring to a contemporary analysis of procreation by the Reform theologian Eugene B. Borowitz. In his many works focusing on modern Jewish thought and Reform Judaism, Borowitz crystallizes how the interfacing of modernity, Jewish ethics, and tradition poses a challenge to the Judaism of the late twentieth and early twenty-first centuries.

The essence of Judaism, according to Borowitz, revolves around what he terms "Covenantal decision making" and "Covenantal obligations."[105] Not universal ethics, Borowitz claims, but the covenant with God grounds the Jewish person, undergirding the decisions a Jewish individual makes.[106] How is one to respond, then, when a conflict arises between duty to God and covenantal obligations? "Duty to God" indicates the realm of ethics, while "Covenantal obligations" are commandments arising from the classic rabbinic texts. Borowitz writes, "[T]he primal ethical thrust of classic Judaism now demands greater weight than it once had in determining our Jewish obligations. . . . [I]ts immediate consequence is a greatly increased regard for the dignity of the individual. . . ."[107] It is in this context of a possible conflict of values that Borowitz mentions contraception and the birth of Jewish children. On the one hand, he says, ". . . I realized the ethical unsupportability of the Jewish duty to procreate."[108] There is an intrinsic "special danger" to which a Jewish child is subjected. "All the joys and advantages of being a Jew cannot ethically compensate for loading this ineradicable disability on another."[109] Yet there is a clear covenantal responsibility not only "to proclaim the duty to have Jewish children,"[110] but indeed to bring Jewish children into this world. The continuity of the Covenant (a term that Borowiz capitalizes) requires the biological continuity of generations.

Borowitz discusses contraception in two additional contexts. First, in *Choosing a Sex Ethic: A Jewish Inquiry,* an entire chapter is devoted to contraception as an ethical necessity. Borowitz argues the parameters of premarital sex, analyzing types of relationships and contraception as "the ethical prerequisite to any justified premarital sexual intercourse."[111]

Part of this volume was reprinted as "When Is It Moral To Have Intercourse?" in *Exploring Jewish Ethics;*[112] here the emphasis is on creating committed relationships. Borowitz shows how the modern world offers a freedom that is at once exhilarating and dangerous and how "decency" has replaced living by Jewish covenantal standards: "[D]evoted Jews . . . will live the Covenant by sanctifying every aspect of their existence and most certainly their sexual behavior."[113] For Borowitz, sexuality in Judaism is a central means of serving God. In addition, he writes that since the Covenant depends upon "Jewish biologic-historic continuity" he has "no choice but to proclaim the Jewish duty to have children."[114] Thus sexuality on its own, as well as procreation as an outcome of sexuality, are essential values. As Borowitz proclaims, "Though the overwhelming majority of Jews worldwide have given up the authority of halakhah, they still manifest a will to Jewish continuity."[115] In the second reference, Borowitz puts forth an interpretation of Lauterbach's responsum that is quite surprising. He affirms that Lauterbach's analysis, though written in 1927, remains timely and relevant for Reform Jews because "Lauterbach concluded his search of the *halakhah* with a straightforward appeal to conscience unbutressed by talmudic citation or precedent."[116]

As indicated above, I read Lauterbach as using traditional methods of rabbinic adjudication to arrive at a lenient reading of the sources. When Lauterbach writes, "We have the right to judge for ourselves which view is the sounder and which authorities are more correct,"[117] who is the "we"? Is it the *posek* (specialist in rabbinic law), or is it every individual person? As halakhah precedent in Reform Judaism serves as guidance rather than command, Borowitz understands Lauterbach to be explaining how he arrived at his suggestion, which may be one among several to be weighed by the individual. Even if the Jewish view in Reform decision-making carries greater weight than other considerations, it remains one factor among several. Critical moral reasoning is left to the discretion of each person. Is Lauterbach giving a "straightforward appeal to conscience" without grounding his view in talmudic precedent? No. Rather, what appears to have happened is that Borowitz has interpreted Lauterbach in a way consonant with his own view of the centrality of autonomy, one of the vertical polarities now to be discussed.

The Vertical Polarities

Public and Private Spheres

This analysis of issues surrounding birth and birth control has summarized the classic rabbinic sources and examined how each movement in contemporary Judaism uses these sources within its own ideological framework. The public/private polarity further illuminates the views presented here. Surely the capacity to carry life and give birth to children, in a strict biological sense, implies certain social roles. Childbirth has an impact on the body, which needs to heal from the birthing process. The need for healing, as well as the subsequent lactation, have social consequences as to a woman's "role" or "status" in the public domain, since healing and lactation generally occur within the home. But these realities do not necessarily point to an essentialist understanding of masculinity and femininity, in which the domestic domain is the primary arena of female creativity, while the public sphere remains almost exclusively male.

While the Bible proposes a perfected monotheistic society as its ideal aim, the reality of biblical society, as embedded with the cultural milieu of the ancient Near East, was that women were subordinate to men in law and in custom, as they were throughout the ancient world. Woman's purpose was often seen as limited to reproduction. Female contributions to cultural development were rare (or not recorded). Property rights and financial independence were limited. But as pointed out by the contemporary scholar of the Hebrew Bible, Tikva Frymer-Kensky, "[T]he Bible presents no characteristics of human behavior as 'female' or 'male,' no division of attributes between the poles of 'feminine' and 'masculine'. . . . As far as the Bible presents humanity, gender is a matter of biology and social roles, it is not a question of basic nature or identity."[118] Thus Frymer-Kensky argues, based on her study of the Bible itself, against the concept of the presumably more private nature of women.

Judith Hauptman, in her analysis of women in talmudic literature, makes a similar claim. She derives her view from the text of the Tosefta (written at the same time as, but not included in, the Mishnah), which suggests a blurring of domestic/private and public spheres. The Tosefta describes the many artisans and workmen who visited the home, which thus appears not to have been a reclusive female arena, but rather the center of a variety of important economic and creative activities. The mistress of the household often supervised both male and female servants. She visited friends, went to the marketplace, the baths, and public lectures.[119] While rabbinic literature tends to portray women and men as segregated, the historical reality of the period indicates more fluid boundaries.

The gendered spheres of public and private come about as a result of the birthing capacity of women, upon which an entire social mythology has been constructed.[120] When women cling to the traditional female role, with its locus in the domestic sphere, it is often because this role offers them power, even if not the power usually held by men. Public submission reaps the reward of private power.[121] This "bargain" is exemplified in many anecdotes about women now in their seventh or eighth decade. The kitchen was their domain, and men's lack of facility in it was constantly derided. Children often were not permitted to be involved in the preparation of food. This occurred even in households in which the woman may have held a job (usually part time, low-level) outside the home. Although exceptions always existed, it was very difficult to resist the prevailing cultural myths of appropriate male and female spheres of influence.

In some instances, however, social history undermines these myths. For it is well known that until the nineteenth century and the development of industrialization, the home was not a restricted, sequestered domestic domain, but the center of a lively and vibrant economy in which women's skills were highly valued. That is, reason, which was regarded as a masculine activity[122] characteristic of "public" culture, comes to be viewed as that which undergirds the "private" arena of home, albeit in different fashion. All thinking arises and is derived from the activities and practices in which people engage. While birthing and the subsequent caring for a newborn leads to thinking informed by connection and nurturing, and thus seems to emphasize the private, this is not to say that maternal thinking and practice, aside from the act of birthing itself, is restricted to women. Men can surely be "mothers" responding to the reality of a small child within a particular social world.[123] Taking on this responsibility as a daily task is indeed the work of "mothering" or, in broader parlance, "parenting." Birthing labor is a uniquely female activity;[124] mothering, however, is work that transcends gender. The realm of the private, then, inasmuch as that realm excludes physical birth and lactation, can be said to be both masculine and feminine.

However, as has been noted across the disciplines, "Women may be important, powerful, and influential, but it seems that . . . women everywhere lack generally recognized and culturally valued authority."[125] Thus when the gendered spheres of public and private are examined, not only is the content of activities significant, but also the value, power, and authority a society will ascribe to each domain. Almost across the cultural board,[126] the public arena is more highly valued. This is seen in the patronizing phrase often used by men to describe the demands of child-rearing and running a home: "women's work." It is seen in the structure of the United States social security system, which does not regard mothering—or parenting—as equal to a paid profession.

The higher value usually given to the public sphere may be related to its being the result, almost entirely, of human effort. The public domain is that of political, social, and artistic institutions—in short, culture. The private arena, with birthing as its foundational event, is viewed as closer to nature and usually considered of lesser value. This may be a consequence of the Greek denigration of the physical, which spread in Western culture as a part of Christian thinking. Another reason for the greater value accorded culture over nature may be male envy of the extraordinary act of birthing. If God is the creator, the female body, in its capacity to carry and give birth to new life, has the aura of divinity. Men's jealousy at their exclusion from this Divine process may have led them to place their cultural creations, far removed from the blood and physicality of birthing, on a level even higher than the coming into existence of life itself. Clearly, the concatenation of circumstances that led human life to be divided into gendered spheres of public and private is complex. It is related to property rights, economics and sources of production, views of the body, and uses of power.[127]

That gendered spheres are also associated with the presumed greater proximity of the female to nature leads anthropologist Sherry B. Ortner to three possible interpretations. First, a woman's position may be viewed as a middle one on the scale from culture down to nature; this meaning would explain woman's almost universal lower status. Or second, it may be seen as a mediating component between the two domains, which would account not only for lower status, but also for restrictions upon woman to prevent the investing of culture with more of nature. And third, woman's more significant physicality (in terms of birthing) and thus closeness to nature, may be understood as ambiguous, causing women sometimes to be seen as aligned with culture while other times interwoven with nature.[128] Implied in the discussion of public and private domains is a description of male/female activites as seen through a gendered lens and its resulting hierarchy of values. The uni-gendered perspective of each of these spheres will gradually dissipate—indeed the process already is in motion—as culture/nature and public/private are seen as integrative rather than disparate, interwoven rather than distinct.[129]

Community and Autonomy

The polarity of community/autonomy has a specifically Jewish dimension as well as general philosophical aspects. While the Jewish community shares much with all communal structures, especially those of other religious groups, it also has some unusual characteristics. The notion of the "Jewish community" or the "Jewish people" is both a halakhic and historical concept deriving from later rabbinic as well as earlier biblical texts. In the liturgy, for instance, there is the prayer of the individual praying alone, the prayer of the individual recited while in the presence of the community, and the prayer of the community itself.[130] One is admonished not to keep aloof from the community.[131] The community in medieval times[132]—up to and including our own era—served as an overall social service agency, organizing communal needs such as kosher meat, education, burial, interest-free loans, care of the poor. As both a people ("the children of Israel," "the nation of Israel") and a religious group, Jews have a deep commitment to the ongoing survival of Judaism. While this has always been the case historically, the post-Holocaust era—even now, more than fifty years since the end of World War II—has added a profound poignancy and an urgency to the strong desire to perpetuate Jewish religion and culture. The Holocaust created a sense of a special responsibility to sustain Jewish survival. Hitler should not, one prominent Jewish theologian wrote, be handed a "posthumous victory."[133]

The ethical obligation to be part of the community devolves upon both men and women, but in different ways. In Orthodox Judaism, only men constitute the minyan, or minimum prayer quorum, which is intended to be a microcosm of the community. But in all denominations, even when women are ordained as rabbis or serve as cantors, even when women hold some leadership positions in Jewish organizations, the higher positions of power within the community are usually held by men. A report by the Jewish Welfare Board in 1984, for instance, indicated that 4 women held positions as executive directors compared with 112 men. In addition, salary disparities continue to exist between men and women who choose Jewish communal work.[134]

Thus a paradox exists. Men usually not only define Jewish community, but are also more powerful within it. Yet the everyday tasks of community—the acts of *hesed,* or loving kindness—tend to be considered more the province of women. Women visit the sick, prepare the food for mourners, care for children, make bridal showers. A recent posting on the listserv of the Women's Tefillah Network (WTN) admonished women not to be concerned about their exclusion from public prayer within Orthodox synagogues. After all, the writer concluded, during prayer services on Shabbat, a woman can be doing many acts of *hesed,*[135] even being good to herself by sleeping late. Her comments elicited learned, lively, and almost entirely negative responses. Yet the mitzvah (commandment) of *hesed* devolves upon Jewish men and women; it surely is not the exclusive, or even the central, aspect of feminine activity. Every person is commanded to "repair the world" *(tikkun olam)* through acts of kindness, both required and offered voluntarily.

What has happened here is that the notion of community is seen in two ways. There is the official community—the (Orthodox) prayer quorum, the leaders of organizations and synagogues, the power structure—and then there is the concept of community as focused within the home and in the family. Within this latter sense, women are seen as preeminent, while in the former, male autonomy predominates, and women in Jewish public life still battle for equal status.

In regard to the general philosophical perspectives, one must clarify the very meaning of autonomy. How does one make sense of the concept of autonomy if it is not to be understood simply as independence from a community relationship? An autonomous person can be one who exists apart from communal interactions and context, but can also be defined as one who manifests initiative within the framework of the community. Immanuel Kant's practical, ethical "autonomy" delineates principled independence, decisions determined on the basis of one's individual will as an expression of universal reason.[136] Can there be principled initiative in which the individual expresses human dignity, independence, and resourcefulness, yet remains connected to and not separate from community? This would mean that moral principles become the rationale for certain styles of interaction that are inclusive of community rather than indicate a solitary enterprise. In the Kantian system, the truly ethical person relies on the self, but does so within the context of ethical law. The good or ethical will is self-legislating, self-generated, and therefore autonomous. This is to be distinguished from the contemporary notion of autonomy, which is no longer tuned in to the Kantian overtones of the term. In popular parlance, autonomy has come to mean "no one can tell me what to do," or "anything I want to do is okay as long as I don't hurt another person."

Thus one can discern three levels of autonomy. At the lowest level is the popular notion described above, which is not of concern here. Then follows the Kantian philosophical concept with its emphasis on the self as both the source and object of the moral law. In our post-Holocaust age, this grand view of reason as the determinant of all that is "good" cannot but be seen as the overly optimistic extension of Enlightenment ideas.[137] Surely Kant's model has had a "melancholy fate"[138] in the wake of nineteenth- and especially twentieth-century history. But while the Kantian concept is anachronistic—we no longer see reason as sovereign—Kant's view of self-determination as central to human identity has become an integral part of modern consciousness. Certainly in American society, liberty is seen not only as the right to be free from interference, but also as the right to choose, whether it be one's political loyalty, communal affiliation, or religious identification. In short, liberty as autonomy is understood as the freedom to define the self.[139] Kant's definition of "autonomy" has been transformed, sometimes into the unsophisticated notion of private pursuit, but more generally into the quest for an understanding of the dialectic that exists between group consciousness and individual agency.

The philosophical conundrum between religious systems and individual choice is the third level of autonomy. This issue has particular poignancy in regard to Judaism, since the Western philosophical tradition attempted to demonstrate the irrelevance of Judaism to the modern world by declaring that the rabbinic writings were founded on a heteronomous rather than an autonomous basis of law. In the writings of Kant and Hegel,[140] Christianity is a moral religion, relying more than any other on reason, while Judaism is a statutory religion, heteronomous and not self-legislating. This view, part of the Enlightenment attempt to demonstrate the supremacy of Christianity, has been undermined.[141]

Yet other aspects of the philosophical conundrum persist. The self is not only rational, as in Kant's description, but also social. No self, to paraphrase John Donne,[142] is an island. Each person is a unique individual, but simultaneously and inseparably a part of subsets of communities and of all humanity. This interweaving of all persons while maintaining the individuality of each thus becomes the basis of both personal autonomy and community life. The resulting "tapestry" creates and depicts the variety of human groups, including the structured community of fellow believers. In modern expositions of Judaism, the Enlightenment notion that full human dignity requires thinking for oneself works in tandem with an understanding of covenant and the social ramifications of private responsibility.[143] Indeed, this dialectic is found within biblical and classical rabbinic sources.[144]

Moshe Z. Sokol's analysis of the concept of autonomy largely overcomes the imprecision that often characterizes its use. Sokol, a contemporary philosopher, demonstrates the complexity of the concept by distinguishing three categories. These he calls "nomic autonomy," "epistemic autonomy," and "haeretic autonomy."[145] "Nomic autonomy" refers to a person's autonomy with respect to the law (the Greek word for law is *nomos*), a concept incorporated into Kantian ethics. "Epistemic autonomy" refers to an individual's autonomy with regard to knowledge. One might claim, for instance, that one can truly know something only if it is proven; one cannot really "know" anything based on someone else's authority. Autonomy in regard to personal decisions and choices Sokol calls "haeretic autonomy." If one makes a choice based more on social conformity than clear thinking and problem solving, one would be relinquishing one's haeretic autonomy.

Sokol draws a further distinction applicable to each of these three broad categories: "hard" and "soft" autonomy. Hard autonomy is "the strict view that wherever autonomy is at all wanting, all is lost." For example, "a law is no law at all if not autonomously imposed *(Hard Nomic Autonomy).*"[146] 'Soft autonomy,' in contrast, is "the more moderate view that considers departures from the ideal of autonomy to be significant, but not fatal."[147] While the nuances of Sokol's discussion cannot be further explicated here, his conclusions regarding the issue at hand, community/autonomy, are significant. Sokol sees Judaism as affirming different conceptions of "the good"[148] in a way that constitutes a hierarchical pluralism. The role of personal autonomy, then, is felt "in the choice each individual makes of a personal conception of the good."[149] Soft personal autonomy, Sokol affirms, is consistent with traditional Judaism; people make choices and take responsibility for their consequences.

That Sokol postulates a hierarchy of conceptions of the good leads him to draw a philosophic demarcation between what he understands as the religious conception of personal choice and that of secular liberalism and humanism. Within a religious framework, there is much room for personal choice of norms based on what might be termed an ethic of virtue. Such an ethic is construed as the recommendation of certain attitudes and principles of judgment that lead to decision making. That is, while halakhah, or Jewish law, governs behavior and deed, an ethic of virtue, delineating the inner qualities and fostering the development of a good, compassionate person, is embodied in many aspects of the tradition.[150] Judaism directs people not only to act certain ways (the *mitzvot* or commandments), but also to create a particular ethical disposition. Examples would be the commands to: "Let the property of your friend be as dear to you as your own";[151] "Be among the disciples of Aaron, loving peace and pursuing it";[152] "You shall be holy, for I the Lord your God am holy."[153] These ethical recommendations, together with prescribed actions that are behavioral reinforcements, provide guidelines for individual decisions. Ultimately the task of becoming a good, ethical person is grounded in personal choice. Thus one dialectic is set up between shared practice and personal initiative in terms of action and another between external action and inner attitude, objective behavior and belief/motivation. In the first, individual initiative becomes part of following prescribed practices, while the second contrasts action taken and intention. An example of the latter would be doing the right action for the wrong reason.[154]

Sokol claims that secular humanism accepts multiple views of the good and lacks principles for ordering them.[155] He thus advocates a theistic model. However, secular humanism may be conceptualized in two distinct ways. There is the pure proceduralist ethical system, which is neutral with regard to a preferred theory of the good. But such a system describes how to proceed fairly in the absence of such a theory.[156] There is also the variety of conventional ethical views which are nontheistic. These are less concerned with procedure and more culturally embedded and substantive. For example, family and country might be primary values, but not God or religious tradition.[157] In deciding to make choices according to certain nontheistic principles of morality, one is simultaneously choosing to become a certain kind of person. Similarly, in a theological framework such as in Judaism, determined by a hierarchy of good, the element of personal choice, autonomy, and initiative remains a significant aspect of personal identity and development of the self.

In applying the polarity of community/autonomy to the issues of birth and birth control, one confronts directly the view prominent in Western history and religion that the man is an independent being; he is a subject, an agent. That is, he is autonomous, largely determining his own goals. In contrast, the woman is bound by her reproductive capacity to the needs of family and community. For her, subjectivity and agency develop primarily within the context not of self-development, but of self-sacrifice.

A good example of this demarcation of masculine and feminine roles is manifested in everyday family dynamics: usually the woman is responsible for creating family celebrations, obtaining birthday gifts, sending anniversary cards. She is the "social secretary," so to speak, the person who maintains and strengthens family ties. She is often considered more responsible than the male for acts of kindness, even outside the family. Development of the self in terms of social/communal support and the family has usually been much more emphasized for women. Even in instances when men have pursued such goals, they have often done so in the context of a profession: becoming a social worker, psychologist, or teacher. Self-development within the context of the larger community is surely the ideal aim of political philosophy and religious traditions for every individual. Yet the woman, historically limited by economic dependence and her reproductive capacity, has had a role which de-emphasizes cultivation of the autonomous self. It stresses instead her designation as "enabler" for husband and children and keeper of the hearth for extended family and friends.

Demographic studies demonstrate the persistence of this trend within the general population and among Jewish families across the denominational spectrum. "In 1992," one study avers, "70 percent of mothers of children under six worked full-time. . . . [W]hile most men have one job, most women have two." Women's steadily increasing share in economic responsibility within the family has not been matched by an increase in men's domestic responsibilities.[158] Demands of home and family often fall disproportionately upon women who have joined the labor force.

The slow advancement for women evident in all levels of the work world is due not only to deep-seated reservations held by men in power, but also to the de-emphasis upon fostering female autonomy. While considerable progress has been made in some fields,[159] recent studies verify facts that Jewish women have long known: female professionals in the Jewish communal world trail behind women in comparable fields. A new initiative of the Trust for Jewish Philanthropy[160] is working to correct the obvious disparity in advancement between male and female staff.

Freud, who aroused the fury of so many feminists with his theories of penis envy and intrinsic female passivity, nonetheless influenced our culture with insights both formative and formidable. Every person needs, Freud commented, *"Lieben und arbeiten,"* love and work.[161] Surely in our increasingly egalitarian world, Freud's words, whatever their original intent, may be understood as offering a prescription for optimal *human* development and contentment. Yet even in our twenty-first century, "love" and family are often seen as more the province of women, while "work," especially work in the public setting, remains the primary arena of self-definition for men, even if they are fathers. That sphere comes to define "society," and "culture," which then assume normative value. The domestic domain is dominated by women whose tasks include much of the affective, emotional, and relational aspects of familial and societal bonding, as well as the physical work related to home and children.[162] Men's work is considered productive, women's reproductive. Society offers economic rewards to productive work, in the form of salary, medical benefits, and Social Security, commensurable benefits lacking for those who plan birthday parties, buy new shoes, and sit in the pediatrician's waiting room. In each domain, different kinds of power are developed.[163] Feminine roles are generally less public and more kin-based. They tend to mediate between the social and cultural, the latter defined by men. This is not to say that the boundaries between these spheres are not crossed; clearly they often are. But the role characteristics may remain nonetheless.

How might this continuing imbalance be corrected? How might women come to see themselves as pursuing the development of an independent, autonomous identity while remaining embedded within familial and communal structures? How might men do the same, valuing connectedness as much as achievement? Could what has become two separate terrains, especially in the postindustrial age, be melded so that they become more mutually empowering?

Melanie Klein, Nancy Chodorow, and Dorothy Dinnerstein are among the thinkers who have struggled with this issue.[164] Klein's theories, adapted by Chodorow and Dinnerstein, are rooted in Freudian psychoanalytic development, but with significant changes. Klein affirms that the traditional family structure is based on the historical reality of mothers—women—being the primary nurturers and caregivers of children. In order for a son to develop appropriately, he would eventually model himself after his father, breaking away from mother, who represents the breast, food, physical closeness, emotional warmth, the affective realm. Father, in contrast, signifies the outside world, achievement, rationality, history, and culture. The male child, then, leaves the world of intimacy and pursues autonomy. Being independent from his mother—from the world represented by women—becomes the goal. The daughter, however, identifies with her mother, learning how to read emotions, be sensitive to feelings, care for and nurture others. The female child specializes in intimacy—how to be close to another—and is generally less equipped to attain independence. According to Klein and her followers, then, men tend to seek autonomy and avoid intimacy, while women usually pursue intimacy and fear autonomy, a theory borne out by numerous psychological studies. This pattern derives from the developmental experiences of the young boy and girl. How might this model, taken as an essentialist standard almost throughout human history, be altered? How might men learn to feel more comfortable with intimacy and human connectedness and women not fear competition and accomplishment?

Klein's theory describes a transformed model of the family. Were both mother and father, in the nitty-gritty of everyday life, to exemplify connectedness *and* achievement, the line of demarcation of male/female as autonomy/intimacy would begin to blur. A fully actualized female would be schooled in both domains, as would a fully realized male. Intimacy and autonomy would be seen as complementary within each person, rather than as more or less separate domains necessary for society as a whole, one primarily the province of men, the other of women. In this altered paradigm of the earliest and continuing love relationships—that of parents and progeny—children would experience both mother and father as sources of warmth and nurturing as well as models of work in the world outside the home. This structure, Klein and her followers claim, would alter the community/autonomy polarity. The polarity would be a balancing of interests or priorities within each man or woman, not a division of labor with an attached hierarchy of value. Similar to the public/private vertical category, man *and* woman would be community oriented (in its two senses) as well as autonomous persons.

The changed paradigm of family life described by Klein evolves together with significant transformations in the nature of work itself. For if both man and woman are to nurture within the family and do work unrelated (except financially) to the home, then the rules of the workplace will need extensive readjustment, a process that has already begun. What is implied conceptually is that family/home/community be valued equally with work/workplace. This does not mean mere lip service but actual change and involvement. The more private domain with its connectedness and intimacy will be as significant as the public sphere of work. Theoretically, this means the breakdown of the old hierarchy of values and the construction of a new, transformed axiology. Practically, this entails welcoming women into the public world of work on equal terms and in ways that recognize the value—and accommodate the reality—of the distinctive female contribution to reproduction and the creation of the family.

The long, slow process of pragmatic changes waxes and wanes but continues to move forward. The mitzvah to "be fertile and increase," the impetus to reproduce—to plant, grow, and nurture a child—affects men and women differently. "That child rearing may be the center of the soul does not mean there isn't room for other things. . . . It has done us no service to have work opposed to our child rearing," remarks a contemporary author. It is true, she continues, that men neither carry nor expel the fetus. But just as the child is also theirs, the world of work is also the woman's. "I resent" this writer goes on, "work vs. child arguments because both are possible, both are necessary to most of us, both make the world turn round. . . . Both require the most individual personal stamp of our souls."[165]

Some of the different "stamp[s] of our souls" have been explored in this chapter and the preceding one. Within the religious framework, conception and birth, ideally, are a consequence of individual decisions *and* the will of God. Birth control surely creates a much stronger sense of autonomy for women. There is choice and control to the extent scientific knowledge offers. But contraception also affects the man in important ways. A child can represent commitment, in the most fundamental way, to joint parenting, to equal nurturing, and to the community. The gift of a child is the ultimate human challenge.

Chapter 3

Fertility and Infertility

If I were to tell the story of my life it wouldn't be about the conflict between being a mother and a feminist but about being a feminist mother and a mother feminist.

Anne Roiphe, Fruitful

Not to have a child, not ever to have a child, the idea echoes down the corridors of my mind as if I were playing with fire, arsonist of my life. To conceive and bear a child alters, reframes, collapses the old self and sets all kinds of limits on the new.

Anne Roiphe, Fruitful

What is the work of one's hands? They are one's sons and daughters.

T.B. Ketubot 71a

Their faces look back at me as I stand in our long hallway, my body turned toward the wall of family photos. In 1928, in Poland, having a photograph taken was a formal event, and the faces reflect that seriousness. Yet years later, in 1980, when I questioned my late mother about why no one in the photographs from Poland smiled, her response was, "Life was hard." Except one, they are all there: my maternal grandparents; Uncle Aaron, killed by the Nazis with his wife and two young sons; Uncle Jacob and my mother, both now deceased; and Aunt Hannah, the "baby," eighty-nine years old when she recently died. Only Uncle Benny is missing; he had already left for America. The sepia brown matted picture, the traditional frame, the poses of that moment in time: I love how they capture a slice of my family history.

This is what comes to mind when I think about fertility: family, continuity, the chain of tradition and of kinship; the intertwining of the personal, the communal, and the peoplehood of Israel; a series of concentric circles; a spiral, twirling toward some unknown destination; the feel of an infant's skin; the sensations of nursing; the delicious smile on a baby's face; the arduousness and joys and tribulations of parenting.

This chapter will examine some of the rabbinic sources on the meaning of family and children,[1] analyze several texts which speak of the longing for progeny, and look at aspects of contemporary sociology as they illuminate the issues of fertility and infertility within the Jewish community. It will not delineate the increasingly sophisticated methods of infertility treatment and their halakhic and ethical implications; these questions have been dealt with in great detail in other studies.[2] The chapter will also describe various ways contemporary Jews are coping with the issue of infertility.

With its usual concrete imagery, the midrashic literature expresses the abstract concepts of historical memory, legacy, transmission of tradition, and children as our immortality. Both the verse in Psalms 8:3, "Out of the mouth of babes and sucklings have You [God] found strength," and that in Proverbs 6:1, "My children, if you have become a pledge for your neighbor," refer, according to the Midrash, to the giving of the Torah. *Matan Torah,* or the giving of the Torah, is understood traditionally to have taken place in the Hebrew month of Sivan on the festival of Shavuot, or Pentecost. "When God sought to give the Torah to the Jewish people," the Midrash states, God said to them:

Give me guarantors that you will fulfill the Torah. They said to God: Are not our ancestors [literally, patriarchs] guarantors for us? God said: "They are indebted to Me; would that they be able to stand for themselves." This is analogous to someone who needs a loan. This person was told: "Bring a guarantor and take as much as you wish." Whereupon the person went and brought someone who was also indebted to the lender. The would-be creditor then said: "You have brought someone who is indebted to me. Would that this person could stand on his/her own. Go and bring someone who is not indebted to me." Thus did God say to Israel: "Have you brought Me your ancestors [the patriarchs], who themselves owe Me debts, as guarantors? Rather, give Me guarantors who are not indebted to Me. And who are those who are not indebted to Me?" God said to them: "The children." Immediately the people brought the children and God said to them: "Do you stand as guarantors that if I give your parents the Torah, they will observe it; and if not, will you be responsible for them?" They answered, "Yes!" and God declared : "I am the Lord your God." They answered, "Yes!" After every Divine Commandment [of the Decalogue] they answered either "yes" or "no" in accord with the respective utterance. God then said to them: "Through your mouths I give the Torah to My people," as it is written in Psalms, 8: "From the mouths of babes and sucklings you have founded strength." And there is no strength other than Torah, as it is said, "The Lord shall give strength to His People."[3]

This midrash beautifully conveys the intergenerational aspect of the tradition. Children guarantee that Judaism will continue. Thus in Judaism are children not seen only as a means to human growth and the fulfillment of individual immortality, nor only as a cementing of the spousal relationship in that nurturing moves away from focus upon the adult partners to the child in need of care. Children are also links in the historical community of Israel, necessary ingredients for spiritual continuity in the national and religious sense. Indeed, fertility—children—make possible the very establishment of the tradition itself. The Torah could not have been placed in a human, historical, faith community had not the children been offered by their parents—and themselves accepted—commitment to the text and its meanings.

Obligating only men in the commandment of procreation precluded women from initiating a divorce. But the result was to make it possible for the woman to choose to have children or not. Perhaps this legal twist, which permitted the woman use of birth control, also presumed her great desire to procreate, born from a teleological view of female nature. Yet it simultaneously offered her a sense of autonomy, limited though it may have been in the absence of reliable birth control and in the presence of social pressure. Surely the woman was more, much more, than a baby-making machine. The legal parameters express great concern not only for her physical health, but, in an era when infant mortality was high, her emotional health as well.

Children are links in the march of history—individual history, family history, communal and national history. But if history appears at times to be linear, other human patterns partake of the cyclical. The patterns of nature are cyclical, as is the diurnal cycle of body time. Menstruation, as an aspect of fertility and infertility, is a reminder of the ebb and flow of the blood of life as it maintains its own cycle within the broader framework of history. Menstruation is also a concrete sign of the particular role women play in this history. Women carry and bear life: creative—indeed sacred—work. If human beings arc seen as partners with God in the ongoing creation of the world, women who give birth are partners in a distinctive way. Judaism values families as structural units that produce and educate the next generation of Jews and especially values women as mothers. The institution of the family has always been primary in Judaism; it is the central social unit upon which both private and public good depend.[4] The tradition is decidedly pronatalist.[5]

Given these cultural parameters, several issues complicate the fertility/infertility conundrum. First, to what extent is having children an intrinsic part of a satisfying life for women—and for men? Is the desire to have children a social construct, like gender? And second, in what way(s) does the increased public role of women create conflicts for women, for men, for children? Are such conflicts good? Are they resolvable? What are their impact in the Jewish community? Third, what new rituals have developed that connect with fertility/infertility?[6] Regarding these issues, do Orthodox, Conservative, and Reform Jews have different approaches? This chapter will respond to these queries and their underlying concepts rather than follow the format of the other chapters.

From the days of Margaret Sanger, the great advocate of readily available and safe birth control,[7] feminism has advocated choice with regard to pregnancy. Indeed, the control of conception has been a significant theme of human history for centuries. But control of conception had—and has—a different resonance from the issue of professional development/career/job while mothering. Feminism does not seem to have lessened the complexity of the mother-daughter relationship,[8] but it has heightened the involvement of fathers.[9] Surely the fact that many fathers are increasingly equal partners not only in child care, but also in the running of the household,[10] can lead to decisions different from when these tasks were almost always the exclusive province of the woman. In addition, the feminist movement has led to women who are more independent and who seek satisfaction not only from family, but also from work, a widespread female pattern in preindustrial societies.[11] At times the work is not primarily a source of new challenges but of economic need.

An example of the literature that views childbirth as intrinsic to "female nature" is found in a booklet by Dr. Eli Schussheim, a physician associated with an Israeli right-to-life program, Efrat. The booklet on marriage features a section entitled "Health and Beauty for the Woman," in which Schussheim states:

The happiness that comes from having children strengthens the emotional health of the person and has a positive influence on physical health. The absence of these elements, because of failure to fulfill the natural function of the family, can result in absence of satisfaction, in stress and tension, that harm the emotional health of the person and so have a bad influence on the physical health as well. There are those who are concerned that bearing many children causes damage to the mother. But reality proves that the opposite is true. The facts prove that mothers of many children, who run their lives according to the biological nature of bearing children, are emotionally healthy and physically strong.[12]

Particularly interesting in Schussheim's words is the subtle shift of the basis of his argument. He begins by speaking of "the natural function of the family," relating physical and emotional health to fulfilling the desire for offspring, the existential need to reproduce and love that which is of oneself, literally or figuratively.[13] The presumption is that an intrinsic need exists to create the next generation, to have "all one is" imprint itself on a being yet in formation. This presumption is generic; Schussheim is writing of the *human* hope of continuity. But midway he switches gears; he moves from men and women "having children" to women "bearing many children," "mothers of many children." These latter, he avers, "run their lives according to the biological nature of bearing children." From the human expectation of children Schussheim proceeds to advocate that women have many children, not only because doing so is their "biological nature," but also because actualizing that "nature" leads to physical and emotional health.

Thus he uses an essentialist understanding of female "nature" to justify a pro-life position. The threat of barrenness is also used by members of the Efrat organization to discourage abortion. In addition, infertility is emphasized not only as a possible consequence but also as a "punishment" for abortion, even though other venues of persuasion and influence to discourage abortion are available.

Schussheim's essentialist perspective contrasts vividly with the interpretation of Isaac Arama, the fifteenth-century biblical commentator, of Genesis 30:1–2, quoted at the beginning of the previous chapter. Arama explains Jacob's angry response to Rachel as a result of Rachel's misperception, her cognitive error; in her desire for progeny, she had forgotten the essential purpose of her existence, which exactly parallels that of a man. In contrast to Schussheim, who views the bearing of many children as an intrinsic aspect of female physical and emotional health, Arama stresses the universality/genderlessness of moral choice, the primary human struggle, and views the female capacity for childbearing as ancillary. Childlessness for a woman, he states, is the same as childlessness for a man. Here essentialism is transformed to the bold human desire for continuity through children. Arama explains Rachel's lament as her veering away from the egalitarianism that undergirds not only the fullest flowering of the individual but also the very notion of family.

The ontology of human nature manifested in Arama's comment on Genesis 30:1–2 is diametrically opposed to the analysis of Schussheim and those of similar sentiment. Cognizance of this spectrum of underlying concepts is helpful in understanding the transitional status of Jewish women with regard to family and fertility, a status described in recent demographic and sociological studies. A transition may be defined as "the often prolonged process of passage from an initial and rather stable situation to a different one (which may also become stabilized in the long run)."[14] The changes affecting women over the last decades, especially in Western societies, affect Jewish women greatly. Jewish culture has always moved toward change through the dialectic of internal principles and external, historical circumstances and influences.[15]

The effects of sociohistorical movements upon Jewish women with regard to fertility can be clarified by examining recent data. In Israel, Jewish fertility levels have been both stable and rather high compared to those in other developed countries,[16] measuring around 2.6 children per family. In the diaspora, using the United States as an example, fertility rates among Jewish women since the 1960s have declined due to overall transformations in American society. The increased emphasis on individual development, greater material expectations, and the higher public visibility of women, especially in the labor force, helped create this decline. Except among Orthodox families, in which large families tend to predominate, "U.S. national and Jewish fertility trends have tended to run in parallel,"[17] clearly demonstrating the intertwining of broader societal social patterns and those of the Jewish community.

In the diaspora, fertility rates among Jews generally were below the replacement level,[18] while in Israel, as noted, the level is above replacement. This is so despite the large number of working women and improved availability of both contraception and higher education. Some attribute the higher fertility rate in Israel to several underlying assumptions about women and family in Israeli society. These include the rabbinic construction of motherhood and fatherhood in classical texts, the strong sense of "replacing" the six million Jews murdered in the Holocaust, the strengthening of the Jewish state, and the state's interest in promoting childbearing and protecting the health of pregnant women through subsidization of various medical and social services relating to maternity.[19]

Could it be that in Israel the notion of Jewish continuity has deeper resonance? Perhaps the higher birthrate is also related to better child-care facilities and social security benefits, the latter depending on the number of offspring. Certainly these can ease the child-rearing process. Sociological studies indicate that a higher fertility rate is associated not only with a more friendly child/parenting infrastructure, but also with a greater involvement by fathers in child care. This increased gender balance is expressed legally in paternity leaves and concretely in the daily tasks of parenting.

Demographers use statistical methods to measure gender performance, a measurement that relates to fertility. Called the Gender Empowerment Measure (GEM), it assesses "the relative empowerment of women and men in *political* and *economic* spheres of activity" (emphasis in original). It consists of an average of three variables: women's share of total administrative and managerial jobs, professional and technical positions, and parliamentary seats. Israel's total ranking is high (twenty-fourth out of 102 countries), reflecting the high levels of female education and accomplishment.[20]

However, when it comes to the first variable—women administrators and managers—Israel's rating drops to fiftieth out of 103 countries. This lower ranking reflects the social obstacles against which women struggle in the public sphere, as well as perhaps encouragement to pursue activities in the more private and peripheral arenas, even professionally.[21] The GEM ranking of Israel accords with other studies of this anomaly. Indeed, "the status of women in the United States and in Canada was rated higher than in Israel with regard to seven of the eight measures" in the Index of Gender Development.[22] Does this dovetail with the higher Israeli fertility rate of 2.6 children? Some see a direct correlation, while others view the measures of Israeli gender empowerment as demonstrating that "there need not . . . be an unbridgeable gap between paid work and conventional household roles."[23] But "paid work" and positions of power are not the same. The dual role of many contemporary Jewish women—maintaining Jewish continuity through the family and achieving in the socioeconomic spheres—does not necessarily result in greater power.[24] There is more responsibility but not concomitant authority. That is, despite the emphases on children and childbearing, the position of mother often is less culturally valued, and women may be systematically excluded from public positions of prestige and power.[25] This discrepancy may fade away as society moves toward greater equality—or it may be the impetus for continued struggle.

Mary Wells Lawrence, the first female C.E.O. of a company traded on the New York Stock Exchange, reflected, in a recent interview, on women in positions of power, male and female working styles, and children. "I have to say that in my life the most satisfying thing has been my two girls," she states,[26] thirty years after breaking the glass ceiling that kept women from heading such high visibility companies. Responding to why she thinks there are still so few women in positions like hers, she offered several insightful comments. First, she said, male clients tended to be supportive and felt relaxed with her; she had mastered the business and could speak competently in terms familiar to them. Second, they didn't see her as competitive, as they tended to see other men. Third, she is married to a successful, good-looking, and well-known man; this, she said, was protective. Her fourth reason was that while women tend to think horizontally, men are usually vertical in their approaches. This leads to male single-mindedness, an aggressive devotion to successful realization of whatever work ideal predominates in a particular profession or job. Interestingly, Lawrence says women, as they move up, look at that intense focus on work and think, "What's so great about that?"[27]

Women, according to Lawrence, derive pleasure from satisfying their horizontal outlook and therefore tend to seek broad and variegated challenges rather than narrow and focused ones. For many, motherhood is a desired part of one's life choices. This despite the fact that the rosy glow surrounding motherhood—indeed, parenthood—prevalent in the 1980s has been subdued by more down-to-earth and realistic assessments of parenting in recent discussions and memoirs. [28] These echo a rabbinic comment that refers to child-rearing as *"tzar gidul banim"*[29]—the pain of raising children. This phrase calls attention to both the physical strains and emotional stress of the many tasks connected with parenting.

Buried in first-wave feminist ideology is a paradox: workplace and professions were more open to women; independence was an attainable goal—but in the face of these often heady accomplishments, mothering seemed a letdown. According to a recent report, "[A] typical thirty-two-year-old prospective mother has had a ten year career and has made her own decisions since college. Although motherhood has always entailed sacrifice—of time, of the ego, of one's sex life—contemporary mothers are sacrificing more: careers, salaries, status."[30]

Here is where fathers and social institutions that encourage parenthood by providing needed services play an important role.[31]

Some women feel feminism has led them astray.

We haven't planned our lives to accommodate our children, and yet having children has proved to be one of the most profound and satisfying experiences of life. We're afraid to give ourselves over to motherhood—to drop out of the workforce. Motherhood is great and important and something I want to do.[32]

This is to conceptualize maternal ambivalence as falling within the ongoing debate about working moms and stay-at-home mothers. Yet many American women are able to find a balance between the demands of both mothering and working, especially if fathering is a high priority for a male partner. Some see feminism as having had a positive impact on family relationships, causing traditional gender boundaries to become permeable and blurred.

In contrast to Schussheim's view of female nature, a recent anthropological study claims that the much debated "maternal instinct" may be more a function of learning to nurture, a result of tending and caring for, rather than an inherent capacity. Experiences—pregnancy, birth, lactation, childcare—ground the feeling.[33] While these experiences can predispose women to what is called "the maternal instinct"—or offer a "head start," so to speak—the practicalities of caring for a child elicit a powerful "paternal instinct." The notions are both abstract and practical. Whatever innate aptitude for parenting one has is further activated by the many acts of attentiveness to the emotional and physical needs of a child. In this sense the desire for children is genderless and involvement in childcare a social construct. The historian Gerda Lerner makes an analogous statement regarding to the generalized understanding of male-female differences. Arguing from her understanding of who the Jewish people are ("Thus, what makes Jews 'Jews' is their historically developed experience"), Lerner reasons that what makes "female persons gendered women is not their biological, but their historically developed experience."[34]

How do these aspects of fertility play out within the parameters of the American Jewish community? Interestingly, research has demonstrated that in the post-World War II period, birthrates for Catholic, Protestant, and Jews all declined. This was attributed to the waning influence of religion in American life as well as to improved contraceptive methods. While statistics for Jewish families show that Jews manifest the general social patterns present in American society,[35] studies indicate one difference: the "Jewish birthrate declined far more than the other two." The National Jewish Population Study of 1970 revealed that Jews had 2.8 children per family compared with an average of 3.5 for the American non-Jewish family.[36]

Social research into contemporary American Jewish life manifests a continuation of this trend. As in the post-World War II period, the transformation of American Jewish families today follows that of American society at large, with some specific differences. There are fewer married Jews and those who are married tend to marry later, even more so than other white Americans, all of whom delay marriage more than they did half a century ago.[37] The nostalgic notion of the large, immigrant family—bustling, creative, often poor—lingers, as in Harriet Rosenstein's wonderful short story about her great-grandmother:

There were, in the beginning, seven children, each rising out of my great-grandmother's darkness every twelve or thirteen months, like little full moons. The sons came first: Mendel, Mischa, Isaac, and Schmuel. And then the pale and round-faced daughters: Sarah, Fraychie, and Sosiesther. My great-grandmother conceived and bore them, I am told, with bemused passivity, as tolerant as the moon must be of her own swellings and thinnings and equally unconscious. Four babies. Seven. A miscarriage or two. . . . The number became finally a matter of indifference. . . . [38]

The often fatalistic attitude toward pregnancy of the immigrant generation is echoed in Sydney Stahl Weinberg's study of Jewish immigrant woman, *The World of our Mothers.*

Poor women with many children aged rapidly. "I do think my mother had a wasted life," Ruth observed sadly. At thirty-eight, her mother had borne eleven children and lost six of them to illness and accidents. The trials of constant childbirth and child-rearing drained her energies and ruined her health.[39]

Contemporary sociological research, however, cites a very different birthrate as the first decade of the twenty-first century gets under way. Numbers are not "a matter of indifference," even if there exists a wistful longing for an idealized past. Birth control is now an integral aspect of American Jewish culture, both individually and communally. Recent research indicates that "even among ultra-Orthodox Jewish women, contraceptive usage is the norm; however, women in that environment do not begin using birth control until after they have had five children.[40] Generally, the closer a woman is to the religious right, the larger the number of children. Currently, most Orthodox-affiliated women have children above replacement level.[41]

As a group, then, American Jewish women have a fairly low fertility rate. But the centrality of family in Jewish culture nonetheless remains strong. Few Jewish women state a desire to remain childless,[42] although many delay starting a family. The relationship between education and childbearing among American Jews is inversely proportional to that of the general population; the more education a Jewish woman has, the more children she is likely to have.[43] Jewish women are deeply committed to the idea of family. But similar to other white, middle-class women, they often postpone pregnancy, seeking a modicum of financial security or, more usually, completion of educational demands. Highly educated Jewish women sometimes don't have as many children as they thought they would and unintentional infertility is one reason. "Fertility," as one sociologist states, "is not an even playing field bounded on one side by menarche and on the other side by menopause."[44]

Feminism has altered the timing of childbearing, leading to complications. For reasons not yet well understood, conception is optimal when a woman is in her twenties. As she grows older, the chances of her becoming pregnant decrease. Age is an important factor in female infertility, although infertility also can affect men and younger women. The particular poignance of infertility derives not only from the powerful sense of family and continuity embedded within Jewish tradition, but also from the historical consequences of the Holocaust. An older friend whose children were born in the 1950s told me years ago that she and her husband had decided they wanted at least five children to compensate, in some way, for those who had been murdered. Indeed, they became the parents of three boys and two girls. Such a highly developed sense of communal responsibility resonates with some. For others, however, individual needs, consciously or unconsciously, are prominent. Often the larger issues are given their due in thinking pregnancy will happen when one is "ready." Thus the deep pain of unintentional infertility—and of all infertility.

A couple struggling with infertility must cope not only with their own feelings but also with those of their parents and even of communal leaders who may be insensitive to the complex issues involved. Financial burdens, sense of identity, feelings of failure, questions about self and community all converge as a couple grapples with hope and fear, anger and resentment.

Jews of all denominations have worked to develop strategies, some rooted in traditional ritual, that can ameliorate the pain of infertility. An Orthodox woman describes two hypothetical scenarios involving infertility, one of a modern Orthodox couple, the other of a couple with a more fundamentalist orientation. Despite the differences in outlook, certain similarities prevail. "[T]he religious Jewish community is centered around the family. . . . It is almost unthinkable to choose child-free living," the author states.[45] The modern Orthodox couple is likely to wait before beginning a family, wishing to establish greater marital closeness, complete educational demands, and/or become more financially secure. In such circumstances, certain forms of birth control are considered acceptable.[46] For the couple more to the right religiously, postponing a family is highly unlikely and becoming pregnant during the first year of marriage is common. In cases of infertility, the former couple is usually more attuned to the biological clock, while the latter often is faced with friends who are the parents of four or five small children.

Therapy may be advised for couples confronting the multiple stresses of infertility, and using therapists familiar with Jewish culture is decidedly advantageous. Nonetheless, despite the greater acceptability of therapy in the Orthodox community, a stigma greater than that within the general community still exists.[47] Some Orthodox Jews, if they choose psychotherapy, prefer using a person who is Jewish as well as religiously observant—someone who understands the parameters that structure their lives. Finding such a professional is much easier in large urban areas. A national infertility organization called "RESOLVE" has over fifty chapters. It offers a variety of services, such as support groups, lectures on aspects of infertility, and informal networking.[48] The modern Orthodox couple will be more inclined to participate in such a group, while the other couple, coming from a more insular environment, generally would not.[49] Conservative and Reform Jews, taking individual personalities and preferences into account, would both consult therapists, if deemed needed, and participate in available support groups.

It is interesting that sometimes within the Orthodox community, which stresses modesty not only of garb but also of words, the emphasis on pregnancy becomes grist for the gossip mill in ways that clearly traverse the acceptable boundaries of modest, appropriate behavior. Such social—and religious—infractions invade privacy and cause pain. They often come from unmannered or insensitive people. A twenty-five-year-old single friend of the family of a newly married twenty-year-old woman looks her up and down upon seeing her seven months after the wedding and says, "What, not pregnant yet?" The rabbi of a prominent yeshiva says to the mother of a twenty-two-year-old man, married a little over a year, "I hope there will be a *simcha* (celebratory occasion), a *bris* (or *brit milah,* circumcision), soon." Not only is the rabbi expressing overt sexism—implying that the birth of a girl is not cause for celebration in the same way as that of a boy—but he is speaking of the most intimate matters of a young couple to a parent who knows him only slightly, in the capacity as school administrator.[50] Clearly gossip and rude behavior cross all religious or social divisions, but the pressure in certain circles to reproduce can make what is impolite to some seemingly more acceptable to others.

Revolving around infertility is a vortex of issues, especially emotional ones, that contemporary religious leaders and laypeople have sought to address through prayer and the creation of new rituals. Transforming tradition in ways that address the specific sadness, pain, and sense of loss associated with miscarriage, failure to become pregnant, stillbirth, and even the birth of exceptional children, recent compilations of suggested prayers and ceremonies, as well as guidelines in some rabbinic manuals, indicate a new communal sensitivity toward what previously had been an isolating, anguishing experience.

Appealing to the Orthodox community, as well as to other communities, is an anthology of unusual prayers titled *Otsar Tefillot Yisrael,* or *A Treasury of Jewish Prayer* (my translation).[51] The first volume of this three-volume work offers several prayers/meditations for infertile couples.[52] Similarly, *Shaarei Dimah* [Gates of Tears] (my translation), has a petitionary prayer for coping with infertility. This volume, reprinted from a 1873 text, demonstrates the nineteenth-century concern with infertility in the traditional Jewish commu-nity.[53] Although speaking in a range different from that of the contemporary voices of women, it recognizes the need to deal with the feelings of disappoint-ment and sorrow when conception fails to occur. A recent essay, "Mourning My Miscarriage," laments the lack in Judaism of established ritual for preg-nancy loss.[54] These new—and newly reprinted—anthologies help fill the void.

The newest edition of *Moreh Derekh,* the rabbi's manual of the Conservative movement, contains a variety of directions and recommendations for rabbis to use when encountering difficult family situations relating to infertility.[55] Sand-wiched between the chapters on divorce and conversion is one titled *"Tsar hae-bur vehaladah,"* or "The Pain of Pregnancy and Birth" (my translation; original in Hebrew only). Sections include "The birth of exceptional children," "Mis-carriage," "Memorial ceremony for neonatal death and burial," "A grieving rit-ual following termination of pregnancy,"[56] and a ritual called "Coping with in-fertility." Almost all biblical passages, verses from Psalms, reflections, and poetry may be used by either a man or a woman, or both. Following is an exam-ple from this text, a meditation or recitation after a stillbirth (only the English is quoted):

Seeing (his/her) days are determined, the number of (his/her) months are with You, You set (him/her) limits that (he/she) could not pass. [After Job 14:5]
... Healer of the brokenhearted:
We mourn, today; we grieve with You,
For the one who could have been,
You grieve too.
We mourn that living being
Who never knew the joy of simple breathing.[57]

The final entry in this section of *Moreh Derekh,* "Coping with infertility," be-gins with an explanatory paragraph.

This is a ritual which may be done in the home or in the rabbi's study. It may be per-formed with the couple alone or in the presence of others. Moving to accept infertility is a moment that begins healing, releases pain, and, at its best, restores a full measure of hope to the marriage.[58]

It includes suggested comments of the rabbi and offers the opportunity for the man, woman, or couple to make a personal statement. The rabbi may say (among other possibilities):

Infertility is not abandonment by God, not a curse and not a punishment. . . . Infertility is an aspect of our own vulnerability. . . . We fear that our sadness may be transformed into despair and hopelessness. . . . We search for ways to find those aspects of life that will help us become whole and integrated. . . . [59]

This is followed by the traditional *Mi shebarakh,* or prayer for healing, usually recited when illness is present. In the manual, however, the *Mi shebarakh* is specifically designated as a "prayer for emotional healing," which "may be appropriate" at this time.[60] Traditional sources are mined for relevant texts and venues germane to the complex emotions such situations elicit. Subjective judgments in pastoral care and individual need combine with the use of objective sources and empathetic words that offer acknowledgment of sorrow, comfort, and the possibility of healing.

Although neither the 1979 nor the 1988 manual for Reform rabbis mentions ceremonies for infertility or related circumstances,[61] a 1994 publication of the Reform Central Conference of American Rabbis specifically addresses them. In a section called "The Path of Life," there is a reflection/prayer for "a couple who fear they may be infertile." Under "Illness and Recovery" are suggested prayers: "After a stillbirth or upon the death of a young child" and "Upon terminating a pregnancy."[62] In addition, two volumes have been published by a Conservative rabbi, one historical and one designated a "spiritual companion," which reflect a woman's perspective on these and related issues. The first, *Out of the Depths I Call to You,*[63] was written for an Italian Jewish bride in 1786 and offers prayers to be said as a woman follows the path from wife to mother. Although infertility is not addressed as such, some of the prayers are interpreted as referring to the anguish of a woman "with empty arms who desperately desires a child."[64] There are prayers to be recited during the first forty days of pregnancy, during the ninth month, at the onset of labor, the beginning of delivery, following a safe delivery, and when assisting in childbirth.[65] The book includes a reflection for when the woman goes to the *mikvah,* or ritual bath, prior to resuming sexual relations with her husband. But it does not directly deal with the disappointment, sorrow—or perhaps relief—a woman may feel should conception not occur. Rather, once she has become pregnant, prayers for different stages of her pregnancy are suggested.

The second volume is born out of Rabbi Cardin's own experience with infertility and the yearning for comfort and solace from a Jewish perspective. As Cardin writes, she "desire[d] to uncover the hidden ways of women's traditions in loss and fertility."[66] With sensitivity and creativity, Cardin speaks to the needs of women, although one section contains a prayer for a prospective father. To mark a miscarriage, Cardin suggests a variety of mourning rituals, from the *mikvah,* planting, speaking to the lost baby, and baking. Given in great detail is a *havdalah,*[67] or separation ritual to indicate the demarcation between being pregnant and no longer being pregnant. A brief chapter contains prayers for husband and wife acknowledging the sorrow of male partners[68] and the toll of infertility on the marriage relationship. The chapter also addresses miscarriage and stillbirth. This volume can offer something to all Jews seeking solace when coping with infertility and related issues.

Other contemporary texts dealing with these aspects of the female life cycle—and their larger impact—are Debra Orenstein's *Lifecycles: Jewish Women on Life Passages and Personal Milestones*[69] and Tikva Frymer-Kensky's *Motherprayer.*[70] The "Beginnings" section of Orenstein's book contains prayers and poems for pregnancy and childbirth, similar to what is found in Frymer-Kensky's volume. In the latter, Frymer-Kensky uses her broad training as an Assyriologist and historian of religions to gather texts often long forgotten, texts that validate and focus on the complex of feelings and thoughts associated with a woman's pregnancy. As Frymer-Kensky writes in her introduction, "This book is not written to convince women to have children; it is written to provide women who have chosen this path with religious imagery and language to maximize the spiritual dimensions of this choice."[71] Frymer-Kensky's collection offers the modern woman ancient texts that address concerns that seem contemporary but indeed are timeless: the voices of women, often hidden or silenced in history, here ring out.

Orenstein's second section, "Infertility and Early Losses," offers four meditative essays on infertility, stillbirth, and miscarriage[72] and a "Fruits of Creation" ceremony "created as a response to not giving birth, which is sometimes, but not always, a choice."[73] Fittingly, the preferred time of the ritual is on Rosh Hodesh, or the festival of the new moon. Rosh Hodesh marks the beginning of a new Hebrew month and is designated as a woman's holiday.

The Jewish community, in all its denominational manifestations, is increasingly providing tools for those women (and couples) for whom having children may be an agonizing problem of short or very long duration. The above-mentioned volumes can offer solace and support. Synagogues, Jewish community centers, and various organizations are working toward enlarging the concept of the Jewish family to a more pluralistic model, one that includes the couple without children. This greater sensitivity on all fronts is welcome.

One of feminism's first tasks was to help break the link between biology and destiny in a way Freud could never have imagined. Cutting this connection enlarged women's freedom of action; women now, for the most part, choose to have children. Babies usually don't appear regularly every twelve or thirteen months "like little full moons."[74] Birth no longer defines women, although a woman may choose to have pregnancy and childbirth as part of her human identity. That birth is now an option is due both to safe contraception as well as to increased opportunities for women to participate in all spheres of society. That broader public role (and voice) has led to many changes in how fertility and infertility are viewed. A pregnant woman is no longer automatically dismissed as soon as her pregnancy is visible. (On the contrary, designer maternity clothes can satisfy the most exacting of executive standards.) Infertility is no longer a hidden topic, but is handled with openness, empathy, and support.

Still, the debate about mothering and working, rather than parenting and working, rages on.[75] Indeed, those who argue that family must come first are of course correct; family in its broad sense must be the first priority for both men *and* women. "[T]he conflict between family and work," writes Lisa Schiffren, is not resolvable. Rather, she states, "it is simply part of the human condition."

As long as there are only 24 hours in a day, taking care of one's family will clash with serious professional ambition. The sooner that fact is recognized, the better equipped young women [and men] will be to make the choices that best suit their temperaments and aims. Some will give up children in order to make millions; some, in the time-tested way, will give up work for children. Others—the great majority—will try to strike the best balance they can, either simultaneously or sequentially. . . . To pretend . . . that women can have everything and sacrifice nothing—is a recipe for widespread misery.[76]

Feminism is not only about careers and economic parity but also about emotional growth, independence, broad opportunities, relationships, and shared vision. Modern Judaism of all denominations reflects this transformation. Birth has become rebirth.

Chapter 4

Simhat Bat: Celebrating the Birth of a Daughter

In Betar, they had a custom. When a baby boy was born, they planted
a cedar tree, and when a baby girl was born, they planted a pine tree.
When [a boy and girl] wed, [the people] would cut down [their trees]
and make the wedding canopy out of the wood.

B.T. Gittin 57a

When our children were born over thirty years ago—two girls and a boy—it never occurred to me that our daughters, or their parents, were missing something in the way they were welcomed into our family, our community, and the Jewish people. They were duly named by their father while I was still in the hospital—at that time one received five days of wonderful postnatal care in Ontario hospitals; grandparents magically appeared, different ones coming and going over a number of weeks. Friends came over to see the new little people and eventually we sponsored a *kiddush* in our synagogue.

It was the 1960s. I was young and naive, bursting with the love of new motherhood and the joy of creating a family. The revealing rip in our otherwise seamless happiness was that my father did not come for months to see his first grandchild. A Polish immigrant, owner of a small business, he would have come had the baby been a boy; a grandfather must be at a grandson's *brit milah*. But since the baby was a girl, he could wait for a more convenient time to close the store.

It was years later, when the social activism and sense of justice so much a part of the legacy from my mother became allied with the beginnings of the feminist movement, that I began to reconsider what my husband and I had, and had not, done to welcome our daughters into this world, and into their world— the world of Jewish tradition.

This chapter is concerned with what rabbinic sources state about the birth of a daughter and of a son in terms of the parents, the community, and social value. Its particular focus is how the rabbinic literature conveys strict views of the future public role of the boy and the primarily private role of the girl, through discussion of a social event and mitzvah celebration such as the welcoming of a new child. It will explore as well how Jewish daughters are now being welcomed into the tradition and reflect upon the conceptual changes indicated by contemporary birth-covenant ceremonies for girls. Recent years have seen the proliferation of ceremonies welcoming a baby girl into the covenant of Abraham and Sarah.[1] These ceremonies parallel in some way the ancient ritual of circumcision, long established as the hallmark of the public welcome of an infant boy into the Jewish community.

While the development of *simhat bat* (Joy of a Daughter) or *brit banot* (Covenant of the Daughters) ceremonies can be traced to the feminist movement beginning in the early 1960s, their contemporary sources in fact go back to the early Reform movement in Germany, which, with its many changes, began ever so slowly to break down the barriers between the male public domain and the female private domain. But the theories it proposed, while admirable, did not find their fit in the social structure of the nineteenth and twentieth centuries. That "fit" had to wait for the impetus of the feminist movement of the 1960s, spawned, perhaps most visibly, by Simone de Beauvoir's *The Second Sex*.[2]

In the Romantic theology of Fredrich Schleiermacher, one finds a great emphasis on the birth of a child as a gift bestowed by God upon the love between a man and a woman. Schleiermacher is repudiating the traditional practice of wanting children for reasons of family line and inheritance and in viewing progeny as the needed outcome of politically expeditious unions. Schleiermacher's view is that children should not be understood as serving any human purpose but rather as a sign of God's grace and love. But surely this notion, while praiseworthy in some respects, is unrealistic in others. Halakhic sources discuss the transformative effect of the birth of a son or daughter precisely in terms of human purpose, emphasizing especially the role of inheritance, in both its tangible and figurative meanings.

When a woman gives birth to a boy child, both parents are required to recite a blessing of praise *(birkhat hodaah)* called *"hatov vehametiv."* The blessing states: "Blessed are you our God, King of the universe, who is good and does good," or "who does good [for me] and causes good [for others]."[3] Each is required to recite the blessing even if, as might occur, they are separated when the husband hears the news. The wife recites the blessing at the time of completion of delivery; the husband, if he is not with her, whenever and wherever he hears the news.[4] Even if the couple already has several sons, each must still recite the blessing upon the birth of yet another boy child.[5]

The sources state that only the parents may recite this blessing upon the occasion of the birth, since they have *hanaat toelet* from the child (the pleasure of a benefit or advantage or usefulness from a son).[6] This benefit is that he is a *yoresh* (he inherits from the parents). The blessing of *hatov vehametiv* is made only in cases where the benefit is a shared one—in this case shared with the mother and father—and in which the object that causes the blessing to be made, namely, the child, leads to an advantage, a practical use, for those making the blessing. Here the benefit is to have an inheritor, one who by virtue of his maleness will gain the family property and is required to recite kaddish after their deaths.

But what is the text implying? Is it affirming an advantage in the utility of having male progeny because of the laws of inheritance? The case is unclear. Despite inequities in the laws of inheritance due to the economic structure of a tribal and patriarchal society, widows and unmarried daughters always had first claim on any estate in the event of the death of a husband/father.[7] The text points beyond property per se to mean property in the cultural sense. That is, since a daughter will become part of another family through marriage, the family legacy, in terms of name and public role, will remain with the sons. Reciting the blessing then is acknowledgment of the possibility of continuing the family traditions and legacy not only through one's teachings—which clearly include one's daughters—but also concretely through the ones who, until current practice, continued to carry the family name in the community.

There are some provisos given in the halakhic literature, however, regarding the recitation of the blessing *hatov vehametiv*. After stating that the parents must recite the blessing for the reason *"sheyesh lahem hanaat toelet meben"* ("they have the pleasure of a practical benefit from a son"), the sources continue, *"veode"* ("in addition"). The appearance of this term in halakhic texts, similar to Rashi's stating in his commentary to the Pentateuch, *"vedavar acher"* ("and another matter"), indicates that the first reason given is incomplete in some way, needing an additional support to clarify and validate the halakhic ruling. And what is the *"veode"*? The text continues, *"Veode, shehu cayerech haav vehaem.* In addition, he [the boy child] is the progeny, the seed of the father and mother, and all persons desire successors or heirs."[8] This point of additional clarification can be seen both as supporting and detracting from the original halakhic ruling. It is supportive in that it emphasizes the human desire to continue oneself through one's children. But it weakens the conclusion that the blessing must be said only upon the birth of a boy child, because this human need clearly supersedes any gender boundaries. It is easily seen that this halakhah, given the circumstances of our culture and our modern sensibilities, can and should be enlarged to include the birth of girls. The original ruling, however, restricts the recitation of the blessing of *hatov vehametiv* to the birth of a boy.

Surprisingly, this is the case as well with the blessing of *shehechiyanu,* although the sources themselves amplify the ruling that focuses on male infants. The blessing thanks God "who has granted us life, sustained us, and permitted us to reach this season." The blessing of *shehechiyanu* is both a *birkhat hodaah* (blessing of praise) and a *birkhat zeman* (a blessing that notes a special time interval and/or a particular occasion).[9] It is recited, for example, at the yearly celebration of Passover, the wearing of new clothing, or the eating of a new fruit. Sources suggest that both mother and father should recite *shehechiyanu* after the birth of a daughter, as well as after the birth of a son. One source states that even though it is not required that either blessing—*hatov vehametiv* or *she-hechiyanu*—be recited after a girl is born, when a father sees his new daughter for the first time, he should nevertheless recite *shehechiyanu*. Since the blessing is said upon seeing a good friend one has not seen for at least thirty days, one surely can proclaim *shehechiyanu* upon seeing one's newborn daughter for the very first time![10]

Although the language sounds strange—can one, after all, really compare wearing new clothes to welcoming one's daughter into the world?—the text needs to be considered as written by men for men, in the kind of language for which Carol Gilligan criticized Lawrence Kohlberg.[11] In a legal text, context, relationship, and affect are expressed in an indirect and abstract manner. The claim is that although the blessing of *shehechiyanu* is not required, it nonetheless *should* be recited because of the joyfulness that characterizes the birth of any child. A recently published booklet on birth published by JOFA, the Jewish Orthodox Feminist Alliance, states, "Traditionally, a baby girl was greeted only with the blessing of *shehechiyanu*."[12] But to my knowledge reciting *shehechiyanu* is not yet a widespread religious practice. The same guidebook declares that R. Nahum Rabinowitz, head of the yeshiva at Maaleh Adumin, has said that "today parents of girls feel the great joy that warrants recitation [even] of the blessing '*hatov vehametiv*.'"[13]

The issue of *brit,* or covenant, is central to an understanding of celebrating the birth of a daughter. Are female infants members of the covenant even though they do not undergo a mark on the flesh, the circumcision that is the sign of the covenant, as given to Abraham in Genesis 17:10?[14] Despite dispute as to when (how early) circumcision becomes completely identified with covenant[15] in the biblical text, by the time of the codification of the Mishnah,[16] the rite and its meaning are inextricably intertwined. Although a most personal rite since the genitals are its focus, at the same time the rite is neither private nor official. It is a public act of identification. Given then that no marking of the flesh is required of female infants, what does this say of their membership in the covenant community?[17] Is the girl child a full member in good standing? Is her membership in some way derivative? Is she excluded from and therefore peripheral to the community? In a multitude of examples, women are assumed to be integral to the covenant community.[18] But how does the girl child enter, since no direct statement of her membership is given in the biblical text and no rite is described as requisite for her entry?

There are four ways in which the entry, or lack thereof, of a girl child into the covenant can be understood.

1. Genesis 17:16, the verse that follows the change of Sarai's name to Sarah, states: "And I will bless her and also give you a child [son] from her; and I will bless her and she shall be a mother of nations, kings of peoples will be of her." That is, in this verse Sarah becomes a full partner with Abraham in the promise of the covenant. Since no rite is required of Sarah, she is subsumed under its aegis upon the transforming of her name. Thus, just as Abraham's male descendants follow him in being circumcised upon the eighth day as an external sign of an internal covenant, Sarah's female descendants embody the covenant's meaning in the absence of an external sign.

2. The B.T. Avodah Zarah 27a contains a detailed discussion of who is qualified to perform circumcision. Part of the discussion revolves around the meaning of the principle "He who is circumcised shall circumcise" (Genesis 17:13) and the verse "And as for thee, thou shalt keep my covenant." The analysis comes around to the question of whether or not a woman is classed among the circumcised and is therefore qualified to perform the rite. Using the example of Zipporah (Exodus 4:25), the Gemara states, "[F]or a woman should be classed among the circumcised." Since she cannot by definition undergo circumcision, she is considered circumcised without the external sign.

3. Another source appears in the commentary of Tosafot to the B.T. Berakhot 20b. The text is discussing whether the obligation of women to recite the grace after meals is of biblical or rabbinic origin.[19]

   One reason the obligation may be rabbinic is that the grace after meals includes the statement "on the land that you [God] have given us," and land parcels—the line of inheritance being patriarchal—were not given to female descendants (although financial support was of course mandated). But, Tosafot says, if that is the reason, the priests and Levites, who also were not given land, should also have an obligation that is rabbinic and not biblical. However, that is not the case. But, says Tosafot, there is another possibility: the verse in the grace after meals that states "on the covenant which you [God] have sealed in our flesh." On the basis of this, should the ruling be that women's obligation is rabbinic? Tosafot says this may be, but one can also rule that women's obligation is biblical because the category of the sign of the covenant simply does not pertain to women. Tosafot's discussion reminds us that in all the cases of covenant in the Bible there is both the covenant itself (its content) as well as the sign of the covenant. This is evident with Noah and with the *brit bain habetarm* (covenant of [between] the pieces) made with Abraham in Genesis 15:9–20. What makes circumcision different is that the marking of the sign becomes a mitzvah, a commandment. Therefore, the content of the covenant is "I will be their God" (Genesis 17:8), and the nonrelevance of the mark of the covenant with regard to women is not an exclusion from the meaning of its content.

4. According to Howard Eilberg-Schwartz, circumcision played three roles in the cultural system/context of biblical society.[20] First, it marked a boundary between Abraham and his male descendants on the one hand, and Abraham's father and male ancestors on the other; between those who embraced monotheism and the idolatrous culture from whence they came. The covenant begins only when Abraham and his male heirs mark their flesh as a sign of their distinctiveness. Second, it combined its symbolic reference to male fertility—take note of the verses that promise Abraham's descendants will be as numerous as the stars[21]—with the need to guarantee that the genealogical line would continue. Finally—a point of great interest—according to Eilberg-Schwartz, circumcision demonstrated symbolically the history of patrilineal over matrilineal descent. Leaving aside the many aspects of this tripartite claim that call for further analysis, it is important to see what happens when the rabbis radically reconstruct the rite of circumcision, moving it well beyond the biblical roots outlined above.

A fine discussion of this transformation is given by Lawrence A. Hoffman in his recent volume, *Covenant of Blood: Circumcision and Gender in Rabbinic Judaism.* Hoffman's approach to analyzing circumcision is anthropological, following the methodology formulated by Clifford Geertz.[22] Cultural and religious groups usually take their ceremonies and rituals for granted, assuming their meanings and meaningfulness rather than necessarily exploring them. Geertz writes about "sorting out the structures of signification"[23] in other cultures as an outside observer. Hoffman's aim is to be anthropologist to his own religious culture.[24]

What is this documentary evidence that we have inherited from times past if not constructions of reality; and who are the authors, if not each generation's experts in the rules governing the propriety of Jewish ritual and in the interpretation of its religious signification? We must learn to utilize the discussions and reports in ancient and medieval sources as if they were answers to hypothetical anthropologists, ourselves, whose task it is to go back in time and ask, What are you doing, and why?"[25]

According to Hoffman, the rabbis "retained the biblical precedent of circumcision as a covenant rite for males . . . but then outfitted it with a liturgy of the word that no biblical Jew could remotely have predicted. They thereby adumbrated a new conception of the Jewish compact with God. Gone is the agricultural imagery . . . and the fertility concern that had so motivated earlier generations. Instead, we get the rabbinic notion of salvation symbolized by the blood of circumcision, which saves."[26] Hoffman's research demonstrates a transition in the meaning of circumcision from that of fertility to that of salvation. Some sources claim that the circumcision liturgy found in geonic prayer books around the ninth century also appeared in nonextant versions of the Palestinian Talmud around the year 500 c.e. Hoffman asserts, then, that the blood of the *brit milah* came to be seen as central due to its saving power: "By your blood, live" rather than "in your blood, live" (Ezekiel 16:6).[27] The rabbis read Ezekiel as guaranteeing that Israel lives by virtue of its blood that is shed in covenant.[28]

Thus the blessing of fertility offered to Abraham is transformed conceptually into one of salvation. This is seen clearly in a contemporary halakhic guide, *Bris Milah,*[29] which states: "Circumcision is an affirmation of Abraham's ancient and still vibrant covenant and an expression of confident hope in a *redemption* [emphasis mine] that will return man [*sic*] to the pedestal on which Adam once stood."[30] In some rabbinic texts, the expression *brit milah* (covenant of circumcision) becomes *brit dam milah* (covenant of the blood of circumcision), emphasizing blood as a sign of salvation.

Hoffman asks the incisive question: since the context of Ezekiel is not related to circumcision, what is its link with circumcision—and even more so, with redemption? Through meticulous analysis of passages in *Pirkei de Rabbi Eliezer,* geonic sources, the Mekhilta as well as *Targum Yonatan,* Hoffman demonstrates that the interpretive link between the covenant of circumcision, circumcision blood, and that blood as a symbol of salvation is tannaitic in origin, continuing through the talmudic period into the geonic era[31]—indeed, into the tapestry of our times.

The contemporary bibiblical scholar, Jon D. Levenson, offers a sharp critique of Hoffman's approach. He writes:

Hoffman . . . misses the fact that the covenant is with the nation collectively and not with Israelites as individuals, and that circumcision symbolizes but does not effectuate this covenant. To say, as he does in a nearby passage, that women are party to the covenant "only in a secondary way" is like saying that American citizenship applies only to those who fly the stars and stripes on their flagpoles, everyone else being a second-class citizen.[32]

Levenson is correct that "circumcision symbolizes but does not effectuate this covenant." But his analogy with American citizenship and flying the flag does not hold. Displaying a flag is a voluntary manifestation of patriotism, not an obligation of citizenship. As demonstrated in the sources analyzed above, women's being "party to the covenant" is almost by default. It seems not incorrect, therefore, to label female inclusion as "secondary."

Three possible sources are given above to provide explanations of how a girl might be considered as having entered the covenant. It never occurred to me when our daughters were born that they could not be included: of course they were part of *klal yisrael,* both the *brit goral* and the *brit yeud* [33] (the covenant of historical destiny and that of moral witnessing). How could it be otherwise? But if this is so, why were they not welcomed—overtly, publicly, with ceremonial song and formula and prayer—into that community? Such ceremonies were just beginning to be thought about. The three options described seem an effort—undoubtedly sincere—to let females in through the back door since the front entrance is locked. These options are creative ways of reading women into that from which women were left out.

A survey of the history of the noncircumcision of Jewish women offers insight into aspects of this issue. The writer, a historian, says he "would like to understand when and why the non-circumcision of Jewish women became a question that required answers, and what answers were advanced by the Jews of antiquity."[34] The author is fully aware that his words are a male construction of both maleness and femaleness. "[N]o sources tell us," he states, "how ancient Jewish women explained the absence of a covenantal mark from their bodies."[35]

Male circumcision among Jews can be seen as part of a broad phenomenon in the ancient Near East. Among those societies engaging in this practice were not only Israel, but also Egypt, Ethiopia, Syria, Phonecia, Edom or Idumea, Amman, Moab, and Arabia.[36] Thus Jewish practice arises not in a vacuum,[37] but as a part of a broad cultural, historical phenomenon. But the question as to why only men are circumcised is addressed by the first-century c.e. Jewish philosopher and exegete, Philo. In his commentary on Genesis 17 in *Questions and Answers on Genesis,* Philo gives two answers to this question. The first is that circumcision "serves to check male lust, which is much stronger than the female's, in fact a little too strong." And second, circumcision curbs male pride, "which has its origin in the fact that males contribute the more important part in the process of generation."[38] Yet that half of all Jews are not circumcised seems not to trouble Philo, who "nowhere says that circumcision is an essential criterion for membership in the people of Israel."[39] Shaye Cohen argues that Philo's discussions of circumcision were a response to the debates about the practice among Greek-speaking Jews. The most notable first-century Jewish critic of circumcision was Paul, but his conversion of physical circumcision to a spiritual state is beyond the scope of this chapter.[40]

Both Philo and Paul believed males and females operated in different spheres and that of females was inferior. In the first five centuries after

Christianity began, noncircumcision of women led Christian anti-Jewish polemicists to formulate three arguments against Judaism. The first, put forthrightly by Justin Martyr in the second century c.e., says: "If righteousness before God requires circumcision, why are women not circumcised?"[41] The second argument avers that Christian baptism is superior to Jewish circumcision, "since baptism applies to both men and women while circumcision applies only to men."[42] Augustine's defense of Christian doctrine leads him to ask, "[S]ince Jewish women are not circumcised, are they Jews at all?"[43] The arguments put forward by these three Christian authors are not answered by Philo's rationales, as they assume circumcision "affects one's status both in the community and in the eyes of God, while Philo makes no such assumption."[44] Classic rabbinic sources, however, while cognizant of the gender implications of circumcision, seem unperturbed by its male exclusivity. Cohen offers three responses the rabbis might have presented to the Christian polemicists "had they chosen to do so."[45] These responses lead back to the central focus of this chapter, celebrating the birth of a daughter.

The first response is that Christianity is a community formed by faith in Christ, by belief in a specific creed. Judaism, in contrast, is an "ethnic" community, attained through birth. The central liturgical statement of Jewish prayer portrays God as the guiding force of Abraham, Isaac, and Jacob, as well as Sarah, Rebecca, Rachel, and Leah, and the Jewish people as descendants of this distinct ancestry. One is born into the Jewish people whether one is male (and circumcised) or female. Second, Cohen views the applicability of circumcision only to males as an indication of the lesser legal status of women indicated both in Torah (Pentateuch) and the Talmud. The use of the term "Jew" in classical Judaism was taken to mean the free adult male Jew,[46] comparable to the use of "Athenian" to mean male Athenian citizen. "Women of citizen status," Shaye Cohen points out, "could not participate in the activities of the public sphere."[47] In a sense, then, only men were "real" Jews, and the mark of circumcision could be understood as the physical sign of a legal identity. The third point relates to the first. In rabbinic literature, circumcision does not confer Jewishness. Circumcised gentiles (or the early Christians who had been circumcised) are not Jews. Circumcision, that is, does not parallel baptism as a sine qua non for entry into the religious community. Thus Jewish women are Jewish even if not circumcised. This may also be the case with a Jewish man who, for medical reasons, cannot undergo circumcision.[48]

As Shaye Cohen notes in his conclusion, however, the questions put to Jews by Christian polemicists in the early centuries of Christian development arise again in the High Middle Ages. Without this external challenge, he claims, the noncircumcision of women would not have been an issue for medieval rabbinic authorities.

For both Philo and the rabbis, the fundamental inferiority, marginality, and Otherness of women were so self-evident that the presence of a covenantal mark on the bodies of men, and its absence from the bodies of women, seemed natural and inevitable.[49]

Circumcision is given as a mitzvah in the Torah with the sole purpose being the establishment of a *brit* between God and Abraham. *Milah* (circumcision) is analyzed in several ways in the history of *taamei hamitzvot* (ascribing reasons or purposes to the commandments). The reasoning given above by Philo is echoed in medieval discussions. Saadia Gaon understands circumcision to be an act of perfecting the (male) body. He writes:

[O]ne might wonder, apropos of the individual precepts, how it could be that as long as a man's body is in its complete natural state he is not perfect, whereas, when something is cut off from it, he becomes perfect. What I have reference to is the [rite of] circumcision. Let me explain, then, that the perfect thing is one that suffers from neither superfluity nor deficiency. Now the Creator created this part of the body with a redundancy, with the result that, when it is cut off, the redundancy is removed and what is left is in a state of perfection.[50]

Maimonides, however, disagrees with Saadia and, in true Aristotelian fashion, ascribes the purpose and merit of circumcision to a decrease in sexual desire, leading to less frequent sexual intimacy.

Similarly with regard to circumcision, one of the reasons for it is, in my opinion, the wish to bring about a decrease in sexual intercourse and a weakening of the organ in question, so that this activity be diminished and the organ be in as quiet a state as possible. It has been thought that circumcision perfects what is defective congenitally. This gave the possibility to everyone to raise an objection and to say: How can natural things be defective so that they need to be perfected from outside, all the more because we know how useful the foreskin is for that member? In fact this commandment has not been prescribed with a view to perfecting what is defective congenitally, but to perfecting what is defective morally. The bodily pain caused to that member is the real purpose of circumcision. None of the activities necessary for the preservation of the individual is harmed thereby, nor is procreation rendered impossible, but violent concupiscence and lust that goes beyond what is needed are diminished. The fact that circumcision weakens the faculty of sexual excitement and sometimes perhaps diminishes the pleasure is indubitable. For if at birth this member has been made to bleed and has had its covering taken away from it, it must indubitably be weakened.[51]

Nahmanides refers to the reason given by the Radak in his commentary on Genesis 17:9, where he states:

Now they [the Radak] have said concerning the reason for the commandment of circumcision that He has thereby placed a reminder in the organ of lust, which is the source of much trouble and sin, in order that it should not be used excepting where it is commandatory and permissible.[52]

And according to S. R. Hirsch, circumcision demonstrates the intrinsic function and social value of the male in contrast to that of the female. The command in Genesis is given to *"kol zakhar"* ("every male") not because he is incomplete or in order to lessen his sexual desire, but because he is the paradigmatic carrier, the *z-kh-r,* rememberer and transmitter of the moral and spiritual legacy of the Torah. This is why, Hirsch maintains, the command of *limud Torah* (study of Torah) is exclusive to males, while the female task is *leatzev,* to form, mold, or fashion the concrete world under the aegis of Torah concepts.[53]

From this survey of reasons for circumcision, what can be deduced about the covenantal status, the intrinsic value, and the halakhic place of the female? Shaye Cohen posits an underlying acceptance of women's lesser status as "natural." Another scholar claims "certain arrangements of gender asymmetry" that took root in formative rabbinic Judaism are now amenable to change.[54] A third examines talmudic sources solely as a history of legal development rather than a reflection of social realities, concluding that rabbinic law created a "benevolent patriarchy."

Even though it placed men in charge of women, it also permitted men to make changes that benefitted women and that showed concern for women in general and even respect for individual women of accomplishment (as measured in male terms).[55]

Not possessing the "redundancy" of the foreskin, is the woman then presumed, according to Saadia's premises, to be born in a state of perfection? Or does she indeed have a physical redundancy that one is not commanded to remove and therefore remains less "perfect" than the male? Or shall it be assumed, as one might with both Philo and Maimonides, that only male sexual desires needs curbing, while female lust is no danger to society?[56] Nahmanides ascribes to circumcision the purpose of a reminder to control sexual desire rather than a procedure that actually leads to its weakening. In this way Nahmanides is closer to the meaning of *ot,* a sign or a reminder. As in Maimonides, implied is the underlying concept that female sexuality does not require restraint, even in the form of a "reminder." It is of course fascinating that none of these analyses of circumcision as the sign of the covenant mentions the female. Only Hirsch, who divides male/female according to strictly essentialist definitions, even mentions the woman. But he does so specifically with regard to ascribing a function to her, not in terms of her relation to the covenant.

Each interpreter of the purpose of circumcision as the first commandment in the Torah speaks out of a specific historical matrix, be it that of first-century Alexandria (Philo), twelfth-century Aristotelianism (Maimonides), or late-nineteenth-century German bourgeoise society (Samson Raphael Hirsch). The same may be said of Lawrence A. Hoffman in his analysis of the meaning of *milah*. Hoffman's interpretation is that the blood of circumcision manifests the controlled release of blood, first related to fertility, subsequently to salvation. In a fascinating analysis, Hoffman demonstrates how the controlled drawing of blood in a male-dominated ceremony[57] on the male genitalia contrasts with the free flowing, ofttimes unpredictable appearance of blood in the female's menstrual cycle. His claim is that circumcision, among other halakhot, supports the divisions presented by Sherry B. Ortner in her well-known essay, "Is Male to Female as Culture is to Nature?"[58] Hoffman's analysis is thorough and convincing.

Hoffman's examination is relevant to this discussion as it focuses upon the conceptual and sociological underpinnings of the *brit milah* to which contemporary parents are responding as they insist their daughters enter the covenant through the front door. *Brit milah,* with its attendant *seudat mitzvah* (festive meal celebrating fulfillment of a *mitzvah*) and invited guests,[59] puts a public persona on that which remains more subdued and private when the welcomed child is female. It would seem that the public/private axis in Judaism, almost always bifurcated along male/female lines,[60] is presaged in the welcome—or lack thereof—accorded the boy or girl child. One might say that the boy is welcomed through circumcision into the public role he is accorded in halakhah. The girl, in contrast, is *assumed* to be part of the covenant; she carries no *ot* (sign), and halakhah does not prescribe an entry point or rite that demarcates the absence of covenant status from its conferral.[61] The lack of such a designated entry point with its concommitant public aspects indicates to many a lack of value.[62] Were a daughter's value equal to that of a son, she would enter the *brit* in a public ceremony.

It is this conundrum that has led to the remarkable development of *simhat bat* or *brit banot* ceremonies over the past thirty or so years. This is not a matter of emulating male ceremonies and/or feeling excluded; it is a far more complex phenomenon—religiously, sociologically, and psychologically. One focus is the social-cultural context, which grounds lived experience and which delimits the choices available in any given historical period. A second is the uniqueness of individual lives—their singularity and distinctiveness, their existential import. Both individual complexity and cultural groundedness must be considered. One needs to ask: what is at stake here for those who find the tradition lacking? What meaning are they seeking that may have been present in earlier times—indeed, may be present today for some—but is no longer for them? If the social-cultural context and the meaningfulness of individual lives are seen as two aspects of the legitimate religious experience, the critical reductionist tendencies (i.e., "modern Orthodox women are self-absorbed, etc.") can be seen for what they are: fear of loss of power and the inability to listen empathetically to the pain of another.

Critics of Orthodox feminism have often demeaned the motivation of its adherents. Orthodox feminists are said to be like the rebels who supported Korah;[63] they are narcissistic and self-absorbed, desiring only personal pleasure,[64] or they wish to obtain "their full share of the so-called good life: money, prestige, power, and indulgence in physical pleasure" and "undermine the spirit of rabbinic Judaism."[65] None of these ad hominem attacks deals with the fundamental issue: the tradition itself is deficient and the voices of women, once silenced, are finally being heard; that which once worked is now found wanting. Women's voices have begun to correct the deficiency present both axiologically and sociologically.

Some contemporary studies of rabbinic sources address the incompleteness within the structures of the tradition.

The relative exclusion of Jewish women from the experience of circumcision, *Torah* learning, and other features of Jewish identity, must affect the nature of their identity as Israel. . . . If she is excluded from the distinctive *praxis* of Israel as defined in rabbinic sources, what then is her Jewish identity, namely her experience of "being Israel" (or "daughter of Israel") supposed to consist of?[66]

Understanding female Jewish identity, however, depends upon experiences ascribed to women in rabbinic sources. That is, rabbinic sources were written by men and for men; they indicate, therefore, what the sages thought were the experiences of women. The dearth of primary sources authored by women, the absence of a women's history written from within the tradition, affects the view of a woman's "being Israel."[67]

Indeed, the male authorship of many texts is a significant factor in clarifying the references to circumcision in which women—and women's Jewish identity—seem to be ignored. At the very least, these sources seem to affirm the ancillary cultural status of the Jewish woman. Circumcision, some midrashic sources affirm, is a sine qua non for success in prayer and study of Torah.[68] In other texts where those born already circumcised are identified—such as Jacob in contrast to Esau—*milah* comes to be seen as "intrinsic to Israel."[69] There appears to be a glorification of the mitzvah of *milah* as connected to an inherent sense of Jewishness. This is illustrated in the comparison of Israel to grains of wheat "because they are split in the middle, just as the penises of Israel are split."[70] In this imagery, circumcision seems almost a quality of the Jewish body as a communal, historical entity. Wherein then does the Jewishness of females lie? The public welcoming of a girl child into the covenantal community of Israel is a response to this question, both its theoretical aspect and its practical thrust.

As the very concept of mitzvah indicates, it is insufficient to know X; X must be realized in the realm of the concrete. Similarly, merely knowing that a daughter is valued and is considered part of the tradition is inadequate; having her father name her and receiving mazal tov wishes at a kiddush is inadequate.[71] The concrete, the experiential—a rite, ritual, or ceremony in the public domain—serves as a corrective for that which has been lacking. It is love of Judaism and deep commitment to the covenant that impels parents to articulate, through ritual, the joy of bringing a girl into their family and the community of Israel.

As early as 1978, strong objections were made specifically about the development of welcoming ceremonies for newborn girls. Moshe Meiselman, in a revealingly entitled chapter, "Nonhalakhic Approaches to the Divine,"[72] inveighs against the creation of new ritual, comparing it to the transgression of Nadab and Abihu, who considered themselves "superior servants of God."[73] Meiselman's formulation manifests both ambivalence and invective. "The introduction of new rituals may not be absolutely forbidden, but it is certainly an exercise in futility, a series of meaningless activities."[74] It is striking that someone would tell a person who finds X not only meaningful, but also a source of delight and joy, that it is "meaningless"—indeed, a mirage, an error of affect, an emptiness. Meiselman continues:

An even more ridiculous ceremony, often referred to as a *britah,* has recently been introduced on the eighth day of a girl's life. It too is invested with a detailed ritual. In some places, the blessing of *koret habrit,* "maker of the covenant," is recited without mentioning God's name. This ceremony mocks the very concept of *brit.* A *brit,* or covenant, cannot be unilateral, it must be bilateral. . . . [A] sign of the covenant cannot be initiated by man [*sic*]. A unilaterally executed covenant with God is, at best, a *meaningless* form of spiritual autoeroticism. . . . [T]he Talmud tells us that a woman becomes a member of the covenant automatically at birth.[75] (emphasis mine)

Meiselman approves of the backdoor approach, labeling the sincere attempts to enter through the main portals as "ridiculous" and delegitimates the contemporary welcoming rituals as "autoerotic," a kind of "spiritual masturbation." This kind of criticism, both logically imprecise and vitriolic in tone, is characteristic in discussion of religious practices that affect women. Indeed, if females are already members of the covenant at birth, a ritual designed to mark this status is not unilateral; the girl child's status has already been divinely initiated and sanctioned. A ceremony merely completes the process much as aspects of *brit milah,* having evolved over time, can be seen as a completion of the minimum requirements of this mitzvah. In addition, since Meiselman acknowledges that creating a *simhat bat* is not "absolutely forbidden,"[76] he is recognizing, albeit reluctantly, the role of a strong subjective element in religious life. The many analyses of *minhag,* or custom, in halakhic sources are discussions precisely of such a subjective element.[77]

Some early attempts to celebrate the birth of a daughter tended to follow closely the format of the male circumcision, suggesting that the ritual take place on the eighth day and even—in one suggestion made in the early 1970s—that the ceremony incorporate the blood and genital aspects of *brit milah* and consist therefore of a ritual breaking of the hymen. While provocative for several reasons, including Hoffman's analysis of the symbolism of blood, this suggestion has not been followed.[78] More recent formulations, however, have abandoned the *brit milah* paradigm in its physical sense, arguing, as did the rabbinic sources analyzed above, that *milah* obviously cannot pertain to a woman.

How then to concretize in ritual form the spiritual transformation that signifies female entry into the covenant of the Jewish people? Two symbols have become popular. One, the water/ritual bath immersion is based not only on the concept of mikvah as described in Leviticus, but also on a well-known suggestion of the medieval commentator, the Meiri,[79] who states that when Abraham was circumcised, Sarah underwent ritual immersion in order to enter the covenant.[80] Both circumcision (in the case of males) and immersion are required of converts to Judaism, signifying transformation, commitment to new responsibility, and change of status. One covenant ceremony for a new daughter thus involves immersion in the ritual bath.

Another focuses upon the new moon, or Rosh Chodesh, traditionally designated as a woman's holiday. It relates female spirituality to the cycles of the moon and uses the first Rosh Chodesh after the child's birth as the appropriate time to welcome her. Both of the above—the immersion and the Rosh Chodesh celebration—relate in some way to female sexuality, reminding us of menstruation and *niddah* (ritual impurity). Perhaps it is important to reevaluate the ritual bath, long denigrated by some feminists, and treat it with the same reverence given to *milah:* an alternative means of spiritual transformation rooted in female uniqueness, as *milah* is grounded in male sexual specificity.

What is unusual about the ceremonies that celebrate the birth of a daughter and welcome her as a member of the convenantal community is their comparative novelty. The first published collection of *simhat bat* ceremonies dates back to 1977 when the New York Jewish feminist group Ezrat Nashim published their booklet of welcoming rituals. The development of these ceremonies parallels the spread and influence of the feminist movement. Since this initial publication, rituals of welcome and celebration for girl babies have become an integral part of Jewish life, except within the most right-wing Orthodox groups.

Celebrating the birth of a baby daughter provides an opportunity to use established traditions within an altered context. One aspect of the transformed circumstances involves an egalitarianism that has been part of *simhat bat* or *brit banot* ceremonies from the very beginning. Not only is the ceremony itself in honor of a new female member of the Jewish people, but it has also developed at a time when female participation in ritual has been increasing. There is no long history of male rabbis conducting *simhat bat* ceremonies.

The lack of established tradition has both disadvantages and benefits. The task of creating one's own ceremony can seem daunting even for one familiar with liturgical and rabbinic texts. Bringing a new life into the world can be overwhelming without having to devise a distinctive way of welcoming the child. But anthropology has enlarged the understanding of the constitutive elements of ritual, and this broader awareness, together with knowledge of Jewish tradition, has helped inform the many ceremonies parents have created.

Ritual is a means of rendering "vivid and palpable our ideas and wishes."[81] In human history it usually develops to mark individual or communal points of anxiety, uncertainty, or chaos. Transitions, especially the significant moments of one's life, are always noted by what is termed a life-cycle ritual. Generally, rituals integrate verbal modes with the "presentational . . . so that our senses are aroused and flood us with phenomenological proof of the symbolic reality which the ritual is portraying."[82] In ritual we rely on that which is predictable and represents continuity. Thus the relatively new *simhat bat* or *brit banot* ceremony arouses its own level of anxiety, as novelty is wont to do. At the same time, however, it calls forth our creativity. Religious rituals link the participants not only with each other but also with a shared past and common vision of the future, thereby enhancing the sensibilities of the participants. New ritual transforms reality, calling forth emotion, imagination, and insight. In the paradigmatic ritual, the symbols coalesce with their underlying meanings, connecting to deeply embedded patterns of human life.

The development of ritual ceremonies in a celebration of the birth of a girl are the culmination of a groundswell among Jewish men and women deeply committed to moving a previously pallid and mostly private occasion of joy into the public arena. Often the mother and infant girl were not present when the father named the child, and a small repast was offered to congregants after the services. This contrast to the communal joy evidenced at *seudat mitzvah,* the meal in celebration of fulfillment of the commandment of *brit milah,* needed to be bridged. In addition, the traditional blessing offered upon the birth of a boy, "May you be blessed to lead your son to the study of Torah, to the marriage canopy, and to doing deeds of loving kindness," was usually altered when recited for a girl: "the study of Torah" was omitted. From that moment the community viewed the girl not only as technically exempt from the study of Torah,[83] but also as having a home-centered role within the tradition. That these blessings are now identical in all but right-wing communities evidences the communal commitment to advanced Jewish education for women and the gradual diminishing of essentialist notions. In addition, the infant girl was traditionally named as the daughter of her father, while contemporary ceremonies specify both parents.

The dozens of naming covenant ceremonies on file at the Jewish Women's Resource Center, New York section of the National Council of Jewish Women,[84] illustrate the creativity, imagination, and love expended in designing new rituals to counterbalance traditional rituals that seem to express a higher valuation of males than females. The new rituals rectify the perceived imbalance both socially, by having an equally big celebration, and symbolically, by using ceremony, liturgy, biblical verses, and rabbinic sayings as lamps of entry to guide the journey of the new child as she enters the Jewish community through the ancient covenant. Following are the complete texts of three such ceremonies.[85] While one is specifically designated as "Orthodox," it is clear that in many ways the ceremonies are transdenominational. They indicate the richness, diversity, creativity, and religious sensitivities of some who labored not only to bring forth a child, but also to celebrate that child's entry into the covenant. The fourth ceremony cited here derives from Sephardic customs. Hebrew sections are omitted.

Ceremony I
Preserving Tradition by Expanding It:
The Creation of Our Simchat Bat

by Gary and Sheila Rubin

The creation of a birth ceremony for our daughter, Michal Sarah, presented us with a sharp contradiction: We wanted very much to induct her into a tradition that provided no entry point for her, save a rather perfunctory formula recited at the Torah reading following her birth. We felt both sides of this contradiction very strongly. As practitioners of Orthodoxy, we believe it is important to maintain traditional Jewish laws and customs, since this guarantees the continuity of the Jewish people, both across space to Jews in other lands and across time to previous generations that observed similar customs. But we also felt the lack of established birth ceremonies to be terribly unfair to newborn daughters and to parents who have no ritualized means within the tradition to express their joy at having produced a Jewish girl.

The challenge we faced, then, was how to induct a girl into a meaningful tradition that had neglected to provide a place for her. Our strategy for dealing with this problem attempted to address both sides of this dilemma. We would create a ceremony for our daughter, but it would embrace traditional sources and follow as closely as possible

Jewish ceremonial patterns. We would draw on tradition and shape it, without distorting it, to fit the needs of parents seeking an authentic Jewish experience to mark the beginning of a Jewish woman's life.

Our readings for the ceremony consisted solely of Jewish sources. We both have read widely in world literature and poetry and find much of it beautiful and meaningful. But for this occasion, we resisted using non-Jewish texts since the goal of our *Simcha* was induction into the Jewish community. We drew exclusively on material from the Bible, the Siddur (prayerbook), and the Midrash. Another key aspect of our ceremony was the participation of our family and close friends. We felt it was particularly important to give prominent roles to our parents, since the transmitting of the tradition would be best represented by involving three generations of our family in a common ritual. Finally, the language of the ceremony held deep meaning for us. Since we had non-Jews and non-Hebrew-speaking Jews in attendance, we translated the service into English. But we also performed the entire text in Hebrew, the language in which the tradition has always been transmitted.

We began, as do most Jewish ceremonies, with a hymn of thanksgiving. We chose Psalm 98, which begins, appropriately, "Sing a new song to the Lord." This psalm, with its evocation of the seas thundering their praises, the rivers applauding, and the mountains singing, captured for us our joy and gratefulness at our daughter's birth. Gary's brother read this section.

Psalm 98

Sing a new song to the Lord, for he has done wonders; his right
    hand, his holy arm, has brought him triumph.
The Lord has made known his saving power; he has let the
    nations see his justice.
He has remembered his kindness and faithfulness to the house of
    Israel, all the ends of the earth have seen the saving power
    of our God.
Shout praise to the Lord, all the earth; break into music, be
    jubilant and sing.
Praise the Lord with the harp, with the harp and the voice of song
With trumpets and the sound of the horn, shout praise before the
    King, the Lord.
Let the sea and all its fulness thunder praise, the world and those
    living in it.
Let the rivers applaud, let the mountains sing in chorus, before the
    Lord who comes to rule the earth!
He will rule the world with righteousness, and the peoples with
    justice.

Next, following the traditional pattern of Jewish prayer, we marked the occasion with three blessings. The first is recited at joyful times, the second thanks God for sustaining us to the season of our happiness, and the third sanctifies the moment by blessing the wine, a central element in most Jewish ceremonies. Each of these blessings is listed in the Siddur in connection with a particular event or service, but we found them relevant to our situation and incorporated them into our Simcha. Sheila performed this part of the service.

> Blessed art thou, Lord our God, King of the universe, who art good and beneficent.
> Blessed art thou, Lord our God, King of the universe, who has granted us life and sustenance and permitted us to reach this season.
> Blessed art thou, Lord our God, King of the universe, who createst the fruit of the vine.

Gary then explained why we had chosen the name (Michal Sarah) for our daughter. He began by citing the biblical and midrashic origins of the name. The biblical Michal was Saul's daughter and David's wife. She defied her father to save David's life when Saul plotted to kill him. After her marriage, she rebuked King David for what she considered inappropriate public behavior when he danced in front of the Ark as it was being transported to Jerusalem. For this she was cursed. In each instance, she stood up to authority to defend what she thought was right. In rabbinical literature the story of Michal is elaborated. In the Midrash, Michal is described as exceedingly beautiful. Her independence receives emphasis in the assertion that Michal was one of the few women to put on *tefillin* (phylacteries). In addition, her generosity is exemplified in her extraordinary concern and care for children born to another woman. Finally, the sources express Michal's piety by noting that she is one of the 22 righteous women in honor of whom sentences in the *Eiyshet Hayil* or Woman of Valor chapter of Proverbs are written. These characteristics of Michal are especially fitting for our daughter because she is named after Gary's maternal aunt, who exhibited the values of piety, beauty, and generosity attributed by the rabbis to the original Michal.

Our daughter's middle name, Sarah, also has both biblical and family antecedents. The biblical Sarah was the Matriarch of the Jewish people, just as Gary's great-grandmother Sarah was the matriarch of her entire extended family. In addition, Sarah's experience figures strongly in attitudes toward all Jewish births. Sarah, like many biblical women, was naturally barren; it required Divine intervention for her to have a child. Tradition has it that all Jewish women similarly do not conceive except with G-d's help. In this way, every Jewish birth is considered a miracle, and we certainly feel that way about our daughter (as we did about our son three years earlier).

After explaining the name, we proceeded to confer it on our daughter. Our parents recited the Jewish formula for giving a name, and in so doing passed on to our daughter both the tradition inherent in this ceremony and the particular meaning of the name for our family.

> Sustain this child for her father and mother and let her name be called in Israel Michal Sarah, daughter of Gary and Sheila Rubin.

At this point, the entire group of family and friends assembled in our house (about 90 people) recited in unison the next section, which symbolizes the community's acceptance and blessing of the newborn child.

> As she has been inducted into the community of the people of Israel, so shall she be introduced to the Torah, to the marriage canopy, and to a life of good deeds.

Then Sheila's brother read the next verse, which expresses the parents' joy at the birth of their offspring.

> May the father rejoice in his offspring, may the mother rejoice in the fruit of her womb, as it is written: "Let your father and mother be happy, let she that gave birth exult."

To close out this section of the service, we gave our own parental blessing to Michal. To do this, we read the formula with which the father traditionally blesses his daughter on Friday evenings, upon returning from the synagogue, saying that God should guide her to grow up like the Matriarchs of Israel. Because this is one of the few places in the traditional liturgy in which female role models are emphasized we considered it especially appropriate for this occasion.

> May the Lord make you as Sarah, Rebecca, Rachel, and Leah.

The penultimate section of the service consisted of biblical readings arranged in such a way that the first letter of each sentence would form an acrostic spelling in Hebrew of Michal Sarah. For text, we chose the *Eiyshet Hayil* (Woman of Valor) chapter of Proverbs. The verses in Proverbs are written in alphabetical order. We simply chose the appropriate ones and arranged them so that they spelled out Michal Sarah's name. Significantly, though picked for alphabetical reasons, the sentences we recited express the values of piety, generosity, and beauty that the Midrash attributes to the original Michal. Each of these verses was read by a close friend of ours.

> She makes her own tapestries
> Her clothing is fine linen and purple
> She sets her hands to the distaff;
> Her fingers hold the spindle
> She stretches out her hand to the poor;
> She reaches out her arms to the needy.
> She is not afraid of the snow for her household,
> For all her household is clad in scarlet wool.
> Charm is deceptive, and beauty is vain;
> Only a god-fearing woman shall be praised.
> "Many women do worthily,
> But you excel them all."
> She is like the merchant ships—
> She brings her food from afar.

To close out the service, we followed the general practice of ceremonies performed in the Diaspora to pray for the welfare of Israel and Jerusalem. For this, we chose Psalm 122, which expresses the grandeur of a rebuilt Jerusalem and prays that it will realize its aspirations to represent peace and justice. Though this psalm had the primary purpose of praying for the Jews' homeland and chief city, within the context of our celebration it also held a family meaning. We are the first generation of Jews in over 2000 years never to have known a world in which the State of Israel was not a reality. Our children, Ari and Michal, are the first generation in two millenia whose world has always included a united Jerusalem. In reading this psalm, we pray that its full description will be realized so that our children's children will know only a world in which the Holy Land is at peace.

Psalm 122

A Pilgrim Song by David. I was glad when they said to me: "Let us go to the house of the Lord." Our feet are standing within your gates, O Jerusalem; Jerusalem that is rebuilt like a city that is compact altogether; whither the tribes went on pilgrimage, the tribes of the Lord, as a testimony of Israel, to offer praise to the name of the Lord. There, indeed, were set the seats of justice, the thrones of the house of David. Pray for the welfare of Jerusalem; they will prosper who love you. May all go well within your walls, within your palaces. For the sake of my brethren and friends I pray: "May all be well with you!" For the sake of the house of the Lord our God I seek your good.

In making up our *Simchat Bat,* we strove to preserve the tradition by embracing it, expanding it, and opening up the possibility of our daughter's full entry into it. By performing this ritual, we hope that we have launched Michal into a life in which she will always be dedicated to her heritage and alert to opportunities to make it relevant to increasing numbers of people.

Ceremony 2

Welcome. These sheets contain an explanation of this morning's ceremony as well as the texts for the *siyyum* and naming. Thank you for participating in this joyous event.

David and Devora

The Day

We name our daughter on her fifteenth day. This is based on Leviticus 12:1–5, which describes the length of a woman's period of impurity after childbirth. If she gives birth to a son, she is impure for seven days; if to a daughter, for fourteen days. The passage seems to connect the baby boy's circumcision on the eighth day to the conclusion of the mother's seven day period of impurity. (Compare Leviticus 22:27, which says that a new-born animal must remain with its mother for seven days, and on the eighth day and on-ward it is acceptable as a sacrificial offering.) It seems, then, that for the first seven days of a little boy's life, and the first fourteen days of a little girl's life, the child and mother are still closely linked, and both remain separate from the larger family and community. Then, on the eighth day of her son's life, and on the fifteenth day of her daughter's life, the mother begins to rejoin her family and community, and the child too becomes incor-porated as a member of the family and community. That is why a baby boy's father be-comes obligated to circumcise his son only on the eighth day, and why the child first re-ceives his name as his *brit milah;* it is then that the child becomes a member of the community of Israel. On our daughter's fifteenth day, we come together as a family and as a community to welcome this new member, and to give her a name.

The *Siyyum*

A *siyyum* is a ceremony marking the completion of the study of a tractate of the Tal-mud, and rededicating the participants to a commitment to further study. We name each of our children at a *siyyum* celebrating our joint study during the period of time that we are expecting the birth of our child. This is both a way of privately rededicating ourselves to Torah study and a way of publicly welcoming our children into a commu-nity joined together in the study of Torah.

The Naming Ceremony

Our daughter enters and leaves the room to the singing of biblical verses excerpted from blessings to children. The first song begins with Genesis 48:16, from the passage in which Jacob blesses Joseph and his sons, Menasheh and Ephram: "May the angel who has redeemed me from all evil bless the lads, and let my name and the name of my fa-thers Abraham and Isaac be called on them, and may they grow into a multitude in the midst of the earth." The song continues with Deuteronomy 1:10, from the introduc-tion to Moses' address to the children of Israel: "The Lord your God has multiplied you, and, behold, you are this day like the stars of heaven for multitude." The second song is from Genesis 27:28, the beginning of Isaac's blessing to Jacob: "May God give you of the dew of heaven and of the fat of the earth and an abundance of grain and wine."

Our daughter is named and blessed with a prayer which incorporates biblical verses celebrating the miracle of birth:

> Our Lord and the Lord of our ancestors, bless this girl, and let her name in Israel be called
> _____ daughter of _____ and _____ . May the father be glad
> in that which came forth from his loins and the mother rejoice in the fruit of her womb,
> as it is written: *May your father and your mother be glad, and may she who bore you rejoice.*

(Proverbs 23:25) Protect her with your abundant grace, as it is written: *But the grace of God is from everlasting to everlasting upon those who fear him, and his righteousness to children's children.* (Psalms 103:17) And it says: *But now, God, you are our father; we are the clay and your are our shaper, and the work of your hand are we all.* (Isaiah 64:7) And it says: *For you have formed my inner parts, you have knit me together in my mother's womb. I will praise you because I am fearfully and wonderfully made; wonderful are your works, and my soul knows that well.* (Psalms 139:13–14) And it says: *Let them praise God for his grace, and his wonders to human-kind* (Psalms 107:7) *Give praise to God, for he is good, for his grace endures forever.* (Psalms 118:1) [The congregation responds: Give praise to God, for he is good, for his grace endures forever.]

May he who blessed our ancestors, Abraham, Isaac, and Jacob, Sarah, Rebecca, Rachel, and Leah, bless _____ daughter of _____ and _____, and may her father and mother merit to raise her to Torah, the marriage canopy, and good deeds.

After the child is named, the mother recites *birkhat hagomel,* in gratitude for a healthy delivery. Both parents then recite the blessing "who is good and does good." They then bless their child with the traditional blessing for daughters and the priestly blessing.

The Meal

All the participants join together in a *seudat mitzvah,* which is concluded with the Grace after Meals with a special *zimmun* and the insertion of special prayers, blessing the parents, the child, and the participants, and praying for peace.

Ceremony 3
An Orthodox Simchat Bat

Joseph C. Kaplan

When my wife, Sharon, gave birth to our first child a short time ago, we were over-joyed that our prayers appeared to be answered and that we were blessed with a healthy baby. In addition, the fact that our firstborn was a daughter had, at this time in our lives, an additional special personal and religious significance; it gave us the oppor-tunity to express our joy and our thanks, on this most joyful and thankful of occasions, in a religious ceremony of our own choosing and design. As Orthodox Jews, we of course confined ourselves to work within the halachic tradition but we felt certain that we could prepare and perform a *simchat bat* in a manner that would be within the tra-ditional framework while still giving expression of our own deeply felt emotions, thoughts, and desires.

And so we did. On the Sunday following Thanksgiving (a singularly appropriate day), we celebrated, together with about 100 of our relatives and friends, a *simchat bat* in honor of our daughter Micole Seanne (or in Hebrew, Sara Michal). Although we consulted with our rabbi, Steven Riskin, as to the appropriateness of the ceremony and received his approval, it was our ceremony, saying what we wanted to say, and bringing our daughter into the covenant between God and the Jewish people in a way that we hope she will appreciate as she grows older.

The following outline (written for the sake of clarity in the third person) is a summary of the ceremony as it was actually performed.

1. Micole was brought into the room by her grandmothers, and was then passed from her aunts and uncles to Joseph's grandparents who, as the senior members of the family, ceremonially presided over the *celebration*. Her voyage to the front table (where she was laid on a white pillow upon an antique silver platter) was accompanied by her uncle's singing of two verses from the Bible which, by starting and ending with the first and last letters of her Hebrew names, symbolize them:

    (a) Hatred stirs up wrath, but love covers all transgressions (Proverbs, 10:12)

    (b) How good are thy tents O Jacob, thy dwelling places O Israel (Numbers, 24:5)

2. Joseph explained the section of the Talmud (Gitin, 57a) which recounts a custom in ancient Israel. Upon the birth of a daughter, her parents would plant a pine tree, with the prayer and the hope that their daughter too would grow strong and fragrant. And the tree they planted would not be cut until their daughter was engaged to be married, so its branches could be used for the chupah under which she and her beloved would stand. In order to perpetuate this ancient, beautiful and very meaningful—although unfortunately neglected—custom, it was announced that both sets of Micole's grandparents planted a tree in Israel in her honor, in the hope and prayer that she would be raised to be a source of pride to her family and the entire Jewish people, and that all who celebrate at her *simchat bat* would be together once again as she stands under the chupah (marriage canopy). The tree symbolizes life.

3. As we planted for the future, Sharon thanked God for the past and present by reciting the two blessings symbolizing this gratitude: the *birkhat hagomel,* thanking God for bringing her through this wonderful experience in good health, and the *birkhat shehechiyanu,* thanking God for bringing all to that day of joy and simcha.

4. Sharon then compared Micole's birth to the blessings over the Torah. Before the Torah is read, we refer to it as "His Torah" *(torato)* ; only after it is read, after we have had a personal experience of Torah, do we call it a "Torah of

Truth, a tree of life" *(torat emet, chayai olam)*. So too with Micole. While we appreciated and loved our many nieces, nephews and children of friends and relatives, it took the birth of Micole, our own child, for us to understand and appreciate more deeply what it means to care for, raise and love a child. Meaning is created through prayers and blessings.

5. Sharon, her sister, Joseph's sister and their sister-in-law (all mothers), then read from the prayer of Hannah (Samuel I, 2:1–10), whose words of gratitude to God upon the birth of a firstborn are one of the most striking and touching prayers recorded in the Bible.

6. Although all of Israel is a nation of priests, since Joseph is *kohayn* (of the priestly class), Micole was born into a family of priests, and thus was privileged to be blessed by her paternal grandfather with the traditional Priestly Blessing (Numbers, 6:24–26).

7. Micole's maternal grandfather, a practicing rabbi, then recited the special prayer from the Song of Songs, and the *mi shebayrach* (with certain minor emendations) found in the Spanish and Portuguese Prayer book. Once again, her name was proclaimed as a true daughter of Israel (as was her namesake, Sharon's paternal grandmother). While the aforesaid was being recited, Sharon inscribed Micole's name into a family tree prepared especially for this occasion, so Micole could take her rightful place in the family, and hopefully follow in the tradition that was set for her.

8. Joseph again thanked God for all the good he bestowed upon them by reciting the blessing of *hatov vehamaytiv*. (The God who does Good).

9. The blessing was recited over the wine (which was shared by Micole and Joseph), words of Torah were spoken by Rabbi Riskin and Micole's grandfathers and great-grandfather, and, as in all traditional Jewish ceremonies, a sumptuous homemade spread, indeed a *yom tov* (festive) feast, was enjoyed by all.

This was our ceremony; it said what we wanted and felt should be said. Others need not follow it; they should say and do what they want and feel. But if they truly appreciate their daughter and her relationship to the People of Israel and its covenant with God, they must say and do something; they must sanctify her birth and her becoming part of that covenant with a religious ceremony of gratitude to God.

· · ·

The following brief ceremony, *Seder Zeved Habat* (the Celebration for the Gift of a Daughter) is a naming ceremony for daughters that appears in the daily and Sabbath prayer book edited by Dr. David de Sola Pool (published by the Union of Sephardic Congregations, New York). This ceremony, although unknown in Ashkenazic communities, is a very popular one at the Spanish and Portuguese Synagogue in New York. It is held at a date and time of the parents' choosing.

Ceremony 4

When the mother comes, or brings the child, to the synagogue, follow the service of *Hagomel* (Thanksgiving for Recovery).

From the Song of Songs:

> O my dove in the rocky clefts,
>> In the covert of terrace high,
>> Let me see thy countenance,
>> Let me hear thy voice
>> For sweet is thy voice
>> And thy countenance comely.

The Hebrew originally reads, "male children." We suggest changing this to "children" or "sons and daughters."

If the child be the first born, add

> One alone is my dove, my perfect one,
>> The darling of her mother,
>> The choice one of her who bore her.
>> Daughters saw her, they acclaimed her,
>> Queens and consorts, they sang her praises.

May He who blessed our mothers Sarah, Rebecca, Rachel and Leah, Miriam the prophetess, Abigail, and Esther the queen, bless also this darling babe. . . . May He bless her to grow up in wealth, health, happiness. May he give to her parents the joy of seeing her happily married, a radiant mother of children, rich in honor and joy to a ripe old age. May this be the will of God, and let us say, Amen.

. . .

Another Orthodox ceremony is described in the 2001–2002 calendar published by JOFA, the Jewish Orthodox Feminist Alliance, whose aim is to expand spiritual opportunities for women within the framework of Jewish law. These include intellectual, ritual, and political aspects of Jewish life and are manifested in the ceremony featured for April 2002/Nisan/Iyar 5762. This ceremony, composed by Rabbi David Silber and Dr. Devorah Steinmetz for the *simchat bat* ceremonies of their daughters, features four blessings beginning with the traditional *"harahamon"* ("May the compassionate God"); six such blessings are part of the *brit milah* for boys. The first blessing states: "May the compassionate God bless the father and mother of this girl child, and may they merit to raise her and educate her and bring her to wisdom through good deeds, the holiness of marriage, and the study of our trustworthy and complete Torah." (my free translation)

I am indebted to Rabbi Marc Angel of the Spanish and Portuguese Synagogue for information about a Sephardic ceremony known as *las fadas.* As he describes it, "The parents would have a banquet to which they would invite relatives and friends, among whom would be a rabbi. The rabbi would hold the infant on his lap and would recite a blessing for the child's good health and happiness. He would also announce the girl's name as chosen by her parents. The baby was then passed around to the guests, all of whom wish her and her parents long life." According to Rabbi Angel's source, "The term *fadas* derives from the Spanish *hadas,* meaning 'fairies.' It was a custom among non-Jewish Spaniards to have a child blessed by various good fairies. Sephardim apparently adopted the Spanish custom, giving it a Jewish, religious symbolism."[86]

The various appellations that signify the celebration ceremony indicate two ideological strands regarding the birth of a daughter. These two approaches are reflected in the rabbinic sources examined earlier.[87] Avodah Zarah 27a and Berakhot 20b, which consider a woman part of the *brit* without the external bodily sign, call the ceremony *simhat bat* or *zeved habat.* These celebrations focus on recitation of psalms, blessings, and prayers of thanksgiving; a naming of the daughter; and usually the mother's recitation of *birkhat hagomel.*[88] Others view the ceremony as parallel to circumcision insofar as it represents the public induction of their daughter into the covenant between God and the Jewish people. In this case the designation of the ceremony includes the word *brit* and may be *brit bat* (covenant of the daughter), or *brit banot* (covenant of the daughters).[89] Contemporary Orthodox discussions point out that the welcoming ceremony for a girl, while religiously significant, is optional and not halakhically equivalent to a *brit milah.*[90]

The third *simhat bat* includes reference to the ancient *zeved habat* ceremony, long a part of Sephardi custom. Correspondence with Rabbi Marc D. Angel of Congregation Shearith Israel of New York[91] led to the discovery that all known versions of the blessing in Hebrew contain the words *bevanim zecharim,* asking God to bless this newborn female with male children. The English of the de Sola Pool translation, however, requests that she be blessed as a "radiant mother of children."[92] Rabbi Angel indicated that the Hebrew will be changed to accord with the more appropriate English in the forthcoming edition.[93]

The actual naming of the baby girl can take different forms depending upon denomination. The new *Rabbi's Manual* for the Conservative movement, for instance, includes two ceremonies for naming a girl, "The Conventional Ritual" and "The Innovative Ritual." The former, however, differs in several ways from namings, part of every *simhat bat,* in most forms of the Orthodox tradition. The Conventional Ritual states:

May God who blessed our ancestors, Abraham, Isaac, and Jacob, Sarah, Rebecca, Rachel, and Leah, bless _____ and _____ and their newborn daughter. Let her be known among the people Israel as _____, daughter of _____ and _____. May the parents be privileged to raise their child to womanhood and may _____ enjoy the blessings of Torah, *huppah,* and a life of *ma'asim tovim,* good deeds. And let us say: Amen.[94]

Here both the patriarchs and matriarchs are specified, both parents are named, and the child is to be known as the daughter of both father and mother.

The Orthodox Birnbaum siddur (prayerbook), published originally in 1949 and reissued in 1977, has the following: "On the occasion of naming a newborn daughter":

He who blessed our fathers Abraham, Isaac and Jacob, Moses and Aaron, David and Solomon, may He bless the mother and her new-born daughter, whose name in Israel shall be [name of child]. May they raise her for the marriage canopy and for a life of good deeds; and let us say, Amen.[95]

The patriarchs are mentioned in addition to Moses, Aaron, David, and Solomon. The matriarchs, as well as Miriam, are not specified as historical models, as having received God's blessings, thus being themselves a source of blessing for the newborn girl. In addition, Orthodox custom usually names the mother as the daughter of her father (e.g., Eliana, the daughter of Meir), as well as the infant as the child of her father (e.g., Adina, the daughter of Reuben). The mothers are generally not included. In addition, the blessing of Torah is omitted.

This traditional structure for the naming of a baby girl, in somewhat different form, is followed in the now widely used (in Orthodox synagogues) Artscroll prayerbook.

He Who blessed our forefathers Abraham, Isaac, and Jacob, may He bless the woman who has given birth (new mother's Hebrew name) daughter of (her father's Hebrew name) with her daughter who has been born at an auspicious time, and may her name be called in Israel (baby's Hebrew name) daughter of (baby's father's Hebrew name) for her husband, the infant's father, will contribute to charity on their behalf. In reward for this, may they raise her to (Torah), marriage and good deeds. Now let us respond: Amen.[96]

In this version only the patriarchs are named, not "Moses, Aaron, David, and Solomon," and the text specifies that both the new mother and newborn child be designated only with their father's name. Several elements in this prayerbook manifest the move to the right in contemporary Orthodoxy, including this naming formula. The version in the older Birnbaum prayerbook leaves the *how* of the naming up to the family; the Artscroll takes a stand, foregoing other options. In the Orthodox *simhat bat* presented earlier in this chapter (Ceremony 3), no naming formula is included. The child's name was probably given soon after her birth, while the *simhat bat* took place on Thanksgiving. How the baby was named—whether with the blessings of matriarchs and patriarchs, whether with her mother's name as well as her father's—is not indicated.

Tradition, however, records a naming formula for girls used in neither the Birnbaum nor the Artscroll prayer books. It is to be found at the back of the *Tikkun Lakoreim,*[97] the text used for preparation of chanting the Torah text with proper cantillation, and combines contemporary and traditional elements. While the original edition of this *tikkun* was published in 1946, the naming rite is much older. It reads:

> May God who blessed our matriarchs, Sarah, Rebecca, Rachel and Leah, bless the mother who has given birth (X the daughter of X) and her daughter, born to her in good fortune *[mazal tov]*. And may her name in Israel be called (X the daughter of X), since her husband, the father (Hebrew name), pledges charity on her behalf.
>
> From this merit, may God grant him life and watch over him, his wife, and newborn daughter. May this (girl) child follow in upright ways. May God be with her and grant her wisdom, understanding, and insight; life, loving kindness, blessing, and peace. And may her ancestors *[avoteinu;* literally "fathers"] raise her to marriage and good deeds, and let us say, amen. (my translation)

This formula, it is clear, is based on the tradition of a father naming a girl baby upon being called to the Torah in synagogue, a custom independent from the modern *simhat bat* ceremony. Yet the structure of the naming delineated here surely could be incorporated into a *simhat bat*. It differs from the Birnbaum/Artscroll formulas by focusing entirely on the matriarchs.[98] It does not specify that only the father's name be used, as does the Artscroll, but it does not offer the newborn girl the blessing of "Torah," always designated for a newborn boy. Modern Orthodox parents, however, usually modify this, so that the blessing of Torah—Torah learning, transmission, and the more public role such knowledge entails—is, from her birth, part of the role and legacy of Jewish daughters. One reason that this formulation uses only the names of the matriarchs is that it is understood not only as a naming of the child but also as a blessing for the well-being of the mother. Petitions for health and well-being customarily specify the mother of the ill person.

In Conservative Judaism, the prayer for the well-being of the mother of a newborn daughter (or son) specifies both patriarchs and matriarchs, includes mother and father, and offers the blessing of Torah:

> May God who blessed our ancestors, Abraham, Isaac, and Jacob, Sarah, Rebecca, Rachel, and Leah, bless [mother's name] and her newborn daughter. May it be Your will that the (parents/mother) be privileged to raise (their/her) child to adulthood, and to

witness the blessings of Torah, *huppah* [marriage], and a life of *ma'asim tovim,* good deeds. And let us say: Amen.[99]

Rabbi's Manual for the Reform movement offers a suggested format, entitled "Covenant Service for a Daughter," which includes a naming rite. Interestingly, it is somewhat different from the ceremony specified in the manual as "Naming a Child in the Sanctuary." This begins with a general prayer.

Naming a Child in the Synagogue

RABBI

Our God, Source of all life: We Thank You for the countless blessings You have given us. We thank You especially for the sacred joy and privilege of parenthood, which adds profound meaning and purpose to our existence.

Grateful for Your gift of new life [parents' names] have come into Your sanctuary to thank You and to ask Your guidance in the upbringing of their newborn son/daughter.

Grant to these parents wisdom, patience, and devotion, that they may raise their son/daughter to live in accordance with Your Torah.

In this synagogue and in the presence of this holy congregation, we give to this newly born child the name _____ , ben/bat _____ Ve-_____ .

May it become a name honored in the household of Israel.

Extend Your shelter over him/her and give to him/her love, health, and understanding. May he/she so grow and live as to become a blessing to his/her parents and family, to the Jewish people, and to all humanity.

Let us all say: Amen.[100]

The blessings following the naming are identical for a baby boy and baby girl, except of course for the distinctions made in the Hebrew grammar. Following is the blessing "For a Girl."

May God who blessed our ancestors, Abraham, Isaac, and Jacob, Sarah, Rebekah, Leah, and Rachel, bless this child with life and health. May she be a joy to her parents. May she live to bring honor to the House of Israel, blessings to humanity, and glory to the name of God.[101]

The literal translation of the Hebrew differs from that given in the manual: for purposes of comparison with the Conservative and Orthodox versions cited above, I offer my own translation.

May God who blessed our fathers/patriarchs, Abraham, Isaac, and Jacob, and our mothers/matriarchs, Sarah, Rebecca, Rachel, and Leah, bless this tender (girl) child. May her father and mother be privileged to raise her, to educate her, and to transmit wisdom to her. May her hands and her heart [express/realize] the faithful God. And let us say, Amen.

Matriarchs as well as patriarchs are noted, but "Torah, marriage, and good deeds" are absent. The Hebrew does not say "House of Israel," while the translation/paraphrase in the manual does. Perhaps this is to include the particularity assumed by transmitting the blessings through the matriarchs and patriarchs. But then why not include the phrase "House of Israel" in the Hebrew? The omission of this phrase, as well as the exclusion of the traditional expression "Torah, marriage, and good deeds," make this naming formula more universal and less rooted in the peoplehood of Israel, despite the stated ancestral history of matriarchs and patriarchs.

A number of years ago, my husband and I gave a young couple, children of good friends and parents of a new baby girl, a silk screen done by a talented artist. On a lovely mauve background was inscribed the traditional blessing for a newborn boy: *"keshem shenikhnas labrit, ken tekanas letorah, lechupah ulemaasim tovim."* The young man, ordained at Yeshiva University and holding a professional degree from Columbia University, looked straight at me: "I'm sorry," he said, "we cannot accept this. A girl is not part of the *brit.*" Even disregarding his rudeness (the gift should have been accepted and then done with as they wished), it is hard to forget even now the certainty—even arrogance— with which this young man excluded all women from the covenant of Israel.

It is thus all the more poignant that Lawrence A. Hoffman cites tannaitic sources for the existence of *Shevua habat,*[102] an ancient birth celebration for new daughters. Perhaps contemporary rituals[103] designed to welcome a girl child into her family and her community and to affirm her status as a fully covenanted member of the Jewish people are but a harking back to history. What an occasion my father would have missed had we, long ago, had a *simhat bat.* Or, far more likely, had he been asked to participate in such a celebration, he would have been there—without hesitation or delay.

These excursions into the rabbinic and contemporary constructions of celebrating the birth of a daughter lead once again to a consideration of the axes of sexuality and gender, public/private spheres and community/autonomy.

Sexuality and Gender

Rabbinic sources claim the infant girl as a full member of the covenant between God and the Jewish people, a connection that an increasing number of contemporary ceremonies makes explicit. The absence of a physical sign of the covenant is understood by some to be a comment on the less aggressive nature of female sexuality or the greater inherent perfection of the female. This latter explanation, however, is apologetics and fails to deal with the issue. It is exactly analogous to the view that the Mishnah exempts women from positive time-specific mitzvot—because women, being in some ways superior to men, do not need the reminders that obligation imposes.[104] Others understand circumcision, the mark of the covenant, to be a proclamation of the male role in the public transmission of the tradition: the male carries the tradition's cultural and intellectual legacy.

These explanations, while attempting to clarify a central male ritual in Judaism, nonetheless do not put forth an unequivocal theory of essentialism. While gender remains a hierarchical category (as it is in all societies, at least empirically) and while rabbinic sources—especially midrash—generalize about male and female differences, there is no straightforward theory of essential difference between male and female. Rather, the descriptions of essentialist distinctions are embedded in sociohistorical perspectives. Such theories are to be found primarily in right-wing publications, which proclaim the woman intrinsically private, more suited to nurturing (especially parenting), and even less intellectual. This is in contrast to the man, who is inherently a public person ingrained with broader intellectual talents. Not unexpectedly, this description of the underlying theory of essential male/female difference is found in just about all fundamentalist interpretations of religious traditions;[105] it maintains traditional gender roles. This is not to argue that physiological differences do not exist; certainly they do.[106] But constructing a rigid societal model upon such differences limits radically the possibilities of human growth.

Thus, the girl child needs a public celebration, one that welcomes her into the community of Israel as a full-fledged member, one that opens to her all possibilities of personal growth within the larger Jewish and human communities. She is appointed a representative of the tradition in the public as well as private realms. She becomes a carrier of the intellectual and cultural legacies of an ancient people. She is free to fly wherever her talents, gifts, propensities, and education may take her. Being a responsible member of her people, she becomes, with them, a partner in the ongoing creation of a more just world. While socially constructed gender roles will undoubtedly be part of her experiences—and perhaps expectations—the *simhat bat* celebrates both the joy of her family and people as well as the many possibilities that lie before her.

Public and Private Spheres

That the *simhat bat* has become a public event—whether a *kiddush* in synagogue or a more elaborate party—signifies the increasing acceptance within the Jewish community of the greater public role, both in Jewish life and in society at large, of its female members. Even in traditional circles, women are reaching for and attaining religious and professional positions rare in earlier generations. For years teaching was considered a female profession; the dearth of bright young women in teaching today is loudly lamented. But even as women move on to accounting, law, medicine, and doctorates in many fields, the teaching expertise of women in Judaica must be viewed as a substantial move forward. My grandmother in Poland could not have taught Bible, Prophets, Mishnah, or Jewish history with the textual skills and mastery available to today's young women. Women of all denominations of Judaism have been carving out for themselves a larger and larger piece of the public pie.

Nonetheless, the arguments supporting the more restrictive and allegedly private status of women persist, advocated both by men and women. An interesting example found its way onto my e-mail in an article entitled "Right vs. Right."[107] The author, now an Orthodox Jew, explains why she can neither understand nor share the concerns, complaints, and anger of contemporary Jewish women who persist in "demanding equality in Judaism." She contrasts the political interactions of democracy, with its emphasis on equal rights, to the legal structure of halakha, which stresses obligations. Acknowledging that the Oral Law includes mechanisms for interpretations, she nonetheless states that such interpretation cannot have its source in "human notions or desires." "Fairness and equality, . . . are wonderful," she writes "but holiness and Torah occupy a different universe." This is a strange statement. Not only does the Torah insist on the primacy of justice, as manifested in the verse, "Justice, justice, you shall pursue" (Deuteronomy 16:20); but the very rabbinic tradition of interpretation the author insists "cannot be amended" reconstructs biblical marital law to give women greater equality and protection. Written by a woman with an Ivy League undergraduate education, law degree, and current position as an adjunct law professor at Touro Law School, this essay defends the private role of women in Judaism in eloquent, but inadequately analytic language, and manifests a lack of understanding of the rabbinic legislative process.

The supporting claims of the author are several. Halakhah cannot be amended; even when interpreted, human concepts or desires are absent from the interpreters. Jewish women who seek religious equality are beset with "a paradigm of entitlements" intrinsic to a "conceptual short circuit" in which "the 'equal rights' mindset has crossed wires with the 'divine obligation' reality." True axiological equality, the author affirms, "is not measured by equivalent religious roles." A woman's "true power" derives from being commanded in the mitzvot (commandments) that address her.

Such pronouncements echo the statements of some (female) students in an advanced seminar I teach called "Women and Religion: Judaism and Christianity." Every year several insist that they are not feminists. "Feminism," it seems, is a word with implications unacceptable to many. A young woman considered feminist is thought to be antimale, against marriage, and uninterested in having children. A feminist thus not only disdains patriarchal hierarchy, but is also responsible for the break-up of established family structures. [108]

What a heavy burden for a young female adult to carry! The students absolutely believe in equal pay for equal work. They assume that gender will not influence their graduate school or job applications. They plan to study theatre, ministry, college administration, musicology, law, business management. They don't compartmentalize as readily as the author of the above essay. But fear of what has become known as the "F word," or "feminism," is sufficient for these students to disclaim inclusion within the broad and variegated category of feminists. Surely if a law professor with an Ivy League undergraduate education fears feminism, the apprehensions of nineteen or twenty year olds become more comprehensible.

The rhetoric of equal value necessarily implies both gender egalitarianism and equal opportunity. A century ago the author of "Rights vs. Right" could neither have attended nor taught at an Ivy League undergraduate institution or law school. She could have worked in a factory at a salary considerably less than her male counterpart with little possibility of advancement. Her entry—or that of her daughter—into the Jewish community might have elicited a cursory *mazal tov* (congratulations) at an early morning synagogue service or even a happy welcome by some men as they hurried from synagogue to work. The noncommunal and private nature of the newborn girl's initiation into Judaism would have been but the first of many instances educating and guiding her toward domesticity as her proper sphere and away from the public domain.

The "true power" of Jewish womanhood consists in transferring "the paradigm of entitlements" from higher education and job qualifications to the religious/spiritual community. This indeed requires the courage to recognize and appreciate one's "greatest potential." The communal celebration of *simhat bat* for a female child is the initial declaration of her public persona.[109]

But this text, advocating an apologetic stance, bears further comment. The distinction between ancient societies and modern Western cultures must be part of the analysis of the public/private argument. In the matter of gender valuation, contemporary ideas cannot be superimposed upon societal structures radically different from our own. "Early Israel," the anthropologist Carol Meyers maintains, "might readily be termed an egalitarian society."[110] While Western industrialized societies ascribe inferior status to the female private sphere and superior value to the male-dominated public arena, this classification is incompatible with social interaction in small, agricultural societies. In such communities, public society and the domestic sphere overlap to a large extent and the domestic role of women is both necessary and significant. Women's work in such societies is directly related to economic life, and the centrality of the household gives women authority and power. The public and private are intersecting sets in a much more obvious way than in contemporary culture.[111]

Anthropology thus cautions us to avoid generalizations regarding patriarchy and oppression in looking at early Israelite women in biblical narrative. But the author of "Rights vs. Right" wishes to maintain a religious system based on public/private separation in the postindustrial twenty-first century. She wishes to compartmentalize her life, functioning as a high-level professional in the public arena but restricted to the private in religious practice. This will no longer work. The very recognition of compartmentalization becomes a means for moving forward toward greater coalescence of public endeavor and private activity, both practically and axiologically. The *simhat bat* for a female newborn is the beginning of this larger and more extensive intersection.

While all societies distinguish between women's work and men's work, it is only since the nineteenth century that "woman's place" has been defined in a way that excludes her from substantial participation in communal life beyond the domestic sphere. As a contemporary historian states, "The nineteenth-century cult of domesticity . . . revolved around a new glorification of motherhood."[112] But this devotion to maternity was complemented by women's voluntary involvement in the public world, manifested most obviously by benevolent and philanthropic organizations, anti-slavery and temperance groups, women's suffrage and prison-reform societies, and church societies dedicated to a variety of purposes. The National Council of Jewish Women was founded in 1893, the General Federation of Women's Clubs in 1890, and the National Association of Colored Women in 1895 (preceding by fifteen years the establishment of the NAACP).[113] Thus women's participation in significant work within the public sphere became a widespread cultural phenomenon in tandem with social and political forces moving toward women's suffrage. The *simhat bat* is a poignant reminder that the separation of home and workplace, domestic and public spaces, must be challenged. While one cannot revert to the household production of small, agricultural societies—whether early Israelite or medieval Christian—integration of professional work and family life is a valuable cultural goal, one that would bring greater human wholeness to both men and women. The workplace needs to be reconfigured around the needs of the family.

In Judaism this would mean an altering not only of practical activities, their functions and availability to both men and women, but also a reassessing of axiology. The implied lesser value of domestic and child-care tasks in the mitzvah system must, without apologetics, be realigned. The increasing prevalence of the *simhat bat* expresses both a practical and an axiological transformation.

Leah Shakdiel, an Israeli feminist, analyzes an interesting aspect of the public/private discussion. She argues that the concept of democracy has increasingly come to be identified with liberal democracy as manifested in the political system of the United States, in which an emphasis upon individual rights remains the central focus.[114] This contrasts with French republicanism, which stresses equal participation in national public spheres, a subtle and different nuance in democratic political theory. Shakdiel sees the latter model as more akin to the problematics of halakhah and human rights. For Shakdiel, the terminology of "human rights," which implies the collective good, is preferable to that of "individual rights," which seeks to appease the good of every individual limited only by the conflicting interests of other people. However, she sees republican democracy as having the inherent risk of re-creating a patriarchal system. In addition, she points out that while feminism in the United States has been experiencing a "disappointing fallout of the younger generation,"[115] the opposite is true of Israeli feminism, especially of the halakhic variety. That which Shadiel designates "halakhic feminism" is experiencing an "outburst of energy," especially with regard to Torah study by women. This "outburst," in Shakdiel's estimation, moves away from the notion of "automatic egalitarianism of the first generations of religious Zionism," indeed of the socialist basis of the Zionist movement in general. Rather, she claims that perhaps "the Israeli context makes it easier for halachic feminists . . . to accept the idea that empowerment of halachic women goes hand in hand with [that of] halachic men, both working on equity, not egalitarianism."[116] Equality appears to include Torah study, which surely empowers women.

Shakdiel asserts that in halakhic feminism, egalitarian ideology should be used selectively "since it does sometimes collide with halacha." The feminist critique of modernism is lacking, she affirms, if it views the overriding issue as inadequate egalitarianism. The focal problem of second-wave radical feminism, on the contrary, is "superficial blanket license to modernist egalitarianism," which shortchanges all groups by using the "elite male" as paradigm.[117]

Yet cannot one have *adequate* egalitarianism that is *not* superficial? Do equity and egalitarianism coalesce? Indeed, increased egalitarianism leads to greater equity. This significant notion, while abstract, is realized in the *simhat bat* celebration, which provides an egalitarian—and thus a just—public welcome to newborn Jewish daughters.

A final note to the discussion of the public/private axis as it pertains to celebrating the birth of a daughter concerns the role of custom. Jewish legal decisions are not only handed down to the people by scholars but also develop, through custom, at the grassroots level. When rabbinic authorities are divided as to the appropriate course of action, the Talmud advises, "Go out and see what the people are doing."[118] This principle has informed numerous rabbinic rulings and, interestingly, played a prominent role in the controversy regarding women's suffrage, both passive and active,[119] in Palestine under the British Mandate. R. Yehiel Weinberg[120] wrote two responsa on this issue. The first, written in 1932, affirms that

religious law provides no grounds for prohibiting suffrage. . . . Even so, we all agreed that the election of women in public life is against Jewish custom and morality, since the Jewish woman should tend her home and attend to the education of her children, and should not be vociferous or a gadabout to squander her strength, destroy her modesty, and lose her charm and appeal by engaging in political and public disputes and quarrels. . . . However, the peace and unity of the community should not be broken if its powerful and influential members prevail to introduce suffrage. . . . [121]

R. Weinberg found no halakhic reason to preclude either active or passive suffrage. The single obstacle was "custom," which viewed the woman as symbolizing the purity, innocence, and virtue of home and family—the private sphere—as compared with the allegedly less truthful and more corrupt public life. Nineteen years later, in 1951, R. Weinberg penned a second responsum on the same subject. After quoting the pro and con opinions in the halakhic literature, he opines: "So why should I thrust myself into the controversy between those who permit and those who prohibit; let time take its course and render its decision."[122]

With regard to *simhat bat,* it has. Custom, that is, has led the community to adopt a course of action commensurate with its history: legal, cultural, and current historical reality—with its pulls and pushes, its variegated influences—has confronted legal opinion and yielded its own verdict. The cultural context from which custom emerges has already affected the increasing presence of women in public spheres once regarded as the exclusive purview of men. The variety of *simhat bat* ceremonies testifies to the appropriate public welcome now being proffered to Jewish girls whose rightful place is the home and beyond.

Community/Autonomy

As indicated in discussions in earlier chapters,[123] autonomy has often been understood as alienation from, if not outright rebellion against, established communal authority. This is especially so when autonomous actions challenge religious traditions as embedded within law and custom. While autonomy is construed variously in different theories of moral psychology, these theories all view authority as that state from which one tries to escape. A recent study of autonomy in moral psychology, however, proposes an alternate reading, one that supports and enhances all aspects of the *simhat bat* as celebrated today.[124]

The most superficial understanding of autonomy is "self-rule as independence from directives by authorities." Thus "the person" is pitted against the broad social meanings of conventional behavior and prescriptions. A second level of autonomy invites "discretion" within limits prescribed by moral norms as conditions of cooperation. The central difference between this level and the first is that here the determining unit is the community rather than the individual. The third and most complex concept of autonomy may be described as "initiative in negotiating normative consensus/participation in norm elaboration."[125] This view acknowledges authority as a prerogative in which the individual might share. It implies a mutually negotiated rather than an imposed authority.

In moral psychology, autonomy has been elucidated from various theoretical approaches. The two-voices theory of Carol Gilligan is one example.[126] Gilligan contrasts the ethics of justice, seen to be conventionally male, with the ethics of care, viewed primarily as female. In this view, autonomy emphasizes gender stereotypes, including disconnection and separation. It pays particular attention to the role of gender socialization in the development toward autonomy.

In contrast to Gilligan's two-voices theory is the formulation of the three domains of social cognition. These are morality, social convention, and personal preference. Autonomy in each domain focuses upon the individual, who, through social conflict, develops preferences and initiatives. Another formulation focuses upon culture-based norms as found in three types of moral codes. These codes are autonomy, community, and divinity.[127] This structure is familiar, for in liberal-centered cultures, such as Western culture, it implies a socially constructed rights-based ethical code. Thus autonomy is understood here as rights-based. Kohlbergian theory, the bête noire of Gilligan's constructions, emphasizes reasoning maturity. In this perspective autonomy emerges as the identification of moral norms as norms for the self.[128]

Each of these theories of moral psychology, while construing autonomy differently, nonetheless captures important insights about this area of moral functioning. The argument of Don Reed is that combining and integrating these perspectives leads to a fuller, more adequate account of autonomy. That more-elaborated narrative supports the notion of *simhat bat* as signaling the public entry of a girl child into the Jewish people. Her official welcoming is public, as will be her role within the tradition. Autonomy as understood within moral psychology undergirds the notion of the girl/woman as both public and private person.

Perhaps most applicable to the significance of *simhat bat* as related to the community/autonomy perspective is Jean Piaget's account of autonomy.[129] Piaget stresses social participation in norm formation. That is, rather than acceptance of ready-made prescriptions, the individual becomes part of the very process that obligates him/her. In such a construction, authority is based upon expertise in clarifying, articulating, and elaborating norms. Autonomy becomes not alienation from or rebellion against authority, but rather participation in a cooperative and focused venture: "participatory initiative."[130] Authority itself changes in response to and with the contributions of autonomous people who are deeply connected to that which constitutes the authority. Thus the autonomous person is neither alienated from nor rebelling against established structures; rather, he/she is an integral part of exploring the constituitive elements of the authority itself. Community authority and individual autonomy in this model are interactive. Initiative exists *within* the connecting interaction, not apart from it. This paradigm supports what may be termed "principled initiative," in contrast to the Kantian ideal of principled independence.

Drawn from various theories of autonomy in moral psychology, this model illuminates a prototype of the halakhic process. It blurs the distinctions between heteronomous and autonomous law and forges a complex, rich interaction among community, custom, legal/religious authority, trained experts, and individual participants within established social/religious structures. This interplay is readily evident when applied to the development and contemporary interpretations of *simhat bat*. The increasing public role of women in general society and the new opportunities for women to study rabbinic texts combine to give Jewish women a public voice and presence new to our times. The multiple implications for Jewish communal life of educating women have been apparent at least since the beginning of the twentieth century.[131] The Jewish woman—increasingly even the Orthodox Jewish woman—is a public person. More and more, the gendered spheres of public/masculine and private/feminine have become androgynous. Time and custom, history and creative ritual, have rendered their decision.[132]

II

Death

Chapter 5

Mourning: Kaddish and the Funeral

Everyone dies at the end of some counting,
Long or short,
Everyone falls in a war,
They all deserve a wreath and a ceremony and an official letter.
When I stand at my mother's grave
It's like saluting
And the hard words of Kaddish a salvo
Into the summer skies.

Yehuda Amichai, "My Mother Died on Shavuot"

It was *isru chag,* the day after the eighth day of Passover, 1982. Now everyone would know what I had been doing for the last nine days, unobtrusive among the multitude of holiday *shul*-goers. I had been saying kaddish (mourner's prayers) for my mother.

My mother had died two days before Passover. My in-laws were already at our home in the Midwest, awaiting the celebration of the seder with us. I had left the hospital in New York four days earlier to return to my husband and three children. Together with my younger brother, I had stood vigil that entire last night in New York, sensing we could lose her at any moment, knowing this could be the last time I would see her alive. I fed her Jell-O, sponged her face, comforted my father, who several weeks earlier had undergone neurosurgery. And late that afternoon I had returned to our Midwestern home, leaving the tasks of caregiving to others. "Can't anything be done?" my older brother lamented on the way to Kennedy Airport. The certainty of imminent death can lead the most intelligent among us to be unrealistic.

And so she died two days before the *chag* (holiday). All of us flew to New York, the last plane to land before the airports were closed during that early April blizzard. We buried her, eerily surrounded by mounds of snow, sat shiva (the official time of mourning, usually seven days) for fewer than twenty-four hours, and arrived back home six hours before candlelighting.

I knew I was going to say kaddish for my mother. What my brothers did or did not do was not my concern. I did not want to say kaddish because my mother, perhaps, would need someone to do so for her.[1] I wanted to say kaddish because—how could I not? How could I not honor her memory in this most traditional way? I wanted to say kaddish because I *needed* to say kaddish: it was a sine qua non of my grieving. I would be in the midst of my community; I would have a daily task on which to focus, to give structure to the inner despair and intense isolation I felt. An internal compass pointed clearly in the obvious direction. I knew I would say kaddish. For me, there was no other option.

Being a halakhically committed Jew, it seemed to me at the outset that my reciting kaddish on a daily basis could not be a problem. I had studied all the halakhot (Jewish legal discussions) and some responsa and knew that while my presence at minyan (the prayer quorum, traditionally composed of ten men) might be unusual, it was definitely halakhically acceptable. I was thus completely unprepared for the attitudes I encountered in a presumably centrist Orthodox synagogue, one affiliated with the Young Israel movement. Looking back, they are all the more astounding in light of a very different experience saying kaddish for my father two years later, also in a Young Israel synagogue. At that time, in 1984, we were living in a suburban Long Island community.

In the Midwest, it was clear that the rabbi disapproved of my decision to be present at the daily morning minyan. When I arrived at 7 A.M., the lights were never turned on in the women's section. No one spoke to me. And the rabbi deemed it "immodest" to grant my request that the *tzedakah* (charity) box, when passed around during the repetition of the *amidah* (long silent prayer), be offered to me as well. This was the synagogue where I had prayed for three years, every Shabbat (Sabbath) and for all the holidays. The experience was isolating and humiliating. My work schedule made it impractical to attend a different shul (synagogue), so I decided to fight, if I had to, to get what should have been graciously proffered.

After six weeks of turning on the lights myself (after searching for the main switches, hidden in a back closet), I phoned the president of the shul. "David," I said, "when the *gabbai* [lay caretaker] arrives at 6:45 A.M. every morning, have him turn on the lights for me." From then on, the lights were on when I arrived. When the rabbi went to a conference, I spoke with the lovely elderly gentleman who looked after the *tzedakah* box. Of course, he said with a smile, he personally would see that the box came around to me every morning. And he did.

On Long Island, in a community where we had lived less than a year, I came daily to recite kaddish for my father, who had died exactly seven days after our daughter's wedding. It is difficult to describe the warmth and solace this group of (mostly) men extended to me. In accordance with established custom, Mishnah was studied regularly in my father's memory. The men spoke to me about my father, about me. They understood the deep need to express my grief the same way they were accustomed to articulating theirs: through the time-honored tradition of reciting kaddish. Caring and comfort reached out to me, and little by little my soul began to heal. I will never forget their kindness.

Both these synagogues are centrist Orthodox. What cause can one ascribe to the blatant differences in responding to a fairly new situation?[2] It seems to me that rabbinic leadership is the key. The rabbi in the Midwest felt threatened by my presence; my being at morning minyan made him intensely uncomfortable, a discomfort manifested by his passive-aggressive behavior. His own lack of sensitivity led him to enforce nonexistent strictures and lose the opportunity of modeling compassion for his congregants. The rabbi on Long Island under-stood my deep religious commitment and longings: my need to affirm myself as part of *klal Yisrael,* the Jewish people; to honor my father's memory by tak-ing on the recitation of kaddish as an obligation . A man of consummate sensi-tivity, he is a person who respects human dignity. Both rabbis had studied the same halakhah, yet they conveyed antithetical attitudes toward me, a woman, doing that which had traditionally been performed mostly by men.

What is kaddish? How did it develop and what is its purpose? How is its role understood in Orthodox, Conservative, and Reform Judaism, especially with regard to the recitation of kaddish by women?[3] This chapter will trace the de-velopment of the responsa literature regarding women and kaddish, analyzing the grounds and lines of argumentation. Especially interesting are the divergent directions expressed in the halakhic literature of the last decade in response to this issue. Within Orthodoxy, the increasingly restrictive attitudes, often cou-pled with attacks on those legal authorities who arrive at more lenient conclu-sions, testify in my view to an underlying fear of the influences of feminism upon halakhic Judaism. This is the case in both right-wing as well as centrist Orthodoxy and is at the core of decades of discussions and controversy in the Conservative movement. The tension expressed in the responsa strongly re-sembles that which appeared regarding the Bat Mitzvah controversy several decades ago.[4] That which was once a point of contention and dispute within the traditional Orthodox community—whether a twelve-year-old girl should cele-brate her reaching the age of Bat Mitzvah in any fashion—is now de rigueur, even within right-wing sects. All the life-cycle events, together with Shabbat and the holidays, form the bases from which Jewish identity and community emanate. Surely, then, the discussion of women as mourners, women confront-ing the finality of the death of a loved one, requires careful examination and analysis.

While women according to Jewish law are mandated to observe all the ha-lakhot of mourning, such as the rending of one's garment, the meal of condo-lence, the prohibitions of bathing or sexual intimacy during shiva, the one act often discouraged is the public declaration of the doxology of kaddish. Both

men and women mourners are required to manifest public and private mourning behavior. During the shiva, they sit on low stools, keep the mirrors in their
homes covered, avoid business or professional involvement and even such
mundane tasks as food preparation.[5] The latter are assumed by non-mourners,
thus allowing men and women equally to deal with their grief. Haircuts generally are not allowed for thirty days, and attendance is prohibited at joyous occasions (especially those with live instrumental music), in the case of the death of
a parent, for twelve months. In traditional Judaism, however, only men are required to recite the kaddish, while women are not.

The earliest known responsum in which the issue of women and kaddish is
discussed appears in the late-seventeenth-century work of R. Yair Bachrach,
known as the *Chavot Yair*. Based on a particular set of circumstances in Amsterdam, R. Bachrach's responsum became known simply as "the Amsterdam
case." It is referred to in nearly all subsequent discussions of women and kaddish. While rabbinic authorities agreed that the answer given in the Amsterdam
case was the right one for that particular situation, other questions arose in
other cases. The later responsa literature manifests two trends: one that restricts
the premises and conclusions of the Amsterdam case, and a second that ex-
pands upon them.

Kaddish has come to serve not only as a memorial prayer but also as a cathartic connection of the community in the working through of grief. The question is: did the ofttimes unavailability of kaddish to women have to do with the
rabbinic general exclusion of women from participation in public prayer (in
rabbinic sources and in Orthodox synagogues today), or were women able to—
and did they in fact—recite kaddish? In examining the halakhic parameters of
this issue, theological, philosophical, and sociological factors come into play.
As in all decision-making processes, the personality of those in positions of
power also plays a crucial role. While the nuances of halakhah demonstrate the
underlying theology and philosophy, an important aspect of the sociological
factor would include an analysis of the positions of religious leadership. Leaders in religious communities both maintain and transform tradition, a dual role
dependent upon many variables, including personality.[6]

The Origin and History of Kaddish

The kaddish prayer, which has four forms, was originally not part of the synagogue service. It had no connection to the prayer service for the dead. The B.T.
Sotah 49a notes that it was the concluding prayer with which the teacher or
preacher (always a male) indicated the end of his public discourse or lecture. It
was formulated in Aramaic, as was the discourse itself. The first reference to
kaddish as part of the synagogue service—indeed, the first instance in which

this doxology is termed kaddish—is in *Soferim* (16:12, 19:1, 21:6). This tractate, written in the sixth century after the closing of the Talmudic canon,[7] also records the use of kaddish at funerals, the first reference to what became accepted custom. Addressed to all assembled, it was spoken in the Babylonian vernacular, Aramaic. A further association of kaddish with the dead noted in *Soferim* is that it was recited at the end of the seven-day period of mourning (shiva) as part of a concluding ceremony of which learning and expounding texts were also part.

Originally the recitation of kaddish at the end of shiva was reserved for those of scholarly accomplishment. Later, however, in order not to put anyone to shame, it became the accepted practice for everyone.[8] An additional reference to the connection between kaddish and mourning is given in *Soferim* 19:12. The text reads, "The reader after *musaf* [the additional service on Shabbat and holidays] goes behind the synagogue door, or in front of the synagogue where he finds the mourners and their relatives. He comforts them with the *berakha* [blessing][9] and then he recites the *kaddish*." During these centuries the kaddish was understood to be, and was recited, as a doxology and justification of God's ways.

In a geonic source,[10] however, called the *Ottiyot de Rabbi Akiva,* a new purpose is ascribed to kaddish; it is said to have the power of redeeming the dead from the sufferings of Gehenna. This term originally referred to the Valley of Ben-Hinnom, south of the walls of Jerusalem, but came to mean "Hell."[11] Two references are given. In one, Akiva is said to meet a spirit in the guise of a man carrying wood. The wood, the man relates, is for the fire in which he is burned daily as punishment for his mistreatment of the poor. He would be released from this suffering, however, if he had a son to recite *barekhu*[12] and kaddish before a congregation that would respond with the praise of God's name. Upon discovering that the man had neglected his son, Akiva cares for and studies with the young man until one day the son stands before a congregation, recites *barekhu* and kaddish, and releases his father from Gehenna. The idea that a son, by virtue of his piety, may exert a redeeming influence on behalf of a parent who has died is mentioned as well in other sources contemporaneous with or later than the *Ottiyot de Rabbi Akiva.* An example is in the collection of midrashim[13] known as *Tanna debe Eliyahu Zuta,* where R. Yochanan ben Zakkai, not R. Akiva, is the central figure.[14]

Mishnaic and talmudic sources state that the torture of Gehenna lasted twelve months;[15] hence originally kaddish was recited for that length of time. Later, however, it was deemed inappropriate for progeny to presume that the soul of a parent was in Gehenna; the obligatory period of time for the recitation of kaddish was then reduced to eleven months. The practice of regular recitation of the kaddish by mourners seems to have become firmly established during the thirteenth century in response to the severe persecutions against Jews in the Crusades. Kaddish is also recited on the *yahrtzeit,* or the anniversary of a death.[16]

Once kaddish entered into the halakhic structure as a memorial prayer for the dead, how were women affected? First, since kaddish is part of the liturgy that requires a minyan, women were excluded as nonmembers of the representative group.[17] Second, Henrietta Szold's famous response to a male friend who volunteered to say kaddish upon the death of Ms. Szold's mother implies that the recitation of kaddish is a positive time-specific commandment, a *mitzvat aseh shehazman graman,*[18] albeit of rabbinic origin, from which women are customarily exempted according to mishnaic sources. Ms. Szold's statement expresses the ethical core of Judaism and reflects upon autonomy and equality, issues with which the community is still struggling. She says:

> The *Kaddish* means to me that the survivor publicly manifests his wish and intention to assume the relation to the Jewish community which his parent had, and that so the chain of tradition remains unbroken from generation to generation, each adding its own link. You can do that for the generations of your family. I must do that for the generations of my family. I believe that the elimination of women from such duties was never intended by our law and custom—women were freed from positive duties when they could not perform them, not when they could. It was never intended that . . . their performance of them should not be considered as valuable and valid as when one of the male sex performed them. And of the *Kaddish* I feel sure this is particularly true.
>
> My mother had eight daughters and no son; and yet never did I hear a word of regret pass the lips of either my mother or my father that one of us was not a son. When father died, my mother would not permit others to take her daughters' place in saying the *Kaddish,* and so I am sure I am acting in her spirit when I am moved to decline your offer. . . . [19]

The connection Szold proposes between the custom of the exclusion of women from kaddish and the mishnaic exemption of women from positive time-specified commandments,[20] however, is not legally correct. Significantly, in all the responsa on kaddish, *mitzvat aseh shehazman graman* is never cited as a reason for women's nonobligation to say kaddish. But since kaddish became closely allied with public prayer, perhaps the association was implicit rather than explicit. Or perhaps kaddish was not regarded at all as a *mitzva derabbanan,* a rabbinic enactment, but rather as a *minhag,* or custom, which gained the strength of social expectation, an expectation that did not devolve upon women.

Before examining some of the responsa literature, it is important to note several things. First, the midrash citied earlier regarding R. Akiva speaks about son and father. As in many sources, the male is considered paradigmatic; *ben,* being both the neuter and masculine in Hebrew, is also almost always translated as "son" rather than "child" or "offspring." A good example is found in the Passover Haggadah, an early section of which refers to "the four *banim*"(plural of *ben*). A quick survey of several editions of the Haggadah demonstrates the propensity to translate in the masculine that which can be neuter. Of the five editions I examined, only one, *The Yeshiva University Haggada* (1985), refers to "The Four Children": the wise child, the evil child, the simple child, and the one who does not know how to ask.[21]

The problems caused by language are known; they are complex, profound, and difficult, and affect the innermost perceptions of ourselves, and ourselves in relation to others—especially others of the opposite sex. In an intricate system of jurisprudence such as that of Jewish law, the repercussions are serious indeed. Critical feminist thinkers from Simone de Beauvoir to Judith Plaskow have addressed the issue.[22] The midrash mentions only *ben,* in every translation and interpretation understood as "son," and *av,* as "father." The other six relatives for whom one would also be required to say kaddish are not enumerated (mother, spouse, brother, sister, son, daughter).[23] But there is a saving specification here. If son and father are paradigmatic, then clearly others are not excluded but merely not enumerated. That is, as a son would say kaddish for a mother, a daughter might recite kaddish for a father *or* a mother. While this is true theoretically, it should be noted that in Eastern European culture a son was often called "my little kaddish" or "*kaddisle,*" a name once applied by my late father, born in Poland, to my son, then seven years old. It is also interesting to note that the geonic and early postgeonic discussions of kaddish deal almost exclusively with the child (or son) saying kaddish for a parent—an eleven-month proposition. But what about the other relatives for whom traditional mourning takes place? For them (sibling or spouse, for instance) kaddish is said for only thirty days. Is there any relationship between the thirty-day recitation and release from Gehenna? No source I am aware of makes this connection. The parent-child relationship here receives decided emphasis.

Second, once kaddish became an established part of the observance of mourning, it came to serve important psychological functions. It compels the mourner to reaffirm connection with the community through daily prayer precisely when despair and alienation are most profound. The frozen glaze of grief begins to soften and heal, supported by the focus of kaddish and the embrace of the community. As part of the community, the mourner testifies to his/her continuation within the tradition of which the deceased was a part. This is in accordance with the talmudic dictum in Sanhedrin 104a: "A child can endow a parent."[24] And in its most abstract sense, kaddish serves as a statement of the unknowability and justification of God's ways. Kaddish becomes a significant component—a cathartic yet simultaneously self-affirming exercise—of the bereavement process. While the other laws of mourning were clearly designed with a psychological aspect in mind, that kaddish would also serve this purpose seems not to have been the motivation for requiring its recitation; benefit accruing to the soul of the departed, specifically the parent, was the original intent. Yet its psychological effects have long been acknowledged.[25]A third and last point to keep in mind: during and after the Holocaust, women all over Europe said kaddish. It was accepted, perhaps even expected and encouraged. A poignant example is given in a testimony found in the Yad Vashem Archives, in which Rahel Fulda writes what she witnessed one day upon return to the Telz (Lithuania) ghetto from the Geralai work camp.

In the ghetto there was also a synagogue, where we prayed and where we said the first *kaddish* after the holy sacrifices [mass murders]. At the reader's stand stood a young woman who recited *kaddish* in the congregation *[betsibur]*. This *kaddish* I will never forget as long as I live. No one could move [from the place]. The heartwrenching cries went directly to heaven. Who could imagine that there stood a community *[edah]* of women in synagogue who recited *kaddish* in the congregation? These were the last Jews of Telz.[26]

Another instance is to be found in the memoir of Pearl Benisch, about a group of Bais Yaacov girls. The Bais Yaacov (House of Jacob) schools for girls, founded by Sarah Scheinirer in 1918, took their name from the verse in Exodus 19:3 in which "House of Jacob" is said to refer to the women. By 1937, 250 Bais Yaacov schools served 38,000 students, nearly all of them Orthodox.[27] Upon liberation from Bergen-Belsen by the British, Benisch relates, a former Bais Yaacov student led a group of assembled survivors in reciting "a collective *Kaddish*."[28]

So we have behavior that contravenes much of the halakhic literature. The problem seems to be this: women are unilaterally included in all requirements of mourning, of which kaddish is one. Reciting kaddish is consonant with a woman's identity as mourner, human being, Jew. But kaddish operates within the arena of public prayer from which, according to traditional rabbinic rulings, women were proscribed as participants equal with men. Hence the dilemma.

Orthodox Responsa

That only sons said kaddish seems to have been the norm, a practice supported by both sociological and religious factors. However, in the *Havot Yair*, R. Yair Bachrach, writing in the late seventeenth century, brings an important precedent. He says:

An unusual and well-known event occurred in Amsterdam. A man died without a son, and before his death commanded that ten should study in his home every day for twelve months, and after the learning his daughter should say *kaddish.* And the scholars and lay officials of the community did not prevent her from doing so. Even though there is no proof to contradict the matter, being that a woman is also commanded in *kiddush Hashem,* and even though there is a quorum (minyan) of males called *bnei Yisrael* [the children/sons of Israel], and even though the incident of R. Akiva, which is the source of mourner's *kaddish,* refers only to a son, it is nonetheless logical that a daughter's *kaddish* is also purposeful, for it comforts the soul of the deceased, since she is also his progeny. However, one must be concerned for the fact that should this become prevalent, it might lead to a general weakening of the customs of our people, which are like Torah itself; then everyone would be erecting his own pulpit according to his own logic and deriding rabbinic enactments, which they would come to scorn.[29]

In the responsum, R. Bachrach analyzes why the rabbinic authorities and lay officials in Amsterdam permitted the daughter of the man in question to say kaddish, obviously an unusual occurrence. He begins by stating that there is no "proof to contradict the matter," that is, there are no compelling reasons that would contravene the decision. From a halakhic perspective, he is saying, a woman's saying kaddish is acceptable, permissible, and in the case under discussion, desirable. How is this so, given that the very existence of the responsum demonstrates that reciting kaddish was not customary for women? That may be, R. Bachrach asserts, because the source for kaddish, the incident with R. Akiva, clearly refers, according to him, to a son (he understands *ben* in its masculine, not neuter sense). But there is halakhic precedent that overrides this linguistic limitation of considering *ben* as referring only to a son: a woman is commanded in the mitzvah (commandment) of *kiddush Hashem* (sanctifying God's name), which in some instances requires the presence of ten men—the *minyan.* As she can perform the mitzvah of *kiddush Hashem* in the presence of ten men, she can likewise recite the mourner's kaddish in the presence of ten men.

Kiddush Hashem, or sanctification of God's name, has three aspects in Jewish law. It can refer to martyrdom, to ethical perfection beyond the minimum standards set by rabbinic law, or to liturgical formulations that emphasize sanctifying God's name. This last type of *kiddush Hashem* pertains especially to the two formal prayers of *kedushah*[30] and kaddish. In kaddish, the congregational response "May God's great name be blessed forever and to all eternity"[31] is considered a *kiddush Hashem.* Since, that is, a woman has an obligation to perform the mitzvah of *kiddush Hashem* should the opportunity arise, she certainly can recite kaddish,[32] which is an essential manifestation of the *mitzvah.*

Five other conclusions may be drawn from this responsum. First, kaddish was said in the home, and not in the synagogue. Second, despite the efficacy of the daughter's kaddish and the solace it brings both her and her deceased father, there is caution in the face of the new. What if this change from established practice leads to other, less palatable, perhaps less legitimate (although valid, according to the halakhah) practices? It is interesting that this concern is expressed before the general encounter of European Jewry with modernity, and certainly before even the earliest echoes of feminism. The custom until the time of the Amsterdam case was obviously that women did not recite kaddish. Despite the halakhic permissibility of women doing so, R. Bachrach discerns the overlap of religious law and social or cultural behavior and is concerned about a general loosening of, or change within, the dominant modes of religious behavior. His reservations and uneasiness in the face of possible change reflect an important component of the transformation and development of all religious systems. Third, the elders of the Amsterdam community consented to the dying man's request in the absence of a son, or sons, to say kaddish. Had there been sons, their decision might have been different. Fourth, the responsum refers to what appears to be an unmarried young woman *(na'arah)*. The decision may have been otherwise in a circumstance involving a married daughter.

And fifth, why did the father request that the ten men study in his home and then have his daughter recite kaddish there? There are several possibilities. Women usually didn't attend synagogue, certainly not daily services. Going to and from the synagogue may have been difficult, unusual, dangerous, or simply impractical for an unaccompanied single Jewish woman. Saying kaddish in a home after study of a text would be less controversial than at the prescribed intervals during the daily morning prayers. And finally, perhaps the structure of the synagogue, in which women were separated either in a balcony or in an adjoining room, would not allow the woman to be heard by the male quorum.

Whether the reasons were practical or sociological, or a combination thereof, kaddish at home was requested and accepted. Interestingly, and not surprisingly, this became a precedent in subsequent responsa. An example is that of R. Yaacov Risher, who wrote and published the *Shevut Yaacov,* a halakhic compendium in Lemberg in 1880. He cites the *Chavot Yair* in his decision that women may certainly recite kaddish, in the presence of a minyan, at home.

The *Be'er Heitev* commentary[33] on the *Shulhan Arukh* cites the *Kenesset Yehezkel,*[34] the responsa of Ezekiel Katzenellenbogen, who comes to a similar conclusion. He says: "a daughter doesn't say *kaddish* at all in the synagogue. But if they [the male community] wish to make a *minyan* for her at home, they certainly can." Women here are excluded from the synagogue, although the right to say kaddish is not questioned.

The *Gesher haChaim*[35] takes what seems to have been based on practical considerations—a woman reciting kaddish at home rather than at the synagogue—and adds a completely new, and in my opinion untenable, dimension. Quoting R. Akiva, he states that a son carries out the essential function of kaddish. But a daughter may, of course, say kaddish. If she is under twelve years of age, she may say it in the synagogue; some, however, would prohibit her doing so. If, however, she is twelve or over, she is not permitted to recite kaddish in the synagogue. In either age group, kaddish may be said at home. The *Gesher ha-Chaim* is adding a sexual element—puberty—although there is no evidence it is relevant. What makes the intrusion of a sexual element especially interesting is that it is completely unnecessary—one may understand the logic of a daughter saying kaddish at home, rather than in the synagogue, as reflecting a synagogue protocol different from our own and different from that which predominated in 1947. In modern synagogues, the custom is for all the mourners to recite kaddish together. The original custom, however, was for one mourner, chosen according to a system of priority, to say kaddish. Since women were nonparticipants in synagogue prayer, here the best option would be to recite kaddish at home. In Orthodox synagogues today, however, when all the mourners say kaddish together, the issue of a female mourner possibly representing and displacing the male mourners is not an issue. Hence the female voice of kaddish in synagogue can be heard, albeit from the women's section.

But not all contemporary responsa concur. While the halakhic legitimacy of women's recitation of kaddish is undeniable, it is nonetheless not universally accepted. The late R. Uziel, former Sephardi Chief Rabbi of Israel, quotes the opinion of the *Chavot Yair* that the recitation of kaddish by a daughter elevates the soul(s) of her parents and that she is obligated in *kiddush Hashem*. But he notes that grandsons may say kaddish if there are no sons. "From all that has been said," he continues (despite the opinion of the *Chavot Yair*), "we learn that this custom [to recite kaddish] is only for sons, for they are his [*sic*] progeny; parents, who are the cause of his [*sic*] existence, are rewarded through their sons' merit" (of reciting kaddish).[36]

R. Shlomo Halevi Wahrman cannot bring himself to accept women's recitation of kaddish. If the permissive view is adopted, he writes,

then those of our contemporaries who are out to cause confusion—their aim being to create a new Torah and, God forbid, change our traditions, are always seeking a nail on which to hang their nonsense—will rely on this to count a woman in a *minyan,* saying that the most strict have already permitted it.[37]

R. Wahrman is prepared to eliminate the possibility of women's participation in the saying of kaddish based on his fear of being misconstrued and misunderstood. How interesting that in the post-Enlightenment period, with the development of Reform and, later, Conservative Judaism, decisions that were (at least in some cases) acceptable are retracted as a matter of public policy.

The words of R. Wahrman echo those of the *Chavot Yair,* expressing concern about "the general weakening of the customs of our people."[38] The former Chief Rabbi of Tel-Aviv-Yaffo, R. Chaim David haLevi, writes an astounding responsum. After discussing in what circumstances *ben* and *banim* refer to the masculine or the neuter and analyzing some of the earlier legal enactments, he renders a decision that a woman is prohibited from reciting kaddish even at the cemetery because it may cause "sinful thoughts to the simple-minded." This is extended to kaddish in the synagogue. She may, however, recite the kaddish at home, in the presence of family members only. "The evil inclination," he concludes, "is present even in a mourner's home."[39] From seventeenth-century Amsterdam, where a woman said kaddish at home and not in the synagogue for practical reasons only, we have arrived three centuries later at a place where sexual polarity enters the human question of how to structure the grieving process so as to permit equal access and opportunity to all. The *Be'er Heitev, Gesher haChaim, Mishpetei Uziel,* and *Aseh Lekha Rav* all manifest a restricting of the decision in the Amsterdam case. While they may agree that the outcome in the Amsterdam case was acceptable in the particular circumstances relevant to it, they are dealing with different situations and a transformed social context. Thus they use the variant details as part of the justification for limiting the original decision. R. Bachrach's fear of change is taken up and projected to a much greater degree than the legal reasoning explaining his judgment.

But such fear of women—or fear of change clothed as such—is absent in a vocal minority of halakhic decisions. R. Joseph B. Soloveitchik ruled that a woman, be she even the only female present, may say kaddish in the synagogue.[40] That a woman may say kaddish with a group of ten or more men, even if she is the only person doing so, is consistent with R. Bachrach's analysis of *kiddush Hashem.* R. Aaron Soloveitchik, in a 1993 publication, argues against the *Chavot Yair* on the grounds of the changing nature of the Jewish community.[41] That is, he explicitly brings historical context to bear in his reasoning. In positing his argument, R. Aaron (as he was known) incorporates precisely the thinking of another Chicago rabbi in an earlier era, R. Moshe Leib Blair.[42] Both the responsa recognize the alienating quality of some of the responsa cited above. They are cognizant as well of the political repercussions of holding fast to legal abstractions that ignore the fundamental Jewish concept of woman as person created in the image of God. The more recent responsum is that of R. Aaron Soloveitchik. He begins by quoting the *Chavot Yair* and then continues:

It seems now that some Jewish men and women are fighting for the equality of women with men with regard to *aliyot* [being called up to the Torah] for women. Since this is the case, if Orthodox rabbis will prevent a woman from reciting *kaddish* in a place where doing so is a possibility, the influence of Conservative and Reform rabbis will greatly increase. Therefore it is prohibited to prevent a woman [daughter] from saying *kaddish.*[43]

This responsum acknowledges that the halakhah can recognize, and indeed has recognized, the right of women to recite kaddish. It does not deal with the reasons offered in the earlier responsa that rule in the negative but clearly asserts the positive option as being within the realm of Jewish law. That halakhic authorities must rule leniently is due to the changing status of women as it has been interpreted in both Conservative and Reform Judaism. The argument is that to prohibit that which is permissible in the context of mourning rites is to cause estrangement from the (Orthodox) tradition. Gender should not, in this case, be the grounds for witholding from women the time-honored way in which the state of mourning has been marked in Judaism.

R. Blair's responsum is more detailed than R. Aaron's. He begins by enumerating three reasons why a woman (he refers specifically to a daughter) should be *obligated* to recite kaddish. First, she is obligated in all the laws of mourning of which kaddish is an integral part. Second, the reasons for saying kaddish—giving solace to the soul of the deceased and redeeming the dead from Gehenna through sanctifying God's name—definitely apply to a woman. R. Blair here used R. Bachrach's argument of *kiddush Hashem* to support his stance. And third, kaddish may be considered not only as part of the obligations of mourning but also within the category of prayer. As such, women are not exempt but are obligated.[44] Then he brings earlier precedents, primary among which is the Amsterdam case. He proceeds to argue against the interpretation of *ben* as "son" rather than "offspring" and to lament the practice of hiring a man to say kaddish in the absence of male progeny. In both cases he brings strong evidence to make his case.

Special note must be taken, however, of the last section of R. Blair's responsum, which alludes to the issue of the relationship of historical context and religious change. In it he offers an unusual and sharp interpretation of the last part of R. Bachrach's argument in the Amsterdam case. He states:

The last words of the *Chavot Yair* require explanation. R. Bachrach is speaking of a case in which the father directed that ten men learn Torah in his home for twelve months and after the learning [each time] the daughter should say *kaddish.*

This is truly erecting one's pulpit and rescinding the custom of Israel, because also in the synagogue only men, and not women, say *kaddish* after learning. But he is not speaking about the *kaddish* of eleven months that a woman says from the woman's gallery or even during the time of *shiva* in her home when at least ten men are praying. On this certainly it is inappropriate to say that it "derides rabbinic enactments."[45]

The narrow focus of R. Blair's responsum is to obligate a daughter's recitation of kaddish in the case where there are no sons. He ends a main section of his discussion by inveighing against the practice of hiring a man to recite kaddish when there is a surviving son.[46] "Certainly," R. Blair concludes,

This frivolous action [of hiring a stranger] most decidedly applies to a daughter, since she is obligated according to the law, and she is able to come to the synagogue to say *kaddish.* Therefore, in my humble opinion, it is important for all rabbis of our time to explain to a daughter who is mourning a parent that since there is no son, it is upon her that the obligation falls to come to synagogue to say *kaddish* and not to hire anyone.[47]

But the broader center of interest is the recitation of kaddish by a woman— spouse, daughter, mother, or sister—even in cases where she is *not* the sole mourner. In our twenty-first century, what R. Blair writes may seem obvious to most: the woman is an autonomous person whose need/desire to express her sorrow and honor the deceased requires the same religious options as that of a male; those options are for people, not gendered beings. But forty or so years ago this was not so apparent and among some Jewish groups even today is not accepted.

R. Blair summarizes his position in four brief statements. He says:

It is not my intention to be unduly stringent with regard to the mourning of a daughter, but merely to uphold the law that the daughter is obligated to recite *kaddish.* On the contrary, in my opinion her obligatory recitation is a leniency, and in the laws of mourning the more lenient view prevails.[48] Also, if there will not be ten women in the women's section to answer "Amen," this also would not preclude her saying *kaddish,* since the law *[din]* is that all those who recite *kaddish* should recite it together in unison; if so, the "Amen" with which the men respond applies as well to her *kaddish.* And when it is said that custom *[minhag]* erases law *[halakhah],* this is only in the case of a communal enactment *[takanat tzibur],* and we do not find such an enactment regarding the circumstance of a daughter's saying *kaddish* when there is no son.

I want to emphasize here to the rabbis of our country who oppose this legal decision *[pesak halakhah]* that in the time of the Geonim when the custom to recite *kaddish* began, many sages of Israel, such as Rav Hai Gaon, were opposed. And what do we see now? That the *kaddish* is included in the general category of mourning and is as important in mourning as a commandment of biblical origin *[mitzvah de'oraita].*[49] The *kaddish* brings many male Jews to the synagogue and causes them to become more involved in Judaism. This will occur also with female Jews; we would bring them closer to Jewish life and to our holy Torah.[50]

Both R. Blair and R. Aaron Soloveitchik recognize the political ramifications of excluding women. R. Blair's concern is focused on the alienation of women not only from traditional Judaism, but even from the Jewish community itself. R. Aaron is worried about defections to the Conservative and Reform denominations. Although not without their own struggles, Conservative and Reform Judaism offer greater legal and ritual equality to women.

Orthodox rabbinic misgivings are rooted in reality. Founder of *Ms.* Magazine, Letty Cottin Pogrebin, was estranged from Judaism for fifteen years when the male minyan ejected her from the room when prayers during shiva were to take place. Grieving the loss of her beloved mother as an adolescent of fifteen at the time, Pogrebin's brusque exclusion led her to reject any connection to the Jewish community. She writes:

The turning point in my spiritual life was the night I was rejected from the minyan that said Kaddish for my mother. I could point to the *shiva* experience . . . [and] . . . say my father sent me into the arms of feminism. No woman who has suffered through the anguish and insult of exclusion on top of the tragedy of her bereavement forgets that her humiliation was inflicted by Jewish men.[51]

Another woman relates that she was fourteen years old when her father, only forty-two, died suddenly in 1961. When she expressed her need and desire to say kaddish, her grandfather agreed to pick her up after school every day and take her to the late afternoon and evening services. He too was reciting kaddish, but, of course, for his son. While her Cleveland family belonged to a Conservative synagogue, it was more convenient, due to the grandfather's working hours, to go to the Taylor Street Synagogue, which was (and still is) Orthodox. To this day she retains a vivid and painful memory of how the men, while greeting her grandfather, made her feel invisible. Not only did they not address her grief; they acknowledged her presence only as an irritant to the usual way the services were organized, i.e., in an all-male setting. The afternoon/evening prayers were held in the small sanctuary with no *mehitzah,* or dividing partition between the men and any women who might attend. This was because women rarely, if ever, participated in the early morning or afternoon/evening services at the synagogue. If they prayed on a daily basis, they did so at home. Thus there was no physical place, i.e., no women's section, to accommodate her.

She recalls even now the rudeness with which men shook their fingers at her and "shooed" her to the back. Because she was unable to share her feelings with her grandfather, he remained unaware of her distress and suffering. When she could bear it no longer, she stopped coming and recited kaddish only on *Shabbat* in her own synagogue.[52] A Maryland woman writes: "My brothers have been hugged, invited home for meals, and made life-long friends in the year they said Kaddish. Women I know have been laughed at, had the synagogue door shut in their faces and told their parents would burn in hell for doing the very same thing."[53] Essays, stories, and e-mail communications are replete with the pain of Jewish women who have been told, both overtly and covertly, that Jewish rituals often have a "For Men Only" label attached.

Citing the case of R. Hai Gaon, R. Blair indicates that movement, evolution, and development are intrinsic to the halakhic process, the nature of which is to apply eternal ideals and principles within specific historical contexts. R. Hai Gaon's opposition to kaddish did not alter its eventual inclusion as part of mourning. Neither should contemporary opposition to women's reciting kaddish deter its establishment, if not as halakhic obligation, the way R. Blair would prefer, at the very least as strongly encouraged social and religious custom.[54]

The case for expanding the logic implicit in the Amsterdam case (that, if a woman can say kaddish at home, it is understood that she most certainly can and should recite kaddish in the synagogue) is supported by another discussion of the issue in a fairly recent article by R. Yehuda Herzl Henkin. R. Henkin writes:

> Certainly the reciting of *kaddish* by a woman is not a difficulty from the responsa of the *Shevut Yaacov* and *Knesset Yechezkel,* who wrote that a woman may not recite *kaddish* at all in the synagogue, *since they wrote only according to their custom.* . . . [55] (emphasis mine)

R. Henkin makes clear reference to social custom as a significant factor in determining the acceptability or discouragement of behavior that is permissible, but may not, in certain historical periods, have been widespread.[56] R. Henkin's discussion is of especial note because it engendered a sharp response in an essay written by R. Reuven Fink.[57] Fink's analysis is a paradigm of the male exercise of power masquerading as piety. It recalls the statement of a modern writer that women's selfhood depends upon her "ability to act in the public domain."[58] Fink finds intolerable the desire of traditional women to participate in kaddish, in the public—and male—domain of community prayer. His words merit examination not only because they represent a restrictive view among modern Orthodox Jewish leaders, but also inasmuch as they manifest both a fear of women and the patriarchal need to retain control. The positions and rebuttals in the Henkin-Fink exchange illustrate well the tug-of-war within halakhic circles with regard to what seems a minor issue: a woman coming to the synagogue to recite kaddish. Fink and others in his mode seem to view the "freedom" to grieve given to women as a grave threat to the tradition. Fink, in fact, ends his analysis by stating:

> It would therefore seem that an attempt to "improve" or alter our sacred traditions . . . [is] both pernicious and dangerous. . . . Tampering with the synagogue's customary practices is clearly a step fraught with great danger.[59]

What are Fink's objections? First, he claims, when women say kaddish from the *ezrat nashim* (the women's section in a traditional synagogue), they are not part of the prayer community. This is an astonishing claim. It would invalidate women as even passive participants in the prayer community of the Jewish people. It would banish to the land of Oz all traditional women who come to pray, to hear the weekly Torah reading, and occasionally to recite *birkhat hagomel.*[60] To say that women come to synagogue but are not technically *in* synagogue is to exclude forever all females from the prayer community. There is a patent absurdity in this claim (as well as a large dose of arrogance), which through legal abstraction denies the reality of real people and relegates the synagogue to the status of an exclusive men's club. Fink's claim is halakhic cavil.

The second objection Fink puts forth is that R. Yehuda Henkin gives inadequate support for his interpretation of his grandfather's *pesak,* or legal decision, about women and kaddish. This objection may be dismissed outright, as Fink does not even refer to R. Yosef Henkin's original discussion in his footnotes.[61] R. Yosef Henkin's argues that the early responsa prohibiting women from reciting kaddish, especially in the synagogue, were based on synagogue practice of the time. Prevailing custom was for one mourner to say kaddish on behalf of all mourners present and to stand at the prayer leader's table while doing so. A woman, according to rabbinic tradition, could not be this representative.[62] This predominant practice had some variations, however, in both Europe and later the United States. Historical records indicate that sometimes young women reciting kaddish entered the men's section and stood in the front with the other male mourners.[63] "Despite this strict separation of the men and women," reports a study of the American synagogue from 1901 to 1925, "a young girl, perhaps sixteen years old, would enter the men's section to recite the Kaddish for a parent. No one ever made a protest or even a comment."[64] While some communities and communal leaders were flexible and less stringent, these practices remained unusual. Current custom, R. Yosef Henkin continued to argue, is for each person to say kaddish in his place, a place that may surely also, then, be *her* place.

Fink's language is sharp and brusque and does not hold up to scrutiny. Indeed, the transformation in custom noted by R. Yosef Henkin indicates, very simply, that changes in religious ritual, observance, and law occur all the time. Fink's notion that recent discussions of women and kaddish camouflage an attempt to "improve" Jewish traditions is, on one level, a distorted reading of the very halakhic processes he claims to wish to protect. On another level, the motivation for change often is the desire to make things better. Customary practices today will not necessarily be customary practices tomorrow.

A recent discussion of women's recitation of kaddish by an Australian Orthodox rabbi contravenes R. Fink's rigid stance. The author, R. J. Simcha Cohen, argues against the stance in the ArtScroll book *Mourning in Halacha,* disputing not only its interpretation of the opinion of the *Chavot Yair* but even its translation. Rather, R. Cohen states, the views of R. Yosef Eliyahu Henkin, R. Moshe Feinstein, and R. Yosef Dov Soloveitchik are determinative, since they "permeated the essence and formed the standards of synagogue life in America." In addition to generating "a firm dedication to the traditional reverence given to the departed" in Judaism, the author reports that "it may well have been an ancient practice for women to say kaddish in synagogues after services" (no sources are given for this tentative claim). Therefore, concludes R. Cohen,

Women who wish daily to attend religious services and to recite kaddish should be acknowledged as faithful adherents to our heritage. They are not . . . innovators seeking to restructure or liberalise halachic practices [but rather to give] kavod [honor] to loved ones.[65]

It seems one must disclaim a liberal or lenient or historically variant reading of the sources in order for one's opinion to be acceptable.

A final word from Orthodox decisors is to be found in the responsa of the current Ashkenazi Chief Rabbi of Israel, R. Meir Lau. He writes a fairly lengthy analysis, quoting and commenting upon the earlier precedents in the halakhic literature. He cites the *Mateh Ephraim,*[66] in which R. Ephraim Margoliot prohibits a woman from reciting kaddish in her home, after Torah learning, in the presence of ten men, as is permitted in R. Bachrach's responsum. The reason? "A woman's voice is *ervah*"[67] (sexual incitement). This explanation makes no appearance in earlier discussions; thus it is surprising to find it here. One could conjecture that it represents the use of a legal mechanism/principle to silence the female voice of kaddish, to disallow to women that which, in many circles, was accepted practice. Instead of women's actively reciting kaddish, the *Mateh Ephraim* recommends that women come to synagogue and respond "amen" to the kaddish recited by a member of the male quorum.

That a woman's voice can be sexually stimulating to a man is a notion that has undergone several permutations in the halakhic literature. These transformations, resulting from varying interpretations over the centuries, are a paradigm both of the axiom that law changes in historical context and of the use of gender in the construction of religious traditions. The most thorough overview of the historical development of *kol isha* (the voice of a woman), as the concept is known, is given by Saul J. Berman in the essay "Kol 'Isha."[68] In order to understand R. Lau's use of this notion (as well as that of the *Mateh Ephraim* a hundred years earlier) as a means of silencing women from reciting kaddish, a brief summary is in order.

The statement ascribing sexual quality to the female voice appears twice in the corpus of the Talmud, in two very different contexts. The first is B.T. *Berakhot* 24a, as part of a discussion of whether or not the Shema, the central liturgical affirmation of God's unity (with correlative ethical implications and commandments),[69] can be recited in the presence of a nude person. The analysis concludes with four statements concerning sexual incitement, one of which avers, "A woman's voice is sexually arousing." The same statement appears in a completely unrelated context in B.T. Kiddushin 70a.[70] In this instance, it is part of an exchange between two rabbinic sages in which one attempts to challenge the scholarly authority of the other. The conversation might even be construed as banter: whatever opinion *A* affirms, *B* will undermine. A related talmudic comment is found in B.T. Sotah 48a with regard to the broad prohibition against singing at festive gatherings instituted after the destruction of the Second Temple in 70 c.e. On the basis of this last reference, the geonim[71] recommended against having female entertainers at festive gatherings of men, be they vocalists or instrumentalists.[72]

However, the assertion that a woman's voice is sexually arousing, *kol b'isha ervah,* is never mentioned in the discussion of the geonim. The choice not to use this general statement confirms that the judgment inherent within it need not—perhaps cannot—be viewed as a general description of the intrinsic nature of all women's voices. Rather, however, it represents a specific limitation regarding recitation of the Shema when concentration must be paramount. R. Hai Gaon, who lived in the ninth century, rules this way in his compendium.[73] In the history of the development of halakhah, the geonim are viewed as innovative. One source states, "The *geonim* were not satisfied with halakhic conclusions derived from the Talmud; they also made new regulations regarding contemporary needs."[74]

In the period of the early halakhic decisors, for those who follow the geonim and are called rishonim, the principle of *kol isha* came to be understood as referring to female singing voices in a specific context or situation. Also, the rishonim articulated the principle that the novelty of exposure to a woman's voice constituted its arousing aspect; were a man accustomed to a particular female voice, erotic arousal would be unlikely. The issue of focusing on prayer without distraction and the prohibition against female performers at exclusively male festive gatherings remained separate and distinctive rulings for nearly 850 years, until a responsum written by the Hungarian decisor, R. Moshe Sofer, in 1814. Interestingly, the question submitted to R. Sofer was whether the synagogue in Vienna could sponsor a mixed choir (i.e., male and female) during a reception it was to host for the Congress of Vienna in the autumn of 1814.[75]

For R. Sofer, as for other aharonim,[76] distraction from prayer and Torah study, which require attentiveness, is not the essential motive of the statement in the Talmud. Rather, for them, that statement ("a woman's voice is sexually arousing") becomes an affirmation that the female singing voice, in all circumstances, is equivalent to nudity. Understanding this jump in reasoning requires a knowledge of historical context. R. Sofer was writing at the time of the incipient Reform movement in Germany, which had instituted mixed choirs, organs in the synagogues, and mixed seating in the synagogue.[77] He saw himself as—and indeed he was—a defender of traditional Judaism (just then beginning to be termed "Orthodox" Judaism), Judaism as it had always been practiced until the innovations of the incipient Reform movement began in Germany. The advocate of tradition in the face of radical transformation,[78] R. Sofer proclaimed, "That which is new is prohibited from the Torah!"[79] Born in Germany (but the rabbi in Pressburg, Hungary, for many years) R. Sofer was a stubborn and vocal opponent of modernism in any form. The dictum above, expressing hostility to any and all innovation, is used even today by ultra-Orthodox leadership as justification for resistance to change.

R. Sofer's responsum on *kol isha* led to an increase of strictures; the occasions in which a woman's voice might be heard by men was narrowed even further. Some recent responsa, however, attempting to create a more balanced perspective, further empower Orthodox women by reinstating the original context of the early legal discussions (i.e., function); they take greater cognizance of historical circumstance in the issuing of halakhah. These responsa work in two directions: preventing additional restrictions and returning to the analyses of the decisors preceding R. Sofer, the rishonim.[80] The rishonim were less restrictive and more flexible than the *aharonim,* or later decisors. Perhaps these responsa will lead to a reexamination of the original talmudic texts in light of contemporary concepts of sexuality and gender: is a woman's singing voice a distraction from men's prayer and Torah study in a manner different from a male singing voice;[81] or is it different from a male singing voice heard when women are praying or learning? And is the singing voice of a woman in all circumstances a tool of sexual arousal in a way that might lead to an illicit sexual encounter, a concern expressed by some? The underlying concept is that of possible lack of focus during male prayer and Torah study, and that which constitutes distraction can change. Much as R. Blair and R. Aaron Soloveitchik expressed apprehension lest severe restrictions on female recitation of kaddish alienate women from tradition, the silencing of women's voices raised in song leads to a similar concern.

Let us return now to R. Lau's discussion of women and kaddish. R. Lau agrees with the *Mateh Ephraim,* in which R. Margoliot's reason for prohibiting a woman from saying kaddish, even in *her own home* (emphasis mine), is *"kol b'isha erva."* This demonstrates, in my view, a distortion of even the more restrictive analyses found in the rabbinic literature from 1814 onward. For it assumes the congruence of the female singing voice and female recitation of a prayer, the kaddish, within a congregation. Such a leap has no basis in the original texts. It represents the use of religious authority to disempower women, to silence female expression of grief and mourning under the pretense of reducing a woman—even her sorrowful, speaking voice—to a tool of sexual enticement. Put another way, it expresses the male fear of male sexuality projected upon the female and is articulated as the banishing of women from *any* role in male public prayer, even participation in the ritual of public mourning. One might ask: what is the difference between the female voice that responds "amen" to the male recitation of kaddish and the female voice that reaffirms the faith by saying the kaddish on her own? R. Lau's use of the principle of *kol isha* is thus both political (it excludes women from reciting kaddish) and sexist (even women's speaking voices are arousing and men need to be protected from such stimulation). One wonders how R. Lau's view accords with the presence in girls' religious high schools of male teachers, who listen every day to the voices of mature young women.

The view that presumes a woman's voice speaking in prayer to be sexually arousing is undermined by the Talmud itself. "Our rabbis taught," the text states that

all are qualified to be among the seven [who read the Torah], even a minor and a woman. But the sages said that a woman should not read because of the honor of the congregation *[kevod hatzibbur]*.[82]

In the lengthy halakhic literature on this passage specifically in regard to women reading from the Torah, the statement that "a woman's voice is sexual incitement" is never mentioned. This might be because until the second half of the twentieth century, women were not called up to and did not read from the Torah scroll in the synagogue. That is, the text describes a theoretical possibility already precluded due to the acceptance of *kevod hatzibbur* as a reason for women's noneligibility. However, were *kol isha* to be a legitimate justification for preventing women from exercising their theoretical right, the text would have listed it. In addition, the cantillation of Torah reading is a singing or chanting, not a speaking, which would strengthen the use of *kol isha* as an argument. But such an argument does not appear. "The underlying concern," as one scholar writes with regard to a related context, "is not about sexual license but about the effect of gender equality in secular society on the system of gender complementarity that constructs and justifies different roles and statuses for men and women in Orthodoxy."[83]

The summation at the end of R. Lau's responsum represents well the increasing restrictions prevalent among Orthodox leaders, often even seemingly centrist Orthodox rabbis. R. Lau claims one cannot rely upon the more moderate stance of R. Yehudah Henkin, and therefore, "one may not permit women to recite *kaddish* in any form."[84] He fears this traditional expression of grieving by women will lead to changes evident in the other denominations of Judaism; in Conservative and all Reform congregations, women are counted as part of the minyan, and men and women sit together. While R. Lau articulates anxiety about the slippery slope of change in religious traditions, the essential component of his argument entails a different paradigm. He says: "The son, in his deeds, words, and place in the midst of the community,[85] represents continuation of the personhood of the father. . . . [H]e takes his [the father's] place in the holy community *[eidah]* of a holy people." Since this designation as replacement of a member of the prayer quorum is clearly open only to males (sons), "therefore daughters cannot recite *kaddish* in the community *[tzibur]*." Their obligation, R. Lau continues, is to honor "their father" by performing good deeds, deeds of lovingkindness and charity, as exemplified by their parents.[86] Reading R. Lau's responsum makes palpable the invisibility of women and the underlying philosophical essentialism used to justify it. Males operate in the public realm; as constituent parts of the prayer quorum, they represent the microcosm of the Jewish community. Women are commanded in prayer but are not officially part of the prayer community.

This ideological invisibility was articulated in a brusque remark by a well-known contemporary rabbi. "Orthodox women should know," he said, "that in synagogue they're welcome guests, but they're guests. Their presence is not required. It's not their role, to modify the service so that they can participate more fully."[87] In contrast to the designated male role in reciting kaddish, the relational sphere, that of deeds of kindness, becomes a primary expression of female connection to God, even when the connections sought concern a woman's grief and sorrow. Women are not part of the community (in all the variant terms R. Lau uses: *eidah, tzibur,* and *am kadosh*), and the designation of "mother" is not used in R. Lau's responsum. Since the son also recites kaddish for his mother (or sister, wife, or daughter), how does he take *her* place within the community?

A more gentle and sensitive depiction of the conflict inherent in this issue is found in a tale by M. Rotenberg titled "The Daughter Who Recited Kaddish."[88] Myrna Steinberg, a young girl, is brought to synagogue by her father to recite kaddish for her recently deceased mother. Both the sexton and the rabbi initially oppose her doing so. The conversations between the father and the synagogue authorities reveal many of the arguments, both for and against, already discussed. For example, the father says, "It seems to me that the legal opinions of the rabbis are often relative. When it is convenient they are regarded as law *[din]*, but other times custom supersedes the law."

The daughter does not miss one kaddish the entire eleven months. The rabbi and sexton defend her to the principal, who does not believe the reasons for her sometimes late arrival at school. Noticing the difficulty the elderly sexton is having with the phylacteries, Myrna instinctively assists him, and continues to do so everyday. At the conclusion of the eleven months, the sexton, on behalf of the congregation, gives her a *Tanakh,* or Hebrew Bible. In presenting it to her, he says:

I wish to thank Rabbi Berger for the gift he has bestowed upon us—Myrna. The soul of her mother has surely merited eternal peace due to her recitation of *kaddish.* May we all be worthy of daughters and granddaughters like Myrna.[89]

The memoir of Myrna ends happily. Unfortunately this is not always the case.

An overview of the halakhic literature finds Orthodox decisors, for the most part, adopting the restrictive interpretations of the Amsterdam case. The legal literature is predominantly negative, despite—and perhaps partially due to—the increase of this practice in many synagogues. Were kaddish not being recited by women, legal decisors would not have to inveigh against its being said in a female voice. As noted by a contemporary sociologist, "the simple reality of women reciting *kaddish* on a regular basis has provoked some reactionary thinkers to heat up the opposition." In doing so, often "they distort facts or resort to perverse arguments."[90] This has been demonstrated in some of the analyses above. Ironically, as this sociologist comments, "the *kaddish* issue has galvanized many Orthodox women to become much more feminist in their outlooks than they otherwise might be." In addition, it has tended to unify Orthodox women with women of other denominations.[91] In some Orthodox synagogues, female friends will accompany to daily services the woman who has decided to recite kaddish. The female voice of kaddish *is* being heard among Orthodox women, although the attempts to silence it are powerful.

A recent posting on the listserv for the Women's Tefillah (prayer) Network eloquently, and sadly, describes the resistance to gender transformation. A woman writes:

I was in my local *mincha* [afternoon service] *minyan* in the hospital near my job [she is a neurologist] saying kaddish for my father. . . . As usual I was the only woman there, but this time nobody else was saying *kaddish*. The men knew me already and knew why I was there. Nevertheless, they would not answer my *kaddish* until the rabbi came up and said it himself. While I was walking out, a chassidic-dressed man came over to me and asked if I could find a male relative to say *kaddish:* "It's better for the *neshamah* [the soul of the deceased]," he said. . . . I told him I disagree, but thanks anyway. He apologized. I felt that he really meant well.[92]

Despite experiences such as this, the gradual transformation of kaddish practices, influenced by articles, studies, and more open discussion relating to women and kaddish, gives subdued hope for the greater acceptance in Orthodox synagogues of grieving mourners who happen to be female.

Conservative Response

The perspective of contemporary Conservative Judaism with regard to women's recitation of kaddish is precisely summarized in a lengthy responsum by R. David Golinkin, director of the Institute of Applied Halakhah of the Conservative movement and dean of its rabbinical school in Jerusalem.[93] The Institute was founded in Jerusalem in 1996

in order to create a library of Conservative/Masorti[94] halakhic literature in Hebrew, English, and other languages which will help foster the study and observance of *halakhah.*

The Institute plans to publish English responsa of Conservative rabbis during past seventy years, the Hebrew responsa of the Va'ad Halakhah [Law Committee] of the Rabbinical Assembly of Israel, Hebrew and English guides to practical *halakhah*, and books of the philosophy of *halakhah*. With the help of Bet Midrash [the Seminary of Judaic Studies in Jerusalem] students and graduates, it will also serve as a center of halakhic research to assist Conservative/Masorti rabbis and laypeople with their halakhic problems.[95]

An Israeli woman affiliated with the Conservative/Masorti movement posed the following query to R. Golinkin:

My mother died a short time ago and I have sought a synagogue in which to say *kaddish*. Some of the Orthodox synagogues say it is prohibited or "it is not customary." Some tell me to recite *kaddish* in a whisper. And others say it is preferable for my husband to say *kaddish* for my mother. Are they correct? Is there a halakhic reason that a woman should not recite mourners' *kaddish* for her parents or other relatives?[96]

The question expresses in broad strokes several of the viewpoints described in the previous section. It notes, for instance, the opinion that a man (in this case the husband) should take upon himself the obligation to recite kaddish for his wife's relative, a practice criticized by R. Blair[97] and other Orthodox decisors. R. Blair alludes to the belief—erroneous, in his judgment—that one can hire a male stranger to say kaddish in lieu of a daughter/wife/sister. This parallels the equally mistaken notion that a man may recite *birkhat hagomel,* the prayer of thanksgiving after overcoming a situation of danger,[98] after childbirth.

R. Golinkin begins his responsum with a summation of the earlier literature. "This question," he begins,

was first asked in the seventeenth century and has been dealt with since by many authorities. . . . Generally one may divide the legal opinions into three categories: those that prohibit, those that are lenient, i.e., permit under certain circumstances, and those that permit women to recite *kaddish*. We will see further on that the first two groups don't find any *internal* halakhic reason to prohibit a woman from reciting mourner's *kaddish;* therefore they ascribe *external* halakhic reasons or *general sociological* concerns. Indeed, the *halakhah* is mandated to deal with sociological factors, but there is nothing in these concerns to preclude a simple permissive ruling *[heter].* In addition, these social concerns from the seventeenth century are no longer relevant (literally: do not exist in our day). On the other hand, there are many good reasons to rely upon the permissive opinions, as will now be discussed.[99] (emphasis in original)

Primary among the category of prohibitors is R. Yair Bachrach. As already discussed, he offers several reasons why women should be permitted to say kaddish.[100] However, his final ruling is to prohibit the practice because it may lead people to think they can create customs as they wish and will weaken the historical traditions. This is surprising, however, as R. Golinkin points out, because mourner's kaddish itself is an innovation, having begun as a new custom in the thirteenth century, during the Crusades. In addition, R. Golinkin argues, customs by definition flow from the people, not the rabbis or religious leadership. "A large percentage of our religious life was created by the people," R. Golinkin asserts, "and the people continue to develop and transform their customs."[101] Examples of such changes, in addition to the mourner's kaddish itself, are Simchat Torah, the celebration of the completion of the annual cycle of reading the Torah on the last day of Succot; *yizkor,* the prayer in commemoration of relatives who have died, recited on the three major festivals and on Yom Kippur; and the many liturgical formulations which have undergone modifications over the centuries. Nevertheless, R. Bachrach's restrictive opinion was quoted by many with approval.

Another prohibitor discussed by R. Golinkin is R. Shimon Frankfurter,[102] who offers a long list of justifications. Among his reasons are *kevod hatzibur* (the honor of the congregation),[103] which in the sources precludes women's reading the Torah in the presence of men; *kol isha,* the idea that a woman's voice is *ervah;*[104] and in the text referring to R. Akiva, interpreting *ben* meaning "son" or "child," in the masculine only. R. Frankfurter's concluding words leave no doubt as to his opinion: "A daughter certainly has no part in kaddish and all this [discussion] is only the piety of fools, a ludicrous idea." The idea of imagining a girl/woman in the synagogue even in a muted active role was clearly beyond R. Frankfurter's ability.

Rabbi Golinkin analyzes other prohibitors as well[105] and concludes that none of the secondary reasons they proffer stand up to careful scrutiny. Their explanations are forced, desperate attempts to disallow the custom at any cost. All the prohibitors, R. Golinkin avers, rely on ancillary sociological reasons to prohibit that which even they acknowledge is indeed halakhically acceptable. This is evident in their language: a woman may not say kaddish "in case someone would think," "because of the possibility of," and so on.

The second group consists of those who permit the female voice of kaddish only under certain circumstances. An example is the responsum of R. Elazar Flekeles,[106] who approved the custom in Prague of girls, aged five or six, saying kaddish in the antechamber of the synagogue after the Book of Psalms. But, he wrote, he never saw—and he strongly opposed—girls/women reciting kaddish in the men's section of the synagogue. This is because, he states, according to the Zohar, a work of the Jewish mystical tradition, "a woman in the house of God is like placing an idol there."[107] Despite his quoting this misogynistic comment in the responsum, R. Flekeles sees nothing inherently wrong with the female voice of kaddish; his objection is to women's recitation in the men's section of the synagogue. His assumption is that a woman is not able to say kaddish from the women's section.[108] The reasons may have been structural or practical, as discussed earlier. The fierce comment taken from the Zohar may also have been occasioned by his opposition to the developing Reform movement in Germany, which did away with synagogue seating separated by sex. R. Golinkin enumerates and analyzes the reasons for leniency given by authorities in this group. Some legal decisors discuss women's obligation to sanctify God's name or draw a distinction between a girl under the age of twelve and one who has already reached puberty. Others say kaddish recitation is permitted at home but prohibited in the synagogue.

Those who neither express reservations nor put restrictions upon their permissive ruling cite both halakhic and sociological reasons. Among such reasons: women are obligated to sanctify God's name; honoring one's parents by saying kaddish is for any child, male or female; mourner's kaddish symbolizes the child's commitment to other mitzvot (commandments) and to the tradition in general; *ben* in the R. Akiva legend means "offspring" or "progeny"; and finally, women, in fact, actually *do* recite kaddish in many places. This is in accordance with the talmudic dictum to "go out and see what the people do."[109] R. Golinkin concludes his responsum by citing the words of Henrietta Szold, using her as a model.[110] "Henrietta Szold," he comments, "recited mourner's kaddish for both her parents. We are convinced that this is the *halakhah* and so it is fitting to act."[111]

R. Golinkin's analysis of women and kaddish manifests the philosophy of halakhah as expressed in Conservative Judaism, which has always asserted the validity and merit of halakhah while simultaneously acknowledging its adaptability. Indeed, without the flexibility built into the legal processes of halakhic development, Judaism would have atrophied. A viable legal system must take historical context into account; otherwise it becomes a historical relic, an anachronism, and not a living, dynamic entity. Expositions of the Conservative philosophy of halakhah have emphasized the tradition's ability to reach out into contemporary circumstances—historical, social, psychological, scientific— and express both the ethic and the practice required for a meaningful Jewish life. Discussions of the attitude of Conservative Judaism towards halakhah emphasize the theophany at Sinai as the "commencement, not the conclusion of Revelation."[112] R. Robert Gordis quotes talmudic texts that demonstrate the nonstatic quality of Jewish law. Of particular relevance is the following well-known passage:

Moses found God adding decorative crowns to the letters of the Torah. Upon asking the reason, the Lawgiver was told, "in a future generation, a man named Akiva ben Joseph is destined to arise, who will derive multitudes of laws from each of these marks." Deeply interested, Moses asked to see him and was admitted to the rear of the house of study where Akiva was lecturing. To Moses' deep distress, however, he could not understand what the scholars were saying and his spirit grew faint within him. Then he heard

Akiva say, "This ordinance that we are discussing is a law derived from Moses on Sinai." Upon hearing this, his spirit revived.[113]

Thus revelation is conceived of as an ongoing process, one in which God and human being are partners. A corollary of this concept is the faith that Torah can "meet all the problems of life, however radically conditions may become altered."[114] R. Gordis's essay, written in 1950, describes in detail the various legal strategies and principles used by halakhah to maintain its flexibility. His views are a continuation of the lengthy study he wrote in 1944 titled "Authority in Jewish Law."[115] His views are affirmed in a more current exposition of the underlying concepts of Conservative Judaism. Published in 1988, *Emet ve-emunah [Truth and Faith]: Statement of Principles of Conservative Judaism* expresses in sixteen concise chapters the foundations upon which the trajectory of Conservative Judaism is based. This statement of principles incorporates many opinions espoused by earlier scholars in the Conservative movement, including R. Gordis. The 1988 statement devotes five pages to halakhah, declaring:

Halakhah consists of the norms taught by the Jewish tradition, how one is to live as a Jew. . . . Since each new age requires new interpretations and applications of the received norms, Halakhah is an ongoing process. It is thus both an ancient tradition, rooted in the experience and texts of our ancestors, and a contemporary way of life, giving value, shape, and direction to our lives. . . . It is, in fact, the primary way in which God and the Jewish people exhibit their love for each other.[116]

In its brief discussion titled "On Women," the statement alludes to the differences of opinion within the movement about "the role of women in Jewish ritual." At the same time, however, it affirms the "dignity of every human being" and the "equality of the sexes." "All the various views on the specifics of women's roles and rights accept Halakhah as the governing framework for Jewish life." R. Golinkin's responsum on women's recitation of kaddish clearly expresses this philosophy. Some maintain, however, despite the analyses offered in 1991 and 1994 by R. David Golinkin,[117] that Conservatism does "not provide a rationale for maintaining it [i.e., halakhah]."[118]

At the same time there is a noticeable gap between theory and practice in Conservative Judaism that is not present in Orthodoxy. While the 1988 statement proclaims that the ideal Conservative Jew be committed to observe the mitzvot and her/his life "pulsate with the rhythms of daily worship,"[119] the laity in general does not approach ideal religious behavior. When I asked a colleague from the East coast about the kaddish practices in her large Conservative synagogue, she responded, "My impression . . . is that, despite the interesting responsa on the subject, the vast majority of Conservative Jews, male and female, do not say kaddish daily either for thirty days or for eleven months."[120]

This concurs with my experience. My parents lived just a half block from a Conservative synagogue, which they sometimes attended, although they usually went to a Young Israel (modern Orthodox) synagogue. But when my father retired in the late 1970s, he would often receive a phone call at 7 A.M. to come to the Conservative synagogue to help make the minyan of ten—despite the fact that the synagogue had over eight hundred members. Perhaps once women were included in the minyan, the male participants were joined by a steady group of female attendees at daily morning services. Even if this were so (the above communication indicates its unlikelihood), that an elderly man had to be called to complete the quorum of ten does not indicate commitment to daily communal prayer.

The rabbi of a large (1,150 families) Midwestern synagogue offers another view of contemporary kaddish practices in Conservative Judaism. The synagogue prayer services (which in the Conservative movement includes women) meet twice a day, morning and late afternoon/evening, with a customary attendance of fifteen to twenty people in the morning, twenty to twenty-five in the evening. Of those who are mourners, the rabbi estimates 40 to 50 percent recite kaddish every day, for either thirty days or eleven months, while 75 percent will say kaddish sporadically, when they are at services, probably on Shabbat or holidays. Many women come to recite kaddish, but in this rabbi's long experience, men are more likely to attend services regularly.[121] A woman in a similarly large Conservative congregation in Maryland reports that she felt a sense of obligation to recite kaddish after recent losses, and that "in [her] Conservative synagogue, it is customary for both men and women to recite kaddish for both thirty days or eleven months. There is a morning and evening minyan daily. . . ."[122]

This variety of views and practices is validated by a recent study about Conservative Judaism.[123] In a section titled "Fostering a More Serious Halakhic Movement," the authors describe the "great ambivalence towards *halakhah*" found in their research among Conservative Jews and in Conservative congregations.[124] Conservative Judaism, it declares, "presents a public face as a *halakhic* movement, but with much private inconsistency."[125] Both leaders and laity must work, the authors proclaim, "to make *halakhah* a living reality in the Conservative Movement."[126] The disparity in observance between the lay and rabbinic leaders and the mass of synagogue members was noted fifty years ago by the sociologist of the American Jewish community, Marshall Sklare,[127] and reaffirmed twenty years later in a study titled *Conservative Judaism: The New Century*.[128] Synagogue members, by and large, tended not to be knowledgeable about the ideology of Conservative Judaism and were far less observant than their leaders.

The battle over the ordination of women, resolved in 1983 after a long, simmering period of conflict, nonetheless united disparate groups within the movement. The commitment of the movement is to remain in the center. Like

Orthodoxy and unlike Reform, halakhah is regarded as indispensable. The view of the ongoing development of halakhah is given more weight and has greater practical repercussions than in most Orthodox responsa. However, the gap between the leaders and the led is still present to a considerable degree. While R. Golinkin's responsum cuts through the restrictive tendencies evident in some recent Orthodox analyses of women and kaddish, and while he enunciates clearly the connection among the sociological, historical, and halakhic, his efforts may be more theoretical than practical unless more Conservative women take on the recitation of kaddish.

Reform Responsa

The reciting of kaddish in Reform Judaism is an option, not an obligation. This is in accordance with Reform ideology, in which the rabbi advises congregants of the tradition and then "helps them come to the place where they are comfortable."[129] That is, in almost all cases Reform Judaism embraces individual choice over ideology, coherence, and discipline. In ritual matters, men and women function equally; thus there is no issue regarding women's recitation of kaddish. Rather, the place of kaddish itself within Reform practice requires examination.

A survey of the relevant responsa begins with discussion at the Breslau Conference in 1846. A motion was made that declared certain mourning practices "contrary to our sentiment and . . . [necessary] to be eliminated." These include *keriah,* the rending of the mourner's garment, usually done prior to burial.[130] The mourner is advised to stay at home for the first three days after internment. The document proclaims the mourning practices in use in traditional Judaism "until now" as "offensive" and incapable of offering solace. "Indeed," it continues, "it is self contradictory to *prescribe* [*sic*] mourning practices."[131] The motion to eliminate these mourning practices passed. While kaddish is not specifically mentioned in this document, the underlying concepts articulated about mourning can be seen to apply as well to the recitation of kaddish. That is, there is no obligation to say kaddish. Indeed, perhaps kaddish is viewed as among those practices which no longer "express properly the sentiments and feelings of the mourner."[132]

Another exchange about mourning occurred at a conference of the Union for Liberal Judaism held in Posen in 1912. After acrimonious debate, various documents were adopted, with the qualification that the final arbiter was to be the conscience of each individual. The section referring to kaddish states:

During the year of mourning . . . of the closest relatives, pious sentiments should be expressed through the old memorial customs, through participation in the worship services with its kaddish prayer, and through pious donations.[133]

Here one is advised to ("should") say kaddish; the frequency of recitation is left to the individual. This reliance on personal proclivity is borne out in anecdotal evidence. In a large Reform synagogue in the Midwest, practice varies among congregants, from those who say kaddish only on the day of burial to the very few who will do so regularly for eleven months. This latter option is of recent origin, since this particular synagogue has had a daily prayer service (in the evening) for only one year. Daily services are unusual in Reform synagogues. This synagogue is 155 years old and has just begun the practice; it is, in addition, the only Reform congregation of the four in the city to do so.[134] Other Reform rabbis confirm similar variations in practice due to individual preferences.[135]

An interesting responsum relating to kaddish was written in 1914 by the scholar and well-known spokesman for Reform Judaism, Kaufmann Kohler.[136] First, R. Kohler reviews the history of kaddish and then deals with the question of standing during its recitation.[137] R. Kohler rules that the custom of standing, based "on the old idea of the mourner reciting *Kaddish* before the congregation still exists" and should be continued if at all possible. In addition, he advocates the congregation's standing as well during the mourner's kaddish as a symbol of its "consideration and sense of sympathy" for the mourner.[138]

More recent responsa also review the history of the development of kaddish and confirm that "[a]t first, only a son recited Kaddish for his dead father," but later, "according to Ashkenazi custom, a daughter was similarly permitted to recite Kaddish."[139] The authors of this 1980 responsum do not refer to the discussions and controversy that followed the proclamation of the Amsterdam case.[140] Citing the rabbinic texts enumerating those seven relatives for whom one would observe mourning, the authors state:

Some would extend this list even further, and certainly, we could agree that it may be so extended as prompted by individual feelings. We would include scholars or people who had particular influence on an individual's life. . . . Kaddish for the dead should be recited at daily services . . . whenever such services are held on a daily basis . . . for a period of twelve months.[141]

Twelve months rather than eleven are specified because Reform Judaism regards the notion of Gehenna as found in the original sources of kaddish as a superstition based on a concession to the fears of ordinary folk.[142] It is interesting to compare this interpretation with the statement of a professor of religion who is a modern Orthodox feminist. Currently reciting kaddish for her father, she writes:

There are two distinct functions to mourning and death rituals. Clearly, there is a sense of aiding the grieving mourners and slowly moving them back into the sphere of a fully active life after an encounter with loss. But there is also a very important Jewish attitude of aiding the *neshama* [soul] of the deceased. *Kaddish* as well as acts of *hesed* [loving-kindness] are performed in order to promote the return of the *neshama* to its source. Doing these acts of prayer and *hesed* will bring merit to the soul/spirit in its ascent to "heaven" [*sic*]. . . . So my *kaddish* is not for my benefit—though I clearly benefit on many levels. But rather I say it as tradition tells me I should, *l'eelui nishmato*, for the elevation of his soul. If in the process I gain prayer time, time to think about my dad and especially a wonderful opportunity to praise God, then I am blessed. And our tradition accepts that and even praises it.[143]

The two interpretations articulated here clearly demonstrate different theologies and views of the purpose and efficacy of kaddish.

Other recent Reform responsa regarding kaddish concern whether one may say kaddish for a convicted criminal who committed a heinous crime or for a pet.[144] The author's conclusion, after analyzing various sources in the Talmud and legal codes, is "*Qaddish* [*sic*] should . . . be recited for an executed or deceased criminal by those normally obligated to do so. The obligations of children do not change through any act committed by the parents." Despite the 1981 date of this responsum, however, Jacob refers twice, both in the beginning and at the conclusion, to the "son's" obligation; in the last paragraph he states, "It remains the responsibility for the son to recite *qaddish* [*sic*] for such an individual as for a righteous mother or father." Women have been ordained in the Reform movement since 1973 and as early as the Breslau Conference of 1846 women were declared required to observe all mitzvot "even though they pertain to a certain time, insofar as these *mitzvot* have any strength and vigor at all for our religious consciousness."[145] The reference to "sons," even though Jacob concludes by noting the "obligations of children," is thus surprising.

Finally, the 1984 discussion of reciting kaddish as part of one's mourning for a much loved pet affirms the affection felt for animals, but declares it vastly different from "the greater love and respect for a human life." At the weekly Friday night services in Reform congregations, the custom is to recite the names of those for whom congregants are mourning, such as, parents within the twelve-month period and other relatives within the designated thirty days, on what is called the "kaddish list." The responsum concludes:

It would be absolutely wrong, and a mockery, to include the name of a pet in the weekly *qaddish* [*sic*] list. Mourners would be shocked and angered to see their father and mother listed alongside a dog or cat. Whatever mourning for a pet may occur should be conducted privately and outside the purview of Judaism.[146]

A recent discussion of kaddish in Reform Judaism is to be found in a volume published in 1979 specifically as a practical guide to Jewish life-cycle events and in the latest edition of the manual for congregational rabbis. The language manifests the current trend in Reform Judaism toward a stronger sense of obligation and an increasing incorporation of ritual and mitzvot. The life-cycle guide states:

It is a *mitzvah* for *mourners* to recite the *Kaddish* prayer in memory of the dead at daily services during *shivah* at home and thereafter in the synagogue. If there is not daily service in the synagogue, mourners should recite *Kaddish* with their families or privately. . . . In Reform Judaism the *mitzvah* of *Kaddish* is incumbent on men and women equally. It is a *mitzvah* to recite *Kaddish* for parents for a year and for other members of the family for a month. As the memory of loved ones inspires the performance of such *mitzvot* as prayer, charity, and study, the dead are immortalized in the lives of those who remember them.[147]

The rabbi's manual offers some of the historical background of kaddish and then declares:

Irrespective of its supposedly mediatorial character, the *Kaddish Yatom* [mourner's *kaddish*] deservedly plays an important part in the religious life of the Jewish people. It expresses faith in the everlasting God in the fact of death and resignation to God's will. It also betokens pious regard for the memory of the departed. As such, it serves to strengthen both the religious sentiment and the ties of family union.

The manual describes the custom of reciting kaddish not only for parents and teachers/religious mentors (the person who has taught one Torah), but also for "grandparents, children, relatives, friends, and even strangers." Children and some relatives, such as siblings, are designated in rabbinic sources, while friends and strangers are not. The text continues:

In congregations which conduct daily worship services, mourners should be encouraged to attend . . . and recite the Kaddish throughout their period of mourning. In congregations which do not conduct daily services, the mourner is expected to recite the Kaddish on Sabbaths and holy days. . . . We would encourage the practice of saying *Kaddish* for all close members of the family.[148]

On the one hand, Reform Judaism declares the recitation of kaddish a mitzvah, thus connoting a sense of obligation. On the other, it "encourages" its observance. The ambiguity of language in these text manifests the equivocal attitudes present within Reform Judaism. First, in general, if X is an obligation (e.g., a mourner reciting kaddish every day), then a demand of equal strength devolves upon the community to provide the means for carrying it out (for example, having daily prayer services). However, as indicated above, daily prayer services in a Reform congregation are very rare. And second, in the teeter-totter of "oblige" and "encourage," Reform leaders are attempting to maintain the emphasis upon individual choice and autonomy, even while they recommend observing a specific religious tradition and try to inculcate a sense of obligation. This ambivalence reflects the tension between community and autonomy within Reform ideology.[149]

The question of the recitation of kaddish as an essential aspect of Jewish mourning practices serves as a paradigm in Reform Judaism for unresolved philosophical questions. The issue here is not gender; women are as free as men to observe or not observe as they wish.[150] But by advocating that each person pick and choose from the tradition as she or he sees fit, is Reform Judaism abandoning the establishment of parameters for normative religious behavior? Pluralism within Reform is surely a desirable goal, but if the boundaries are so very wide, then coherence dissipates. As one leader of the movement wondered, "Is there *any* ideology that is beyond the pale of Reform? Just what is essential to a Reform outlook, what is optional—and what, if anything, is forbidden?"[151] Reform offers all options of observance of ritual, ceremony, and halakhah to women but is often unclear as to what those options are.

The Funeral

With an attention-getting headline in bold print, a 1998 story in the *Jewish Week,* a New York newspaper, proclaimed its subject: "Mourning Glory." The article describes the unusual work of Jennifer Martin, from Queens, New York, ". . . the only Orthodox female funeral director in the city, the country, and, perhaps, the world."[152] Ms. Martin arranges funerals and helps the bereaved, tasks aided by her balance of sensitivity, sympathy, and professionalism. Her appointment has broken down another barrier for Jewish women, who have not usually been in positions of authority with regard to funerals. This has been the case not only in the profession of funeral director but also when women have been official mourners or simply attending a funeral as a friend or relative of the deceased. This section will deal with the general issue of women and funerals and then comment upon four specific practices/roles: the eulogy, the pallbearers, the shoveling of earth on the coffin by those attending the funeral, and the lines *(shurot)* through which the mourners pass when leaving the cemetery.

The general issue arises because of customs developed over the years in different countries regarding women, public ritual, religious authority, and even superstition. This section will deal with the broad issue through examination of a responsum to a question posed in 1986 to the Law Committee of the Masorti, or Conservative, movement in Israel. The committee offered a careful and forthright discussion of the halakhic literature, delineating the areas of concern in both Orthodox and Conservative practice. The question, posed by a rabbi in

Ashkelon, refers to customs prevalent in Israel. However, these practices, as well as their underlying conceptual bases, apply as well to groups within the Orthodox and Conservative communities elsewhere.

The Ashkelon rabbi states:

> In different places in Israel there are various customs whose purpose is to separate men and women at funerals or to prevent the participation of women in the burial service. One custom uses a physical mehitzah [dividing barrier] to separate men and women during the eulogy. Another separates the participants into distinct men's and women's groups in proceeding to the burial place.[153] In a third, the Hevra Kadishah [group responsible for preparing the body for burial and in Israel for the burial as well] keeps even women who are members of the immediate family away from the grave, so that they may not participate in the burial ceremony. In a fourth instance, women are totally excluded from the funeral as well as the burial. These patterns—especially the latter—often generate bitterness on the part of the mourner and real anguish to the female relatives of the deceased. What is the source of these customs? Are they mandatory? May one rule otherwise?[154]

The responsum begins by quoting R. Joseph Caro, author of the *Shulhan Arukh.*[155] R. Caro cites the two places in the Talmud that refer to women and funerals and that make clear that women certainly were participants in funeral rites in the time of the Talmud. The T.B. Sanhedrin 20a states: "In a place where it was the custom for women to walk before the bier, they do so; after the bier they do so." The Jerusalem Talmud in Sanhedrin 2:4 mentions the same custom, recording in addition a dispute about the proper order. The opinion of those who advocate that women precede the men and walk immediately after the dead was based on the claim that "women brought death into the world,"[156] while those who maintained that the men must walk ahead of the women did so to protect "the dignity of Jewish women and prevent men from looking at them." Although R. Caro offers these talmudic sources, he concludes by citing a passage from the Zohar, or *The Book of Splendor,* the central work in the literature of Jewish mysticism.[157] This passage advises that women should be prevented from going to the cemetery because their presence "causes evil in the world."[158]

R. Caro puts aside the clear historical record of the Talmud as to female participation in funerals in favor of a mystical source with far less authority in terms of legal precedent. While the influence of mystical thought on R. Caro in sixteenth-century Safed was clearly very powerful, that many later decisors, or aharonim, followed his opinion is puzzling. Their connection to Kabbalah, Jewish mysticism, was undoubtedly less intense than that of R. Caro. But they may have followed his view because it fit the historical/social/political circumstances of the time[159] or was accepted as authoritative due to his stature.

Those who adhere to R. Caro's view of women at funerals divide into two groups. Several permit women to walk after the bier but not to enter the cemetery, while the larger number prevents women from doing either. One authority writes that the true reason underlying the stringency of the Zohar was to keep men and women separated due to possible *hirhur,* or improper thoughts. The actual statement in the text as cited by R. Caro, this person avers, was simply a strategy to convince the ordinary folk.[160]

Some aharonim claimed that women don't go to the cemetery when they are in the state of *niddah,* or menstrual impurity,[161] as additional validation of R. Caro's position. However, until the time of R. Caro, no source mandated separation of the sexes during the eulogy,[162] and the Zohar itself only cautions the men not to gaze at the women during the funeral and actual burial; no prohibition is involved and women's participation in funerals and burials is assumed. Indeed, when a contradiction exists between a source in the Babylonian Talmud and the Zohar, the legal ruling must follow the Talmud, which presumes that fear of sexual arousal was not an issue at a time of grief and mourning. In addition, no source prior to the nineteenth century connects participation at a funeral and burial with *niddah.* This is so even though certain fears and superstitions found a place in the legal literature.

There are two other reasons to reject R. Caro's view. First, an individual may choose the stricter opinion of the Zohar over the Talmud but cannot coerce the public to follow this stringency. Second, the customs that limit female participation compel women to violate three talmudic principles. First, if one sees a funeral taking place and doesn't join the procession in order to honor the dead, one is guilty of *loeg larash,* or "scoffing at the unfortunate." Surely if this is true of a stranger, it applies to female relatives and friends of the deceased. Second, the principle of *kevod haberiyot,* or "the honor accorded all creatures of God," supersedes both biblical commandments and rabbinic enactments.[163] How much more so does it apply to customs deriving from a superstitious core? Lastly, the very purpose of the *shomrim* (those who stay with the body prior to burial), as well as of the eulogy and other aspects of funeral rites, is *kevod hamet,* "honoring the dead," giving honor to the vessel that held the soul. To prevent the full participation of female mourners, relatives, and friends not only offends the living but also dishonors the dead.[164]

Thus the only restrictive custom for which there is a strong basis, a source in the Talmud, is the separation of men and women while escorting the coffin to the burial place. According to some, its origin may be based on Greek custom.[165] Whatever its cultural roots, however, Jewish tradition claims this separation as custom and not as either commandment or obligation. Even this custom, the Masorti document concludes, may be overridden by the ethical principles of "honoring God's creatures" and "honoring the dead."[166]

As this responsum demonstrates through its thorough analysis of classical rabbinic sources, the Conservative movement gives women a full and equal role in all funeral practices, be they the mourners, friends, or relatives of the deceased. Similar principles inform funerals coordinated through modern or centrist Orthodox congregations. In more right-wing Orthodox groups, however, where separation of the sexes is often de rigueur even for social gatherings, the views of the aharonim hold sway.

A contemporary compendium relating to Reform Judaism and halakhah also offers a survey of the sources and discusses R. Caro's use of the Zohar.[167] The author concludes by citing decisors who not only allow, but even encourage, female participation in funeral processions and burial services. Among them are R. Jacob ben Samuel, head of the religious court in Susmir in the seventeenth century,[168] and R. Isaac bar Sheshet of Algeria in the nineteenth century, who, like R. Caro, are Sephardi (and therefore follow the customs of Jews from the Iberian Peninsula). The latter ruled that if it is a custom in a certain locale "for men and women to stand together during a funeral, the members of the burial society cannot prevent them from doing so."[169] The author of this collection (interpretations of traditional rabbinic sources from a Reform perspective) concludes by stating, "Anyone who believes in this superstition about women and the angel of death in the cemetery may act accordingly in his or her private life, but may not impose such customs on others who reject these superstitions."[170]

In all branches of Judaism except right-wing Orthodox, women's increasingly public role in general society has influenced her more public role in Jewish funeral practices. Women—and not only women rabbis—often eulogize the deceased, are honored as pallbearers, and share equally with male participants the task—part of *kevod hamet,* or "honoring the dead"—of shoveling the earth over the coffin. Halakhah requires that the community bury its dead. Thus develops the mitzvah of covering the coffin with earth until the coffin is no longer visible. Called *tzurat hakever* (the earth taking on the shape of the grave), this practice constitutes fulfillment of the mitzvah of burial. Men, historically, were the ones who so honored the dead. At some funerals people quietly stand in line, awaiting a turn with the two or more shovels; the silence and earnestness are an elegaic tribute to the deceased. Women may hesitate to take the shovel, accustomed to standing back and not participating. But often one or two women taking their turns allows others to see the possibility as actual and encourages greater female participation.

In Israel, the issues relating to women and mourning are complicated by the dominance of Orthodox burial societies, which impose their authority on all aspects of the funeral. While the Israeli Supreme Court ordered the Ministry of Religious Affairs to permit pluralistic non-Orthodox ceremonies, only one—in Beersheva—is operational at this time. The burial societies generally interpret halakhah stringently; female mourners are often not permitted at the graveside, are prevented from reciting kaddish, covering the coffin with earth, or walking through the lines to receive words of comfort. In Jerusalem, for instance, there are thirteen Orthodox burial societies. Women's participation, they claim, cannot be accommodated.

Public and Private Spheres

The overview of responsa literature in Orthodox, Conservative, and Reform Judaism clearly demonstrates how perspectives regarding sexuality and gender contribute to decisions about women's recitation of kaddish. Traditional Jewish law treats men and women in mourning identically in many ways. Both are required according to halakhah to exhibit public and private mourning. During shiva, for instance, they are expected to wear the garment torn at the funeral, to cover mirrors, to avoid bathing and sexual intimacy, to sit on low stools, and to avoid dealing with business or professional matters as well as such daily home-based needs as shopping and food preparation.[171] The mourner is freed from mundane activities in order to focus on grieving. This means that all household tasks are taken over by non-mourners, who provide meals and often child care. For a month following the funeral, it is customary for neither men nor women to cut their hair; for twelve months, participation in joyous celebrations (with some exceptions) or live musical performances is prohibited for both females and males. But with regard to recitation of kaddish, as has been demonstrated above, men and women are treated differently. This difference is most apparent in Orthodox Judaism, but can manifest itself in some Conservative synagogues as well. In Reform Judaism, since saying kaddish is a personal choice rather than a religious obligation, and since men and women participate equally in all ritual, the practical implications of how one expresses mourning, as described above, vary greatly from those discussed in Orthodox and Conservative practices.

A central aspect of reciting kaddish is the public affirmation of the mourner's honor and devotion to the deceased, as well as to Jewish tradition and peoplehood. The unfriendly, even hostile, attitudes at times encountered in Orthodox (and some Conservative) synagogues, therefore, come as a brusque shock to women sufficiently committed to attend daily services and especially vulnerable due to their recent loss. As reported at the beginning of this chapter and in a recent sociological study of the Orthodox community, changes are occurring, but reactions differ from community to community.[172]

This example stems from personal experience. After my mother's death in 1982, I one day entered the synagogue (where I came early every morning to recite kaddish) to find painters busy at work. The (male) quorum had moved to the social hall. In an effort to be sensitive to the synagogue practices, I went to the back and stood behind a table. But this gesture was insufficient for the rabbi, who had been unhappy with my presence since I had begun to attend daily morning services. While I stood there—and without looking at or saying anything to me—he ordered the men to pile folding chairs on the table. The pain and humiliation I felt was deep—"like an animal in a cage," I lamented to my husband. The rabbi's behavior demonstrated not only insensitivity, opposition to my commitment, and an abuse of authority, but also a palpable sense of male ownership of public religious turf. "The Orthodox synagogue," as a (male) friend has remarked, "is the last men's club, and even a Supreme Court ruling can't change it."

Indeed, the examination of Orthodox responsa discloses the clear dichotomy of public space (in the synagogue) as male, and private space (in the home) as female. The public/private dichotomy is based on an essentialist foundation. "Views of woman's 'natural' differences from man justify a status quo that divides work, psychological qualities, and family responsibilities into 'his' and 'hers,'" states a contemporary psychologist.[173] She continues: "Those who are dominant have an interest in maintaining their difference from others, attributing those differences to the 'harsh dictates of nature,' and obscuring the unequal arrangements that benefit them."

In her fascinating study, this psychologist, Carol Tavris, investigated the question of male and female differences. She summarizes her findings in the following table:

Do Men and Women Differ?

Where the differences aren't	Where the differences are
Attachment, connection	Care-taking

Cognitive abilities
  Verbal, mathematical,[a] reasoning,
  rote memory, vocabulary,
  reading,[b] etc.
	Communication
	  interaction styles, uses of talk,
	  power differences

Dependency	Emotions
	  Contexts that produce them
	  Forms of expression
	  "Feminization of love"
	  "Feminization of distress"

Emotions Likelihood of feeling them	
Empathy	Employment, work opportunities

Moods and "moodiness"	Health and medicine
	  medication and treatment
	  longevity differences

Moral reasoning	
Need for achievement	Income

Need for love and attachment

Need for power

Nurturance[c]

Pacifism, belligerence
(e.g., depersonalizing enemies)

Sexual capacity, desire, interest

Verbal aggressiveness, hostility

Care-taking

Communication
interaction styles, uses of talk,
power differences

Emotions
Contexts that produce them
Forms of expression
"Feminization of love"
"Feminization of distress"

Employment, work opportunities

Health and medicine
medication and treatment
longevity differences

Income

Life-span development
effects of children
work and family sequence

Life narratives

Power and status at work, in relationships,
in society

Reproductive experiences

Reproductive technology and its
social/legal consequences

"Second shift": housework, child care,
family obligations

Sexual experiences and concerns

Violence, public and intimate

Weight and body image

---

a. Males excel at highest levels of math performance; in general population, females have slilght advantage.
b. Males are more susceptible to some verbal problems. However, many alleged sex differences seem to be an artifact of referral bias: More boys are *reported* for help than girls, but there are no sex differences in the *actual* prevalence of dyslexia and other reading disabilities (see Shaywitz et al., 1990).
c. As a capacity; in practice, women do more of the actual care and feeding of children, parents, relatives, friends.

Tavris's research relates the public/private polarity to issues of power. Meaningful differences between women and men are far more frequently related to context than to one's essential "nature" or "personality." "Context," Tavris explains,

includes everything in the environment of a person's life: work, family, class, culture, race, obligations, the immediate situation . . . the likelihood of experiencing violence and discrimination, access to health care and education, legal status, and so on. These factors not only affect sex differences . . . they are responsible for differences and conflicts *within* each gender.[174]

While the list in the left-hand column is the subject of study and dispute, as Tavris's chart demonstrates, the significant differences turn up in the right-hand column, in which the persistent disparities of income, power, and family obligations are listed. Men and women exhibit flexible capacities in varied contexts. This experiential observation is much more valuable in constructing our inner and outer worlds than the question as to what women or men "essentially" are. Male and female contexts or cultures are not "separate but equal." Rather, "they are vastly unequal in power, resources, and status."[175] The notions of public and private are an important factor in these divergent cultures.

Women were (are) restricted in the recitation of kaddish, first and foremost, because the synagogue, until the twentieth century, was entirely a male space. As the survey of traditional responsa demonstrates, sensitive rabbinic decisors struggled with how—and sometimes whether—to accommodate the ordinarily private, female voice of grieving within the public, male turf of traditional synagogues.

Orthodox Jews may be divided into three categories.[176] The first, often working-class Eastern European immigrants, were not particularly learned in Judaism. But Orthodoxy was the tradition they knew, the way they practiced tradition and identified religiously; they were, one might say, Orthodox by default. The second category, modern Orthodox Jews, demonstrates the viability of halakhah for contemporary Jewish life. Modern Orthodoxy seeks a synthesis, an integration, a coalescence.[177] The *Torah umadda* (Torah and general knowledge) emblem of Yeshiva University expresses the ideology of this group, which also seeks to find commonality with all other Jews. The third category is comprised of sectarians who create a subcommunity that isolates them not only from modern culture but also from non-Orthodox Jews.

The modern Orthodox articulates conceptions of gender and the public/private dichotomy that explain some of the responsa about women and kaddish analyzed here. This centrist community, as it is often called, within Orthodoxy attempts to challenge certain contemporary values and assumptions, even while subscribing to many modern attitudes and practices. It incorporates modern conceptions of feminism, pluralism, and rationalism at the same time as it strongly adheres to traditional ways. The responsa of R. Blair, R. Aaron Soloveitchik, and R. Henkin articulate this balancing act; those of R. Fink and R. Lau are more sectarian. The former find a place—even a welcoming place—for women within the public, male space of the synagogue. The latter demand male exclusivity, using reasons of "tampering with . . . customary practices" (R. Fink) and alleged sexuality, or *kol isha* (R. Lau), to banish the female mourner. When the place of public prayer is viewed as exclusively male, women can only be intruders or guests, welcomed or not.[178] The modern Orthodox viewpoint can also reveal an essentialism that R. Ephraim Buchwald deftly describes:

Men and women have roles and basic areas of responsibility. That's incontrovertible. Nothing can be used to rationalize that away. The woman basically is ascribed the responsibility for the raising and nurturing of children. The men are assigned the responsibility for the cognitive education of the children.[179]

Although articulated by a spokesperson presumably espousing a centrist perspective, these words express rigid gender roles. Roles are "incontrovertible"; "raising and nurturing" the children are a woman's—not a parental—task, and that task *excludes* "cognitive education" (emphasis mine).

Sometimes the viability of this religious worldview is articulated as an allegiance to tradition and community allied with a compatibility to the individualism of the dominant culture. If such a partnership is to be a synthesis rather than a compartmentalization,[180] integration on the theological/philosophical level must occur. The religious ideology of Orthodoxy must both reflect and support the reality, the lived experiences, of being a traditional Jew within, rather than isolated from, our culture. The conceptual move toward such a synthesis is articulated with unusual clarity by the philosopher Dr. Tamar Ross.

In a series of public lectures and published articles,[181] Dr. Ross characterizes Orthodox feminists who tend to blur the public/private dichotomy as a group that regards "the particular conception of the nature of woman used as a premise for various *Halakhot* [as] . . . the function of a sociological situation that is gradually becoming obsolete, and cannot be equated with Absolute Truth or some eternal norm."[182] Orthodox antifeminists, in contrast, generally "confirm the direct relationship between the two, which is why sociological or historical explanations of Halakhic positions are often regarded as sacrilege" and rabbinic sages of all generations are seen, somehow, as operating in an historic vacuum. This view presumes halakhic discourse as "hermetically sealed against passing environmental influence."[183]

Examples of this view abound. A 1997 essay by Mayer Twersky is replete with antifeminist declarations. "Any attempt to blur these [gender] differences inevitably diverts men and women from the path of God," Twersky proclaims.[184] The feminine role is usually "private and supporting," he continues, and "[the woman] cannot be energized by the excitement and acclaim of public life," since her life is characterized by "modesty and self-effacement."[185] Twersky's tone becomes venomous when describing the ideas of Orthodox feminists, who use "rampant, misleading rhetoric" and fail to realize the "unbridgeable chasm," the irreconcilability of Torah norms and "secular" feminism."[186] Should we, he inquires, "presumptuously challenge the provision which disqualifies women from positions of formal religious authority? . . ." While Twersky asserts the "divinely authentic" restriction of women in the public religious sphere, Ross eschews the simplistic approach of a defensive attitude and offers a subtle, nuanced explication of halakhic discourse as contextual. "I do not believe," she writes,

there is any necessary connection between the time-bound features of the Torah and its eternally binding nature. Thus, I do not believe that the sanctity of tradition depends upon proving that it has been hermetically sealed against outside influences. . . . Traditionally, the nature of Torah has been expressed so as to include both a dynamic and a static element.[187]

Ross puts forth a concept of revelation as the unfolding of the divine within history,[188] delineating a conceptual framework rooted in the writings of R. Abraham Isaac Kook, the first Ashkenazi Chief Rabbi of modern Israel (then called Palestine).[189] R. Kook, in contrast to R. Sofer's pronouncement prohibiting anything new, maintained that the new must be embraced, but selectively, in such a way that it is integrated into and indeed enhances the religious perspective.[190] Ross describes a "stringently Orthodox [haredi] society" in which women's roles have sometimes been so transformed that they no longer readily fit the image found in rabbinic sources themselves.[191]

The lives of many Orthodox women—not only among the centrists—belie the rigid defense of tradition exemplified by Twersky's essay. The public sphere has not been exclusively male for a long time. Women *are* leaders and holders of power and authority. There is no going back in history. In some Orthodox families and institutions, the boundaries of public/private may be blurred; in its ideology, however, as exemplified by the responsa on kaddish and analyses of issues relating to funeral practices, Orthodoxy retains the public/private split. The tension between feminist and Orthodox norms continues.

The move of women into the public sphere of Jewish practice is more evident within the Conservative movement. On the issue of separate or mixed pews, the preeminent rabbinics scholar, R. Louis Ginzburg (a descendant of the Vilna Gaon), "told a congregation in Baltimore that if 'continued separation of family units during services presents a great danger to its spiritual welfare, the minority ought to yield to the spiritual need of the majority.'"[192] This argument gives spiritual need "priority over the legal tradition, which from later rabbinic times had separated men and women during prayer, [193] thus delineating a subjective measurement as grounds for halakhic transformation.

By 1948, separate seating was almost universally replaced by mixed pews in Conservative synagogues. [194] As of 1997, almost all synagogues affiliated with the movement counted women in the minyan (83 percent), and had women leading the services (78 percent) as well as reading from the Torah (82 percent). [195] In addition, almost 80 percent of Conservative synagogues have had a woman serve as president within the last two decades. [196] Though the issues relating to gender egalitarianism in religious ritual remain a source of conflict within a small minority of congregations, "by and large, by the close of the 1990s, egalitarianism was the norm in Conservative synagogues." Following decades of strife focused on women's ordination, gender egalitarianism has triumphed. [197]

Interestingly, however, "as it has become normative, gender egalitarianism has lost its association with lenient stands on other matters of Jewish law." [198] This is an important development, indicating that gender equality need not erode, and indeed in this instance has not eroded, commitment to the tradition and the centrality of Jewish law. Ideologically, this commitment remains strong, despite the hiatus both in knowledge and practice between Conservative religious leaders and most of the laity. [199] The view of halakhah that prevails, however, is one in which cultural custom is seen as a driving force with regard to the role of women generally and in the public arena. "[W]e err," writes a scholar of the movement,

if we try to decide issues concerning the status of women in Jewish law on the basis of the texts and legal arguments that have come down to us because they were all *post-facto* reflections of what was determined by custom in the first place. [200]

Prominent Conservative rabbi and scholar Robert Gordis, who traces the principles of change within the contemporary Conservative movement back to its roots in the nineteenth century, offers another approach to confirming the legitimacy of women in the public sphere. The "positive-historical Judaism" of Zacharias Frankel emphasized Judaism as the result of historical development, in which reverence toward and understanding of the rabbinic tradition would lead to organic growth. Thus change would come about slowly, not motivated by convenience or an ill-considered love of progress but firmly rooted in allegiance to Judaic principles and values. [201] R. Gordis applies Frankel's strategies of religious change to the question of gender equality and uses egalitarianism as a normative standard against which halakhah itself must be measured and compared. [202] In his study regarding the ordination of women, R. Gordis declares,

To defend such a principle [the exclusion of women as witnesses] today is, for most people, morally repugnant and sexist. To bring Halakhah in this respect into conformity with *our* ethical standards constitutes part of the unfinished business of contemporary Judaism.[203] (emphasis in original)

This is in clear contrast to the conceptual framework articulated by most Orthodox thinkers, who usually do not openly acknowledge custom or cultural influence and would regard as unacceptable the notion that an ethical principle within general society not only can but indeed ought to affect halakhic change. Conservative Judaism, despite continuing dissent within some segments, acknowledges that the new sensitivities regarding relationships between the genders and the increasingly public role of women within the Conservative movement are a legitimate development of the tradition.

Reform thinkers are well aware of the impact of outside forces on religious development. "Sometimes," Walter Jacob states, changing attitudes toward women in Reform Judaism "was a reaction to external pressures; at other times internal motivations were at work."[204] Jacob sees Reform Judaism as responding to the dramatic changes in the views of gender over the last two centuries since its inception. These changes were "impossible to accommodate within the framework of Jewish tradition."[205] The 1845 rabbinic conference in Frankfurt referred to committee the motion that women be considered equal to men with regard to all religious obligations. The motion was not passed at the 1846 Breslau conference, although it was recommended, together with other suggestions for change pertaining to women. At the 1865 rabbinic conference in Pittsburgh, Kaufmann Kohler asserted that "Reform Judaism has pulled down the screen from the gallery behind which alone the Jewish woman of old was allowed to take part in divine service" and that in all moral and religious spheres, "equal voice [be given] to woman with men."[206]

Two ideas permeate this pronouncement and its subsequent actualization in the practical realm. First, it makes the assumption that Jewish women within rabbinic tradition functioned unequally on the moral level. This premise, however, goes against all halakhic formulations, in which men and women are, and always have been, considered equal in relation to civil law and punishment.[207] Moral equality is derived from being created in the image of God; moral obligations devolve upon men and women without distinction. That which has been unequal, as has been shown, is agency within the public sphere of religious leadership and ritual. Might Kohler have been alluding to a concept close to that articulated by Robert Gordis decades later, that the ethic of woman as private and not public person is itself lacking? Although this seems unlikely, as R. Gordis's statement is based on a view of gender developed over more than a century after Kohler, it remains difficult to narrow down Kohler's definition of "moral." Second, despite the theoretical equality accorded to women so early on, actual equality in the public sphere comes decades later. While mixed seating in the synagogue was de rigueur from 1846,[208] the public debate on women's ordination did not begin until 1922, at which time Jacob Lauterbach's responsum recommending against female ordination carried, despite lively debate. Regina Jonas received Reform ordination in Germany at the end of 1935 and died in Auschwitz in 1944. It was not until 1973 that Sally Preisand was ordained by Hebrew Union College.

During these decades, did women in Reform synagogues recite kaddish and participate equally in funerals? Certainly they were part of the prayer quorum. To what extent women—and men—said kaddish following the death of a relative is difficult to ascertain. While funeral practices may have varied, as in the case of much prescribed religious behavior in Reform Judaism, individual choice took priority over obligation.

Despite advances in all denominations, the progress is uneven with regard to acceptance of women into the spheres of Jewish public religious life.[209] Within the broader Jewish community in North America, only about 25 percent of presidents of Jewish federations are women, and these tend to be concentrated in smaller communities. Women who work professionally in Jewish communal service are often not remunerated equally when compared with their male counterparts. Few female rabbis occupy senior positions in large congregations. Both professionals and laypeople often are uncomfortable with a woman—no matter her qualifications—in a senior executive position or as plenary speaker at large gatherings such as the General Assembly of Jewish Federations.[210] The stance toward greater public roles for women in Jewish life, both professionally and in terms of religious practices, is still unfolding.

Community and Autonomy

She was buried in Israel [writes the novelist Tova Reich of her mother], and, as is the custom [in Israel], we put her in the ground, coffinless, wrapped only in her shroud, and after her body eased itself into its grave as into a familiar bed, and after we covered her with the earth . . . the men, in the Orthodox way, formed two lines for the mourners to pass between and receive the traditional words of consolation. I, too, began to make my way between these lines until a gray-bearded sage redirected me. "Only the men!" he cried. "Only the men!" He was absolutely right, of course. I could not be comforted.[211]

The daughter who, on one level, "could not be comforted" anyway, was not even permitted by this *chevra kadisha* (burial society) to receive words of consolation from her family and friends in the public arena of the cemetery. Her grief was to remain private, unacknowledged, there on the very ground that now embraced her mother's lifeless body. So prevalent is the notion that some mourning rites, including kaddish, are exclusively male prerogatives that

Supreme Court Justice Ruth Ginsburg referred in a 1997 interview to daughters being prohibited from the recitation of kaddish.[212]

Except in stringently Orthodox circles, such a prohibition (whether against reciting kaddish or receiving words of consolation at the cemetery) affects a small number of women.[213] But the underlying concept—that a woman's femaleness can erase the comfort due her as an individual—cannot be reconciled with Jewish concepts of human value; that conflict is part of the struggle found in classic rabbinic sources. Woman as person, individual, and human being—as self-directed, separate, and autonomous—is often submerged into the matrix of community in a manner not required of men. The Jewish community has for centuries been a powerful aspect of Jewish living, whether one thinks of the medieval *kehillah*[214] or its derivatives in post-Enlightenment times, which include the federations of the contemporary organized American Jewish community. The notion of "community" refers not only to its structured social component but also to its structured religious aspect. Traditionally, women were not part of the official prayer community, the microcosm of *klal Yisrael* (the Jewish people). Not only did men represent the Jewish community in prayer, but they also dominated the power structures of its societal aspects. Female presidents of Jewish federations here in the United States, as noted earlier, are still unusual.[215] Yet despite the pervasive denial to women of positions of leadership, the viability of the broader community has often been seen as based on female power as exercised in very specific and significant roles: those that articulate and foster intimacy, nurturance, feelings, family relations. The community/autonomy polarity therefore points to the disparity between women enmeshed within familial structures and women operating as individuals—part of the larger communal structure of power and leadership.

The autonomous person would not usually be denied words of consolation. In the example cited above, sexuality precludes consideration as a person, and the woman is coerced into a private role, the arena designated as appropriate by the religious community. She is not viewed as autonomous, able to determine her own destiny and direct her own development into the self she wishes to be. Her femaleness creates the obstacles that limit her journey. In advocating that girls and women seek to form a deep-rooted sense of autonomy, some theories of psychology caution that autonomy as commonly understood may be seen as a quality drawn from descriptions of male development. The concept itself may need fine-tuning when applied to women.

The writings of Jean Baker Miller provide a good example of such an admonition. In an early work, Dr. Miller, commenting on various studies of psychoanalysis, advises that "notions about women's growth have been limited [by] conceptions derived from male notions of the meaning of maturity."[216] Her later work further explicates this notion. "We need a terminology," she writes, that is not based on inappropriate carryovers from men's situation. Even a word like *autonomy,* which many of us have used and liked, may need revamping for women. It carries the implication—and for women therefore the threat—that one should be able to pay the price of giving up affiliations in order to become a separate and self-directed individual.[217] (emphasis in original)

Indeed, Dr. Miller argues, women "are . . . seeking something more complete than autonomy as it is defined for men, a fuller, not a lesser ability to encompass relationships to others, simultaneously with the fullest development of oneself."[218]

The goal is to foster a society that in turn permits both the development of self and mutuality of personhood for all. In such a society, no women would be denied words of consolation nor have to run an obstacle course in order to recite kaddish. That women as autonomous persons who are part of the Jewish community may, can, and should recite kaddish would be expected and accepted practice. Dr. Miller supports a transformation and restructuring of the nature of relationships so that both partners pursue self-determination as well as nurturing and the cultivation of affect. Male-female relationships have been so structured as to deflect women away from cognizance of what they want and therefore the fulfillment of whatever that is. Women need power for themselves, not necessarily power over others; the existence of the latter has been the bane of women throughout history. Women need power as a "capacity to implement."[219] Because women's nature has been determined by others over centuries of history, developing autonomy means not only fostering individual growth but also initially becoming cognizant of what aspects of the self have yet to grow.

Dr. Miller's observations are echoed in later studies of scholars in other disciplines. The writer and literary historian Carolyn Heilbrun recalls a description she believes aptly applies to women: a "reiterated impersonation." "Is there a better description of women's situation today?" she inquires.

Autonomy for women has sometimes been denigrated by those who see no profit in women's imitation of the male scramble for power at the cost of loving. But [these words, i.e., "reiterated impersonation"] make clear that the danger is not of imitation of men, but of women's internalization of men's signals and institutions, so that woman appears to preserve herself in preserving man's "signals" and institutions.[220]

The notion of a "self" developed in the seventeenth and eighteenth centuries and was both created by and reflected in the philosophical and political theories of the time. Jewish law, with its strong sense of the individual, has always placed the individual within the matrix of community, creating a necessary and supportive dialectic between them. But, much as in a marriage there must be constant realignment between intimacy and separateness,[221] the female self moves between community and autonomy. When the woman has internalized the messages of the male community and those signals form part of her own sense of self, she may become cognizant of possible ambiguities and risks. Then she needs to identify those aspects of self that exist separate from others' signals and move forward to cultivate them.

I recall, in the late 1970s, being at a funeral in Jerusalem at which the burial society forbade the women from approaching the grave at the cemetery. The woman I was with said to me, "Let's go," and we simply walked over and stood quietly with the mourners. How much more so must women break free from those who would deign to "permit" or "forbid" the recitation of kaddish for a loved one. The dialectic of self and religious authority is a palpable process in which movement is never-ending. One might describe autonomy as the position of strength from which a person develops and enters into relationships. That is, autonomy is the process of self-directed individuation leading toward healthier relationships, rather than a self-reliance strengthened by the diminishing of affiliation.[222]

Anthropological studies, as well as theories in psychology, especially those based on the work of Melanie Klein,[223] affirm that

[s]ocieties that do not elaborate the opposition of male and female and place positive value on the conjugal relationship and the involvement of both men and women in the home seem to be the most egalitarian in terms of sex roles. When a man is involved in domestic labor, in child care and cooking, he cannot establish an aura of authority and distance. And when public decisions are made in the household, women may have a legitimate public role.[224]

Historically, women have functioned as the unseen but all-important threads that interweave and bind together the disparate functions of the public community. Woman's identity as private person and enabler has been so enmeshed in community that affirming the self—her own autonomous, self-directed self—has seemed a betrayal of communal ideals. It is only when men *and* women are committed to *both* aspects of human development, that neither femaleness—nor maleness—will be an obstacle to the full expression of one's grief at the death of a loved one and the desire to find comfort within the religious community and its established practices.

Such a transformation of social and cultural constructs is a long and arduous process. This is clearly seen, quite paradoxically perhaps, by examining the view of women in the ideology of the early-twentieth-century Reform thinker, Kaufmann Kohler. While Kohler articulated the spiritual and moral equality of woman and argued against segregated seating in the synagogue, as well as for full female membership in the congregation, female presence in the public space of the synagogue did not lead to the greater religious participation he had anticipated. He laments, in 1906, that "the great revival" of the synagogue had not yet occurred.[225] Yet despite the Reform woman's altered public role, Kohler insisted upon seeing her through a very traditional, culturally rooted prism. "A woman," he states, "without tenderness, without gentleness, without the power of self-suppression to an almost infinite degree, is a creature so anomalous that she cannot fail to do enormous harm, both to her own sex and the other. . . . She becomes a devil in disguise!"[226] The stereotype, as well as the strong language, is surprising, perhaps even shocking. Surely this is not the Reform Judaism that is so familiar; the movement that prides itself on egalitarianism! Yet Kohler's words, part of an article on Esther published in 1900, are of their time. They bespeak the reluctance to accept new views of women that challenge the public/private and community/autonomy polarities. Yes, according to Kohler a woman is not required to sit separately in synagogue, but she still reigns as the center of the family, the manager of the home, the caretaker of the children; she remains a private person characterized by "self-suppression." The vagaries of public life would endanger not only her, but also the established structure of society.

Some contemporary Orthodox responsa about the female voice of kaddish echo Kohler's strong language and manifest a similar defensive posture. In different ways, R. Sofer, R. Lau, R. Uziel, and R. Fink demonstrate the fear of women as separate, autonomous individuals who feel comfortable in the public arena and with the use of sexuality, such as *kol isha* and men's presumably uncontrollable lust, as reasons to restrict women. "Using Modesty as a Gag," the subject heading of an e-mail posting, states the issue succinctly. The writer declares, "There is nothing in my shape or bodily functions which need prevent me from being close to God in the ways prescribed for all Jews—not only for the men—at Sinai."[227]

The journey toward autonomy—the right to define oneself and one's modes of expressions within one's choice of individual or group affiliation, or community—is a task the modern Jewish woman has already begun. Whether or not she decides to recite kaddish or how she chooses to participate at a funeral, it is clear that "the reinterpretation of history and myth is one of the most powerful means women have of demonstrating their historic fitness to play *all* [emphasis mine] the roles in the human drama."[228]

Epilogue

In 1975, after three years of part-time study begun when our children were five, seven, and nine years old, I received my M.A. degree in philosophy. Sharing this news with my mother-in-law brought an unexpected comment.[1] "Oh Rochel," she enthused, "you think just like a man!" Even in those early days of consciousness-raising, I had developed a sense of humor about sexist assumptions and comments. "It's a good thing we're on the phone," I said to my husband; "she can't see me laughing." Such strict gender divisions—the influence of abstract theory upon real-world dynamics—in the Jewish world were held not only by some rabbis[2] but also by ordinary people. In this case, the ordinary person was an American-born statistical typist, a high-school graduate very involved in the Jewish community of Boston, and the mother of three, one of whom happened to be my husband. In her home, the kitchen was solely her domain; even I was refused entry. Essentialist notions of gender were pivotal in her thinking, despite the salary she earned.

This volume has surveyed the rabbinic literature regarding birth and death and how that corpus of work deals with women as those who sometimes bring forth life and sometimes mourn its end. It has analyzed contemporary manifestations of the classic texts as found in general discussions as well as the responsa of Orthodox, Conservative, and Reform Judaism. The conceptual apparatus of the analysis—gender, sexuality, public/private spheres, and community/autonomy—has provided a frame of reference that demonstrates not only the patriarchal assumptions undergirding the classic texts, but also some of the possibilities for moving beyond them. Despite their androcentric impetus, the texts remain the multilayered repository of Jewish communal, historical memory. History cannot be erased; rather, the ongoing processes of interpretation give new insights into the texts. Historical circumstances may change, but the principles of the tradition remain living and vital.

The foregoing chapters have examined aspects of birth and death as they affect women in the life-cycle events of Judaism. They have shown that the

161

tradition, while neither intrinsically misogynistic nor hostile to women, clearly represents the predominance of the male perspective. "[R]abbinic Jewish culture did not base its gender asymmetry on an instinctive, atavistic fear of women's bodies or sexuality," one scholar claims.[3] Another states that to assert either that the rabbis despised women or "loved and respected" them is inaccurate—and simplistic.[4] As this volume has demonstrated with regard to issues surrounding birth and death, the situation is far more complex. Certainly the primary rabbinic sources function from within an androcentric framework in which woman is secondary in social status. At the same time, however, the direction in which most of the sources move is toward greater protection for women achieved through additional legal rights.

A forthcoming book on medieval Jewish women[5] illustrates situations similar to those of the contemporary Jewish woman. The author says, "when I began [the research], I assumed that I would find the medieval Jewish woman to be downtrodden. But the more I researched the more I realized that a revolution had taken place. Women were out there fighting for their rights in the home and community."[6] Women's economic power was the catalyst, in this author's opinion, for the changes that occurred.[7] Other scholars of Jewish women's history have unearthed documents in which women's voices, previously unheard, can now speak to their descendants. Notwithstanding the seemingly ancillary status of women in Jewish society, some women were autonomous, public individuals, despite their gender and in the face of generalized views about female sexuality. Historical instances of such women indicate that the mainstream could function with—and perhaps even accept and admire—that which hovered on its periphery. But mainstream tradition was not much altered by the personalities and actions of a Dona Gracia, the sixteenth-century Portugese Jew,[8] or Urania, daughter of Abraham in medieval Worms.[9] Halakhah, with its androcentric thrust, continued despite exceptions, and its core assumptions and laws remained, for the most part, inviolate.

Economic power in modern feminism is a potent factor. But as in medieval or Greco-Roman times,[10] it alone cannot transform deeply entrenched attitudes. The notion of woman as female in an essentialist way—gendered inherently rather than socially, intrinsically private and lacking independence—simply can no longer stand up to scrutiny. Not only women's intellectual history, but psychology, sociology, and religious studies also demonstrate that gender is socially constructed. Incorporating this understanding of the basic human condition into the self-understanding of religious traditions is a daunting, and at times frightening, challenge. For it necessarily leads to a reassessment not only of texts understood as divinely inspired, but also of their interpretive traditions. Within Judaism, such reassessment has taken different forms within each denomination. The struggle is slow, thoughtful, and impassioned. What is at stake are both the full humanity of women as a sine qua non of the tradition and the integrity of Judaism itself. The issues examined in this volume serve as a paradigm of the broader theological and sociological implications of the transformation in progress.

In the multifaceted world of Orthodoxy, the inroads of feminist thinking vary. Even the most right-wing groups indicate some influences of the modern feminist movement. At the center, within modern Orthodoxy, the effects are stronger, sometimes challenging the theological structures of halakhah itself. A good example is to be found within the work of Tamar Ross. Ross meticulously constructs the foundation for a philosophical reassessment of some of the established legal bases of the rabbinic system. Noting that since the nineteenth century Orthodox thinking has been ahistorical, Ross argues for a move away from a metahistoricism that denies that halakhah evolves and is in a dialectical relationship with social and cultural realities. Orthodoxy must hold together the paradox that "Torah and halakhah are formulated in a time- and culture-bound social mold . . . and that this same Torah is nevertheless the eternal voice of God speaking to us—with every word of that voice equally holy and indispensable."[11]

Ross brings several persuasive examples from the tradition to support her point that a progressive unfolding of the divine in history is consonant with traditional rabbinic understandings of Judaism. The social revolution that is feminism, according to Ross, has elements of genuine value that can only enhance Judaism if they are adapted and incorporated. If Orthodoxy ignores the transforming effects on Judaism of democratic political thinking, with its notions of autonomy, authority, individual, and community, it withdraws from modern history (as much as such a withdrawal is possible). But Jews live *within* history. Jews are bidden to "repair the world *[tikkun olam]*," the world of history, not a Platonic ideal. Feminist thinking cannot readily be sidestepped or ignored. It raises new questions and different perspectives, challenging the structure of hierarchy upon which Western society has been established. Ross maintains that the social revolution of feminism must be "[f]iltered through the prism of tradition in a constructive manner," in a way that deepens the relevance of Torah for our time.[12]

Another Orthodox thinker, Seth Farber, asserts that "the acceptance of the expanding roles of women in Orthodoxy is ultimately limited by the boundaries of *halachah* [*sic*]."[13] He does not offer a newly woven theological tapestry upon which to read ancient rabbinic truths and principles, as does Ross. Yet he acknowledges that while in the past learned Jewish women were isolated cases, the small number of women interested in Orthodox feminism thirty or so years ago has burgeoned into a movement, one with its own network, infrastructure, and resources. Surely this is a new phenomenon. Nevertheless, he states (and many will agree), "The future for this movement is unclear."[14] As religious communities in general move toward the right, modern Orthodoxy itself has become less open to change, more insular and self-protective, more concerned with what those on the extreme right might say. Some movement regarding women and the life-cycle events of birth and death has occurred, as these chapters demonstrate. Its slow pace can be discouraging, but movement forward it is.

The tension evident within Orthodoxy is epitomized by the work of Tzvia Greenfield, subject of an article in the *Jerusalem Report*.[15] *Hem Mefahadim* [They are Afraid], Greenfield's recent book, is a no-nonsense analysis of the Orthodox drift to the political right. Herself a strictly Orthodox woman residing in the Har Nof neighborhood of Jerusalem, Greenfield critiques both the Orthodox establishment and communities for what she calls "'the hijacking of halakhah' by right-wing religious ideologues."[16] She is a feminist who argues against the culture of ignorance, poverty, and extremely large families (she herself has five children), which excessively restricts opportunities for women. She opposes the dependence upon religious leaders fostered in the Orthodox world, a dependence that limits the development of autonomy. Like Ross, she sees the necessity of democratic political theory—and its many consequences—making inroads into the Orthodox community.

These thinkers represent, in different ways, the political/religious center of contemporary Orthodoxy. Historically, this center has almost always been a minority among traditional Jews, especially within the Ashkenazi communities. Earlier generations responded to the Enlightenment, the gradual emancipation of Western European Jewry, the extreme persecutions of Czarist Russia—each of which put its imprint upon how the traditional community understood itself. Feminism and democracy are the cultural forces with which contemporary Orthodoxy must struggle. For birth and death in the Jewish woman's life cycle to be the best experience each can be, Orthodoxy has to shift. The public, autonomous woman must not only be tolerated, but also respected, accepted, and *integrated* within the tradition's view that recognizes, values, and welcomes her full humanity. From a theological perspective, asserts Rachel Adler, this can be achieved most completely by altering the concept that a woman is acquired within marriage.[17] Only then will true partnership and equality be integral to family structure; only then will marriage be a contract between subjects of equal agency and power,[18] autonomous yet enmeshed in community.

Conservative Judaism, in ways similar to yet different from modern Orthodoxy, has begun to meet the challenges of feminism and democracy. Over the years it has struggled with the tensions resulting from its philosophy:

Torah is the eternally binding word of God, but it is also responsive to changing times; the people decide what to change, but the scholars have to inspire the people so that they may know what to change and what to retain. And if any change can be validated only by its ultimate effects years later, how do we know at the outset what to change and what to preserve?[19]

This perspective is fraught with ambiguities. Therein lies both its strengths and weaknesses. Conservative Judaism vacillated about accepting aspects of feminism, struggled with feminism's profound impact, and moved to accord women, as autonomous individuals, public roles within the community structure. As indicated in the previous chapters, the transformation of the place of women within Conservative Judaism has had a definitive effect on how women experience birth and death. The Conservative movement is also working to close the gap between scholars/clergy and laity by increasing support for intensive religious schools. There is, after all, no substitute for knowledge. The more learned and committed Conservative Jews are, the more potent the transformation.

Reform Judaism has moved from the critique of what it calls "strict rabbinism" to philosophy. "The early founders of Reform were convinced they could create a modern, rational, and progressive religion on the grounds of a scientific study of history and culture. The result was often a Jewish ethical culture that had little or no religious content."[20] This has been remedied in recent years by a strong acknowledgment of the need for ritual, ceremony, and the spiritual dimensions they bring. Contemporary Reform Judaism has seen a renewed interest in Jewish learning and in the practice of mitzvot. This reexamination of original principles has led Reform Judaism to invigorate and alter the experiences of birth and death for women.

Birth, contraception, fertility, the welcoming of a new daughter, kaddish, and the funeral are fundamental factors in human life. How a Jewish woman experiences these aspects of the life cycle depends upon how her community understands gender, sexuality, the public/private nexus, and the community/autonomy dialectic. The intersection of these four polarities with the denominations of the Jewish community poses a profound challenge not only to women's development, but also to the vitality of Judaism itself.

Notes

Preface

1. Some other works that deal with this sense of dissonance are Elyse Goldstein, *Re-Visions: Seeing Torah through a Feminist Lens* (Woodstock, Vt.: Jewish Lights Publishing, 1998); Judith Plaskow, *Standing Again at Sinai: Judaism from a Feminist Perspective* (San Francisco: Harper & Row, 1990); Cynthia Ozick, "Notes toward Finding the Right Question," in *On Being a Jewish Feminist: A Reader*, ed. Susannah Heschel (New York: Schocken Books, 1983).
2. See for instance the wonderful study by Natalie Zemon Davis, *Women on the Margins: Three Seventeenth-Century Lives* (Cambridge: Harvard University Press, 1995).

Introduction

1. Susan S. Sered, *Women as Ritual Experts: The Religious Lives of Elderly Jewish Women in Jerusalem* (New York: Oxford University Press, 1992).
2. Judith Hauptman, *Rereading the Rabbis: A Women's Voice* (Boulder, Colo.: Westview Press, 1998).
3. Rachel Adler, *Engendering Judaism: An Inclusive Theology and Ethics* (Philadelphia: Jewish Publication Society, 1998). See also Susannah Heschel's review of Adler's book in *JAAR* 167, no. 2 (June 1999), 473–476.
4. See the various works of Jacob Katz. Also, Gershom Scholem, "Revelation and Tradition as Religious Categories in Judaism," in *The Messianic Idea in Judaism* (New York: Schocken Books, 1971), 282–303; Tikva Frymer-Kensky, *In the Wake of the Goddesses* (New York: Fawcett Columbine, 1992); Paula E. Hyman, *Gender and Assimilation in Modern Jewish History* (Seattle: University of Washington Press, 1995); Hauptman, *Rereading the Rabbis*.
5. See David Novak, "Natural Law, Halakhah, and the Covenant," in his *Jewish Social Ethics* (New York: Oxford University Press, 1992), 22–44; Joseph B. Soloveitchik, *Halakhic Man,* trans. Lawrence Kaplan (Philadelphia: Jewish Publication Society, 1983); Mayer Twersky, "Torah Perspectives on Women's Issues," *Jewish Action* 57, no. 4 (summer 1997): 24–29; and Twersky, "Halakhic Values and Halakhic Decisions: Rav Soloveitchik's Pesak Regarding Women's Prayer Groups," *Tradition* 32, no. 3 (spring 1998): 5–18. See also Moshe Meiselman, "The Rav, Feminism, and Public Policy: An Insider's Overview," *Tradition* 33, no. 1 (fall 1998): 5–30, and subsequent letters to the editor.
6. Sylvia Barack Fishman, *A Breath of Life: Feminism in the American Jewish Community* (Hanover, N.H.: University Press of New England, 1993); Fishman, *Jewish Life and American Culture* (Albany: State University of New York Press, 2000); also, Hershel Schacter, "Go Out in the Footsteps of the Sheep" (in Hebrew), *Bet Yitshak,* 17 (1984–1985), 118–34.

7. Women who complete the Scholar's Circle program at the Drisha Institute in New York have had the same intensive education in rabbinic sources as Orthodox rabbis, but do not function as rabbis. Some have become rabbinic interns. See four articles in the *Jewish Week* by Jonathan Mark, who has followed this phenomenon: "In Uncharted Waters," 11 December 1998; "Torat Miriam, A Work in Progress," 6 February 1998; "Women Take Giant Step in Orthodox Community," 19 December 1997; "Reassessing An Experiment," 26 May 2000.

8. Carol Gilligan, *In a Different Voice: Psychological Theory and Women's Development* (Cambridge: Harvard University Press, 1982); Maggie Scarf, *Unfinished Business: Pressure Points in the Lives of Women* (New York: Ballantine, 1981); Tikva Frymer-Kensky, *Motherprayer: The Pregnant Woman's Spiritual Companion* (New York: Riverhead Books, 1995).

9. See, for instance, Aharon Feldman, *The River, the Kettle, and the Bird* (New York and Jerusalem: Feldheim, 1987); Moshe Meiselman, *Jewish Women and Jewish Law* (New York: Ktav and Yeshiva University, 1978); and Pinchas Stolper, *Jewish Alternatives in Love, Dating, and Marriage* (New York: Orthodox Union and University Press of America, 1967).

10. Michel Foucault, *The Archeology of Knowledge*, transl. A. M. Sheridan Smith (New York: Pantheon Books, 1972). Also, Rachel T. Hare-Mustin and Jean Marecek, "The Meaning of Difference: Gender Theory, Postmodernism, and Psychology," *American Psychologist* 43, no. 6 (June 1988): 455–64. One of several problems with postmodernism is that it deprives the world of any meaning independent of the construction itself; meaning is invested in the construction of meaning. Therefore, the system becomes epistemologically nihilistic. But the logical impasse at which postmodernism may find itself does not invalidate the ways it has illuminated the structure of knowledge and meaning in religion, ritual, and human development. One might say that what is important is not what happens, but how what happens is used to conceptualize gender. See as well the introduction in Joan Wallach Scott, *Gender and the Politics of History* (New York: Columbia University Press, 1999), 1–11.

11. Scott, *Gender*, 49.

12. Ibid., 2.

13. Ibid., 3, 33, 41.

14. Ibid., 48.

15. Saul Horovitz and Louis Finkelstein, eds., *Sifre on Deuteronomy* (New York: Jewish Theological Seminary of America [hereafter JTSA], 1969), sect. 46.

16. Scott, *Gender*, 55.

17. A brief discussion of the effect of religious language on the construction of gender is to be found in "Inclusion in the Myth: The Case of Women," in *Beyond the Text: A Holistic Approach to Liturgy*, by Lawrence A. Hoffman (Bloomington: Indiana University Press, 1987), 145–49.

18. Found in Julia Wolf Mazow, ed., *The Woman Who Lost Her Names: Selected Writings by American Jewish Women* (San Francisco: Harper & Row, 1980), 196–205.

19. Judith Viorst, *Imperfect Control* (New York: Fireside/Simon & Schuster, 1999), 13–32; and Steven Pinker, *The Blank Slate: The Denial of Human Nature* (New York: Viking/Penguin, 2002).

20. Gilligan, *In A Different Voice.* See also Gilligan's *Mapping the Moral Terrain* (Cambridge: Harvard University Press, 1988).
21. The first two essays are found in Anne Fausto-Sterling, *Myths of Gender: Biological Theories About Women and Men* (New York: Basic Books, 1985), the third in Carol MacCormack and Marilyn Strathern, eds., *Nature, Culture, and Gender* (New York: Cambridge University Press, 1980).
22. Carolyn G. Heilbrun, *Reinventing Womanhood* (New York: W. W. Norton, 1981); Jocelyn Hellig, *Toward A Recognition of Androgyny* (New York: W. W. Norton, 1992); Carolyn G. Heilbrun, *Writing A Woman's Life* (New York: Ballantine, 1988).
23. Eleanor Maccoby and Carol N. Jacklin, *The Psychology of Sex Differences* (Stanford: Stanford University Press, 1974).
24. See, for instance, Eleanor Galenson, "Observation of Early Infantile Sexual and Erotic Development," in *Childhood and Adolescent Sexology,* vol. 7 of *Handbook of Sexology,* ed. M. E. Perry (New York: Elsievier Science Publishers, 1990), chap. 9; Sandra Wittelson and Doreen Kimure, "Sex Differences in the Brain," *Scientific American* 267 (Sept. 1992), 118–25. See also Juanita H. Williams, *Psychology of Women,* 3d ed. (New York: W. W. Norton, 1987).
25. An excellent example is Scott, *Gender and the Politics of History.* See also Paula Hyman, "Gender and Jewish History," *Tikkun* (January–February 1988): 35–38; and Hyman, "Feminist Studies and Modern Jewish History," in *Feminist Perspectives on Jewish Studies,* ed. Lynn Davidman and Shelly Tenenbaum (New Haven: Yale University Press, 1994), 120–39; Gerda Lerner, "Reconceptualizing Differences Among Women," *Journal of Women's History* 1, no. 3 (winter 1990): 106–22.
26. Tamar Ross, "Modern Orthodoxy and the Challenge of Feminism," in *Jews and Gender: The Challenge to Hierarchy,* ed. Jonathan Frankel (New York: Oxford University Press, 2000). On p. 5, she writes, "No matter how benign to women, the considerations that are taken into account by male authorities must of necessity remain, on some level, typically male." Also, on p. 6, "[women] have had no official part to play in the legislative and interpretive process."
27. That the masculine hermeneutic affects how women are understood even in antiquity is convincingly demonstrated by Tal Ilan in *Mine and Yours are Hers: Retrieving Women's History from Rabbinic Literature* (New York: Brill, 1997), 51–84.
28. Hauptman, *Rereading the Rabbis,* 11; also 14, n.24.
29. Ibid., 11. Also, Tikva Frymer-Kensky, "The Bible and Women's Studies," in *Feminist Perspectives on Jewish Studies;* Shulamit Valler, *Women and Womanhood in the Stories of the Babylonian Talmud* (in Hebrew) (Tel Aviv: Hakibbutz Hameuchad, 1993); Eliezer Berkovits, *Jewish Women in Time and Torah* (Hoboken, N.J.: Ktav, 1990).
30. Daniel Boyarin, *Carnal Israel: Reading Sex and Talmudic Culture* (Berkeley: University of California Press, 1993), 240–45. Boyarin argues that while rabbinic sources assume gender asymmetry, rabbinic culture is neither misogynistic nor based upon the fear of women's bodies or sexuality.
31. Samson Raphael Hirsch, "The Jewish Woman," in *Judaism Eternal,* vol. 2 (London: Soncino Press, 1959), 49–96; Reuven Kimelman, "The Seduction of Eve and the Exegetical Politics of Gender," in *Women in the Hebrew Bible: A Reader,* ed.

Alice Bach (New York: Routledge, 1999), 241–70; Phyllis Trible, "A Love Story Gone Awry," in *God and the Rhetoric of Sexuality* (Philadelphia: Fortress Press, 1978), 72–143. Also Emmanuel Levinas, "And God Created Woman," in his *Nine Talmudic Readings* (Bloomington: Indiana University Press, 1990), 161–77.

32. Meiselman, *Jewish Woman in Jewish Law,* 11, 14. One problem with Meiselman's book and other books of apologetics is the lack of rigor with which the basic methodology is established. For instance, Meiselman brings the talmudic text of B.T. Shevuot 30a as a supporting text for the essentialist interpretation of Psalms 45:12. But this text does not support his interpretation. Rather, it uses the verse to validate its ruling—or description—of the nonqualification of women as witnesses in court. It is significant that the Gemara, in applying this verse to the legal issue of court appearances of witnesses, states, "it is not the bold way of women to appear in court because 'the honor of the King's daughter is inside/internal.'" Thus the Gemara uses the verse in a sociological context and not as an axiomatic statement of female nature. This is seen also in n.26 to B.T. Shevuot 30a of the Schottenstein edition of the Talmud. The note states: "The honor and dignity of a princess require that she remain in her palace and not go outside and mingle with the common folk. Since it is expected of women to emulate the dignified behavior of a princess, it was customary for women to limit their appearances in public." This interpretation reasons from class differences to gender differentiation. See also Rachel Adler, "Innovation and Authority: A Feminist Reading of the 'Women's Minyan Responsum,'" in *Gender Issues in Jewish Law: Essays and Response,* ed. Walter Jacob and Moshe Zemer (New York: Berghahn Books, 2001), 3–33.

33. For J. B. Soloveitchik, Jewish tradition views true heroism as occurring in the private rather than public arena. This is in contrast to the ancient Greek notion of heroism, in which military might and public acclaim indicated heroic triumph. The private heroism of Judaism is moral. See J. B. Soloveitchik, "Majesty and Humility," and "Catharsis," in *Tradition* 17, no. 2 (spring 1978): 25–37 and 38–54, respectively, esp. 36–37, 41. Also Shoshanna Gelerenter-Liebowitz, "Growing Up Lubavitch," in *Daughters of the King: Women and the Synagogue,* ed. Susan Grossman and Rivka Haut (Philadelphia: Jewish Publication Society, 1992), 238–41.

34. Derived from Deut. 6:7: "And you shall teach them to your children." The word for "children" is in male plural in the text, leading the Talmud to interpret the command as "And you shall teach them to your sons." See B.T. Kiddushin 29a, as well as commentaries of Rashi, Tosafot, and others on that text. The contemporary discussion of this issue is large. Discussion is found in Menachem M. Brayer, *The Jewish Woman in Rabbinic Literature: A Psychohistorical Perspective* (Hoboken, N.J.: Ktav, 1986), vol. 2, chap. 6; Rachel Biale, *Women and Jewish Law* (New York: Schocken Books, 1984), 29–41; Boyarin, *Carnal Israel,* chap. 6; Hauptman, *Rereading the Rabbis,* 22–25.

35. Works investigating women in biblical and rabbinic times are numerous. They include Tal Ilan, *Jewish Women in Greco-Roman Palestine* (Peabody, Ma.: Hendrickson, 1996), Ross Shepard Kraemer, *Her Share of the Blessings* (New York: Oxford University Press, 1992), and Carol Meyers, *Discovering Eve: Ancient Israelite Women in Context* (New York: Oxford University Press, 1988).

36. Gerda Lerner, *The Creation of Feminist Consciousness* (New York: Oxford University Press, 1993); Bonnie S. Anderson and Judith P. Zinsser, *A History of Their Own: Women in Europe From Prehistory to the Present,* vol 1 (New York: Harper & Row, 1988).

37. Women's exemption from time-bound commandments is specified in B.T. Kiddushin 33b. No rationale is offered for the exemption. This important concept, which determines the status of women in halakha (Jewish law), is discussed and analyzed in a number of secondary sources. See, for instance, Biale, *Women and Jewish Law;* Berkovits, *Jewish Women in Time and Torah,* 70–74; Rochelle L. Millen, "An Analysis of Rabbinic Hermeneutics: B.T. Kiddushin 34a," in *Gender and Judaism: The Transformation of Tradition,* ed. T. M. Rudavsky (New York: New York University Press, 1995), 25–38; Judith Romney Wegner, *Chattel or Person? The Status of Women in the Mishnah* (New York: Oxford University Press, 1988), 150–56; David C. Kraemer, *Reading the Rabbis: The Talmud as Literature* (New York: Oxford University Press, 1996), 86–108. See discussion under "Isha" [Woman] in *Encyclopedia Talmudit* (in Hebrew), vol. 2 (1957). Also, Chaim Rapoport, "Why Women Are Exempt From Positive Time-bound Commandments: Is There a Torah-true View?" *Le'Ela* no. 50 (December 2000): 53–64 (published by the London School of Jewish Studies).

38. Wegner, *Chattel or Person?,* 153.

39. Hauptman, *Rereading the Rabbis,* 227.

40. Saul Berman, "The Status of Women in Halakhic Judaism," *Tradition* 14:2 (fall 1973), 2–30.

41. See my discussion of this in "Social Attitudes Disguised as Halakhah: '*Zila milta, Ein havrutan naah, Kevod ha-tsibbur*'" *Nashim: A Journal of Jewish Women's Studies and Gender Issues,* no. 4 (fall 2001): 178–96.

42. Biale, *Women and Jewish Law,* 29–41.

43. *The Memoirs of Glückel of Hameln,* trans. Marvin Lowenthal (New York: Schocken Books, 1977). Glueckel lived from 1646 to 1724. See also Natalie Zemon Davis, *Women On the Margins: Three Seventeenth-Century Lives* (Cambridge: Harvard University Press, 1995), 1–62.

44. Anzia Yezierska, *Bread Givers* (New York: Persea Books, 1925), 136–37.

45. Berman, "The Status of Women in Halakhic Judaism," esp. 23–24.

46. It has been suggested to me that perhaps the structural functionalism of Emile Durkheim was influenced by his Jewish background.

47. 1 Cor. 14:33–36. While there is no serious question about Pauline authorship of 1 Corinthians, some scholars argue that this passage about women being silent was originally a marginal gloss from a later reader that made its way into the text proper; see Jourette M. Bassler, "1 Corinthians," in *The Women's Bible Commentary,* ed. Carol A. Newsom and Sharon H. Ringe (Louisville, Ky.: Westminster/John Knox, 1992), 321–29. Issues of Pauline authorship are discussed in Calvin Roetzel, *The Letters of Paul: Conversations in Context* (Louisville, Ky.: Westminster/John Knox, 1991). My thanks to colleague Barbara Kaiser for these references.

48. *Ervah* literally translates as "nakedness." See Gen. 9:22 and Lev. 18:6f. for the classical biblical uses of the term. The notion that a woman's voice is *ervah* is expressed in T.B Berakhot 24a and Kiddushin 70a.

49. Saul J. Berman, "Kol'Isha," in *Rabbi Joseph H. Lookstein Memorial Volume*, ed. Leo Landman (New York: Ktav, 1981), 45–66. A critique of Berman's analysis is made by Yehuda Henkin, "Kol Ishah Reviewed," in a book of his essays, *Equality Lost: Essays in Torah Commentary, Halacha, and Jewish Thought* (Jerusalem: Urim Publishers, 1999), 66–76.
50. "Dat Yehudit," in *Encyclopedia Talmudit*, vol. 8. (1957).
51. See Berman, "Status of Women in Halakhic Judaism," 18; Meiselman, *Jewish Woman in Jewish Law*, 73–80; Twersky, "Torah Perspectives on Women's Issues," 26.
52. Rochelle L. Millen, "The Female Voice of Kaddish," in *Jewish Legal Writings by Women*, ed. Chana Safrai and Micah D. Halpern (Jerusalem: Urim Publications, 1995), 179–202.
53. For contemporary discussions of classical sources and modern dilemmas, see Biale, *Women and Jewish Law*, 192–97; Rebecca T. Alpert, *Like Bread on the Seder Plate: Jewish Lesbians and the Transformation of Tradition* (New York: Columbia University Press, 1998); Rebecca T. Alpert, Sue Levi Elwell, Shirley Idelson, eds., *Lesbian Rabbis: The First Generation* (New Jersey: Rutgers University Press, 2001).
54. Gen. 1:4,10,12,18,27,31. All of God's creation, including the material world and human physicality, is considered intrinsically "good." Sexual pleasure in itself is regarded as a "good." Compare the discussions in Peter Brown, *The Body and Society: Men, Women, and Sexual Renunciation in Early Christianity* (New York: Random House, 1989), and Elaine Pagels, *Adam, Eve, and the Serpent* (New York: Columbia University Press, 1988). Compare Avivah Gottlieb Zornberg, *Genesis: The Beginning of Desire* (Philadelphia: Jewish Publication Society, 1995).
55. As evidenced in Gen. 1:27–28.
56. T.B. Bava kamma 110b; Yevamot 118b; Kiddushin 7a and 41a; Ketubot 75a.
57. See Susan Aranoff, "Two Views of Marriage—Two Views of Woman: Reconsidering *Tav Lemetav Tan Du Milemetav Armelu*," *Nashim*, no. 3 (spring-summer 2000): 199–227. Also J. David Bleich, "Survey of Recent Halakhic Periodical Literature," *Tradition*, 33, no. 1 (fall 1998): 90–128.
58. See Peter L. Berger, *Invitation to Sociology* (Woodstock, N.Y.: Overlook Press, 1973), esp. chap. 5.
59. See, for instance, J. B. Soloveitchik, "The Community," *Tradition* 117, no. 2 (spring 1978): 7–24; and Eugene B. Borowitz, *Renewing the Convenant: A Theology for the Postmodern Jew* (Philadelphia: Jewish Publication Society, 1991), esp. 254–65.
60. Wegner, *Chattel or Person?*, 168–81.

I. Beginnings

1. The literature on this question is huge. Some sources include Anne Fausto-Sterling, *Myths of Gender* (New York: Basic Books, 1985); Eleanor Galenson, "Observation of Early Infantile Sexual and Erotic Development," in *Childhood and Adolescent Sexology*, vol. 7 of *Handbook of Sexology*, ed. M. E. Perry (New York: Elsevier Science Publishers, 1991); chap. 9, 169–78; Eleanor Galenson and Herman Roiphe, "Pre-Oedipal Development of the Boy," *Journal of the American*

Psychoanalytic Association 28:4 (1980); Carol Tavris, *The Mismeasure of Woman* (New York: Simon and Schuster, 1992), 95–96; Juanita H. Williams, *Psychology of Women: Behavior in a Biosocial Context,* 3d ed. (New York: W. W. Norton, 1987); Doreen Kimura, "Sex Differences in the Brain," *Scientific American* 267 (Sept. 1992): 118–25.

2. Simone de Beauvoir created the terminology of woman as "Other" in her 1949 publication, *La Deuxieme Sexe,* translated into English as *The Second Sex* in 1952. As de Beauvoir herself demonstrates, the presentation of woman as Other is not only a description of social or historical reality, but also an expression of male advantage. Woman as Other in Jewish law has been noted by many, including Rachel Adler, Judith Plaskow, Judith Romney Wegner, Paula E. Hyman, Cynthia Ozick, Rachel Biale, Aviva Cantor, Rochelle L. Millen, and Blu Greenberg.

3. Sherry B. Ortner, "Is Female to Male as Nature is to Culture?" in *Woman, Culture, and Society,* ed. Michelle Z. Rosaldo and Louise Lamphere (Stanford, Calif.: Stanford University Press, 1974), 67–88.

4. See Tamar Ross, "Modern Orthodoxy and the Challenge of Feminism" in *Jews and Gender: The Challenge to Hierarchy,* ed. Jonathan Frankel (New York: Oxford University Press, 2000), 3–38; and in the same volume, Elizabeth Shanks Alexander, "The Impact of Feminism on Rabbinic Studies: The Impossible Paradox of Reading Women into Rabbinic Literature," 101–18. Gerda Lerner, *The Creation of Patriarchy* (New York: Oxford University Press, 1987); Lerner, *The Creation of Feminist Consciousness* (New York: Oxford University Press, 1993); Judith Plaskow, *Standing Again at Sinai* (San Francisco: Harper & Row, 1990); Rachel Adler, *Engendering Judaism* (Philadelphia: Jewish Publication Society, 1998), chap. 2; Hava Tirosh-Rothchild, "'Dare to Know': Feminism and the Discipline of Jewish Philosophy," in *Feminist Perspectives on Jewish Studies,* ed. Lynn Davidman and Shelly Tenenbaum (New Haven, Conn.: Yale University Press, 1994), 85–120. Also see Thelma Jean Goodrich, ed., *Women and Power: Perspectives for Family Therapy* (New York: W. W. Norton, 1990).

5. Simone de Beauvoir, *The Second Sex,* trans. H. M. Parshley (New York: Bantam Books, 1961), 239.

6. Ortner, "Is Female to Male . . . ?" 80.

7. Gerda Lerner, *Why History Matters: Life and Thought* (New York: Oxford University Press, 1997), 146–98. The interweaving of gender and class is explored in Karen Chase and Michael Levenson, *The Spectacle of Intimacy: A Public Life for the Victorian Family* (Princeton, N.J.: Princeton University Press, 2000).

8. *Niddah,* often translated as "ritual impurity," refers to a physical/spiritual state during which one was prohibited from coming to the Temple. For women, this state is connected to menstrual bleeding or bleeding outside of the usual monthly cycle. The laws derive from Lev. 15. See Rachel Biale, *Women and Jewish Law* (New York: Schocken Books, 1984), chap. 6, and Rahel R. Wasserfall, ed., *Women and Water: Menstruation in Jewish Life and Law* (Hanover, N.H.: University Press of New England, 1999).

9. Mishnah Shabbat 2:6.

10. An excellent overview of biblical, rabbinic, and modern Jewish sources on the issue of theodicy is to be found in Zachary Braiterman (*God) After Auschwitz:*

Tradition and Change in Post-Holocaust Jewish Thought (Princeton: Princeton University Press, 1998).

11. Jerusalem Talmud Shabbat 8b.

12. For other, more feminist readings of Gen. 1–3, see Phyllis Trible, *God and the Rhetoric of Sexuality* (Philadelphia: Fortress Press, 1978), chap. 4; Reuven Kimelman, "The Seduction of Eve and the Exegetical Politics of Gender," in *Women in the Hebrew Bible: A Reader,* ed. Alice Bach (New York: Routledge, 1999), 241–70; Adele Reinhartz, *"Why Ask My Name?": Anonymity and Identity in Biblical Narrative* (New York: Oxford University Press, 1998), 86–88, 141–44.

13. An extended discussion of this text can be found in Daniel Boyarin, *Carnal Israel: Reading Sex in Talmudic Culture* (Berkeley: University of California Press, 1993), 90–94. See also Judith Romney Wegner, *Chattel or Person? The Status of Women in the Mishnah* (New York: Oxford University Press, 1988), 155–56.

14. B.T. Shabbat 31b–32a.

15. For a discussion of childbirth as a time of risk, see Rochelle L. Millen, "Birkhat Ha-Gomel: A Study in Cultural Context and Halakhic Practice," *Judaism* 43, no. 3 (summer 1994): 270–78.

16. An overview of sources in given is Shmuel A. Adler, *Aspaklaryia* (in Hebrew), vol. 12 (Jerusalem: Aspaklaryia, 5749/1989), 389–96.

17. My thanks to Barbara Kaiser for this interpretation.

18. T.B. Megillah 13a and Ketubot 446.

19. An alternate version is found in Bereishit Rabbah 73.

20. Among the many references, see, for instance, Exod. 23:1–9; Lev. 19:1–19, 32–37; Deut. 16:18–20; Amos 5–24; Hos. 2:21

21. See Lerner, *Why History Matters,* 8, 199–211; Cynthia Ozick, "Notes Toward Finding the Right Question," in *On Being a Jewish Feminist: A Reader,* ed. Susannah Heschel (New York: Schocken Books, 1983), 120–51; Wegner, *Chattel or Person?*; Judith Hauptman, *Rereading the Rabbis: A Woman's Voice* (Boulder, Colo.: Westview Press, 1998).

22. "[T]he rabbi's upheld patriarchy as the preordained mode of social organization," [as] dictated by the Torah." Hauptman, *Rereading the Rabbis,* 4

23. Bereshit Rabbah 9:9.

24. Daniel Boyarin suggests that "the Rabbis inherited the term 'Evil Instinct' from a first century Judaism much more averse to sexuality than they were, and unable to dispense with it, they ironized the term—'The Evil Instinct is very good' and rendered the concept itself dialectical. . . ." *Carnal Israel,* 63.

25. An excellent discussion of the transformation of the blessing of Gen. 1:28 into legal statute is to be found in Jeremy Cohen, *"Be Fertile and Increase, Fill the Earth and Master It": The Ancient and Medieval Career of a Biblical Text* (Ithaca, N.Y.: Cornell University Press, 1989), chap. 3.

26. The Talmud also uses this same term *derekh* to indicate a man's search for completion, based on Gen. 2:28, the primal myth of Adam's rib. It states: "It is the way of a man to go around searching for a wife, like a person who has suffered a loss" (T.B. Kiddushin 2b); Cf. Phyllis Trible, who reads the term *"Adam"* as androgynous, "the earth creature," until sexual differentiation occurs. This model differs

from the Talmud, which generally assumes "*Adam*" is male. Trible, *God and the Rhetoric of Sexuality,* 88–99.

27. See Elliot N. Dorff, "Custom Drives Jewish Law on Women," in *Gender Issues in Jewish Law: Essays and Responsa,* ed. Walter Jacob and Moshe Zemer (New York: Berghahn Books, 2001), 82–106.

28. The language connotes an androcentric perspective.

29. The rule used in this derivation is called *"gilui milta"* ("merely revealing something"). See Adin Steinsaltz, *The Talmud: A Reference Guide* (New York: Random House, 1989), 150.

30. It is interesting that in Gen. 9:1, the blessing of fertility given to Noah and his sons/children, is not referred to. Two possibilities exist. Either 9:1 is referring only to Noah's sons and not their wives (an interpretation in which *banim* would mean only male progeny) and/or actual children, not spouses of one's children; or R. Joseph wishes to find a prooftext that would validate an already-existing conclusion in the legal tradition.

31. While the Torah contains 613 commandments (mitzvot) that devolve upon Jews, all humankind, according to rabbinic teaching, is mandated in what are known as the seven Noahide commandments. They are derived in T.B. Sanhedrin from the blessings given to Noah in Gen. 9. Observance of the Noahide commandments qualifies one for the world to come, indicating the universal redemption inherent in Jewish teachings. The Noahide laws are: the prohibition against idolatry, blasphemy, murder, immorality, theft, and consuming of flesh from a live animal, as well as the establishment of civil courts. The legal status of procreation as regards non-Jews is examined in Feldman, *Birth Control in Jewish Law,* 56–59, and Jeremy Cohen, *Be Fertile and Increase,* 148–53.

32. See Feldman, *Birth Control in Jewish Law,* 53–56, and Cohen, *Be Fertile and Increase,* 143.

33. Mishnah Shabbat 14:3 and B.T. Shabbat 109b–110a.

34. See T.B. Berakhot 54b. Also Elyakim Ellinson, *The Woman and the Commandments* (in Hebrew), 1 (Jerusalem: The Jewish Agency, 1979), 134–38; and Millen, "Birkhat Ha-Gomel."

35. T.B. Yevamot 119b, "Resh Lakish states . . ." See Susan Aranoff, "Two Views of Marriage—Two Views of Women: Reconsidering *Tav Lemetav Tan Du Milemetav Armelu,*" *Nashim: A Journal of Jewish Women's Studies & Gender Issues,* no. 3 (spring/summer 5760/2000): 199–227; Judith R. Baskin, "Rabbinic Reflections on the Barren Wife," *Harvard Theological Review* 82, no. 1 (1989): 101–14.

36. This issue is analyzed from various perspectives in Biale, *Women and Jewish Law,* chaps. 2 and 5; Hauptman, *Rereading the Rabbis,* chaps. 3 and 6; Wegner, *Chattel or Person?*

37. Rashi on T.B. Baba Metzia 84a: "A woman's passion is greater than that of a man." Cf. "Almighty God created sexual desire in ten parts; then he gave nine parts to women and one to men," Ali ibn Abu Taleb, Muhammad's son-in-law and founder of Shiite sect of Islam. Quoted in Geraldine Brooks, *Nine Parts of Desire* (New York: Doubleday, 1995).

38. T.B. Sanhedrin 7a. The text states: "A man's sexual impulse is out in the open: his erection stands out and he embarrasses himself in front of his fellows. A woman's sexual impulse is within and no one can recognize her [arousal]."

39. That is, she carries and nurses the child. For recent discussion of the father's increased role in child care, see Warren Farrell, *Father and Child Reunion* (New York: Tarcher Putnam Penguin, 2001), and Marc Parent, "A Dad at the Final Frontier," *New York Times,* 16 June 2001.

40. See William H. Masters and Virginia E. Johnson, *The Pleasure Bond: A New Look at Sexuality and Commitment* (Boston: Little Brown, 1974). Also see their work with Robert C. Kolodny, *Masters and Johnson on Sex and Human Loving* (Boston: Little Brown, 1986).

41. It is interesting that the Tosefta seems to promulgate the halakhah according to R. Johanan ben Beroka's opinion. A dispute about how to interpret the Tosefta is found in Hauptman, *Rereading the Rabbis,* 134–35 and 145, nn.7, 10.

42. Mishnah Yevamot 6:60. "A man *[adam]* must not abstain from fruitfulness and increase unless he already has children. The School of Shammai says two sons, but the School of Hillel says a son and a daughter because it says 'male and female God Created them.'"

43. See Tal Ilan, *Mine and Yours are Hers: Retrieving Woman's History from Rabbinic Literature* (New York: Brill, 1997), 204–6.

44. Feldman, *Birth Control in Jewish Law,* 54.

45. Ibid.

46. A sixth possibility is offered in Jeremy Cohen's astute analysis of Gen. 1:28, *"Be Fertile and Increase,"* 162. At the conclusion of chap. 3, Cohen avers that "the rabbinic restriction of the law of procreation to free Jewish males bespoke the contention that *they* were the full-fledged partners of God in his divine covenant" (emphasis in original).

2. Birth Control and Contraception

1. Translation of the verses is mine.

2. Isaac Arama lived from 1420 to 1494 and wrote a commentary on the Pentateuch called *Akedat Yitzchak.*

3. Quoted in Nehama Leibowitz, *Studies in Bereishit (Genesis),* 3d ed. (Jerusalem: World Zionist Organization, 1976), 334.

4. See Joseph B. Soloveitchik, "The Lonely Man of Faith," *Tradition,* 7, no. 2 (summer 1965): 1–69.

5. T.B. Yevamot 12b and 100b; Ketubot 39a; Nedarim 35b, Niddah 45a. This text is referred to in the Gemara as a *baraita,* i.e., it is from the period of the Mishnah, but was not included in the final edited version of the Mishnah; it also appears in the Tosefta. See David M. Feldman, *Birth Control in Jewish Law* (New York: New York University Press, 1968), 169, n.2. David M. Feldman is a (right-wing) Conservative rabbi. Feldman's discussion of this text are in chaps. 9, 10, and 11 of his book. Shorter expositions are given in Hershel Schachter, "Halachic Aspects of Family Planning," in *Halacha and Contemporary Society,* ed. Alfred S. Cohen (Ktav: Rabbi Jacob Joseph School, 1981), 3–30, and Rachel Biale, *Women and*

Jewish Law: An Exploration of Women's Issues in Halakhic Sources (New York: Schocken Books, 1984), chap. 8.

6. A brief overview of the halakhic sources on procreation may be found in Louis Flancbaum, *"And You Shall Live by Them"*: *Contemporary Jewish Approaches to Medical Ethics* (Pittsburgh: Mirkov Publications, 2001), 200–5.

7. TB Yevamot 63a.

8. Feldman, *Birth Control in Jewish Law*, 60–61.

9. The Hebrew term *hash-hatat zera* means "destruction of the seed" and also "corruption of the seed." The term refers not only to coitus interruptus, known as "onanism" based on Gen. 38, but also to a "corruption" or "abuse" of the generative process. A detailed discussion of the term in biblical and rabbinic literature and of its halakhic implications is given in ibid., chaps. 6 and 8.

10. For a detailed listing and analysis of the sources given, see ibid., chap. 10. See also Biale, *Women and Jewish Law*, 204–6.

11. "A man is forbidden to betroth his daughter while she is a minor until she is grown and says 'I wish to marry so and so.'" T.B. Kiddushin 41a.

12. This point is made explicit in the Jerusalem Talmud Pesahim 8:1 as brought by Feldman, *Birth Control in Jewish Law*, 180, n.23.

13. The wording of the text includes risks that may be physical and/or emotional. This is significant in the later literature relating to contraception.

14. This was not the case in early and medieval Church sources. Feldman offers a brief discussion, ibid. 180–82. A more complete analysis is to be found in John T. Noonan Jr., *Contraception: A History of Its Treatment by the Catholic Theologians and Canonists* (Cambridge: Harvard University Press, 1986).

15. T.B. Niddah 27a. As in all ancient sources, the Talmud's anatomical and medical suppositions manifest the limitations of medical knowledge of that time. Nonetheless, the degree of accuracy in many matters is surprising, and the underlying conceptual bases form the foundation of current Jewish bioethics.

16. T.B. Niddah 31a.

17. See T.B. Pesahim 72b. *Onah*, or regular sexual relations, is an obligation of the husband and a right of the wife.

18. William Masters and Virginia Johnson, *Human Sexual Response* (Boston: Little, Brown, and Co., 1966), 166–167. Cited in Feldman, *Birth Control in Jewish Law*, 186.

19. See note 9 above.

20. T.B. Yoma 85b.

21. Feldman, *Birth Control in Jewish Law*, 199.

22. It is important to note that abstinence is never considered an option due to the mitzvah of *onah*.

23. Rabbi Luria, also called the Maharshal, lived from 1510 to 1574 in Poland and was known for the independence of his legal rulings.

24. *Onah* refers to the obligation of the husband to be sexually intimate with his wife and is based on Exod. 21:10. See nn.17 and 22, above.

25. Quoted in Biale, *Women in Jewish Law*, 216. Also see detailed discussion of Rabbi Luria's analysis in Feldman, *Birth Control in Jewish Law*, 210–13.

26. For a detailed analysis of his responsum, see ibid., 213–18.

27. This fact is pointed out in ibid., 213.

28. This comment about R. Eger's responsum is made by R. Moshe Feinstein (d. 1962), ibid., 217.
29. The legal/intellectual trail of ideas is traced in ibid., 219–26. See especially the light shed on R. Luria's interpretation by a recently found responsum of R. Hai Gaon's in the tenth century. R. Hai Gaon affirms the central concern of the three women text to be the possible danger of pregnancy and not the status of the *mokh,* the legal use of which is assumed.
30. The natural sexual act in halakhic terminology generally refers to the insertion of the penis into the vagina with the man on top of the woman.
31. Found in T.B. Berakhot 57b.
32. Mishnah Shabbat, 14:3 and T.B. Shabbat 109b–110a.
33. The story of the development of the pill and its relation to Catholic theology is found in Loretta McLaughlin, *The Pill, John Rock, and the Church* (Boston: Little, Brown, and Co., 1982). See also Malcolm Gladwell, "John Rock's Error," *The New Yorker* 13 March 2000, 52–57.
34. As compared with the higher doses of hormones found in the original formulations.
35. A daring feminist analysis of the emphasis upon motherhood in the modern state of Israel is given in Susan S. Sered, *What Makes Women Sick: Maternity, Modesty, and Militarism in Israeli Society* (Hanover, N.H.: University Press of New England, 2000).
36. Feldman, *Birth Control in Jewish Law,* 297.
37. N. S. Hecht, et al., eds., *An Introduction to the History and Sources of Jewish Law* (New York: Oxford University Press for the Jewish Law Association, 1996).
38. Fred Rosner, "Contraception in Jewish Law" in *Jewish Bioethics,* ed. Fred Rosner and J. David Bleich (Hoboken, N.J.: Ktav, 2000), 105–16.
39. Ibid., 106.
40. Ibid. The designation "immoral" is used three times on pp. 106–7.
41. Ibid., 106.
42. Ibid., 107.
43. Ibid.
44. Ibid., 114.
45. Nisson E. Shulman, *Jewish Answers to Medical Ethics Questions: Questions and Answers from the Medical Ethics Department of the Office of the Chief Rabbi of Great Britain* (Northvale, N.J.: Jason Aronson, 1998).
46. Ibid., 64. The legal rationale is taken from a text edited by David Feldman and Fred Rosner, *Compendium on Medical Ethics* (New York: Federation of Jewish Philanthropies, 1986), 45f.
47. Michael Kaufman, *The Woman in Jewish Law and Tradition* (Northvale, N.J.: Jason Aronson, 1993), 162.
48. Moshe Feinstein, *Iggerot Moshe,* Even Haezer 4:69.
49. Ibid., 4:68.
50. Related to me in 1984 by a young woman then living in Washington Heights, N.Y.
51. Susan Martha Kahn, "Rabbis and Reproduction: The Uses of New Reproductive Technologies among Ultraorthodox Jews in Israel," Brandeis University Working Paper Series (Waltham, Ma.: Hadassah International Research Institute on Jewish Women, 1998), 19.

52. Susan Martha Kahn, *Reproducing Jews: A Cultural Account of Assisted Conception in Israel* (Durham and London: Duke University Press, 2000), 3. See also Sered, *What Makes Women Sick?* 17. Sered writes that "women have no authority over the accessibility of contraception, or . . . whether their husbands are willing to cooperate . . . whether their communities will look askance . . . or (for Orthodox women) whether their rabbis will permit the use of contraception at all."
53. Sylvia Barack Fishman, *A Breath of Life: Feminism in the American Jewish Community* (Hanover, N.H.: University Press of New England, 1993), 107.
54. Ibid.
55. Ben Zion Bokser, "Statement on Birth Control" (in Hebrew and English), in *Proceedings of the Committee on Jewish Law and Standards of the Conservative Movement, 1927–1970*, ed. David Golinkin (Jerusalem: The Rabbinical Assembly and the Institute of Applied Halakhah, 1997), 1451–58. The statement was originally published in 1960. More recent halakhic discussions regarding birth control are not available.
56. Ibid., 1455.
57. Bokser brings Isa. 45:18, brought in rabbinic sources, as a prooftext. Ibid.
58. Ibid., 1456.
59. Ibid.
60. Ibid.
61. In only three sets of circumstances can the priority of the preservation of human life be violated: idolatry, immorality, and murder. See T.B. Sanhedrin 74a.
62. With the exception of the economic factor, as indicated; financial hardship is mentioned in some Orthodox responsa, however.
63. Rabbi Klein became a member of the Law Committee of the Rabbinical Assembly of the Conservative movement in 1935.
64. T.B. Taanit 11a.
65. Isaac Klein, "Science and Some Ethical Issues," in *Responsa and Halakhic Studies* (New York: Ktav, 1975), 161. While this collection was published in 1975, the essay is dated 1959.
66. Solomon B. Freehof, *Reform Responsa for Our Time* (Cincinnati, Ohio: Hebrew Union College Press, 1977), 206–7.
67. Found in Isaac Klein, *Guide to Jewish Religious Practice* (New York: Jewish Theological Seminary, 1979), 415.
68. Klein cites Ben Zion Bokser, David Feldman, and Moshe Feinstein, all of whom have been referred to above. He also cites Robert Gordis, *Sex and the Family in the Jewish Tradition* (New York: United Synagogue, 1967), 36f.
69. The pill as the least objectionable method of contraception according to Jewish law is discussed at length in Feldman, *Birth Control in Jewish Law,* 244. Among legal decisors, or *poskim,* who support this view are Feinstein, *Iggerot Moshe,* Even Haezer 2:17, and Eliezer Waldenberg, *Tzitz Eliezer,* vol. 9, 51:4:14 and vol. 10, 25:10:1.
70. Fishman, *A Breath of Life,* 50.
71. Ibid., 107.
72. Eugene B. Borowitz, "Judaism: An Overview" in *Judaism: A People and Its History,* ed. Robert M. Seltzer (New York: MacMillan, 1989), 3–35.

73. Daniel J. Elazar and Rela Mintz Geffen, *The Conservative Movement in Judaism: Dilemmas and Opportunities* (Albany: State University of New York Press, 2000), 162.
74. Ibid., 168–69. See also Joel Roth, *The Halakhic Process: A Systematic Analysis* (New York: Jewish Theological Seminary, 1986), esp. intro. and chaps. 1, 3, 8, 9, and 11.
75. Bernard Asbell, *The Pill: A Biography of the Drug that Changed the World* (New York: Random House, 1995).
76. The assessment of Lauterbach and his relation to the tradition of responsa in the Reform movement is explored in Solomon B. Freehof, "Jacob Z. Lauterbach and the Halakah," *Judaism* 3 (August 1952): 270–73.
77. Jacob Z. Lauterbach, "Birth Control," in *The Fetus and Fertility in Jewish Law: Essays and Responsa,* ed. Walter Jacob and Moshe Zemer (Pittsburgh and Tel Aviv: Rodef Shalom Press, 1995), 173.
78. Freehof, "Lauterbach and the Halakah." Also Lauterbach's lecture at Hebrew Union College, "Reform Judaism and the Law" reprinted in *American Israelite* 58, n.18 (Nov. 2, 1918) 1.
79. He does not give citations, but merely states, "Some rabbis . . ." Lauterbach, "Birth Control" 173.
80. Ibid., 174.
81. Ibid.
82. Ibid.
83. Ibid., 175.
84. Ibid., 177.
85. Solomon Jehiel Luria, *Yam shel Shelomo* chap. 1, n.8 (Altona, Germany: Aharon ben Eli Kats, 1739).
86. Lauterbach, "Birth Control" 181.
87. Ibid.
88. See Feldman's analysis of this text, *Birth Control in Jewish Law,* 240*ff.*
89. Lauterbach, "Birth Control," 187.
90. According to the School of Shammai, two boys, while the School of Hillel says a boy and a girl, i.e., replacing the couple. There is no recorded opinion that having two girls fulfills the mitzvah.
91. Here Lauterbach brings as sources T.B. Yevamot 61b and Joseph Karo, *Shulhan Arukh,* Even Haezer 1:5.
92. Lauterbach, "Birth Control," 183.
93. T.B. Kiddushin 29b; Moses Maimonides, *Mishneh Torah,* Hilkhot Ishut (Laws of Marriage) 15:2–3; Karo, *Shulhan Arukh,* Even Haezer 1:3–4.
94. Lauterbach, "Birth Control," 185.
95. Feldman, *Birth Control in Jewish Law,* 213–20.
96. Lauterbach, *"Birth Control,"* 186.
97. Feldman, *Birth Control in Jewish Law,* 219–26.
98. An overview of Lauterbach's philosophy of liberal halakhah is given in Walter Jacob and Moshe Zemer, eds., *Dynamic Jewish Law: Progressive Halakhah, Essence and Application* (Pittsburgh: Rodef Shalom Press, 1991), 98–103.
99. Lauterbach uses this phrase throughout his conclusion. See his essay "Birth Control," 188. The quotes in my summary of Lauterbach are from pp. 188–89.

100. Compare the comments of ultra-orthodox wives quoted above on p. 35. Traditionally, a kollel is a community group of (male) Torah scholars.
101. Lauterbach, "Birth Control," 189.
102. In the words of Pamela S. Nadell, Lauterbach, more than his predecessors on the Responsa Committee representing the Reform movement, "linked Reform Judaism to the classical rabbinic legacy of textual interpretation." See Nadell, *Women Who Would Be Rabbis: A History of Women's Ordination, 1889–1985* (Boston: Beacon Press, 1998), 65.
103. At the same time, however, haggadic texts often express, albeit in indirect form, the very theological perspective of the rabbis and therefore can be extremely influential. This is so in regard not only to framework and attitude, but also to halakhah itself.
104. Lauterbach served as rabbi of the Reform congregation in Huntsville, Alabama, from 1910–1911. My correspondence with Mr. Henry Marks, archivist of the synagogue, indicates that the congregation had eight different rabbis between 1892 and 1911 and Marks does not know why Lauterbach left. See also Michael A. Meyer, *Response to Modernity: A History of the Reform Movement in Judaism* (New York: Oxford University Press, 1988), 312. Also, essays in Dana Evan Kaplan, ed., *Contemporary Debates in American Reform Judaism: Conflicting Visions* (New York: Routledge, 2001).
105. Eugene B. Borowitz, *Renewing the Covenant: A Theology for the Postmodern Jew* (Philadelphia: Jewish Publication Society, 1991), 207–35, 297–99.
106. For a general analysis of Borowitz's concept of "Covenant," see ibid., 185, 188–89, 229–30, and Borowitz, *Exploring Jewish Ethics: Papers on Covenant Responsibility* (Detroit: Wayne State University Press, 1990), 18–19, 150–52, 174–75, 181–82. On p. 387, *Exploring Jewish Ethics*, Borowitz writes: "Formally, we [Reform Jews] do not speak of God and duty differently than do other Jews."
107. Ibid., 386. For an analysis of the rabbinic and contemporary views of "dignity," see Rochelle L. Millen, "Social Attitudes Disguised as Halakhah: *Zila Milta, Ein Havrutan Na'ah, Kevod Hatzibbur,*" *Nashim: A Journal of Jewish Women's Studies and Gender Issues,* no. 4 (fall 2001) 178–96.
108. Borowitz, *Exploring Jewish Ethics,* 298.
109. Ibid.
110. Ibid.
111. Eugene B. Borowitz, *Choosing a Sex Ethic: A Jewish Inquiry* (New York: Schocken Books, 1969), 26.
112. Borowitz, *Exploring Jewish Ethics,* 244–57.
113. Ibid., 257.
114. Borowitz, "The Autonomous Jewish Self," in *Exploring Jewish Ethics,* 191.
115. Ibid.
116. Borowitz, "Prospects for Jewish Denominationalism," in *Exploring Jewish Ethics,* 382.
117. Lauterbach, "Birth Control," 189.
118. Tikva Frymer-Kensky, *In the Wake of the Goddesses: Women, Culture and the Biblical Transformation of Pagan Myth* (New York: Fawcett Columbine, 1992), 141.
119. Judith Hauptman, *Rereading the Rabbis: A Woman's Voice* (Boulder, Colo.: Westview Press, 1998), 38–39, 56–57, nn.22, 23, 24.

120. Elizabeth Janeway, *Man's World, Woman's Place* (New York: Dell Publishing, 1971).
121. Ibid., 56.
122. An example is to be found in Aquinas, whose notion of reason as masculine leads to a hierarchy with men at the apex: "Good order would have been wanting in the human family if some were not governed by others wiser than themselves. So by such a kind of subjection woman is naturally subject to man, because in man the discretion of reason predominates." Thomas Aquinas, *Summa Theologica,* vol. 4 (New York: Benzinger Bros., 1947–1948), I, Q92, 276.
123. A contemporary discussion about nurturing fathers is found in Anne Roiphe, *Fruitful: A Real Mother in the Modern World* (Boston: Houghton Mifflin, 1996), esp. 139–59.
124. "To deny the different relations of women and men to human birth founds the entire egalitarian project on an illusion." Sara Ruddick, *Maternal Thinking: Toward a Politics of Peace* (New York: Ballantine, 1989), 49.
125. Michelle Zimbalist Rosaldo, "Women, Culture, and Society: A Theoretical Overview," in *Women, Culture, and Society,* ed. Michelle Z. Rosaldo and Louise Lamphere (Stanford, Calif.: Stanford University Press, 1974), 17.
126. See the discussion of the Ilongots in the Philippines, ibid., 39–42.
127. Peggy Sanday, "Female Status in the Public Domain," in *Women, Culture, and Society,* 189–206. Also in the same volume, Karen Sacks, "Engels Revisited: Women, the Organization of Production, and Private Property," 207–23.
128. Sherry B. Ortner, "Is Female to Male as Nature is to Culture?" in *Women, Culture, and Society,* 83–87.
129. A fascinating philosophical analysis of public/private and the concept of goodness is given by Hannah Arendt in *The Human Condition* (Chicago: University of Chicago Press, 1958), 68–73.
130. Lecture of J. B. Soloveitchik, undated.
131. Mishnah Avot 2:5.
132. Medieval communal structures were referred to as *"kahal,"* or *"kehillah."* See Jacob Katz, *Tradition and Crisis: Jewish* Society *at the End of the Middle Ages,* trans. Bernard Dov Cooperman (New York: New York University Press, 1993).
133. Emil L. Fackenheim, *God's Presence in History: Jewish Affirmations and Philosophical Reflections* (New York: Harper & Row, 1970), 67–98.
134. Fishman, *A Breath of Life,* 216–29.
135. References to the Women's Tefillah Network will be noted hereafter as WTN. This posting was titled "An Open Letter to Rabbi Saul Berman" and dated Feb. 20, 2000. In Hebrew, the root letters *r-h-m* form the word meaning "womb" as well as the term for "compassion."
136. Lewis White Beck, "Kant's Two Conceptions of the Will in Their Political Context," in his *Studies in the Philosophy of Kant* (New York: Bobbs-Merrill, 1965), 215–30. Also Rochelle L. Millen, "Free Will and the Possibility of Radical Evil in Kant" (master's thesis, McMaster University, 1975).
137. Jeffrey Stout argues that the development of the concept of "autonomy" is based on the Enlightenment "flight from authority," especially the breakdown of religious authority and community as manifested in the Reformation and its subsequent

religious wars. See Jeffrey Stout, *The Flight from Authority* (Notre Dame, Ind.: University of Notre Dame Press, 1981), chap. 11.

138. Eugene Borowitz, "The Autonomous Self and the Commanding Community," *Theological Studies* 45 (1984): 37.

139. Gerda Lerner, *Why History Matters: Life and Thought* (New York: Oxford University Press, 1997), 74–92.

140. Immanuel Kant, *Religion within the Limits of Reason Alone,* trans. Theodore M. Greene and Hoyt H. Hudson (New York: Harper Torchbooks, 1960). This was originally published in 1794. Also Emil L. Fackenheim, *The Religious Dimension in Hegel's Thought (*Boston: Beacon Press, 1967), esp. 197–203, and Fackenheim, *Encounters between Judaism and Modern Philosophy* (New York: Basic Books, 1973), chaps. 2 and 3.

141. Ibid., as well as Fackenheim's earlier essay, "The Revealed Morality of Judaism and Modern Thought," in *Quest for Past and Future: Essays in Jewish Theology* (Bloomington: Indiana University Press, 1967), 204–28. Also see David Hartman, *A Living Covenant: The Innovative Spirit in Traditional Judaism* (New York: The Free Press, 1985), 42–60, 229–55.

142. Donne proclaims, "No man is an island, entire of itself. . . ." in Meditation XVII of *Devotions Upon Emergent Occasions,* written in 1623.

143. See Borowitz, "The Autonomous Self and the Commanding Community," as well as his "The Autonomous Jewish Self," *Modern Judaism* 4, no. 1 (February 1984): 39–55. Also Moshe Z. Sokol, "Personal Authority and Religious Authority" in *Rabbinic Authority and Personal Autonomy,* ed. Moshe Z. Sokol (Northvale, N.J.: Jason Aronson, 1992), 169–216.

144. Abraham has the independence to challenge God when bargaining over Sodom. Well-known talmudic texts that reflect human autonomy in regard to tradition are T.B. Baba Metzia 59b and Berakhot 31b. These texts are analyzed in Gershom Scholem, "Revelation and Tradition as Religious Categories in Judaism," in *The Messianic Idea in Judaism and Other Essays on Jewish Spirituality* (New York: Schocken Books, 1971), 282–303, and David Hartman, *A Living Covenant* (New York: Free Press, 1985).

145. Sokol, "Personal Authority and Religious Authority."

146. Ibid., 181.

147. Ibid., 182.

148. He states, "It turns out, then, that in a theological framework one can simultaneously affirm multiple conceptions of the good and provide grounds for arguing that one of these conceptions is superior to the rest, whether for the Jewish people generally or for the individual Jew." Ibid., 213.

149. Ibid., 214.

150. Aharon Lichtenstein, "Does Jewish Tradition Recognize an Ethic Independent of Halakha?" reprinted in *Contemporary Jewish Ethics,* ed. Menachem Kellner (New York: Hebrew Publishing Co., 1978), 102–23; and Elliot N. Dorff and Louis E. Newman, eds., *Contemporary Jewish Ethics and Morality: A Reader* (New York: Oxford University Press, 1995), 9–128, sect. 1 (A–C).

151. Mishnah *Avot* 1:18.

152. Ibid., 1:12.

153. Lev. 19:2. See the dispute between Rashi and Nahmanides on how this verse is to be understood.
154. While the Jewish ideal is for inner attitude and outward action to be in harmony, Judaism recognizes that in human experience, a gap between them often exists. See Nehama Leibowitz's discussion of Ibn Ezra on this ideal in Nehama Leibowitz, *Studies in Shemot* [Exodus], vol. 1 (Jerusalem: World Zionist Organization, 1976), 342–43.
155. Sokol, "Personal Authority and Religious Authority," 215.
156. An excellent example is John Rawls, *Political Liberalism* (New York: Columbia University Press, 1993). This volume is a reworking of Rawls's earlier study, *Theory of Justice*.
157. My thanks to Don Reed for his helpful insights on this issue. For further discussion, see Charles Fried, *An Anatomy of Values: Problems of Personal and Social Choice* (Cambridge: Harvard University Press, 1970).
158. Research within the Jewish community has repeatedly demonstrated that a large majority of Jewish women want both families and careers. Indeed, Jewish women with university degrees tend to want more children than comparable groups of other religious and ethnic communities. The commitment to family and the Jewish community is powerful. Calvin Goldscheider, *Jewish Continuity and Change: Emerging Patterns in America* (Bloomington: Indiana University Press, 1986), 125–30.
159. Judith A. Baer, *Women in American Law: The Struggle toward Equality from the New Deal to the Present* (New York: Holmes & Meier, 1966), 65–121.
160. Led by David Altshuler, the trust is part of the United Jewish Communities. The project, called "Advancing Women Professionals and the Jewish Community," was given funding in February 2001 by Barbara and Eric Dobkin, and the project officially was launched by the trust on October 31, 2001. My thanks to Jackie Jacobs, executive director of the Columbus Jewish Foundation (Columbus, Ohio), for this information. This project is also discussed on p. 3 of the *Forward,* 2 November 2001, in an article titled "Women Leadership Project Launched."
161. Quoted by Erik Erikson in *Childhood and Society,* 2d ed. (New York: W. W. Norton, 1963), 265.
162. An interesting comment of Martin Luther's is quoted by Roland H. Bainton in his biography *Here I Stand: A Life of Martin Luther* (New York: New American Library, 1950), 235. While the neighbors may laugh to see a father hanging out the diapers (and this in the sixteenth century!), nonetheless, Luther says, "God and the angels smile in heaven." Luther's Reformation views of marriage are analyzed in Steven Ozment, "Re-inventing Family Life," *Christian History* 12, no. 3 (1993): 22–26. My thanks to Paul T. Nelson for the references.
163. These kinds of power—masculine and feminine—are astutely analyzed by Jean Baker Miller in "Women and Power: Reflections Ten Years Later," in *Women and Power: Perspectives for Family Therapy,* ed. Thelma Jean Goodrich (New York: W. W. Norton, 1991), 36–47.
164. Another thinker whose work illuminates these issues is Jessica Benjamin, in *The Bonds of Love: Psychoanalysis, Feminism, and the Problem of Domination* (New York: Pantheon, 1988). Examples of melding are flex-time, changes in maternity

leave, and contractual paternity leave. See Judith A. Baer, "The Problem That Won't Go Away," in *Women in American Law,* 318–19; Also, Mary Williams Walsh, "So Where Are the Corporate Husbands?" *New York Times,* 24 June 2001, Money and Business Section. The latter is accompanied by a shorter piece by Eve Tahminciolglu, "As Wives Move Up, Men Fend for Themselves."

165. Roiphe, *Fruitful,* Part III.

3. Fertility and Infertility

1. The biblical command to procreate is analyzed in chap. 2. As indicated there, women's exemption from the command to procreate, while having certain positive aspects, "stems from what one may appropriately call a sexist construction of marriage and divorce." So writes Judith Hauptman in *Rereading the Rabbis: A Woman's Voice* (Boulder, Ohio: Westview Press, 1998), 140. However, Hauptman maintains, the woman is not seen simply as enabler. Rather, she is viewed as full marriage partner having her own needs, "albeit subordinate to her husband," p. 141. Further explication of biblical and halakhic sources are to be found in Jeremy Cohen, *"Be Fertile and Increase, Fill the Earth and Master It": The Ancient and Medieval Career of a Biblical Text* (Ithaca: Cornell University Press, 1989).

2. Examples are Richard V. Grazi, *Be Fruitful and Multiply: Fertility Therapy and the Jewish Tradition* (Jerusalem: Genesis Jerusalem Press, 5754/1994); Walter Jacob and Moshe Zemer, eds., *The Fetus and Fertility in Jewish Law: Essays and Responsa* (Pittsburgh: Rodef Shalom Press, 1995); David M. Feldman, "The Ethical Implications of New Reproductive Techniques," in *Jewish Values in Bioethics,* ed. Levi Meier (New York: Human Sciences Press, 1986), 174–82; Susan Martha Kahn, *Reproducing Jews: A Cultural Account of Assisted Conception in Israel* (Durham, N.C.: Duke University Press, 2000); Nisson E. Shulman, "Sexuality and Reproduction," in *Jewish Answers to Medical Ethics Questions: Questions and Answers from the Medical Ethics Department of the Office of the Chief Rabbi of Great Britain* (Northvale, N.J.: Jason Aronson, 1998), 41–114; Abraham Sofer Abraham, *Nishmat Avraham: Hilkhot Refuah* (in Hebrew) (Jerusalem: Salk-Schlessinger Institute, 1993), vol. 3, 1–73. Articles about modern reproductive technology have also frequently appeared in Jewish newspapers; examples include Seth Mnookin, "Fertility Treatments, On Rise, Prompt New Dilemmas," *Forward,* 2 July 1999, 5, and Tami Bickley, "High-tech Fertility Options Provide Hope For Infertile Couples," *Jewish News of Greater Phoenix,* 14 May 1999, S23.

3. Solomon Buber, ed., *Midrash Shohar Tov* (in Hebrew) (New York: Om Publishing, 1947), 76.

4. Susan Handelman, "Family: A Religiously Mandated Ideal," *Sh'ma,* 20 March 1987.

5. "Marriage is . . . central to the theology of Judaism. The entire success of the covenant rests on the marriage premise and its procreative impulse." Blu Greenberg, "Marriage in the Jewish Tradition" in *Perspectives on Marriage: A Reader,* ed. Kieran Scott and Michael Warren (New York: Oxford University Press, 1993), 380.

6. *Simhat bat,* the celebration of the birth of a daughter, is clearly related to fertility and will be discussed in detail in the following chapter.

7. Margaret Sanger (1883–1966), a trained nurse, was born in Corning, N.Y. She fought tenaciously for the availability of contraceptives, leading the birth control movement here in the United States. In 1914 she established the American Birth Control League, forerunner of Planned Parenthood of America.

8. Conversation with Sylvia Barack Fishman, May 1993. Also, see Karen Payne, ed., *Between Ourselves: Letters between Mothers and Daughters, 1750–1982* (Boston: Houghton-Mifflin, 1983).

9. See Lawrence H. Fuchs, *Beyond Patriarchy: Jewish Fathers and Families* (Hanover, N.H.: University Press of New England, 2000).

10. See Sylvia Barack Fishman, *A Breath of Life: Feminism in the American Jewish Community* (Hanover, N.H.: University Press of New England, 1993), 60–61. Also Ruth W. Messinger, "A Surprising Lesson from those September 11 Obituaries," *Lilith* 27, no.1 (spring 2002): 10.

11. See Rosemary Ruether, "Home and Work: Women's Roles and the Transformation of Values," in *Perspectives on Marriage,* 285–96.

12. Eli Schussheim, *In Anticipation of a Happy Marriage* (Jerusalem: Efrat Organization), quoted in Susan S. Sered, *What Makes Women Sick? Maternity, Modesty, and Militarism in Israeli Society* (Hanover, N.H.: Brandeis University Press and University Press of New England, 2000), 39.

13. Adopted children are of oneself in terms of love and commitment, but not in regard to biology. Similarly, new reproductive technologies may offer biology as a partial factor.

14. Sergio DellaPergola, "Jewish Women in Transition: A Comparative Sociodemographic Perspective," in *Jews and Gender: The Challenge to Hierarchy,* ed. Jonathan Frankel (New York: Oxford University Press, 2000), 209.

15. Examples of this phenomenon are found, for instance, in such works of Jacob Katz as *Exclusiveness and Tolerance: Studies in Jewish-Gentile Relations in Medieval and Modern Times* (New York: Behrman House, 1961), and *The "Shabbes Goy": A Study in Halakhic Flexibility* (Philadelphia: Jewish Publication Society, 1989). Much responsa literature as well manifests this dialectic.

16. DellaPergola, "Jewish Women in Transition," 224. Also see Kahn, introduction to *Reproducing Jews,* 1–8, and Sered, *What Makes Women Sick?,* 1–21.

17. DellaPergola, "Jewish Women in Transition," 225.

18. Ibid., 226; DellaPergola puts the U.S., Canada, Argentina, Australia, and France in this category.

19. Kahn, *Reproducing Jews,* 1–3, and Sered, *What Makes Women Sick?,* 10. Kahn writes: "[R]eproduction as a response to tragedy is one of the most prominent characteristics of Israeli pronatalism," *Reproducing Jews,* 60.

20. DellaPergola, "Jewish Women in Transition," 236.

21. Ibid.

22. Ibid., 237.

23. Ibid., 237–38.

24. See Thelma Jean Goodrich, *Women and Power: Perspectives for Family Therapy* (New York: W. W. Norton, 1991).

25. Ibid., 238.

26. Amy Barrett, "Just One of the Boys," *New York Times Magazine,* 23 June 2002, 13.

27. Ibid.
28. Ambivalent feelings about motherhood have been explored in such recent studies as Naomi Wolf, *Misconceptions: Truth, Lies, and the Unexpected on the Journey to Motherhood* (New York: Doubleday, 2001), and Rachel Cusk, *A Life's Work: On Becoming a Mother* (New York: Picador, 2002).
29. T.B. Eruvin 100b; also quoted in Rashi's commentary on Gen. 3:16. In both of these sources, the phrase is understood as part of God's punishment to the woman subsequent to the sin of disobedience; i.e., the interpreters viewed the woman as the primary caregiver of children.
30. Elizabeth Hayt, "Admitting to Mixed Feelings About Motherhood," *New York Times,* Sunday, 12 May 2002, Style Section.
31. Compare the description of parenting among Jewish immigrant women in the late nineteenth and early twentieth centuries in Sydney Stahl Weinberg, *The World of Our Mothers: The Lives of Jewish Immigrant Women* (Chapel Hill: The University of North Carolina Press, 1988), chap. 11, esp. 211–15.
32. Quoted in Hayt, "Admitting to Mixed Feelings."
33. Sarah Bleffer Hrdy, *Mother Nature: A History of Mothers, Infants and Natural Selection* (New York: Pantheon, 1999). This was reissued in paperback under the title *Mother Nature: Maternal Instincts and How They Shape the Human Species* (New York: Ballantine, 2000).
34. Gerda Lerner, *Why History Matters: Life and Thought* (New York: Oxford University Press, 1997), 208.
35. Sylvia Barack Fishman, *Jewish Life and American Culture* (Albany: State University of New York Press, 2000), 96.
36. Ibid.
37. Ibid., 97.
38. Harriet Rosenstein, "The Fraychie Story" in *The Woman Who Lost Her Names: Selected Writings by American Jewish Women,* ed. Julia Wolf Mazow (San Francisco: Harper & Row, 1980).
39. Weinberg, *The World of Our Mothers,* 38.
40. Fishman, *Jewish Life and American Culture,* 98. Fishman is quoting from an unpublished dissertation by Sarah Silver Bunim, "Religious and Secular Factors of Role Strain in Orthodox Jewish Mothers" (Ph.D. diss., Wurzweiler School of Social Work, 1986).
41. Fishman, *Jewish Life and American Culture,* 99.
42. "[M]arriage without children is very distant from the Jewish ideal of marriage. The letter of the law may permit it, but we must encourage every couple to have at least two children." Written by Reform thinker Walter Jacob, in Walter Jacob and Moshe Zemer, eds., *Marriage and Its Obstacles in Jewish Law: Essays and Responsa* (Tel Aviv and Pittsburgh: Rodef Shalom Press, 1999), 195.
43. Calvin Goldscheider, *Jewish Continuity and Change: Emerging Patterns in America* (Bloomington: Indiana University Press, 1986), 195.
44. Fishman, *A Breath of Life,* 50.
45. Robin B. Zeiger, "Reflections on Infertility," in *Jewish Women Speak Out: Expanding the Boundaries of Psychology,* ed. Kayla Weiner and Arinna Moon (Seattle: Canopy Press, 1995), 83.

46. See chap. 2.

47. Zeiger, "Reflections on Infertility," 91.

48. Ibid.

49. Sara Barris, Ph.D., clinical psychologist in the New York area, is an example of a professional who focuses especially on issues of fertility (primary and secondary) as well as adoption within the Orthodox community. Articles by her are available through the internet.

50. Related to me in 1983 and 1990, respectively (the dates are approximate).

51. Naftali Herz Hacohen Kahane, *Otsar Tefillot Yisrael* (in Hebrew), 3 vols. (Jerusalem and London: n.p.,1993). My thanks to Eli Millen for this reference.

52. Ibid., 93–98.

53. Shmuel Hakatan, *Shaarei Dimah* (in Hebrew) (1873; reprint, Jerusalem: Eshkol Press, 1968). It is possible that the 1873 edition is derived from an earlier original. The petionary prayer concerning infertility is on p. 145. My thanks to Eli Millen for this reference.

54. Peggy Orenstein, "Mourning My Miscarriage," *New York Times Magazine.* April 21, 2002. See also David S. Rosenthal, *The Joyful Mother of Children* (New York: Feldheim, 1988) for a selection of prayers and reflections during pregnancy.

55. Perry Raphael Rank and Gordon M. Freeman, eds., *Moreh Derekh: The Rabbinical Assembly Rabbi's Manual,* vol. 2 (New York: The Rabbinical Assembly, 1998), sect. 1, 3–45.

56. In contrast to Orthodox rabbinic law, the manual states: "According to an official position of the committee on Jewish Law and Standards, a family that experiences the death of a baby prior to the thirty-first day of life may be comforted through the traditional rituals of *avelut* [mourning] as they apply to any death." Ibid., 18.

57. Ibid., 30.

58. Ibid., 42.

59. Ibid., 43.

60. Ibid., 45.

61. Simeon J. Maslin, ed., *Gates of Mitzvah: A Guide to the Jewish Life Cycle* (New York: Central Conference of American Rabbis, 1979), and David Polish, ed., *Maaglei tsedek: Rabbi's Manual,* annot. W. Gunther Plaut (New York: Central Conference of American Rabbis, 1988).

62. Chaim Stern, et al., eds., *On the Doorposts of Your House* (New York: Central Conference of American Rabbis, 1994), 108, 162–63.

63. Nina Beth Cardin, ed. and trans., *Out of the Depths I Call to You: A Book of Prayers for the Married Jewish Woman* (Northvale, N.J.: Jason Aronson, 1995). Written in 1786 for Mrs. Yehudit Kutscher Coen in Italy.

64. Ibid., 93.

65. Ibid., v.

66. Nina Beth Cardin, *Tears of Sorrow, Seeds of Hope: A Jewish Spiritual Companion for Infertility and Pregnancy Loss* (Woodstock, Vt.: Jewish Lights Publishing, 1999), 13.

67. *Havdalah* is the weekly ceremony performed at the end of the Sabbath. It distinguishes between Sabbath and the rest of the week.

68. Here assumed to be husbands.

69. Debra Orenstein, ed., *Lifecycles: Jewish Women on Life Passages and Personal Milestones* (Woodstock, Vt.: Jewish Lights Publishing, 1994).
70. Tikva Frymer-Kensky, *Motherprayer: The Pregnant Woman's Spiritual Companion* (New York: Riverhead Books, 1995).
71. Ibid., xvii.
72. One is by Nina Beth Cardin; another, "A Grieving Ritual Following Miscarriage or Stillbirth," by Amy Eilberg, is also in Cardin's *Tears of Sorrow, Seeds of Hope.*
73. Lynn Gottlieb, "The Fruits of Creation," in Orenstein, ed., *Lifecycles,* 40–44.
74. See n.38, above.
75. An example is in F. Carolyn Graglia, *Domestic Tranquility: A Brief Against Feminism* (Dallas, Tex.: Spence Publications, 1998).
76. Lisa Schiffren, "Lifestyles of the Rich and Infertile," *Commentary* 114, no. 1 (July–August 2002): 54.

4. *Simhat Bat:* Celebrating the Birth of a Daughter

1. Early ceremonies appeared in Michael and Sharon Strassfeld, eds., *The Second Jewish Catalog: Sources and Resources* (Philadelphia: Jewish Publication Society, 1976), and in Liz Koltun, ed., *Response: A Contemporary Jewish Review* VII, no. 2 (summer 1973). A new book, which is a "how to" guide, is Debra Nussbaum Cohen, *Celebrating Your New Jewish Daughter* (Woodstock, Vt.: Jewish Lights Publishing, 2001). Celebrating the birth of a girl is mentioned only in passing in David Novak's essay, "'Be Fruitful and Multiply': Issues Relating to Birth in Judaism," in *Celebration and Renewal: Rites of Passage in Judaism,* ed. Rela Mintz Geffen (Philadelphia: JPS, 5753/1993), 28. Another resource is Debra Orenstein, ed., *Lifecycles: Jewish Women on Life Passages and Personal Milestones* (Woodstock, Vt.: Jewish Lights Publishing, 1994), esp. chap. 3. Also Anita Diament, *The New Jewish Baby Book* (Woodstock, Vt.: Jewish Lights Publishing, 1993).
2. Published originally in French in 1949. The first English edition came out in 1952.
3. See T.B. Brachot 59b.
4. *Rosh* and *Mordecai* on T.B. Brachot 59b. *Rosh* and *Mordecai* are medieval commentaries on the Talmud.
5. *Shulhan Arukh, Orekh Haim* (in Hebrew), Siman 223; *Taz, sief katan aleph,* following the opinion of the Rashba.
6. T.B. Eruvin 70b.
7. See T.B. Ketubot 86b–87a.
8. T.B. Eruvin 70b.
9. A detailed discussion is given in S. Z. Zevin, ed., *Encyclopedia Talmudit,* vol. 4 (1952). 431–51.
10. See *Shulhan Arukh, Mishnah Berurah, sief katan beit.*
11. See Carol Gilligan, *In a Different Voice: Psychological Theory and Women's Development* (Cambridge: Harvard University Press, 1982). The literature on the Gilligan-Kohlberg controversy is extensive. See, for instance, Eva Feder Kittay and Diana T. Meyers, eds., *Women and Moral Theory* (Totowa, N.J.: Rowman & Littlefield, 1987); William M. Kurtines and Jacob L. Gewirtz, eds., *Handbook of Moral Behavior and Development,* vols. 1–3 (Hillsdale, N.J.: Lawrence Erlbaum

Associates, 1991); Susan S. Sered, *Women as Ritual Experts: The Religious Lives of Elderly Jewish Women in Jerusalem* (New York: Oxford University Press, 1992), 46–48.

12. Jennifer Breger and Lisa Schlaff, eds., *The Orthodox Jewish Woman and Ritual: Options and Opportunities—Birth* (New York: Jewish Orthodox Feminist Alliance, 2000), 3.

13. Ibid.

14. See discussion in Lawrence A. Hoffman, *Covenant of Blood: Circumcision and Gender in Rabbinic Judaism* (Chicago: University of Chicago Press, 1996), 30–36. Also Judith M. Lieu, "Circumcision, Women and Salvation," *New Testament Studies* 40, no. 3 (July 1994): 358–70.

15. Hoffman, *Covenant of Blood*.

16. The Mishnah was codified around the year 200 C.E.

17. Since she is obligated in fewer mitzvot as indicated in B.T. Kiddushin 33b and "Greater is [the reward of] the person who is commanded and fulfills the command than the person who is not commanded and fulfills the command" (B.T. Kiddushin 31a and Tosafot to that passage), her mitzvah value, so to speak, is automatically less and can never be that of a male. Joseph Karo reaffirms this in *Shulhan Arukh, Yoreh De'ah* 246:6, where he says, "A woman who has studied Torah has a reward but not as much as the reward of a man, because she is not commanded and performs it [of her own will]." The issue of what I have termed "mitzvah value" does seem to render her axiologically peripheral, at least in theory.

18. Is this mere apologetics? Is this relegating the female to the role of "enabler" of the person essential to maintaining the covenant, i.e., the male? Examples of studies that assume women to be full members of the covenant are Tamar Frankiel, *The Voice of Sarah: Feminine Spirituality and Traditional Judaism* (San Francisco: Harper, 1990); Lynn Davidman, *Tradition in a Rootless World: Women Turn to Orthodox Judaism* (Berkeley: University of California Press, 1991); Moshe Meiselman, *Jewish Woman in Jewish Law* (New York: Ktav, 1978). In these texts, the lack of a sign of the covenant, of any ceremony of acceptance into the covenant for a female child, is not an issue. Cf. Judith M. Lieu, "Circumcision, Women, and Salvation."

19. See Ari Z. Zivotofsky and Naomi T. S. Zivotofsky, "What's Right with Women and Zimun," *Judaism* 42, no. 4 (fall 1993): 453–64.

20. Howard Eilberg-Schwartz, *The Savage in Judaism: An Anthropology of Israelite Religion and Ancient Judaism* (Bloomington: Indiana University Press, 1990).

21. Gen. 15:5.

22. See Clifford Geertz, *The Interpretation of Culture* (New York: Basic Books, 1973).

23. Ibid., 9.

24. Cf. Barbara Myerhoff, introduction to *Number Our Days* (New York: Simon and Schuster, 1978).

25. Lawrence A. Hoffman, *Beyond the Text: A Holistic Approach to Liturgy* (Bloomington: Indiana University Press, 1987), 16.

26. Ibid., 96.

27. This verse, Ezek. 16:6, is central to the circumcision ceremony and is proclaimed when the child is named.

28. Hoffman, *Covenant of Blood,* 101.
29. Paysach J. Krohn, *Bris Milah* (New York: Mesorah Publications, 1985). *Brit,* the Hebrew word for covenant, can also be pronounced *"bris."*
30. Ibid., 30.
31. Hoffman, *Covenant of Blood,* 101–10. Compare the discussion in chap. 8, "The Problem with Foreskin: Circumcision, Gender, Impurity and Death," in David Kraemer, *Reading the Rabbis: The Talmud as Literature* (New York: Oxford University Press, 1996), 109–23. Chap. 7, "Women Categorized," 86–108, gives an interesting analysis of women and time-bound mitzvot.
32. Jon D. Levenson, "The New Enemies of Circumcision," *Commentary* 109, no. 3 (March 2000): 29–38. His essay provoked numerous letters to the editor in *Commentary* 109, no. 6 (June 2000): 1. See also Miriam Pollack, "Circumcision: A Jewish Feminist Perspective," in *Jewish Women Speak Out: Expanding the Boundaries of Psychology,* ed. Kayla Weiner and Arinna Moon (Seattle: Canopy Press, 1995), 171–85
33. These are terms used by Rabbi J. B. Soloveitchick in his essay "Kol Dodi Dofek" (in Hebrew) in *Besod Ha yahid veha yahad,* ed. Pinchas Peli (Jerusalem: Orot, 1976), 331–400.
34. Shaye J. D. Cohen, "Why Aren't Jewish Women Circumcised?" *Gender and History* 9, no. 3 (November 1997): 561.
35. Ibid.
36. Ibid., 562. Cohen also analyzes in some detail the practice of female excision in the ancient world.
37. The claim of Strabo, a Greek of the first century B.C.E., is that Jews are "Egyptians" and adapted circumcision from Egyptian culture. See also Lieu, "Circumcision, Women, and Salvation."
38. Ibid., 565. Cohen notes that "Philo follows the common Greek view that menstrual fluid is the stuff out of which the fetus is created" ("Why Aren't Women Circumcised?" 576, n.20.). The male, in contrast, provides the skill and the cause. Thus he needs a check on his pride.
39. Ibid., 565.
40. Ibid., 566–67. The literature on Paul's transformation of circumcision is large and relates to the general theological framework in which *halakhah* was declared non-salvific.
41. Ibid., 571. See Justin Martyr, "Dialogue with Trypho the Jew," ed. and trans. T. Falls, in *Writings of Saint Justin Martyr: The First Apology* (New York: Christian Heritage, 1948), sects. 16–24. Cited in S. Cohen, "Why Aren't Jewish Women Circumcised?" 577, n.28. Also see discussion of Martyr in Lieu, "Circumcision, Women, and Salvation."
42. S. Cohen, "Why Aren't Jewish Women Circumcised?" 571.
43. Ibid.
44. Ibid.
45. Ibid., 572.
46. See Jeremy Cohen, *"Be Fertile and Increase, Fill the Earth and Master It": The Ancient and Medieval Career of a Biblical Text* (Ithaca, N.Y.: Cornell University Press, 1989), 164. Also note Judith Hauptman's statements, "I do not believe that it

is possible to depatriarchalize the Talmud, but I will show that, within its patriarchal framework, not only is sympathy expressed for women . . . but . . . resolute action taken on their behalf." Judith Hauptman, *Rereading the Rabbis: A Woman's Voice* (Boulder, Colo.: Westview Press, 1998).

47. S. Cohen, "Why Aren't Jewish Women Circumcised?" 574, 573.

48. Some of the sources dealing with this possibility are B.T. Hulin 46 and Mishnah Yevamot 8:1.

49. S. Cohen, "Why Aren't Jewish Women Circumcised?" 574.

50. Saadia Gaon, *The Book of Beliefs and Opinions,* trans. Samuel Rosenblatt (New Haven, Conn.: Yale University Press, 1958), 177.

51. Moses Maimonides, *The Guide of the Perplexed,* vol. 3 trans. Shlomo Pines (Chicago: University of Chicago Press, 1963), chap. 49, 609.

52. Moses Nahmanides, *Commentary on the Torah,* trans. C. B. Chavel (New York: Shilo, 1971), "Genesis," 219. Additional reasons are given in B.T. Shabbat 108a.

53. Samson R. Hirsch, *Pentateuch,* trans. Isaac Levy (New York: Bloch, 1963), 302. See also Hirsch's essays in *Yeshurun,* vols. 4 and 5 (Bene Brak: Tefutsah, 1985), as well as Shmuel A. Adler, *Aspaklarya* (in Hebrew) (Jerusalem: Aspaklarya, 1991), 238. See also n.39, above. Cf. Don Seeman, "The Silence of Rayna Batya," *The Torah U-Madda Journal* 6 (1995–96): 91–128.

54. Daniel Boyarin, *Carnal Israel: Reading Sex in Talmudic Culture* (Berkeley: University of California Press, 1993), 245.

55. Hauptman, *Rereading the Rabbis,* 5. Hauptman describes her study as a "contextualized feminism," (p. 6).

56. An interesting view, given the rite of *sotah* (woman suspected of infidelity). Other reasons given for circumcision may be found in Sander L. Gilman, *The Jew's Body* (New York: Routledge, 1991), esp. 91–92 and 155–57.

57. See Hoffman, *Covenant of Blood,* 179–207. Especially important is Hoffman's citing of sources that verify the custom of mothers holding their newborn sons during the *brit milah.* This was done away with by "the German rabbis from the Maharam to Maharil" (205) and labeled *peritsut* (licentiousness) by the Rama in the sixteenth century. For interesting discussions of Zipporah and Moses in Exod. 4:24–26, see in addition to the classical commentators, Ilana Pardes, *Countertraditions in the Bible: A Feminist Approach* (Cambridge: Harvard University Press, 1992) chap. 5, and Martin Buber, *Moses: The Revelation and the Covenant* (San Francisco: Harper Torchbooks, 1958), 56–59.

58. Sherry B. Ortner, "Is Female to Male as Nature is to Culture?" in *Woman, Culture, and Society,* ed. Michelle Zimbalist Rosaldo and Louise Lamphere (Stanford, Calif.: Stanford University Press, 1974), 67–89.

59. The institution of *shalom zakhor* (welcoming a newborn boy the Friday night prior to his *brit milah*) is also relevant here, but will not be discussed.

60. This bifurcation is clearly indicated in the words of the renowned Torah commentator, Samson R. Hirsch. Frequently using etymological analysis as a guide to insight into the verses of the text, Hirsch explains that a male is *zakhar* in Hebrew based on the root *z-kh-r,* meaning "to remember." This denotes the male role as not only repository but also transmitter of the historical memory of the Jewish people. The female, is contrast, is *nekavah, n-k-v,* a hole or opening through which

her destiny as bearer of new life is fulfilled. See "The Jewish Woman," in *Judaism Eternal: Selected Essays from the Writings of Rabbi Samson Raphael Hirsch,* trans. and annot. by I. Grunfeld (London: Soncino Press, 1959), 51.

61. The notion expressed by some that she doesn't need the *ot habrit* because she is on a higher spiritual level is pure apologetics, comparable to certain explanations given for exemption from time-bound mitzvot.

62. That woman possesses an intrinsic "private nature," which public rites contravene, is, once again, apologetics. See Meiselman, *Jewish Women in Jewish Law,* 11–15.

63. Hershel Schacter, "Go Out in the Footsteps of the Sheep" (in Hebrew), *Bet Yitshak* 17 (1984–1985), 118.

64. See Emanuel Feldman, "Orthodox Feminism and Feminist Orthodoxy," *Jewish Action* (winter 5760/1990): 12–17. Feldman's piece is egregious in its use of stereotypes.

65. Aharon Feldman, "Halakhic Feminism or Feminist Halakha?" *Tradition* 33, no. 2 (winter 1999): 62 and 66. This purported book review is a vituperative attack on the publishers and contributors to the volume *Jewish Legal Writings by Women,* edited by Micah D. Halpern and Chana Safrai (Jerusalem: Urim Publications, 1998). It expresses the fear of female scholarship and power through the projection of ad hominem attacks upon those who, by virtue of writing in and publishing this book, have challenged male rabbinic scholarship and power.

66. Sacha Stern, *Jewish Identity in Early Rabbinic Writings* (New York: E. J. Brill, 1994), 240–41.

67. A corrective to this perspective is offered in Tal Ilan's recent book, *Integrating Women into Second Temple History* (Peabody, Ma.: Hendrickson, 2001). See also Judith R. Baskin, *Midrashic Women: Formations of the Feminine in Rabbinic Literature* (Hanover, N.H.: University Press of New England, 2002).

68. *Pirkei de R. Eliezer* (in Hebrew) notes by David Luria (Jerusalem, 1970), cited by Stern, *Jewish Identity,* 65.

69. Stern, *Jewish Identity,* 64. See also Susan S. Sered, *What Makes Women Sick? Maternity, Modesty, and Militarism in Israeli Society* (Hanover, N.H.: Brandeis University Press and University Press of New England, 2000). On p. 9 she states, "Circumcision brings Jewish men into the covenant community once and for all. . . . Women's status in the covenant community is more precarious, in need of negotiation and testing. . . ."

70. Stern, *Jewish Identity,* 65. The text is "Song of Songs" and the interpretation in *Song of Songs Rabbah* (in Hebrew) (Jerusalem: Levi Epstein, 1960), 7:3. See Stern's n. 113 on p. 65, where other comparisons—to a fig and a nut—are given a similar male-focused reading. Female genitals, however, are also "split."

71. See the wonderful short story by Nessa Rapoport, "The Woman Who Lost Her Names," in *The Woman Who Lost Her Names: Selected Writings by American Jewish Women,* ed. Julia Wolf Mazow (San Francisco: Harper & Row, 1980), 135–45. On the continuing development of new ritual (and its relation to feminism) see *Journey* (fall 2002), published by Ma'yan, the Jewish Women's Project; and the website <ritualwell.org>.

72. Meiselman, *Jewish Women in Jewish Law,* 58–62.

73. Ibid., 58. The biblical references are Lev. 10:1–2.

74. Ibid., 60f.

75. Ibid., 6–62. In his concluding paragraph, Meiselman proclaims, "A Jew does not view his [*sic*] Judaism as the cultural expression of a patriarchal society. . . ."

76. See n.48, above; is it then *somewhat* forbidden?

77. Also see Nahmanides on Lev. 19:2.

78. Orenstein, ed., *Lifecycles,* vol. 1, 63. Also see Hoffman: "I do not mean, of course, that anyone seriously recommends introducing a parallel operation for girls," *Covenant of Blood,* 219.

79. BT Yevamot 46a.

80. Orenstein, ed., *Lifecycles.*

81. Barbara Myerhoff, *Remembered Lives: The Work of Ritual, Storytelling, and Growing Older* (Ann Arbor: University of Michigan Press, 1992), 161.

82. Ibid.

83. See Rachel Biale, *Women and Jewish Law: An Exploration of Women's Issues in Halakhic Sources* (New York: Schocken Books, 1984), 29–43.

84. I wish to thank Mrs. Annette Landau, librarian at the New York section of the NCJW, for her help on May 10, 1999, when I spent several hours reading through the collection of *simhat bat* ceremonies.

85. Ceremonies 1, 2, and 3 are part of the archives at the Jewish Women's Resource Center of the National Council of Jewish Women, New York section.

86. Unpublished paper by Rabbi Marc Angel, rabbi of Spanish-Portugese Synagogue of New York.

87. See pages 74–75.

88. See Breger and Schlaff, eds., *The Orthodox Jewish Woman and Ritual.* Also Rochelle L. Millen, "*Birkhat Hagomel:* A Study in Cultural Context and Halakhic Practice," *Judaism* 43, no. 3 (summer 1994): 270–78.

89. A listing is given by D. Cohen, *Celebrating Your New Jewish Daughter,* 44.

90. See Breger and Schlaff, eds., *The Orthodox Jewish Woman and Ritual.*

91. Personal fax received on January 21, 2000, in response to a series of questions I had faxed Rabbi Angel earlier that same day.

92. David de Sola Pool, ed., *Siddur* [Sephardi], 3d ed. (New York: Behrman House, 1972), 417. See also last page of the fourth ceremony, above, p. 95.

93. It is also of interest that Rabbi Angel indicated that the blessing of "Torah" is not included in contemporary Orthodox Sephardi baby-namings, nor is the mother's name included with the father's.

94. Perry Raphael Rank and Gordon M. Freeman, eds., *Moreh Derekh: The Rabbinical Assembly Rabbi's Manual,* vol. 2 (New York: The Rabbinical Assembly, 1998), F–10.

95. *Ha-Siddur Hashalem,* trans. and annot. Philip Birnbaum (New York: Hebrew Publishing Company, 1977), 372.

96. Nosson Scherman and Meir Zlotowitz, eds., *Siddur Ahavat Shalom: The Complete Artscroll Siddur* (New York: Mesorah Publications, 1984), 443.

97. Asher Sharfstein, *Tikkun Lakoreim* (in Hebrew) (1946; reprinted New York: Ktav Publishing, 1969), 376.

98. It does so as well in the naming formula for a baby boy. The JOFA calendar ceremony states, "May God who blessed Sarah, Rebecca, Rachel and Leah, Miriam the prophet, Abigail, and Queen Esther the daughter of Avichayil . . ."

99. English version of Hebrew text in *Moreh Derech,* F-7. Omitted in the translation is the phrase *"noldah lah be mazal tov,"* (born to her in good fortune).
100. David Polish, ed., *Rabbi's Manual,* with historical and halachic notes by W. Gunther Plaut (New York: Central Conference of American Rabbis, 1988), 16–24.
101. Ibid., 41.
102. Hoffman, *Covenant of Blood,* 179.
103. See, for instance, Michel Klein, *A Time To Be Born: Customs and Folklore of Jewish Birth* (Philadelphia: JPS, 1998), 191–92.
104. For discussion of this rabbinic text, see Rochelle L. Millen, "Analysis of Rabbinic Hermeneutics: B.T. Kiddushin 34a," in *Gender and Judaism: The Transformation of Tradition,* ed. T. M. Rudavsky (New York: New York University Press, 1995), 25–39, and Noam Zohar, "Women, Men and Religious Status: Deciphering a Chapter in Mishnah," in *Approaches to Ancient Judaism,* vol. 5, eds. Herbert W. Basser and Simeha Fishbein (Atlanta: Scholars Press, 1993), 33–54.
105. An example is Mary Todd, *Authority Vested: A Story of Identity and Change in the Lutheran Church—Missouri Synod* (Grand Rapids, Mich.: W. B. Eerdmans, 2000). See also Taliban promulgations regarding women, as well as "Letter of Pope John Paul II to Women" issued on June 29, 1995, and available on the Vatican web page, <http://www.vatican.va/holy_father/john_paul/ii/index>
106. See Josephine Wilson, *Biological Foundations of Human Behavior* (Pacific Grove, Calif.: Wadsworth, 2002).
107. Sent to <wtn@shamash.org> by a member of that listserve on October 4, 2001; article by Elaine M. Viders, J.D., is taken from <Aish.com>. Readers' responses may be found at <http://aish.com/societywork/women/Rights vs. Right.asp>. Ms. Viders is a professor of law at Touro Law School.
108. A similar reluctance among some Israeli feminists is noted in Andrea M. Jacobs, "'Address me as a Woman!': Can Linguistic Structure Influence Strategies for Language Reform? The Case of Contemporary Israeli Hebrew," (paper presented to the Jewish Feminist Research Group of Ma'yan, May 2002), 33.
109. See Christel Manning, *God Gave Us the Right: Conservative Catholic, Evangelical Protestant, and Orthodox Jewish Women Grapple with Feminism* (New Brunswick, N.J.: Rutgers University Press, 1999).
110. Carol Meyers, *Discovering Eve: Ancient Israelite Women in Context* (New York: Oxford University Press, 1988), 169.
111. See Louise Lamphere, "The Domestic Sphere of Women and the Public World of Men: The Strengths and Limitations of an Anthropological Dichotomy," in *Gender in Cross-Cultural Perspective,* ed. Carolyn Brettell and Carolyn Sargent (Upper Saddle River, N.J.: Prentice Hall, 2001), 100–9.
112. Christopher Lasch, *Women and the Common Life: Love, Marriage, and Feminism* (New York: W. W. Norton, 1997), 95.
113. Ibid., 96.
114. For recent discussion of the concept of individualism, see Jennifer L. Geddes, ed., *The Hedgehog Review: Critical Reflections on Contemporary Culture* 4, no. 1 (spring 2002). The issue is named "Individualism" and includes essays by Robert N. Bellah, Amitai Etzioni, Patrick J. Deneen, and Nina Eliasoph.

115. Leah Shakdiel, Women's Tefillah Network (hereafter, WTN), list-serve posting, March 25, 2002 and personal communication, October 31, 2002.
116. Ibid., October 31, 2002.
117. Ibid.
118. B.T. Berakhot 45a; Eruvin 14b.
119. That is, the right to elect as well as to be elected.
120. Weinberg (1885–1966) taught at the Hildesheimer Rabbinical Seminary in Berlin and later lived in Switzerland.
121. *Responsa Seridei Esh* 2, no. 52, quoted in *Jewish Law (Mishpat Ivri): Cases and Materials,* ed. Menachem Elon, et al. (New York: Matthew Bender, 1999), 506.
122. *Responsa Seridei Esh* 2, no. 105, in ibid., 507. See also Zvi Zohar, "Traditional Flexibility and Modern Strictness: Two Halakhic Positions on Women's Suffrage," in *Sephardi and Middle Eastern Jewries,* ed. Harvey E. Goldberg (Bloomington: Indiana University Press, 1996), 119–133.
123. See pp. 10, 46–50.
124. Donald Collins Reed, "Some Observations about How Moral Psychologists Have Construed Autonomy," (paper presented at the Association for Moral Education, Vancouver, British Columbia, October 2001).
125. Ibid.
126. Gilligan, *In A Different Voice.*
127. See Reed, "Some Observations." Also Richard A. Shweder, et al., "The 'Big Three' of Morality (Autonomy, Community, Diversity) and the 'Big Three' Explanations of Suffering," in *Morality and Health,* ed. Allan M. Brandt and Paul Rozin (Florence, Ky.: Routledge, 1997).
128. Reed, "Some Observations." See Anne Colby, et al., *The Measurement of Moral Judgment,* vol. 1 (New York: Cambridge University Press, 1987). The debt of this notion to Kantian ethics is clear.
129. Jean Piaget, *The Moral Judgment of the Child* (1932; New York: Free Press, 1954).
130. Reed, "Some Observations."
131. See Paula E. Hyman, *Gender and Assimilation in Modern Jewish History: The Roles and Representations of Women* (Seattle: University of Washington Press, 1995), esp. 134–70.
132. A recent analysis of how time, history, and custom have affected halakhah is to be found in Aharon Lichtenstein, "The Human and Social Factor in Halakha," *Tradition* 36, no. 1 (spring 2001): 1–25. R. Lichtenstein inveighs against the notion of the *posek,* or halakhic legislator, as a "heartless supercomputer" who, upon receiving the necessary data, "produces *the* right answer." There is no pure standard. Social, economic, and personal factors, he argues, are always part of halakhic decision-making. He acknowledges that sociological considerations play a part in the development of Jewish law, but cautiously advises that there is "nothing in this process to undermine the halakhic order or to challenge its architects," p. 19.

5. Mourning: Kaddish and the Funeral

1. An uncle, a younger brother of my mother, convinced that neither of my brothers would carry out the recitation of kaddish on a daily basis, volunteered to say kad-

dish on my mother's behalf. When I told him I would be doing so, he was adamant. How could I, his niece, fulfill an obligation that in his mind, and in halakhic (Jewish legal) sources, devolved only upon men?

2. It is known from the responsa of R. Moshe Feinstein that it was not uncommon for women sometimes to come to morning prayers in order to recite kaddish on behalf of a family member. See *Iggerot Moshe* (in Hebrew) (Brooklyn, N.Y.: Moriah Press, 1961), Orach Haim 5:12, in which R. Feinstein writes, "[I]n every generation, it has been customary that sometimes . . . a woman who is a mourner will come to *shul* to say *kaddish*. . . ."

3. Some of the discussion of halakhic sources and responsa in this chapter are excerpted, with permission of the publisher, from Rochelle L. Millen, "The Female Voice of Kaddish," in *Jewish Legal Writings by Women,* ed. Chana Safrai and Micah D. Halpern (Jerusalem: Urim Publications, 1998), 179–201. A very early version of this article was published as "Women and Kaddish: Reflections on Responsa," in *Modern Judaism* 10 (1990): 191–203.

4. See Feinstein, *Iggerot Moshe* 1:104, 2:97, 4:36, and 2:30; R. Ovadia Yosef, *Yehaveh daat* (in Hebrew) (Jerusalem: Mahon Ovadia, 1976–1977), 2:29; Yosef, *Yabia omer* (in Hebrew) (Jerusalem: Porat Yosef, 1963–1995), 6:29; R. Yehiel Weinberg, *Seredei esh* (in Hebrew) (Jerusalem: The Committee for Publication of R. Weinberg's Writings, 1999), 3:93. Also Erica S. Brown, "The Bat Mitzvah in Jewish Law and Contemporary Practice," in *Jewish Legal Writings by Women,* 232–58.

5. The covering of mirrors and prohibition of food preparation are more in the sphere of established custom than rabbinic law. One source for the *seudat hav-ra-a,* the meal served by the community to the mourners upon return from the cemetery, is the restriction upon the mourner of food preparation.

6. See Aaron Kirschenbaum, "Subjectivity in Rabbinic Decision-Making," in *Rabbinic Authority and Personal Autonomy,* ed. Moshe Z. Sokol (Northvale, N.J.: Jason Aronson, 1992), 61–92.

7. The Jerusalem (or Palestinian) Talmud was written and edited between 220 and 350 C.E.; the Babylonian Talmud between 220 and 550 C.E. There is slight variation in scholarly opinion about the dates. These are taken from Jacques K. Mikliszanski, *The Saga of Traditional Judaism* (Los Angeles: Zahava Publishing, 1977).

8. This is analogous to the B.T. Moed Katan 27b and Ketubot 8b where the text states, "In earlier times the expenses of burying the dead were harder for his/her relatives to bear than his death [itself]. Finally, Rabban Gamliel [ordered] that he be buried in [simple] linen wrappings. Everyone then followed his example and was buried in linen wrappings" (rather than the more expensive wool garments, which some had used). From this derives the Jewish custom of using white cotton/linen shrouds for everyone, regardless of class and economic status.

9. This refers to the words of comfort extended to the mourners, usually in the format, "May you be comforted among the mourners of Zion and Jerusalem."

10. The geonim (singular: gaon) were the formal heads of the Talmudic academies in Sura and Pumbedita (in Babylonia) from the end of the sixth century to the middle of the eleventh.

11. During the period of the Israelite monarchy, the Valley of Ben-Hinnom was the site

of the cult of Moloch, where children were burned. It then came to refer to the place of torment and punishment reserved for the wicked after death.

12. The recitation in the prayer service of *barekhu,* or "Bless the Lord who is blessed."

13. Midrashim (midrash is the singular) is a genre primarily of sermonic literature compiled between 400 and 1200 C.E. See Barry W. Holtz, "Midrash," in *Back to the Sources: Reading the Classic Jewish Texts,* ed. Barry W. Holtz (New York: Summit Books, 1984), 177–212.

14. See also, however, B.T. Sanhedrin 104a. "A son confers privileges on his father, but a father confers no privilege on a son" (Soncino tranlation).

15. See Mishna Eduyot 2:10 and Rosh haShana 17a.

16. The date of a *yahrtzeit* is calculated according to the Jewish calendar.

17. This aspect of a woman's reciting kaddish is dramatically conveyed in the 1990 documentary *Half the Kingdom,* produced by Francine Zuckerman and Roushellc Goldstein (Kol Ishah Productions and the National Film Board of Canada).

18. An excellent discussion of this category is found in Rachel Biale, *Women and Jewish Law: An Exploration of Women's Issues in Halakhic Sources* (New York: Shocken, 1984), chap. 1. See n.20, below.

19. Quoted in Charlotte Baum, Paula Hyman, and Sonya Michel, *The Jewish Woman in America* (New York: New American Library, 1976), 45.

20. For a detailed analysis of this category, see Biale, *Women and Jewish Law,* 10–43. Also, Rochelle L. Millen, "An Analysis of Rabbinic Hermeneutics: B.T. Kiddushin 34a," in *Gender and Judaism: The Transformation of Tradition,* ed. T. M. Rudavsky (New York: New York University Press, 1995), 25–38. Also see the discussion in Judith Hauptman, *Rereading the Rabbis: A Woman's Voice* (Boulder, Colo.: Westview Press, 1998), chap. 10.

21. Steven F. Cohen and Kenneth Branden, eds. *The Yeshiva University Haggada* (New York: Student Organization of Yeshiva, 1985), 7–9. The other editions I looked at were Chaim Stefansky, ed. *The Carlebach Haggadah* (New York: Urim Publications, 2001); *The Malbim Haggadah,* trans. and adapted by Jonathan Toub and Yisroel Shaw (New York: Feldheim, 1993); Marcus Lehmann, ed., *Lehmann's Passover Hagadah* (New York: Lehmann Books, 1974); and Morris Silverman, ed. *Passover Haggadah* (Hartford, Conn.: Prayer Book Press, 1966).

22. The literature on the relationship between language, religion, and feminism is large. A few examples are Virginia Ramey Mollenkott, *The Divine Feminine: The Biblical Imagery of God as Female* (New York: Crossroad, 1987); Janet Morley, "I Desire Her with My Whole Heart," in *Feminist Theology: A Reader,* ed. Ann Loades (Louisville, Ky.: Westminster John Knox, 1990), 158–165; Janet Martin Soskice, "Can a Feminist Call God 'Father'?" in *Women's Voices: Essays in Contemporary Feminist Theology,* ed. Theresa Elwes (London: Marshall Pickering/Harper Collins, 1992), 15–30; Rachel Adler, *Engendering Judaism: An Inclusive Theology and Ethics* (Philadelphia: Jewish Publication Society, 1998), chap. 3, esp. 70–71. Language and class is addressed by Joan Wallach Scott in *Gender and the Politics of History* (New York: Columbia University Press, 1999), chap. 3; Robin Lakoff, *Language and Woman's Place* (New York: Harper Torchbooks, 1975); Rosemary Ruether, *Sexism and Godtalk: Towards a Feminist Theology* (Boston: Beacon, 1984); Sherry Ruth Anderson and Patricia Hopkins, *The Feminine Face of God* (New York: Bantam, 1991).

23. English language guides to the traditional laws of mourning may be found in Chaim B. Goldberg, *Mourning in Halachah* (New York: Mesorah Publications, 1991), and Maurice Lamm, *The Jewish Way in Death and Mourning,* rev. ed. (Middle Village, N.Y.: Jonathan David, 2000). The classic Hebrew text is Yekutiel Greenwald, *Kol bo al avelut* (New York: Feldheim, 1973).

24. See n.14 above.

25. Some contemporary Jewish discussions of grief, mourning, and kaddish may be found in Letty Cottin Pogrebin, *Deborah, Golda, and Me: Being Female and Jewish in America* (New York: Crown Publishing, 1991), 43, 50–54; Leonard Fein, *Against the Dying of the Light: A Father's Journey through Loss* (Woodstock, Vt.: Jewish Lights, 2001); E. M. Broner, *Mornings and Mourning: A Kaddish Journal* (San Francisco: Harper, 1994); Nessa Rapoport, *A Woman's Book of Grieving* (New York: William Morrow, 1994); Leon Wieseltier, *Kaddish* (New York: A. Knopf, 1998); Judith Hauptman, "Death and Mourning: A Time for Weeping, A Time for Healing," in *Celebration and Renewal: Rites of Passage in Judaism,* ed. Reta Mintz Geffen (Philadelphia: Jewish Publication Society, 5753/1993), 226–51.

26. My thanks to Gershon Greenberg for helping me locate this quotation from the Yad Vashem Archives 03/8515, testimony of Rahel Fulda and Hannah Zak. It is represented in the memorial book, *Sefer Telz: matsevet zikaron li-kehilah kedoshah* (in Hebrew and Yiddish), ed. Yitshak Alperovits (Tel-Aviv: Society of Telz in Israel, 1984). Translation from the Yiddish by Henoch and Rochelle L. Millen.

27. See Deborah Weissman, "Bais Yaacov: A Historical Model for Jewish Feminists" in *The Jewish Woman: New Perspectives,* ed. Elizabeth Koltun (New York: Schocken Books, 1976), 139–48.

28. Pearl Benisch, *To Vanquish the Dragon* (New York: Feldheim, 1991), 417.

29. My free translation from Responsum 222, *Responsa of the Havot Yair* (Jerusalem, 1972). *Kedusha* is the third blessing of the long silent prayer, called the *amida,* which is the focal point of all prayer services. Known also as *kedushat Hashem,* it is inserted at the beginning of the third benediction when the reader repeats the *amida* during public worship.

30. These are the *kedushah* of the *amidah* (silent prayer of eighteen blessings) and that called *kedushah d'sidrah* in the prayer *Uva l'tzion.*

31. My translation.

32. Note that Bachrach's reasoning goes from "obligation" in *kiddush Hashem* to "can," "may," or "is permitted to" say kaddish and not from "obligation" in *kiddush Hashem* to "is therefore obligated to" recite kaddish.

33. Written by Yehudah Ashkenazi of mid-eighteenth-century Frankfurt.

34. Responsa of Ezekiel Katzenellenbogen, *Keneset Yehezkel* (in Hebrew) (Hamburg and Altona, 1732). Reprinted in Bene Brak in the 1980s.

35. Responsa of Jehiel Aaron Tukachinsky, written in 1947.

36. Ben-Zion Meir Hai Uziel, *Mishpetei Uziel* (in Hebrew) (Tel Aviv: Levitski, 1935–1940), Orah Chaim 2:8, 13.

37. Shlomo Halevi Wahrman, *She'erit Yosef* (in Hebrew) vol. 2 (New York: Balsham, 1981), 299f. The translation is mine.

38. See n.24, above.

39. Haim David haLevi, *Aseh lekha Rav* (in Hebrew), vol. 5 (Tel Aviv: Ha-Vaddah Le-hotsaat Kitve H. D. Halevi, 5743/1983), 334–36.
40. See Joel B. Wolowelsky's letter to the editor in *HaDarom* 57 (5748/1988): 157–58, and his *Women, Jewish Law, and Modernity* (New York: Ktav, 1997), 88. Also see Sara Reguer, "Kaddish from the 'Wrong' Side of the Mehitzah," in *On Being a Jewish Feminist,* ed. Susannah Heschel (New York: Schocken Books, 1983), 177–81.
41. Aaron Soloveitchik, *Od Yisrael Yosef Beni Chai* (in Hebrew) (Chicago: Yeshivat Brisk, 1993), 100, n.32.
42. I am grateful to the late Isaac Nadoff of Omaha, Nebraska (formerly of Chicago), for sending me the Blair responsum. Blair was born in Dvinsk in 1897, where he was ordained. He died in Israel in 1967, having written the responsum around 1950 while living in Chicago (e-mail communication from Aviva Cayam, granddaughter of Blair).
43. My free translation from Soloveitchik, *Od Yisrael Yosef Beni Chai* (in Hebrew).
44. Blair analyzes the well-known dispute as to whether prayer is of rabbinic or biblical origin and discusses sources in the Mishnah and Maimonides's *Mishneh Torah.*
45. My translation from Blair's independently printed responsum, *Does a Daughter Have a Duty to Say Kaddish?* (Chicago: 1950). See n.3 above.
46. Blair quotes Yekutiel Greenwald on this question in the *Kol Bo Al Avelut.* Other Jewish legal decisors have also addressed the question. See for instance Uziel, *Mishpetei Uziel.*
47. Blair, *Does a Daughter . . . ?* The phrase "twelve months" in the *Chavot Yair* may refer to the practice of reciting kaddish for eleven months and one day, i.e., into the twelfth month.
48. This principle is enunciated in several places in B.T. Moed Katan, including 18a and b, 22 a and b.
49. A commandment of biblical origin carries greater weight and has more authority than a commandment of rabbinic origin. Despite the rabbinic origins of the recitation of kaddish, Blair is designating it as equal to a commandment whose source is the Torah itself. Kaddish has become so much a part of mourning rites that it is *as if* it were biblically mandated.
50. Blair, *Does a Daughter . . . ?*
51. Pogrebin, *Deborah, Golda, and Me,* 54.
52. Related to me by Karen Moss of Columbus, Ohio.
53. Francesca Lunzer Kritz, "The 'Dangerous' Act of Saying Kaddish in an Orthodox Synagogue," *Forward,* 3 July 1998, 15.
54. The sources analyzing the relationship between historical context and halakhic flexibility are many. Among them are the works of the social historian Jacob Katz and the following essays: Zvi Zohar, "Traditional Flexibility and Modern Strictness: Two Halakhic Positions on Women's Suffrage," In *Sephardi and Middle Eastern Jewries,* ed. Harvey E. Goldberg (Bloomington: Indiana University Press, 1996), 119–33; Nissan Rubin, "Coping with the Value of the *Pidyon haben* Payment in Rabbinic Literature: An Example of a Social Change Process," *Jewish History* 10, no. 1 (spring 1996): 39–62.
55. Yehuda Herzl Henkin, "The Reciting of Kaddish by a Woman" (in Hebrew), Henkin, *HaDarom:* 54 (5745/1985): 34–38, reprinted in Yehuda Herzl Henkin,

Responsa Bnei Banim, vol. 2, responsum 7 (Y. H. Henkin: Jerusalem, 1950) esp. 43, para. 2, and n.1. The cited passage is from page 43.

56. Henkin's analysis is based on a responsum of his grandfather, Yosef Eliyahu Henkin, originally written in 1948.

57. Reuven Fink, "The Recital of Kaddish by Women," *Journal of Halacha and Contemporary Society* (spring 1996), 23–37. See Yehuda Henkin's letter in response in the *Journal of Halacha* (fall 1997), 97–102, and Fink's rebuttal of Henkin's letter.

58. Stated by Myra Jehlen and quoted in Carolyn Heilbrun, *Writing a Woman's Life* (New York: Ballantine, 1988), 17.

59. Fink, "Recital of Kaddish by Women," 37.

60. *Birkhat hagomel* is recited after successfully coming through a situation of danger. Childbirth is one of these categories and is discussed in chap. 1. See Rochelle L. Millen, "*Birkhat Ha-Gomel:* Cultural Context and Halakhic Practice," *Judaism* 43, no. 3 (summer 1994), and Millen, "Communications," *Judaism* 44, no. 1 (winter 1995). Also Henoch Goldberg, "The Obligation of Women to Recite Birkhat Hagomel" (in Hebrew), in *Shana beShana,* ed. Haim Menahem Lewittes (Jerusalem: Heichal Shlomo, 1990), 231–39. Blair also took note of this question.

61. Fink, "Recital of Kaddish by Women," 34.

62. One might ask why the woman could not have been present without being the representative mourner. Then, however, she wouldn't be reciting kaddish.

63. See Joel Wolowelsky, "Women and Kaddish," *Judaism* 44, no. 3 (summer 1995): 286.

64. "The American Synagogue World of Yesterday, 1901–1925," *American Jewish Archives* 42, no. 1 (spring/summer 1990): 72.

65. J. Simha Cohen, "Debate over Women Reciting *Kaddish*" in AJN, the internet edition of the *Australian Jewish News,* 23 January 2002; <http://www.ajn.com.> My thanks to Ari Zivotofsky for informing me of this website.

66. Ephraim Zalman Margoliot, *Mateh Ephraim* (in Hebrew) (Jerusalem: Eisenbach, 1989). Rabbi Margoliot lived in Brody, Russia/Austria, 1760–1828.

67. Cited in Yisrael Meir Lau, *Responsa Yahel Yisrael:Halakhic Insights and Clarifications* (in Hebrew) (Jerusalem: Makhon Masoret A. Y. Yeshivat Haye Mosheh, 5752/1992), vol. 2, 479, n.90.

68. Saul J. Berman, "Kol 'Isha," in *Rabbi Joseph H. Lookstein Memorial Volume,* ed. Leo Landman (New York: Ktav Publishing, 1980), 45–66. Similar issues relating to women speaking, teaching, and praying in public have concerned Christian feminists. Some of the relevant texts are Luke 1:46–55 and 2:36; 1 Tim. 2:8–15 and 3:11; Rom. 16:1–2; 1 Cor. 14:35–35.

69. The Shema consists of verses from Deut. 6:4–9, 11:13–21; Num. 15:37–41.

70. Cited in the name of the same rabbinic scholar, Samuel, who was one of the amoraim, i.e., the scholars living during the period in which the Talmud (both Babylonian and Palestinian) were written and edited (200–600 C.E.).

71. The geonim were the rabbinic scholars who lived 600–1000. See n.10, above.

72. Berman, "Kol 'Isha," 46.

73. *Otzar ha-geonim* (Jerusalem: Mosad Ha-Rav Kook, 1966), Berakhot 102:30. Cited in Berman, "Kol 'Isha," 47, n.12.

74. "Gaon/Geonim" in *Encyclopedia Judaica,* vol. 7, eds. Meir Bar Ilan and Shlomo Zevin (Jerusalem: Talmudic Encyclopedia Publishing, 1972), 316.

75. Berman, "Kol 'Isha," 62.
76. The aharonim, or later rabbinic authorities, are those from the fifteenth century until our day. They are distinguished from the rishonim, or earlier authorities, whose works span the eleventh through fifteenth centuries.
77. See Paul R. Mendes-Flohr and Jehuda Reinharz, eds., *The Jew in the Modern World: A Documentary History* (New York: Oxford University Press, 1980), 140–52; and Michael A. Meyer, *The Origins of the Modern Jew: Jewish Identity and European Culture in Germany, 1749–1824* (Detroit: Wayne State University Press, 1967), chap. 5.
78. The early reformers had suggested doing away with circumcision, eliminating Hebrew in the services, abolishing the *Kol Nidre* prayer of Yom Kippur. Some of these practices were termed "excrescences of the dark ages." See Aaron Chorin, "The Rationale of Reform," in *The Jew in the Modern World,* 167.
79. Selections and citations from Sofer's writings may be found in Mendes-Flohr and Reinharz, eds., *The Jew in the Modern World,* 153–55, and W. Gunther Plaut, *The Growth of Reform Judaism: American and European Sources until 1948* (New York: World Union for Progressive Judaism, 1965), 265–66. Also see Aviezer Ravitsky, "*Hadash Min Ha-Torah?:* Modernist versus Traditionalist Orientations in Contemporary Orthodoxy," in *Engaging Modernity: Rabbinic Leaders and the Challenge of the Twentieth Century,* ed. Moshe Z. Sokol (Northvale, N.J.: Jason Aronson, 1997), 35–56. Sofer took this maxim, which in Mishnah Orla 3:9 refers to not using the produce from a new crop until the *Omer* offering is given, and altered its meaning by vastly broadening its context. Sofer created a pun, a quip, which he and others used to distance themselves from many aspects of modernity.
80. See n.76, above.
81. See Deborah Lipstadt, "Feminism and American Judaism: Looking Back at the Turn of the Century," in *Women and American Judaism: Historical Perspectives,* ed. Pamela S. Nadell and Jonathan D. Sarna (Hanover, N.H.: University Press of New England, 2001). On p. 292 Lipstadt writes: "Another practice that seems to be spreading is the observance of *Kol isha,* the prohibition against hearing a woman sing. It could be argued that this is nothing but a means of limiting the ability of women to make their voices 'fully heard' in community activities." See also Lipstadt, "And Deborah Made Ten," in *On Being a Jewish Feminist,* 207–10, and Faye Kellerstein, "A Feygele Zingt [A Daughter Sings]," in *Lilith* (fall 1997): 21–22.
82. B.T. Megillah 23a. The concept of "the honor of the congregation" is analyzed in Rochelle L. Millen, "Social Attitudes Disguised as Halakhah: *Zila milta, ein havrutan na'ah, kevod hatzibbur,*" in *Nashim: A Journal of Jewish Women's Studies and Gender Issues,* no. 4 (fall 5762/2001), esp. 188–91. Some interpret this phrase as implying sexual distraction, but this is not supported by the sources. Women's lesser social status is the more likely interpretation. Also, "reading the Torah" here does not mean simply reading, but being called up to the Torah scroll during services and making the blessing over the Torah to which the entire congregation responds, "amen."
83. Rachel Adler, "Innovation and Authority: A Feminist Reading of the 'Women's Minyan' Responsum," in *Gender Issues in Jewish Law: Essays and Responsa,* ed. Walter Jacob and Moshe Zemer (New York: Berghahn Books, 2001), 25.
84. Lau, *Responsa Yahel Yisreal.*

85. This refers to his being counted as part of the prayer quorum, which in Orthodoxy is a male privilege.

86. Lau, *Responsa Yahel Yisrael,* 480. All translations are mine.

87. Cited in an article by E. J. Kessler, "Who's Afraid of Orthodox Feminism?" *Forward,* 25 February 2000. My thanks to Shirley Kaplan, Bill Freeman, and Lindsey Taylor Guthartz of the WTN (Women's Tefillah Network) listserv for help in locating the exact source.

88. M. Rotenberg, "The Daughter Who Recited Kaddish" (in Hebrew), *Ha Doar* 54, no. 2 (21 March 1975): 328–29. My thanks to Yossi Galron of The Ohio State University Library for sharing this.

89. Ibid., 329 (my translation).

90. Sylvia Barack Fishman, *Changing Minds: Feminism in Contemporary Orthodox Jewish Life* (New York: American Jewish Committee, 2000), 44.

91. Ibid., 45.

92. Received from <wtn@shamash.org> on March 10, 2002.

93. Golinkin, "Responsum on the Issue of Reciting Mourner's Kaddish by Women" (in Hebrew) in *Responsa of the Va'ad Halakhah of the Rabbinical Assembly of Israel,* vol. 3, ed. David Golinkin (Jerusalem: Institute of Applied Halakhah, 5748/1997), 69–80.

94. *Masorti* is the Hebrew term for Conservative Judaism. Literally, it means "traditional."

95. Title page of *Proceedings of the Committee on Jewish Law and Standards of the Conservative Movement, 1927–1970,* vol. 1, ed. David Golinkin (New York: Rabbinical Assembly, 1997).

96. Golinkin, "Reciting Mourner's Kaddish," 69 (my translation).

97. See text quoted on page 123–24 and n.42, above.

98. See n.57, above.

99. Golinkin, "Reciting Mourner's Kaddish," 69 (my translation).

100. See pages 118–20 above.

101. Golinkin, "Reciting Mourner's Kaddish," 70–71 (my translation).

102. Author of *Sefer Ha-chaim [The Book of Life]* (Frankfurt am Main: n.p., 1834). He died in Amsterdam in 1712.

103. See analysis of this notion in Millen, "Social Attitudes Disguised as Halakhah," in *Nashim: A Journal of Jewish Studies and Gender Issues. Kevod hatzibbur* is discussed on pp. 188–92 of that journal.

104. See Berman, "Kol 'Isha."

105. Yehezkel Katznellenbogen (1714–1749), Ephraim Margoliot (1760–1828), and Abraham B. Zilberberg, a twentieth-century rabbi in Pittsburgh. Zilberberg came from Poland to Pittsburgh in the 1930s and remained there until his death in the 1970s.

106. Flekeles, a resident of Prague for most of his life, lived from 1754 to 1826.

107. Quoted by Golinkin, "Reciting Mourner's Kaddish," 75.

108. Ibid.

109. This is quoted by Golinkin in his exposition of the permissive rulings, ibid., 77. The statement appears several times in the Jerusalem (or Palestinian) Talmud, including Yevamot, 7b. In the B.T. it may be found in Berakhot 41a.

110. Cited here on page 116.

111. Golinkin, "Reciting Mourner's Kaddish," 78.

112. Robert Gordis, "A Modern Approach to a Living Halachah," in *Law and Standards of the Conservative Movement* 3:1138.

113. B.T. Menahot 29b and quoted in Bemidbar Rabbah 19:6, Vilna edition. This famous legend is also cited by other contemporary scholars who wish to emphasize the inherent flexibility built into the halakhic system. See for instance Gershom Scholem, "Revelation and Tradition as Religious Categories in Judaism," in *The Messianic Idea in Judaism: And Other Essays on Jewish Spirituality* (New York: Schocken Books, 1971), 283; and David Hartman, *A Living Covenant: The Innovative Spirit in Traditional Judaism* (New York: Free Press, 1985), 36, 46.

114. Gordis, "A Modern Approach to a Living Halachah," 1141.

115. Robert Gordis, "Authority in Jewish Law," in *Conservative Judaism and Jewish Law,* ed. Seymour Siegel (New York: The Rabbinical Assembly, 1977), 47–78

116. *Emet ve-emunah: Statement of Principles of Conservative Judaism* (New York: Jewish Theological Seminary of America, Rabbinical Assembly, United Synagogue of America, 1988), 21–22.

117. David Golinkin, *Halakhah for Our Time: A Conservative Approach to Jewish Law* (New York: United Synagogue Commission on Jewish Education, 1991), and Golinkin, "A Halakhic Agenda for the Conservative Movement," *Conservative Judaism* no. 46 (1994): 29–39.

118. Tikva Krymer-Kensky, "Toward a Liberal Theory of Halakhah," *Tikkun,* 10, no. 4 (1995): 44.

119. Ibid., 56.

120. E-mail communication with Dr. Pamela Nadell, November 28, 2001. The synagogue is Congregation B'nai Tzedek in Rockville, Md., with a membership of around five hundred families. "Thirty days" refers to the required period of mourning for a spouse, sibling, or child; eleven months is for a parent. Both require the recitation of kaddish and include some other restrictions.

121. Interview with Rabbi Harold Berman of Congregation Tifereth Israel, Columbus, Ohio, November 29, 2001.

122. E-mail from Dr. Peggy Pearlstein of Congregation B'nai Israel, Rockville, Md.

123. Daniel J. Elazar and Rela Mintz Geffen, *The Conservative Movement in Judaism: Dilemmas and Opportunities* (Albany: State University of New York, 2000).

124. Ibid., 167. The methodology of the study is explained on pp. 7–8.

125. Ibid., 167.

126. Ibid., 168.

127. See Marshall Sklare, *Conservative Judaism: An American Religious Movement,* rev. ed. (New York: Schocken Books, 1972).

128. Neil Gillman, *Conservative Judaism: The New Century* (New York: Behrman House, 1993). On p. 99, Gillman writes, "It [Jewish ritual practice] was certainly adhered to by the rabbis but rarely by any but a minority of the congregants."

129. Phone interview with Arthur Nemitoff, rabbi of Temple Israel (Reform) in Columbus, Ohio, November 29, 2001. See Jack Wertheimer, *Conservative Synagogues and Their Members* (New York: Jewish Theological Seminary, 1996), chap. 5.

130. W. Gunther Plaut, *The Rise of Reform Judaism* (New York: World Union for Progressive Judaism, 1963), 223.
131. Ibid., 224.
132. Ibid., 223.
133. Plaut, *The Growth of Reform Judaism,* 71.
134. Phone interview with Rabbi Nemitoff (see n.129, above).
135. Phone interview with Rabbi Marianne Gevirtz of Springfield, Ohio, November 29, 2001. Neither her synagogue nor the Reform congregations in nearby Dayton offer daily prayer services.
136. Kohler (1843–1926) was a staunch advocate of Reform Judaism both in Germany and Cincinnati. In 1885, he convened the conference that led to the Pittsburgh Platform and over the years authored numerous scholarly articles.
137. Cited in Plaut, *The Growth of Reform Judaism,* 309. Also found in Walter Jacob, ed., *American Reform Responsa: Collected Responsa of the Central Conference of American Rabbis, 1889–1983* (New York: Central Conference of American Rabbis, 5743/1983), 380–81.
138. The traditional reason for standing during kaddish is that it is considered *davar shebekedushah,* that is, one of the parts of the liturgy that require a quorum (of ten men in rabbinic sources, of ten persons in Conservative Judaism). These are *barkhu, kedusha,* and *kaddish.*
139. Jacob, ed., *American Reform Responsa,* 377–379. This responsum was authored by Jacob, together with others, in 1980.
140. See pages 118–20.
141. Jacob, ed., *American Reform Responsa,* 377.
142. Cited in a responsum titled "Mourning Customs" written in 1913 by K. Kohler and D. Neumark and published in Jacob, ed. *American Reform Responsa,* 375. See also Moshe Zemer, *Evolving Halakhah: A Progressive Approach to Traditional Jewish Law* (Woodstock, Vt.: Jewish Lights, 1999), 261–81.
143. Dr. Norma Baumel Joseph, WTN listserv, December 3, 2001.
144. Cited in Walter Jacob, *Contemporary American Reform Responsa* (New York: Central Conference of American Rabbis, 5747/1987), nos. 122, 124.
145. Plaut, *The Rise of Reform Judaism,* 254.
146. Jacob, *Contemporary American Reform Responsa,* 186–88.
147. Simon J. Maslin, ed., *Gates of Mitzvah: A Guide to the Jewish Life Cycle* (New York: Central Conference of American Rabbis, 5739/1979), 62.
148. The citations from the manual are from *Maaglei tsedek: Rabbi's Manual,* ed. David Polish and annot. W. Gunther Plaut (New York: Central Conference of American Rabbis, 5748/1988), 255.
149. The strong sense of community within Jewish tradition is expressed in many sources, biblical and rabbinic. A contemporary sociologist articulates it in these words: "Judaism is a communal, not just an individual or family religion; in Judaism, community plays the role that in Christianity is occupied by God's grace. It is the community that 'touches and moves people and brings them back to the faith. And the return to faith, which in Christianity means the acceptance of beliefs . . . in Judaism means the return to the community, which is made holy because it

lives under God's law.'" Nathan Glazer cited in Charles E. Silberman, *A Certain People: American Jews and Their Lives Today* (New York: Summit Books, 1985), 242.

150. In an essay titled "The Woman in Reform Judaism," Walter Jacob writes: "When they [responsa on women's issues] dealt with ritual questions like may women recite *kaddish,* read from the Torah, or be counted as part of a minyan . . . equality was taken for granted and did not need justification." Cited in Jacob and Zemer, eds., *Gender Issues in Jewish Law,* 147.

151. Arthur J. Magida, "A Movement Searching for Its Soul," *Baltimore Jewish Times,* 8 November 1991, as cited in Jack Wertheimer, *The American Synagogue: A Sanctuary Transformed* (New York: Cambridge University Press, 1987), 109.

152. Hilary Larson, "Mourning Glory," *Jewish Week,* 26 June 1998, 17.

153. Jewish law requires that one accompany the deceased to his/her final resting place. In our times this means walking after the coffin as it is carried from the funeral home, where the eulogies usually are given, to the waiting hearse; and at the cemetery, following the coffin as it is carried from the hearse to the grave itself.

154. "The Participation of Women at Funerals," in *Responsa of the Va'ad Halakhah of the Rabbinical Assembly of Israel,* vol. 2 (5747). The authors of this volume are Rabbis David Golinkin, Reuven Hammer, Robert Harris, Joseph Heckelman, and Theodore Friedman. The responsum is in Hebrew on pp. 31–38. This citation is from the short English summary given on p. v. See also Henry Abramovitch, "The Jerusalem Funeral as a Microcosm of the 'Mismeeting' between Religious and Secular Israelis," in *Tradition, Innovation, Conflict: Jewishness and Judaism in Contemporary Israel,* ed. Zvi Sobel and Benjamin Beit-Hallahomi (Albany: State University of New York Press, 1991), 71–98.

155. Karo (1488–1575) lived from 1536 in Safed, a center of Jewish mystical and talmudic thought. The *Shulhan Arukh* is a digest of Karo's longer halakhic compendium, the *Beit Yosef.* It was designed for young students not yet sufficiently versed to undertake study of the more complex and rigorous *Beit Yosef.*

156. This view is brought in the midrashic literature as a way of explaining why three specific commandments are the responsibility of women, especially when two of them can (and sometimes are) performed by men. The three mitzvot are observing *niddah* (separation from one's husband during and for several days after menstruation); *challah,* the taking and burning of a piece of dough when baking bread; and lighting Shabbat candles. The woman was given the mitzvah of *niddah* to atone for the fact that she caused the man to die (i.e. become mortal), his blood to spill. *Challah* is usually her task because she made impure the bread of the world, and the Shabbat candles since she extinguished the light of humanity.

These midrashim connect through various wordplays that are characteristic of the genre. All the sources of the above can be found in Meir Bar Ilan and Shlomo Zevin, eds., *Encyclopedia Talmudit* (in Hebrew), vol. 2. See also Pinhas Kahati, *Mishnah Seder Moed* (in Hebrew), vol. 1, nn.29–30.

The conceptual difficulty that undergirds these texts is their assigning culpability to the woman for the man's action. This view is not amplified in rabbinic literature; on the contrary, it is usually denied. With Augustine, however, it becomes ensconced in Christian doctrine in the notions of original sin and woman as (sexual) tempter of men.

157. Written in the thirteenth century, the Zohar was probably authored by Moses de Leon (d. 1305). See Gershom Scholem, *Kabbalah* (New York: Quadrangle/New York Times Book Co., 1974), 213–43.

158. See page 122.

159. An excellent study making this type of connection in regard to Christian theology is Elaine Pagel, *Adam, Eve, and the Serpent* (New York: Vintage Books, 1988).

160. Golinkin, et al., "Participation of Women at Funerals," 32.

161. Based on Lev. 15. For an explication of the laws of *niddah,* see Biale, *Women and Jewish Law,* chap. 6. Also see Charlotte E. Fonrobert, *Menstrual Purity: Rabbinic and Christian Reconstructions of Biblical Gender* (Stanford, Calif.: Stanford University Press, 2000).

162. Golinkin, et al., "Participation of Women at Funerals," 32 and n.5a.

163. A partial summary of rabbinic sources on *kevod haberiyot* is to be found in Yehuda Moriel, *Barukh Tovim* (in Hebrew) (Jerusalem: World Zionist Organization, 1976), esp. 20–30.

164. Golinkin, et al., "Participation of Women at Funerals," 36–37.

165. Ibid., 39, n.1, cites William Smith, *Dictionary of Greek and Roman Antiquities,* 2d ed. (London: 1865), 558–59.

166. This conclusion brings up the sometimes tangled issue of what custom is and what authority it has in the determining of religious practice. Some sources are Barukh halevi Epstein, *Torah Temimah* (in Hebrew), commentary on the Pentateuch (Israel: Ortsel, 1955); Deut. 19:14 and *Yalkut Shimoni* to Prov. 22:28. See chap. 1 in Daniel Sperber, *The Customs of Israel* (in Hebrew) (Jerusalem: Mossad Harav Kook, 1990). Note the statement "The custom of women is as Torah," found in the Jerusalem Talmud Pesachim 4:1, and also in *Pirkei der Rabbi Eliezer,* 45. The format of this statement parallels that found in the Babylonian Talmud, "The custom of Israel is as law *[din]."*

167. Zemer, *Evolving Halakhah.*

168. Jacob ben Samuel, *Responsa Beit Yaacov,* no. 72, cited in Zemer, ed., *Evolving Halakhah,* 420, n.5.

169. Ibid., 258. Also see n.6 on p. 420.

170. Ibid., 259.

171. The covering of mirrors and refraining from food preparation are deeply ingrained customs, not actual halakhic obligations. The only exception is the *seudat hav-ra-a,* the meal eaten by mourners immediately upon returning from the burial. This repast must be prepared by others.

172. Fishman, *Changing Minds,* 43–45.

173. Carol Tavris, *The Mismeasure of Woman* (New York: Simon and Schuster, 1992), 24.

174. Ibid., 295.

175. Ibid. See also Deborah Tannen, *Gender and Discourse* (New York: Oxford University Press, 1994).

176. See Charles S. Liebman, "Orthodoxy in American Jewish Life," *American Jewish Yearbook* 66 (1965), 21–98.

177. See Sylvia Barack Fishman, *Jewish Life and American Culture* (Albany: State University of New York Press, 2000), chap. 1.

178. Moshe Tendler as quoted in mail.jewish, February 28, 2000.

179. Cited in Lynn Davidman, *Tradition in a Rootless World: Women Turn to Orthodox Judaism* (Berkeley: University of California at Los Angeles Press, 1991), 156.

180. Aharon Lichtenstein, "Legitimization of Modernity: Classical and Contemporary," in *Engaging Modernity,* 3–34. Sylvia Barack Fishman delineates the distinctions between synthesis and coalescence in *Jewish Life and American Culture,* 15–32; Norman Lamm, *Torah Umadda: The Encounter of Religious Learning and Worldly Knowledge in the Jewish Tradition* (Northvale, N.J.: Jason Aronson, 1990).

181. Ross, "Can the Demand for Change in the Status of Women Be Halakhically Legitimated?" *Judaism* 42, n.4 (fall 1993): 478–491; and Ross, "Modern Orthodoxy and the Challenge of Feminism" in *Modern Orthodoxy and the Challenge of Feminism,* ed. Jonathan Frankel (New York: Oxford University Press, 2000), 3–38.

182. Ross, "Can the Demand for Change. . .?" 480.

183. Ibid.

184. Mayer Twersky, "Torah Perspectives on Women's Issues," *Jewish Action* 57, no. 4 (summer 5757/1997): 26.

185. Ibid.

186. Ibid., 27.

187. Ross, "Can the Demand for Change . . .?" 482.

188. See also Ross, "Modern Orthodoxy," 23–27.

189. For background on R. Kook, see the entry under his name in *Encyclopedia Judaica,* vol. 10 (1972). Also see the essays by Benjamin Ish Shalom, Bezalel Naor, and David Shatz on R. Kook in *Engaging Modernity,* 57–118. Also see Rochelle L. Millen, review of *Rav Avraham Itzhak HaCohen Kook: Between Rationalism and Mysticism* by Benjamin Ish Shalom, *Association of Jewish Studies Review,* 21, no. 1 (1996): 216–19, and Benjamin Ish Shalom and Shalom Rosenberg, eds., *The World of Rav Kook's Thought* (Jerusalem: Avi Chai, 1991).

190. This notion is explicated in Walter Wurzburger, "Confronting the Challenge of the Value of Modernity," *Torah U'mada Journal* 1 (1989), 104–12.

191. Ross, "Modern Orthodoxy," 6.

192. Jonathan D. Sarna, "Mixed Seating in the American Synagogue," in *The American Synagogue,* 380.

193. See Bernadette J. Brooten, *Women Leaders in the Ancient Synagogue* (Atlanta: Scholars Press, 1982), chap. 6.

194. Jack Wertheimer, "The Conservative Synagogue," in *The American Synagogue,* 131.

195. Cited in Jeffrey S. Gurock, *From Fluidity to Rigidity: The Religious Worlds of Conservative and Orthodox Jews in Twentieth-Century America* (Ann Arbor: Jean and Samuel Frankel Center for Judaic Studies, University of Michigan, 1998), 4.

196. Wertheimer, ed., *Conservative Synagogues,* 16.

197. Elazar and Geffen, *The Conservative Movement in Judaism,* 57.

198. Ibid.

199. Ibid., 166–67. See also Golinkin, "A Halakhic Agenda" 29–39.

200. Elliot N. Dorff, "Custom Drives Jewish Law on Women," *Conservative Judaism* (spring 1997): 3.

201. See Zecharias Frankel, "On Changes in Judaism," in *The Jew in the Modern World,* 173–76.

202. Cynthia Ozick formulates a similar strategy in her essay "Notes toward Finding the Right Question," in *On Being a Jewish Feminist.* She laments, "But mostly, the social order as given—woman dehumanized, woman as inferior, woman as chattel—remains untouched by the healing force of any grand principle of justice," p. 46.

203. Robert Gordis, "The Ordination of Women," in *The Ordination of Women as Rabbis: Studies and Responsa,* ed. Simon Greenberg (New York: Jewish Theological Seminary, 1988), 55.

204. Jacob, "The Woman in Reform Judaism," 131.

205. Ibid., 130.

206. Ibid., 140.

207. See *Sifri,* Bamidkar, Piska 2; and B.T. Kiddushin 35a, Baba Kama 15a.

208. Jacob, "The Women in Reform Judaism," 141.

209. In addition to evidence discussed here, the *Jerusalem Report* of 22 May 2000, writes about Rachel Levmore, the first woman ever to serve on the directorate of Israel's rabbinical courts. She is one of five senior staffers handling divorce cases.

210. Cited in Lipstadt, "Feminism and American Judaism," 291–308.

211. Tova Reich, "My Mother, My Muse," *New York Times Magazine,* 6 November 1988, 30.

212. Quoted in Jeffrey Rosen, "The New Look of Liberalism on the Court," *New York Times Magazine,* 5 October 1997. See also Ruth Bader Ginsburg, "Reflections on Way Paving Jewish Justices and Jewish Women," *Touro Law Review* 14, no. 2 (winter 1998): 283–94.

213. While Reich is not part of this small group, the burial society was, and therefore enforced its own designated code of behavior. Also see Abramovitch, "The Jerusalem Funeral."

214. For a detailed discussion of the structure of the medieval Jewish community, see Jacob Katz, *Tradition and Crisis: Jewish Society at the End of the Middle Ages,* trans. Bernard Dov Cooperman (New York: New York University Press, 1993).

215. Examples are Miriam Yenkin in Columbus, Ohio, who served a two-year term, 1985–1987, and Shoshana Cardin in New York, chairman of the Council of Presidents of Major Jewish Organizations, 1990–1992.

216. Jean Baker Miller, ed., *Psychoanalysis and Women* (Baltimore, Md.: Penguin, 1973), 387.

217. Jean Baker Miller, *Toward a New Psychology of Women,* 2nd ed. (Boston: Beacon Press, 1986), 94–95.

218. Ibid., 95.

219. Ibid., 116.

220. Carolyn G. Heilbrun, *Reinventing Womanhood* (New York: W. W. Norton, 1979), 133.

221. See Maggie Scarf, *Intimate Partners: Patterns in Love and Marriage* (New York: Random House, 1987).

222. My thanks to Kevin A. Arnold, Ph.D., for this clarification.

223. See earlier, pp. 52–53.

224. Michelle Zimbalist Rosaldo, "Women, Culture, and Society: A Theoretical Overview," in *Women, Culture, and Society,* ed. Michelle Z. Rosaldo and Louise Lamphere (Stanford, Calif.: Stanford University Press, 1974), 39.

225. Cited in Karla Goldman, *Beyond the Synagogue Gallery: Finding a Place for Women in American Judaism* (Cambridge: Harvard University Press, 2000), 164.

226. Ibid., 165.

227. Yvonne Fein, WTN, June 25, 2000.

228. Heilbrun, *Reinventing Womanhood,* 98.

Epilogue

1. How else to handle the (male) plumber who repeatedly called me "sweetheart" or the receipts from donations I gave with my husband's name.

2. Compare Letty Cottin Pogrebin, *Deborah, Golda, and Me: Being Female and Jewish in America* (New York: Crown Publishing, 1991), 236.

3. Daniel Boyarin, *Carnal Israel: Reading Sex in Talmudic Culture* (Berkeley: University of California Press, 1995), 242.

4. Judith Hauptman, *Rereading the Rabbis: A Woman's Voice* (Boulder, Colo.: Westview Press, 1998), 244.

5. Avraham Grossman, *Pious and Rebellious: Jewish Women in Europe in the Middle Ages* (Hanover, NH: University Press of New England, 2003).

6. Rochelle Furstenberg, "Medieval Feminism," *Hadassah Magazine,* 83, no. 10, June–July, 2002, 10.

7. Ibid.

8. Cecil Roth, *Dona Gracia of the House of Nasi* (Philadelphia: Jewish Publication Society, 1977).

9. Rochelle Furstenberg, *"Medieval Feminism,"* 10.

10. See Bernadette J. Brooten, *Women Leaders in the Ancient Synagogue* (Atlanta: Scholars Press, 1982).

11. Tamar Ross, "Modern Orthodoxy and the Challenge of Feminism" in ed. Jonathan Frankel, *Jews and Gender: The Challenge to Hierarchy,* 25.

12. Ibid., 29.

13. Seth Farber, "Expanding Women's Roles in Orthodoxy: The History Behind the Movement" in *Amit* (Fall, 2001), 44.

14. Ibid., 46.

15. Netty C. Gross, "The Dissenter" in *The Jerusalem Report,* no. 2, 12:21, 11 February 2002, 18–20.

16. Ibid., 19.

17. See Rachel Biale, *Women and Jewish Law: An Exploration of Women's Issues in Halakhic Sources* (New York: Schocken Books, 1984), Chapter 2.

18. Rachel Adler, *Engendering Judaism* (Philadelphia: Jewish Publication Society, 1998), esp. Chapter 5.

19. Neil Gillman, *Conservative Judaism: The New Century* (New York: Behrman House, 1993), 61.

20. Peter J. Haas, "Ethical Wills," in ed. Walter Jacob and Moshe Zemer, *Aging and the Aged in Jewish Law: Essays and Responsa* (Pittsburgh: Rodef Shalom Press, 1998), 111–220.

Works Cited

Abraham, Abraham Sofer. *Nishmat Avraham: Hilkhot Refuah* vol. 3 (in Hebrew). Jerusalem: Salk-Schlessinger Institute, 1993.

Abramovitch, Henry. "The Jerusalem Funeral as a Microcosm of the "Mismeeting' between Religious and Secular Israelis." In *Tradition, Innovation, and Conflict: Jewishness and Judaism in Contemporary Israel,* edited by Zvi Sobel and Benjamin Beit-Hallahoomi, 71–98. Albany: State University of New York Press, 1991.

Adelman, Penina. "Citing the Source." *Moment* 22, no. 4 (1997): 26–27.

Adler, Rachel. *Engendering Judaism.* Philadelphia: Jewish Publication Society, 1998.

———. "Feminist Folktales of Justice: Robert Cover as a Resource for the Renewal of Halakhah." *Conservative Judaism* 45 (1993): 40–55.

———. "Innovation and Authority: A Feminist Reading of the 'Women's Minyan Responsum.'" In *Gender Issues in Jewish Law: Essays and Response,* edited by Walter Jacob and Moshe Zemer, 3–33. New York: Berghahn Books, 2001.

Adler, Shmuel A. *Aspaklaryia* (in Hebrew). vol. 12. Jerusalem: Aspaklaryia, 5749/1989.

Alexander, Elizabeth Shanks. "The Impact of Feminism on Rabbinic Studies: The Impossible Paradox of Reading Women into Rabbinic Literature." In *Jews and Gender: The Challenge to Hierarchy,* edited by Jonathan Frankel, 101–18. New York: Oxford University Press, 2000.

Alperovits, Yitshak, ed. *Sefer Telz: matsevert zikaron likehilah kedoshah* (in Hebrew). Tel-Aviv: Society of Telz in Israel, 1984.

Alpert, Rebecca T. *Like Bread on the Seder Plate: Jewish Lesbians and the Transformation of Tradition.* New York: Columbia University Press, 1998.

———. "Sometimes the Law Is Cruel: The Construction of a Jewish Antiabortion Position in the Writings of Immanuel Jakobovits." *Journal of Feminist Studies* 11 (1995): 27–37.

———, Sue Levi Elwell, and Shirley Idelson, eds. *Lesbian Rabbis: The First Generation.* New Jersey: Rutgers University press, 2001.

"The American Synagogue World of Yesterday, 1901–1925." *American Jewish Archives* 42, no. 1 (spring/summer 1990): 72.

Anderson, Bonnie S., and Judith P. Zinsser. *A History of Their Own: Women in Europe From Prehistory to the Present.* Vol. 1. New York: Harper & Row, 1988.

Anderson, Sherry Ruth, and Patricia Hopkins. *The Feminine Face of God.* New York: Bantam, 1991.

Aquinas, Thomas. *Summa Theologica.* New York: Benziger Bros., 1947–1948.

Aranoff, Susan. "Two Views of Marriage—Two Views of Woman: Reconsidering *Tav Lemetav Tan Du Milemetav Armelu.*" *Nashim: A Journal of Jewish Women's Studies and Gender Issues,* no. 3 (spring–summer 5760/2000): 199–227.

Arendt, Hannah. *The Human Condition.* Chicago: University of Chicago Press, 1958.

Asbell, Bernard. *The Pill: A Biography of the Drug that Changed the World.* New York: Random House, 1995.

Bach, Alice, ed. *Women in the Hebrew Bible: A Reader.* New York: Routledge, 1999.

Baer, Judith A. "The Problem that Won't Go Away." In *Women in American Law.* New York: Holmes and Meier, 1991.

———. *Women in American Law: The Struggle for Equality from the New Deal to the Present.* New York: Holmes & Meier, 1991.

Bainton, Roland H. *Here I Stand: A Life of Martin Luther.* New York: New American Library: 1950.

Barrett, Amy. "Just One of the Boys." *New York Times Magazine,* 23 June 2002, 13.

Baskin, Judith R. "Rabbinic Reflections on the Barren Wife." *Harvard Theological Review* 82, no. 1 (1989): 101–14.

———. *Midrashic Women: Formations of the Feminine in Rabbinic Literature.* Hanover, N.H.: University Press of New England, 2002.

Basser, Herbert W., and Simcha Fishbein, eds. *Approaches to Ancient Judaism.* Vol. 5. Atlanta: Scholars Press, 1993.

Bassler, Jourette M. "I Corinthians." In *The Women's Bible Commentary,* edited by Carol A. Newsom and Sharon H. Ringe, 321–29. Louisville, Ky.: Westminster/John Knox, 1992.

Baum, Charlotte, Paula Hyman, and Sonya Michel. *The Jewish Woman in America.* New York: New American Library, 1976.

Beck, Lewis White. "Kant's Two Conceptions of the Will in Their Political Context." In *Studies in the Philosophy of Kant,* edited by Lewis White Beck, 215–30. New York: Bobbs-Merrill, 1965.

———, ed. *Studies in* the Philosophy of *Kant.* New York: Bobbs-Merrill, 1965.

Beck, Mordechai. "And Adam Knew Eve: A Meditation [on marriage]." *Tikkun* 11 (1996).

Benisch, Pearl. *To Vanquish the Dragon.* New York: Feldheim, 1991.

Benjamin, Jessica. *The Bonds of Love: Psychoanalysis, Feminism, and the Problem of Domination.* New York: Pantheon Books, 1988.

Bereishit Rabbah (in Hebrew). Jerusalem: Lewin–Epstein Brothers Publishing, 1960.

Berger, Peter L. *Invitation to Sociology.* Woodstock, N.Y.: Overlook Press, 1973.

Berkovits, Eliezer. *Jewish Women in Time and Torah.* Hoboken, N.J.: Ktav Publishing, 1990.

Berman, Phyllis Ocean. "Recreating Menopause." *Moment* 19, no. 1 (1994).

Berman, Saul. "The Status of Women in Halakhic Judaism." *Tradition* 14, no. 2 (fall 1973): 2–30.

———. "Kol'Isha." In *Rabbi Joseph H. Lookstein Memorial Volume,* edited by Leo Landman, 45–66. New York: Ktav Publishing, 1981.

Biale, Rachel. *Women and Jewish Law: An Exploration of Women's Issues in Halakhic Sources.* New York: Schocken Books, 1984.

Bickley,Tami. "High-tech Fertility Options Provide Hope for Infertile Couples." *Jewish News of Greater Phoenix,* 14 May 1999.

Blair, Moshe Leib. *Does a Daughter Have A Duty to Say Kaddish?* Chicago: [independently printed], 1950.

Bleich, J. David. "The Attitude of American Civil Courts towards Jewish Divorce" (in Hebrew). *Dine Israel* 10–11 (1981–1983): 365–84.

———. *"Avitzur:* A Victory for the *Agunah." Jewish Week,* 25 February 1983.

———. "Jewish Divorce: Judicial Misconceptions and Possible Means of Civil Enforcement." *Connecticut Law Review* 16, no. 2 (winter 1984): 201–98.

———. "Modern Day *Agunot:* A Proposed Remedy." *Jewish Law Annual* 4 (1981): 167–87.

———. "Pregnancy Reduction" Survey of Recent Halakchic Periodical Literature. *Tradition* 29, no. 3 (spring, 1995): 55–63.

———. "Sperm Banking in Anticipation of Infertility." Survey of Recent Halakhic Periodic Literature. *Tradition* 29, no. 4 (summer 1995): 47–60.

———. "A Suggested Antenuptial Agreement: A Proposal in Wake of *Avitzur." Journal of Halacha and Contemporary Society* (spring 1984): 25–41.

———. "Ketubah Issues." Survey of Recent Halakhic Periodical Literature. *Tradition* 31, no. 2 (winter, 1997): 50–66.

Bokser, Ben Zion. "Statement on Birth Control" (in Hebrew and English). In *Proceedings of the Committee on Jewish Law and Standards of the Conservative Movement, 1927–1970,* edited by David Golinkin, 1451–58. Jerusalem: The Rabbinical Assembly and the Institute of Applied Halakhah, 1997.

Borowitz, Eugene B. "The Autonomous Jewish Self." *Modern Judaism* 4, no. 1 (February 1984): 39–55.

———. "The Autonomous Self and the Commanding Community." *Theological Studies* 45 (1984): 34–56.

———. *Choosing a Sex Ethic: A Jewish Inquiry.* New York: Schocken Books, 1969.

———. *Exploring Jewish Ethics: Papers on Covenant Responsibility.* Detroit: Wayne State University Press, 1990.

———. "Judaism: An Overview." In *Judaism: A People and Its History,* edited by Robert Seltzer, 3–35. New York: Macmillan Press, 1989.

———. *Renewing the Covenant: A Theology for the Postmodern Jew.* Philadelphia: Jewish Publication Society, 1991.

Boyarin, Daniel. *Carnal Israel: Reading Sex in Talmudic Culture.* Berkeley: University of California Press, 1993.

Braiterman, Zachary. *(God) After Auschwitz: Tradition and Change in Post-Holocaust Jewish Thought.* Princeton, N.J.: Princeton University Press: 1998.

Brandt, Allan, and Paul Rozin, eds. *Morality and Health.* Florence, Ky.: Routledge, 1997.

Brayer, Menachem M. *The Jewish Woman in Rabbinic Literature: A Psychohistorical Perspective,* Vol. 2. Hoboken, N.J.: Ktav Publishing, 1986.

Breger, Jennifer, and Lisa Schlaff, eds. *The Orthodox Jewish Woman and Ritual: Options and Opportunities–Birth.* New York: Jewish Orthodox Feminist Alliance, 2000.

Brettell, Caroline, and Carolyn Sargent, eds. *Gender in Cross-Cultural Perspective.* Upper Saddle River, N.J.: Prentice Hall, 2001.

Broner, Esther M. *Mornings and Mourning: A Kaddish Journal.* San Francisco: Harper, 1994.

Brooks, Geraldine. *Nine Parts of Desire.* New York: Doubleday, 1995.

Brooten, Bernadette J. *Women Leaders in the Ancient Synagogue.* Atlanta: Scholars Press, 1982.

Brown, Erica S. "The Bat Mitzvah in Jewish Law and Contemporary Practice." In *Jewish Legal Writings by Women,* edited by Micah D. Halpern and Chana Safrai. Jerusalem; Urim Publications, 1998/5758.

Brown, Peter. *The Body and Society: Men, Women, and Sexual Renunciation in Early Christianity.* New York: Random House, 1989.

Broyde, Michael J. "The 1992 New York Get Law." *Tradition* 29, no. 4 (summer, 1995): 5–13.

Buber, Martin. *Moses: The Revelation and the Covenant.* San Francisco: Harper Torchbooks, 1958.

Buber, Solomon, ed. *Midrash Shohar Tov* (in Hebrew). New York: Om Publishing, 1947.

Bunim, Sarah Silver. "Religious and Secular Factors of Role in Orthodox Jewish Mothers." Unpublished doctoral dissertation, Wurzweiler School of Social Work, 1986.

Cardin, Nina Beth, ed. and trans. *Out of the Depths I Call to You: A Book of Prayers for the Married Jewish Woman.* Northvale, N.J.: Jason Aronson, 1995.

———. *Tears of Sorrow, Seeds of Hope: A Jewish Spiritual Companion for Infertility and Pregnancy Loss.* Woodstock, Vt.: Jewish Lights Publishing, 1999.

Chase, Karen, and Michael Levenson. *The Spectacle of Intimacy: A Public Life for the Victorian Family.* Princeton, N.J.: Princeton University Press, 2000.

Chorin, Aaron. "The Rationale of Reform." In *The Jew in the Modern World: A Documentary History,* edited by Paul R. Mendes-Flohr and Jehuda Reinhartz. New York: Oxford University Press, 1980.

Cohen, Alfred S., ed. *Halacha and Contemporary Society.* New York: Ktav, Rabbi Jacob Joseph School, 1981.

Cohen, Debra Nussbaum. *Celebrating Your New Jewish Daughter.* Woodstock, Vt.: Jewish Lights Publishing, 2001.

Cohen, Jeremy. *"Be Fertile and Increase, Fill the Earth and Master It": The Ancient and Medieval Career of a Biblical Text.* Ithaca, N.Y.: Cornell University Press, 1989.

Cohen, Shaye J. D. "Menstruants and the Sacred in Judaism and Christianity." In *Women's History and Ancient History,* edited by Sarah B. Pomeroy, 273–99. Chapel Hill: University of North Carolina Press, 1991.

———. "Why Aren't Jewish Women Circumcised?" *Gender and History* 9, no. 3 (November 1997): 560–78.

Cohen, Simha J. "Debate Over Women Reciting *Kaddish.*" In AJN, the internet edition of *Australian Jewish News* <http:www.ajn.com>. 23 Jan. 2002.

Cohen, Steven F., and Kenneth Brander, eds. *The Yeshiva University Haggada.* New York: Student Organization of Yeshiva, 1985.

Colby, Ann, and Lawrence Kohlberg. *The Measurement of Moral Judgment.* Vol. 1. New York: Cambridge University Press, 1987.

Cooey, Paula M., ed. *Embodied Love: Sensuality and Relationship as Feminist Values.* San Francisco: Harper & Row, 1987.

Cusk, Rachel. *A Life's Work: On Becoming a Mother.* New York: Picador, 2002.

Davidman, Lynn. *Tradition in a Rootless World: Women Turn to Orthodox Judaism.* Berkeley: University of California Press, 1991.

Davidman, Lynn, and Shelly Tenebaum, eds. *Feminist Perspectives on Jewish Studies.* New Haven, Conn.: Yale University Press, 1994.

Davis, Natalie Zemon. *Women on the Margins: Three Seventeenth-Century Lives.* Cambridge: Harvard University Press, 1995.

de Beauvoir, Simone. *The Second Sex.* Translated by H. M. Parshley. New York: Bantam Books, 1961.

DellaPergola, Sergio. "Jewish Women in Transition: A Comparative Sociodemographic Perspective." In *Jews and Gender: The Challenge to Hierarchy,* edited by Jonathan Frankel, 209–42. New York: Oxford University Press, 2000.

Diament, Anita. *The New Jewish Baby Book.* Woodstock, Vt.: Jewish Lights Publishing, 1993.

Dorff, Elliot N. "Custom Drives Jewish Law on Women." In *Gender Issues in Jewish Law: Essays and Responsa,* edited by Walter Jacob and Moshe Zemer, 82–106. New York: Berghahn Books, 2001.

Dorff, Elliot N., and Louis E. Newman, eds. *Contemporary Jewish Ethics and Morality: A Reader.* New York: Oxford University Press, 1995.

———. "'Male and Female God Created Them': Equality with Distinction." *University Papers,* 13–23. Los Angeles: University of Judaism, 1994.

Eilberg, Amy. "A Grieving Ritual Following Miscarriage or Stillbirth." In *Tears of Sorrow, Seeds of Hope: A Jewish Spiritual Companion for Infertility and Pregnancy Loss,* edited by Nina Beth Cardin. Woodstock, Vt.: Jewish Lights Publishing, 1999.

Eilberg-Schwartz, Howard. *The Savage in Judaism: An Anthropology of Israelite Religion and Ancient Judaism.* Bloomington: Indiana University Press, 1990.

Elazar, Daniel J., and Rela Mintz Geffen. *The Conservative Movement in Judaism: Dilemmas and Opportunities.* Albany: State University of New York Press, 2000.

Ellinson, Elyakim. *The Woman and the Commandments* (in Hebrew). Pt. 1. Jerusalem: The Jewish Agency, 1979.

Elon, Menachem, Bernard Auerbach, Daniel D. Chazin, and Melvin Sykes, eds. *Jewish Law (Mishpat Ivri): Cases and Materials.* New York: Matthew Bender, 1999.

Elwes, Theresa, edited by *Women's Voices: Essays in Contemporary Feminist Theology.* London: Marshall Pickering/Harper Collins, 1992.

Emet ve-emunah: Statement on Our Time: A Conservative Judaism. New York: Jewish Theological Seminary of America, Rabbinical Assembly, United Synagogue of America, 1988.

Epstein, Baruch Halevi. *Torah Teminah* (in Hebrew). Israel: Ortsel, 1955.

Epstein, Louis M. *Sex Laws and Customs in Judaism.* New York: Ktav Publishing, 1967.

Erikson, Erik. *Childhood and Society,* 2d ed. New York: W.W. Norton, 1963.

Fackenheim, Emil L. *God's Presence in History: Jewish Affirmations and Philosophical Reflections.* New York: Harper & Row, 1970.

———. *Encounters between Judaism and Modern Philosophy.* New York: Basic Books, 1973.

———. *Quest for Past and Future: Essays in Jewish Theology.* Bloomington: Indiana University Press, 1967.

———. *The Religious Dimension in Hegel's Thought.* Boston: Beacon Press, 1967.

Falk, Ze'ev W. "Gender Differentiation and Spirituality." *Journal of Law and Religion* 1 (1995–1996): 85–103.

Falls, Thomas B., ed. and trans. *Writings of Saint Justin Martyr: The First Apology.* New York: Christian Heritage, 1948.

Farber, Seth. "Expanding Women's Roles in Orthodoxy: The History behind the Movement." *Amit,* Fall 2001.

Farrell, Warren. *Father and Child Reunion.* New York: Tarcher Putnam Penguin, 2001.

Fausto-Sterling, Anne. *Myths of Gender: Biological Theories about Women and Men.* New York: Basic Books, 1985.

Fein, Leonard. *Against the Dying of the Light: A Father's Journey Through Loss.* Woodstock, Vt.: Jewish Lights, 2001.

Feinstein, Moshe. *Iggerot Moshe* (in Hebrew). Brooklyn, N.Y.: Moriah Press, 1961.

Feldman, Aharon. "Halakhic Feminism or Feminist Halakha?" *Tradition* 33, no. 2 (winter 1999): 61–79.

———. *The River, the Kettle, and the Bird.* New York and Jerusalem: Feldheim, 1987.

Feldman, David M. *Birth Control in Jewish Law.* New York: New York University Press, 1968.

———. "The Ethical Implications of New Reproductive Techniques." In *Jewish Values in Bioethics,* edited by Levi Meier, 174–82. New York: Human Sciences Press, 1986.

Feldman, David, and Fred Rosner. *Compendium on Medical Ethics.* New York: Federation of Jewish Philanthropies, 1986.

Feldman, Emanuel. "An Articulate *Berakha* ['. . . Who Has Not Made Me a Woman'; Others Say]." *Tradition* 29 (1995): 68–74.

———. "Orthodox Feminism and Feminist Orthodoxy." *Jewish Action* (winter 5760/1990): 12–17.

———. "Reconciling Opposites: Uncommon Connections in the Halakha of Mourning." *Tradition* 27, no. 3 (1993): 13–20.

Fink, Reuven. "The Recital of Kaddish by Women." *Journal of Halacha and Contemporary Society* (spring 1996): 26–37.

Fishbane, Simcha. "'In Any Case There Are No Sinful Thoughts'—The Role and Status of Women in Jewish Law as Expressed in the Arukh Hashulhan." *Judaism* 42, no. 4 (1993): 492–503.

Fishman, Sylvia Barack. *A Breath of Life: Feminism in the American Jewish Community.* Hanover, N.H.: University Press of New England, 1993.

———. *Changing Minds: Feminism in Contemporary Orthodox Jewish Life.* New York: American Jewish Committee, 2000.

———. *Jewish Life and American Culture.* Albany: State University of New York Press, 2000.

Flancbaum, Louis. *"And You Shall Live by Them": Contemporary Jewish Approaches to Medical Ethics.* Pittsburgh: Mirkov Publications, 2001.

Fonrobert, Charlotte E. *Menstrual Purity: Rabbinic and Christian Reconstructions of Biblical Gender.* Stanford, Calif.: Stanford University Press, 2000.

Foucault, Michel. *The Archeology of Knowledge.* Translated by A. M. Sheridan Smith. New York: Pantheon Books, 1972.

Frankel, Jonathan, edited by *Jews and Gender: The Challenge to Hierarchy.* New York: Oxford University Press, 2000.

Frankel, Zecharias. "On Changes in Judaism." In *The Jew in the Modern World: A Documentary History,* edited by Paul R. Mendes-Flohr and Jehuda Reinhartz, 173–76. New York: Oxford University Press, 1980.

Frankiel, Tamar. *The Voice of Sarah: Feminine Spirituality and Traditional Judaism.* San Francisco: Harper, 1990.

Freehof, Solomon B. "Jacob Z. Lauterbach and the Halakhah." *Judaism* 3 (August 1952): 270–73.

———. *Reform Responsa for Our Time.* Cincinnati: Hebrew Union College Press, 1977.

Fried, Charles. *An Anatomy of Values: Problems of Personal and Social Choice.* Cambridge: Harvard University Press, 1970.

Frymer-Kensky, Tikva. "The Bible and Women's Studies." In *Feminist Perspectives on Jewish Studies,* edited by Lynn Davidman and Shelly Tenenbaum, 16–39. New Haven, Conn.: Yale University Press, 1994.

———. *In the Wake of the Goddesses: Women, Culture and the Biblical Transformation of Pagan Myth.* New York: Fawcett Columbine, 1992.

———. *Motherprayer: The Pregnant Woman's Spiritual Companion.* New York: Riverhead Books, 1995.

———."Toward a Liberal Theory of Halakha." *Tikkun* 10 (1995).

Fuchs, Lawrence. *Beyond Patriarchy: Jewish Fathers and Families.* Hanover, N.H.: University Press of New England, 2000.

Furstenberg, Rochelle. "Medieval Feminism." *Hadassah Magazine* 83, no. 10 (June–July 2002).

Galenson, Eleanor. "Observation of Early Infantile Sexual and Erotic Development." In *Handbook of Sexology,* Vol. 7 of *Childhood and Adolescent Sexology,* edited by M. E. Perry. New York: Elsievier Science Publishers, B. V. Biomedical Division, 1991.

Galenson, Eleanor, and Herman Roiphe. "Pre-Oedipal Development of the Boy," *Journal of the American Psychoanalytic Association* 28, no. 4 (1976), 805–27.

Gaon, Saadia. *The Book of Beliefs and Opinions.* Translated by Samuel Rosenblatt. New Haven, Conn.: Yale University Press, 1958.

Geddes, Jennifer L., ed. *The Hedgehog Review: Critical Reflections on Contemporary Culture* 4, no. 1. (spring 2002).

Geertz, Clifford. *The Interpretation of Culture.* New York: Basic Books, 1973.

Geffen, Rela M., ed. *Celebration and Renewal: Rites of Passage in Judaism.* Philadelphia: Jewish Publication Society, 5753/1993.

Gelerenter-Liebowitz, Shoshanna. "Growing Up Lubavitch." In *Daughters of the King: Women and the Synagogue: A Survey of History, Halakhah, and Contemporary Realities,* edited by Susan Grossman and Rivka Haut, 238–41. Philadelphia: Jewish Publication Society, 1992.

Gilligan, Carol. *In a Different Voice: Psychological Theory and Women's Development.* Cambridge: Harvard University Press, 1982.

———. *Mapping the Moral Terrain.* Cambridge: Harvard University Press, 1988.

Gillman, Neil. *Conservative Judaism: The New Century.* New York: Behrman House, 1993.

Gilman, Sander L. *The Jew's Body.* New York: Routledge, 1991.

Ginsburg, Ruth Bader. "Reflections on Way Paving Jewish Justices and Jewish Women." *Touro Law Review* 14, no. 2 (winter 1998): 283–94.

Gladwell, Malcolm. "John Rock's Error." *New Yorker,* 13 March 2000, 52–57.

Glückel of Hameln. *The Memoirs of Glückel of Hameln.* Translated by Marvin Lowenthal. New York: Schocken Books, 1977.

Goldberg, Chaim B. *Mourning in Halachah.* New York: Mesorah Publications, 1991.

Goldberg, Harvey E., ed. *Sephardi and Middle Eastern Jewries.* Bloomington: Indiana University Press, 1996.

Goldberg, Henoch. "The Obligation of Women to Recite Birkhat Hagomel" (in Hebrew). In *Shana beShana* (in Hebrew), edited by Haim Menahem Lewittes, 231–39. Jerusalem: Heichal Shlomo, 1990.

Goldberg, Hillel. "Philosophy of Halakha: The Many Worlds of Mikve." *Tradition* 30 (1996): 41–64.

Goldman, Karla. *Beyond the Synagogue Gallery: Finding a Place for Women in American Judaism.* Cambridge: Harvard University Press, 2000.

Goldscheider, Calvin. *Jewish Continuity and Change: Emerging Patterns in America.* Bloomington: Indiana University Press, 1986.

Goldstein, Elyse. "Jewish Feminism and 'New' Jewish Rituals: Imitative or Inventive?" *CCAR Journal: A Reform Jewish Quarterly* (summer 1997): 5–110.

———. *ReVisions: Seeing Torah Through a Feminist Lens.* Woodstock, Vt.: Jewish Lights Publishing, 1998.

Golinkin, David. *Halakhah for Our Time: A Conservative Approach to Jewish Law.* New York: United Synagogue Commission on Jewish Education, 1991.

———. "A Halakhic Agenda for the Conservative Movement." *Conservative Judaism* 46 (1994): 29–39.

———. "Responsum on the Issue of Reciting Mourner's Kaddish by Women (Hebrew)." *Responsa of the Va'ad Halakhah of the Rabbinical Assembly of Israel* 3 (Jerusalem: Institute of Applied Halakhah, 5748/1987): 69–80.

———. "Rethinking the American Jewish Experience: The Movement for Equal Rights for Women in Judaism as Reflected in the Writings of Rabbi David Aronson." *American Jewish Archives* 47, no. 2 (1995): 242–60.

———, ed. *Proceedings of the Committee on Jewish Law and Standards of the Conservative Movement, 1927–1970.* Jerusalem: The Rabbinical Assembly and the Institute of Applied Halakhah, 1997.

Goodrich, Thelma Jean, ed. *Women and Power: Perspectives for Family Therapy.* New York: W. W. Norton, 1991.

Gordis, Robert. "Authority in Jewish Law." In *Conservative Judaism and Jewish Law,* edited by Seymour Siegel, 47–78. New York: The Rabbinical Assembly, 1977.

———. "The Ordination of Women." In *The Ordination of Women as Rabbis: Studies and Responsa,* edited by Simon Greenberg. New York : The Jewish Theological Seminary of America, 1988.

———. "A Modern Approach to a Living Halachah." In *Proceedings of the Committee on Jewish Law and Standards of the Conservative Movement, 1927–1970,* edited by David Golinkin. Jerusalem: The Rabbinical Assembly and the Institute of Applied Halakhah, 1997.

———. *Sex and the Family in the Jewish Tradition.* New York: United Synagogue, 1967.

Gottlieb, Lynn. "The Fruits of Creation." In *Lifecycles: Jewish Women on Life Passages and Personal Milestones,* edited by Debra Orenstein, 40–44. Woodstock, Vt.: Jewish Lights Publishing, 1994.

———. *She Who Dwells Within: A Feminist Vision of a Renewed Judaism.* San Francisco: Harper Collins, 1995.

Graglia, F. Carolyn. *Domestic Tranquility: A Brief Against Feminism.* Dallas, Tex.: Spence Publications, 1998.

Grazi, Richard. *Be Fruitful and Multiply: Fertility Therapy and the Jewish Tradition.* Jerusalem: Genesis Jerusalem Press, 5754/1994.

Grazi, Richard, Joel Wolowelsky, and Raphael Jewelwicz. "Assisted Reproduction in Contemporary Jewish Law and Ethics." *Gynecologic and Obstetric Investigation* 37 (1994): 217–25.

Greenberg, Blu. "Marriage in the Jewish Tradition." In *Perspectives on Marriage: A Reader,* edited by Kieran Scott and Michael Warren, 379–396. New York: Oxford University Press, 1993.

Greenberg, Simon, ed. *The Ordination of Women as Rabbis: Studies and Responsa.* New York : The Jewish Theological Seminary of America, 1988.

Greenwald, Yekutiel. *Kol bo al avelut* (in Hebrew). New York: Feldheim, 1973.

Gross, Netty C. "The Dissenter." *Jerusalem Report,* no. 21. 11 February 2002.

Grossman, Naomi. "Getting a Jewish Divorce Can Be an Ordeal for Orthodox Women," *Ms Magazine* 8, no. 5 (March/April 1998): 22–24.

Grossman, Susan. "Orthodox Feminism: A Movement Whose time Has Come." 1st Int'l Conference on Feminism and Orthodoxy." *Tikkun* 12, no. 3 (May/June 1997): 59–61.

———. "Religious Divorce: The Catch-22 for Orthodox Jewish Women." *Ms Magazine* 8, no. 5 (March/April 1998): 22–24.

Grossman, Susan, and Rivka Haut, eds. *Daughters of the King: Women and the Synagogue: A Survey of History, Halakhah, and Contemporary Realities.* Philadelphia: Jewish Publication Society, 1992.

Gurock, Jeffrey S. *From Fluidity to Rigidity: The Religious Worlds of Conservative and Orthodox Jews in Twentieth Century America.* Ann Arbor: Jean and Frankel Center for Judaic Studies, The University of Michigan, 1998.

Haberman, Bonna Devora. "Women Beyond the Wall: From Text to Praxis." *Journal of Feminist Studies in Religion* 13 (1997): 5–34.

Hakatan, Shmuel. *Shaarei Dimah* (in Hebrew). Jerusalem, 1873. Reprint, Jerusalem: Eshkol Press, 1968.

Halevi, Haim David. *Aseh lekha Rav* (in Hebrew). Vol. 5. Tel-Aviv: Ha-Vaadah Lehotsaat Kitve H. D. Halevi, 5743/1983.

Half the Kingdom. Directed by Franchine Zuckerman and Roushelle Goldstein. 59 min. Kol Ishah Production and National Film Board of Canada, 1990. Videocassette.

Halivni, David Weiss. "The Use of K-N-H in Connection with Marriage." *Harvard Theological Review* (1964): 244–48.

Halpern, Micah D., and Chana Safrai, eds. *Jewish Legal Writings by Women.* Jerusalem: Urim Publications, 1998.

Hammer, Jill, ed. *Journey* (fall 2002). Published by Ma'ayan, the Jewish Women's Project of the Jewish Community Center for Manhattan.

Handelman, Susan. "Family: A Religiously Mandated Ideal." *Sh'ma,* 20 March 1987, 2–3.

Hare-Mustin, and Jean Marecek. "The Meaning of Difference: Gender Theory, Postmodernism and Psychology." *American Psychologist* 46, no. 6 (June 1988): 455–64.

Hartman, David. *A Living Covenant: The Innovative Spirit in Traditional Judaism.* New York: The Free Press, 1985.

Hartman, Moshe, and Harriet Hartman. *Gender Equality and American Jews.* New York: State University of New York Press, 1996.

Ha-Siddur Hashalem. Translated and annotated by Philip Birnbaum. New York: Hebrew Publishing Company, 1977.

Hauptman, Judith. "Abortion: Where We Stand." *United Synagogue Review* 42, no. 2 (spring 1990): 17–18.

———. *Rereading the Rabbis: A Woman's Voice.* Boulder, Colo.: Westview Press, 1998.

Hayt, Elizabeth. "Admitting to Mixed Feelings About Motherhood." *New York Times,* Sunday Styles, 12 May 2002.

Hecht, Neil S., B. S. Jackson, S. M. Passamaneck, D. Piattelli, A. M. Rabello, eds. *An Introduction to the History and Sources of Jewish Law.* New York: Oxford University Press for the Jewish Law Association, 1996.

Heilbrun, Carolyn G. *Reinventing Womanhood.* New York: W. W. Norton, 1981.

———. *Writing a Woman's Life.* New York: Ballantine, 1988.

Hekman, Susan J. *Gender and Knowledge: Elements of a Postmodern Feminism.* Boston: Northeastern University Press, 1990.

Hellig, Jocelyn. "A Jewish Woman's Reflections on the Pressures of Secularist and Hedonist Influences on the Traditional Jewish Ideals of Marriage and Family." *Dialog Alliance* 9 (1995): 85–95.

———. *Toward A Recognition of Androgyny.* New York: W. W. Norton, 1992.

———. *Writing A Woman's Life.* New York: Ballantine, 1988.

Henkin, Yeduda. "Kol Ishah Reviewed." In *Equality Lost: Essays in Torah Commentary, Halacha, and Jewish Thought,* edited by Yeduda Henkin, 66–76. Jerusalem: Urim Publishers, 1999.

———. "The Reciting of Kaddish by a Woman" (in Hebrew). *HaDarom* 54 (5745/1985): 34–38.

———, ed. *Equality Lost: Essays in Torah Commentary, Halacha, and Jewish Thought.* Jerusalem: Urim Publishers, 1999.

Heschel, Susannah. Review of Rachel Adler, *Engendering Judaism: An Inclusive Theology and Ethics, Journal of the American Academy of Religion* 167, no. 2 (June 1999): 473–76.

———, ed. *On Being a Jewish Feminist: A Reader.* New York: Schocken Books, 1983.

Hirsch, Samson Raphael. "The Jewish Woman." In *Judaism Eternal: Selected Essays from the Writings of Rabbi Samson Raphael Hirsch.* Vol. 2, 49–96. London: Soncino Press, 1959.

———. *Judaism Eternal: Selected Essays from the Writings of Rabbi Samson Raphael Hirsch.* Vol. 2. Translated and annotated by I. Grunfeld. London: Soncino Press, 1959.

———. *Pentateuch.* Translated by Isaac Levy. New York: Bloch, 1963.

———. *Yeshurun.* Bene Berak, Israel: Tefutsah, 1985.

Hoffman, Lawrence A. *Beyond the Text: A Holistic Approach to Liturgy.* Bloomington: Indiana University Press, 1987.

———. *Covenant of Blood: Circumcision and Gender in Rabbinic Judaism.* Chicago: University of Chicago Press, 1996.

Holtz, Barry W. "Midrash." In *Back to the Sources: Reading the Classic Jewish Texts,* edited by Barry W. Holtz, 177–212. New York: Summit Books, 1984.

———, ed. *Back to the Sources: Reading the Classic Jewish Texts.* New York: Summit Books, 1984.

Horovitz, Saul, and Louis Finkelstein, eds. *Sifre on Deuteronomy.* Annotated by Louis Finkelstein. Berlin: Gesellschaft zur Förderung der Wissenschaft des Judentums, 1939. Reprint, New York, Jewish Theological Seminary of America, 1969.

Hrdy, Sarah Bleffer. *Mother Nature: A History of Mothers, Infants and Natural Selection.* New York: Pantheon, 1999.

———. *Mother Nature: Maternal Instincts and How They Shape the Human Species.* New York: Ballantine, 2000.

Hyman, Paula E. "Ezrat Nashim and the Emergence of a New Jewish Feminism." In *The Americanization of the Jew,* edited by Robert M. Seltzer and Norman J. Cohen, 284–95. New York: New York University Press, 1995.

———. "Feminist Studies and Modern Jewish History." In *Feminist Perspectives on Jewish Studies,* edited by Lynn Davidman and Shelly Tenebaum, 120–39. New Haven, Conn.: Yale University Press, 1994.

———. *Gender and Assimilation in Modern Jewish History: The Roles and Representations of Women.* Seattle: University of Washington Press, 1995.

———. "Gender and Jewish History." *Tikkun* (January–February 1988): 35–38.

Ilan, Meir Bar, and Shlomo Zevin, eds. *Encyclopedia Talmudit* 23 vols. (in Hebrew). Jerusalem: Talmudic Encyclopedia Publishing, 1951–1997.

Ilan, Tal. *Integrating Women Into Second Temple History.* Peabody, Mass.: Hendrickson, 2001.

———. *Jewish Women in Greco-Roman Palestine.* Peabody, Mass.: Hendrickson, 1996.

———. *Mine and Yours are Hers: Retrieving Woman's History from Rabbinic Literature.* New York: Brill, 1997.

Jacklin, Carol Nagy, and Eleanor E. Maccoby. *Psychology of Sex Differences.* Stanford, Calif.: Stanford University Press, 1984.

Jacob, Walter. "The Woman in Reform Judaism." In *Gender Issues in Jewish Law: Essays and Response,* eds. Walter Jacobs and Moshe Zemer, 130–151. New York: Berghahn Books, 2001.

———, ed. *American Reform Responsa: Collected Responsa of the Central Conference of American Rabbis, 1889–1983.* New York: Central Conference of American Rabbis, 5743/1983.

———. *Contemporary American Reform Responsa.* New York: Central Conference of American Rabbis, 5747/1987.

Jacob, Walter, and Moshe Zemer, eds. *Dynamic Jewish Law: Progressive Halakhah, Essence and Application.* Pittsburgh: Rodef Shalom Press, 1991.

———. *The Fetus and Fertility in Jewish Law: Essays and Responsa.* Pittsburgh: Rodef Shalom Press, 1995.

———. *Gender Issues in Jewish Law: Essays and Response.* New York: Berghahn Books, 2001.

———. *Marriage and Its Obstacles in Jewish Law: Essays and Responsa.* Tel Aviv and Pittsburgh: Rodef Shalom Press for Freehof Institute of Progressive Halakah, 1999.

Jacobs, Andrea M. "'Address me as a Woman!'—Can Linguistic Structure Influence Strategies for Language Reform? The Case of Contemporary Israeli Hebrew." Ma'yan: The Jewish Feminist Research Group. (May 2002).

Jacobs, Janet L. "Women, Ritual and, Secrecy: The Creation of Crypto-Jewish Culture." *Journal for the Scientific Study of Religion* 35 (1996): 97–108.

Jacobs, Louis. Review of *Studies in the Development of Halakha* (in Hebrew), by Yitzhak D. Gilat. In *Journal of Jewish Studies* 46, nos. 1–2 (spring–autumn 1995), 323–25.

Jakobovits, Immanuel. "Controlling the Generation of Life." In *Jewish Medical Ethics,* 170–92. New York: Bloch Publishing, 1959.

———. "Jewish Voices on Abortion." In *Abortion and the Law,* edited by David T. Smith, 124–43. Cleveland, Ohio: Western Reserve University Press, 1967.

Janeway, Elizabeth. *Man's World, Woman's Place.* New York: Dell Publishing, 1971.

Jensvold, Margaret F., Uriel Halbreich, and Jean A. Hamilton, eds. *Psychopharmacology and Women: Sex, Gender, and Hormones.* Washington, D.C.: American Psychiatric Press, 1996.

John Paul II. "Letter of Pope John Paul II to Women." 29 June 1995. <http://www.vatican.va/holy_father/john_paul_ii/letters/documents/hf_jp-ii_let_29061995_women_en.html> (May 1, 2002).

Kahane, Naftali Herz Hacohen. *Otsar Tefillot Yisrael* (in Hebrew). Vols. 1–3. Jerusalem and London: n.p., 1993.

Kahn, Susan Martha. "Rabbis and Reproduction: The Uses of New Reproductive Technologies among Ultraorthodox in Israel." Waltham, Mass.: Hadassah International Research Institute on Jewish Women: Brandeis University Working Paper Series, 1998.

———. *Reproducing Jews: A Cultural Account of Assisted Conception in Israel.* Durham, N.C.: Duke University Press, 2000.

Kant, Immanuel. *Religion within the Limits of Reason Alone.* Translated by Theodore M. Greene and Hoyt H. Hudson. New York: Harper Torchbooks, 1960.

Kaplan, Dana Evan, ed. *Contemporary Debates in American Reform Judaism: Conflicting Visions.* New York: Routledge, 2001.

Karo, Joseph. *Shulhan Arukh.* Vilna Rom, 1880. Reprint, Jerusalem: Talmon, 1977.

Katz, Jacob. *Exclusiveness and Tolerance: Studies in Jewish-Gentile Relations in Medieval and Modern Times.* New York: Behrman House, 1961.

———. *The "Shabbes Goy": A Study in Halakhic Flexibility.* Philadelphia: Jewish Publication Society, 1989.

———. *Tradition and Crisis: Jewish Society at the End of the Middle Ages.* Translated by Bernard Dov Cooperman. New York: New York University Press, 1993.

Kaufman, Michael. *The Woman in Jewish Law and Tradition.* Northvale, N.J.: Jason Aronson, 1993.

Kellerstein, Faye. "A Feygele Zingt [A Daughter Sings]." *Lilith* (fall 1997): 21–22.

Kellner, Menachem, ed., *Contemporary Jewish Ethics.* New York: Hebrew Publishing Co., 1978.

Kimelman, Reuven. "The Seduction of Eve and the Exegetical Politics of Gender." In *Women in the Hebrew Bible: A Reader,* edited by Alice Bach, 241–70. New York: Routledge, 1999.

Kimura, Doreen, "Sex Differences in the Brain." *Scientific American* 267 no. 3 (Sept. 1992): 118–25.

Kirschenbaum, Aaron. "Subjectivity in Rabbinic Decision Making." In *Rabbinic Authority and Personal Autonomy,* edited by Moshe Z. Sokol, 61–92. Northvale, N.J.: Aronson, 1992.

Kittay, Eva Feder, and Diana T. Meyers, eds. *Women and Moral Theory.* Totowa, N.J.: Rowman & Littlefield Publishers, 1987.

Klein, Isaac. *Guide to Jewish Religious Practice.* New York: Jewish Theological Seminary, 1979.

———. *Responsa and Halakhic Studies.* New York: Ktav Publishing, 1975.

Klein, Michel. *A Time to Be Born: Customs and Folklore of Jewish Birth.* Philadelphia: Jewish Publication Society, 1998.

Kohler, Kaufmann, and David Neumark. "Mourning Customs." In *American Reform Responsa: Collected Responsa of the Central Conference of American Rabbis, 1889–1983,* edited by Walter Jacob. New York: Central Conference of American Rabbis, 5743/1983.

Kolodny, Robert C. *Masters and Johnson on Sex and Human Loving.* Boston: Little Brown, 1986.

Koltun, Elizabeth, ed. *The Jewish Woman: New Perspectives.* New York: Schocken Books, 1976.

———, ed. *Response: A Contemporary Jewish Review,* no. 18 (summer 1973).

Kraemer, David C. "A Developmental Perspective on the Laws of Niddah." *Conservative Judaism* 38, no. 3 (spring 1986): 26–33.

———. *Reading the Rabbis: The Talmud as Literature.* New York: Oxford University Press, 1996.

Kraemer, Ross Shepard. *Her Share of the Blessings.* New York: Oxford University Press, 1992.

Kramer, Ross. "The Other as Woman: An Aspect of Polemic among Pagans, Christians, and Jews in the Greco-Roman World." In *The Other in Jewish Thought and History: Construction of Jewish Culture and Identity,* edited by Laurence J. Silberstein and Robert Cohn, 121–44. New York: New York University Press, 1994.

Kritz, Francesca Lunzer. "The 'Dangerous' Act of Saying Kaddish in an Orthodox Synagogue." *Forward,* 3 July 1998.

Krohn, Paysach J. *Bris Milah.* New York: Mesorah Publications, 1985.

Kurtines, William M., and Jacob L. Gewirtz, eds. *Handbook of Moral Behavior and Development.* Vols. 1–3. Hillsdale, N.J.: Lawrence Erlbaum Associates, 1991.

Lakoff, Robin. *Language and Woman's Place.* New York: Harper Torchbooks, 1975.

Lamm, Maurice. *The Jewish Way in Death and Mourning.* Middle Village, N.Y.: Jonathan David, 2000.

Lamm, Norman. *Torah Umadda: The Encounter of Religious Learning and Worldly Knowledge in the Jewish Tradition.* Northvale, N.J.: Jason Aronson, 1990.

Lamphere, Louise. "The Domestic Sphere of Women and the Public World of Men: The Strengths and Limitations of an Anthropological Dichotomy." In *Gender in Cross-Cultural Perspective,* edited by Caroline Brettell and Carolyn Sargent, 100–9. Upper Saddle River, N.J.: Prentice Hall, 2001.

Landman, Leo, ed. *Rabbi Joseph H. Lookstein Memorial Volume.* New York: Ktav Publishing, 1981.

Larson, Hilary. "Mourning Glory." *Jewish Week,* 26 June 1998.

Lasch, Christopher. *Women and the Common Life: Love, Marriage, and Feminism.* New York: W. W. Norton, 1997.

Lau, Meir. *Responsa Yahel Yisrael: Halakhic Insights and Clarifications.* Vol. 2, no. 90. Jerusalem: Makhon Masoret A. Y. Yeshivah Haye Mosheh, 5752/1992.

Lauterbach, Jacob Z. "Birth Control." In *The Fetus and Fertility in Jewish Law: Essays and Responsa,* edited by Walter Jacob and Moshe Zemer. Pittsburgh and Tel Aviv: Rodef Shalom Press, 1995, 173–89.

Leibowitz, Nehama. *Studies in Bereishit (Genesis).* 3d ed. Jerusalem: World Zionist Organization, 1976.

———. *Studies in Shemot (Exodus),* Vol. 1. Jerusalem: World Zionist Organization, 1976.

Lehmann, Marcus. *Lehmann's Passover Hagadah.* New York: Lehmann Books, 1974.

Lerner, Gerda. *The Creation of Feminist Consciousness.* New York: Oxford University Press, 1993.

———. *The Creation of Patriarchy.* New York: Oxford University Press, 1987.

———. "Reconceptualizing Differences Among Women." *Journal of Women's History* 1, no. 3 (winter 1990): 106–22.

———. *Why History Matters: Life and Thought.* New York: Oxford University Press, 1997.

Levenson, Jon D. "The New Enemies of Circumcision." *Commentary* 109, no. 3 (March 2000): 29–38.

Levinas, Emmanuel. *Nine Talmudic Readings.* Translated by Annette Aronowicz. Bloomington: Indiana University Press, 1990.

Lewittes, Haim Menahem, ed. *Shana beShana* (in Hebrew). Jerusalem: Heichal Shlomo, 1990.

Levy, Yael V. "The Agunah and the Missing Husband: An American Solution to a Jewish Problem," [divorce]. *Journal of Law and Religion* 10, no. 1 (1993–1994): 49–71.

Lichtenstein, Aharon. "Does Jewish Tradition Recognize an Ethic Independent of Halakha?" In *Contemporary Jewish Ethics,* edited by Menachem Kellner, 102–23. New York: Hebrew Publishing Co., 1978.

———. "The Human and Social Factor in Halakha." *Tradition* 36, no.1 (spring 2001): 1–25.

———. "Legitimization of Modernity: Classical and Contemporary." In *Engaging Modernity: Rabbinic Leaders and the Challenge of the Twentieth Century,* edited by Moshe Z. Sokol, 3–34. Northvale, N.J.: Jason Aronson, 1997.

Liebman, Charles S. "Orthodoxy in American Jewish Life." *American Jewish Yearbook* 66 (1965): 21–98.

Lieu, Judith. "Circumcision, Women and Salvation." *New Testament Studies* 40, no. 3 (1994): 358–70.

Lipstadt, Deborah. "And Deborah Made Ten." In *On Being a Jewish Feminist,* edited by Susannah Heschel. New York: Shocken Books,1983.

———. "Feminism and American Judaism: Looking Back at the Turn of the Century." In *Women and American Judaism: Historical Perspectives,* edited by Pamela S.

Nadell and Jonathan D. Sarna, 291–308. Hanover, N.H.: University Press of New England, 2001.

Loades, Ann, ed. *Feminist Theology: A Reader*. Louisville, Ky.: Westminster John Knox, 1990.

Luria, Solomon Yehiel. *Yam shel Shelomo*. Altona, Germany: Aharon ben Eli Katz, 1739.

Maccoby, Eleanor, and Carol N. Jacklin. *The Psychology of Sex Differences*. Stanford, Calif.: Stanford University Press, 1974.

MacCormack, Carol, and Marilyn Strether, eds. *Nature, Culture, and Gender*. Cambridge, England and New York: Cambridge University Press, 1980.

Magnus, Shulamit S. "Modern Jewish Social History." In *The Modern Jewish Experience: A Reader's Guide,* edited by Jack Wartheimer, 109–122. New York: New York University Press, 1993.

Maimonides, Moses. *The Guide of the Perplexed*. Translated by Shlomo Pines. Chicago: University of Chicago Press, 1963.

———. *Mishneh Torah* (in Hebrew). Annotated and edited by Shabtai Frankel. Jerusalem: Congregation Bnei Yosef, 1975.

Majewska, Maria D. "Sex Differences in Brain Morphology and Pharmacodynamics." In *Psychopharmacology and Women: Sex, Gender, and Hormones,* edited by Margaret F. Jensvold, Uriel Halbreich, and Jean A. Hamilton, pp. 73–83. Washington, D.C.: American Psychiatric Press, 1996.

Malbim Haggadah. Translated and annotated by Jonathan Taub and Yisroel Shaw. New York: Feldheim, 1993.

Manning, Christel. *God Gave Us the Right: Conservative Catholic, Evangelical Protestant, Orthodox Jewish Women Grapple with Feminism*. New Brunswick, N.J.: Rutgers University Press, 1999.

Mark, Jonathan. "In Uncharted Waters." *Jewish Week,* 11 December1998.

———. "Reassessing an Experiment." *Jewish Week*. 26 May 2000.

———. "Torat Miriam, a Work in Progress." *Jewish Week,* 6 February 1998.

———. "Women Take Giant Step in Orthodox Community." *Jewish Week,* 19 December 1997.

Margoliot, Ephraim Zalman. *Mateh Ephraim* (in Hebrew). Jerusalem: Eisenbach, 1989.

Martyr, Justin. "Dialogue with Trypho the Jew." In *Writings of Saint Justin Martyr: The First Apology,* 139–366. Translated and edited by Thomas B. Falls. New York: Christian Heritage, 1948.

Maslin, Simeon J., ed. *Gates of Mitzvah: A Guide to the Jewish Life Cycle*. New York: Central Conference of American Rabbis, 1979.

Masters, William H., and Virginia E. Johnson. *Human Sexual Response*. Boston: Little, Brown, and Co., 1966.

———. *The Pleasure Bond: A New Look at Sexuality and Commitment*. Boston: Little Brown, 1974.

Mazow, Julia Wolf, ed. *The Woman Who Lost Her Names: Selected Writings by American Jewish Women*. San Francisco: Harper & Row, 1980.

McLaughlin, Loretta. *The Pill, John Rock, and the Church*. Boston: Little Brown, and Co., 1982.

Meier, Levi, ed. *Jewish Values in Bioethics*. New York: Human Sciences Press, 1986.

Meiselman, Moshe. *Jewish Women in Jewish Law.* New York: Ktav Publishing, 1978.
———. "The Rav, Feminism, and Public Policy: An Insider's Overview." *Tradition* 33, no. 1 (fall 1998), 5–30.
Mendes-Flohr, Paul R., and Jehuda Reinhartz, eds. *The Jew in the Modern World: A Documentary History.* New York: Oxford University Press, 1980.
Messinger, Ruth W. "A Surprising Lesson from Those September 11 Obituaries." *Lilith* 27, no. 1 (spring 2000).
Meyer, Michael A. *The Origins of the Modern Jew: Jewish Identity and European Culture in Germany, 1749–1824.* Detroit: Wayne State University Press, 1967.
———. *Response to Modernity: A History of the Reform Movement in Judaism.* New York: Oxford University Press, 1988.
Meyers, Carol. *Discovering Eve: Ancient Israelite Women in Context.* New York: Oxford University Press, 1988.
Mikliszanski, Jacques Koppel. *The Saga of Traditional Judaism.* Los Angeles: Zahava Publishing, 1977.
Millen, Rochelle L. "An Analysis of Rabbinic Hermeneutics: B.T. Kiddushin 34a." In *Gender and Judaism: The Transformation of Tradition,* edited by T. M. Rudavsky, 25–32. New York: New York University Press, 1995.
———. "Birkhat Ha-Gomel: A Study in Cultural Context and Halakhic Practice." *Judaism* 43, no. 3 (summer 1994): 270–78.
———. "Communications." *Judaism* 44, no. 1 (winter 1995).
———. "Free Will and the Possibility of Radical Evil in Kant." Master's thesis, McMaster University, 1975.
———. "The Female Voice of Kaddish." In *Jewish Legal Writings by Women,* edited by Chana Safrai and Micah D. Halpern, 179–201. Jerusalem: Urim Publications, 1995.
———. "Social Attitudes Disguised as Halakhah: *Zila Milta, Ein Havrutan Na'ah, Kevod Hatzibbur.*" *Nashim: A Journal of Jewish Women's Studies and Gender Issues,* no. 4 (fall 2001): 178–96.
———. "Women and Kaddish: Reflections on Responsa." *Modern Judaism* 10 (1990): 191–203.
Miller, Jean Baker. *Psychoanalysis and Women.* Baltimore, Md.: Penguin, 1973.
———. *Toward A New Psychology of Women,* 2d ed. Boston: Beacon Press, 1986.
———. "Women and Power: Reflections Ten Years Later." In *Women and Power: Perspectives for Family Therapy,* edited by Thelma Jean Goodrich, 36–47. New York: W. W. Norton, 1991.
Miller, Marlene. "An Intricate Weave: Women Write about Girls and Girlhood." *Lilith* (spring 1997).
Mnookin, Seth. "Fertility Treatments, on Rise, Prompt New Dilemmas." *Forward,* 2 July 1995.
Mollenkott, Virginia Ramey. *The Divine Feminine: The Biblical Imagery of God as Female.* New York: Crossroad, 1987.
Moriel, Jehudah. *Barukh Tovim* (in Hebrew). Jerusalem: World Zionist Organization, 1976.
Morley, Janet. "I Desire Her With My Whole Heart." In *Feminist Theology: A Reader,* edited by Ann Loades, 158–65. Louisville, Ky.: Westminster John Knox, 1990.
Myerhoff, Barbara. *Number Our Days.* New York: Simon and Schuster, 1978.

————. *Remembered Lives: The Work of Ritual, Storytelling, and Growing Older.* Ann Arbor: The University of Michigan Press, 1992.

Nadell, Pamela. *Women Who Would Be Rabbis: A History of Women's Ordination, 1889–1985.* Boston: Beacon Press, 1998.

Nadell, Pamela S., and Jonathan D. Sarna, eds. *Women and American Judaism: Historical Perspectives.* Hanover, N.H.: University Press of New England, 2001.

Nahmanides, Moses. *Commentary on the Torah.* Translated by C. B. Chavel. New York: Shilo, 1971.

Neusner, Jacob. "The Feminization of Judaism: Systemic Reversals and Their Meaning in the Formation of the Rabbinic System." *Conservative Judaism* 46 (1994): 37–52.

Newsom, Carol A., and Sharon H. Ringe, eds. *The Women's Bible Commentary.* Louisville, Ky.: Westminster/John Knox, 1992.

Noonan Jr., John T. *Contraception: A History of Its Treatment by the Catholic Theologians and Canonists.* Cambridge: Harvard University Press, 1986.

Northrup, Lesley A. "Emerging Patterns of Women's Ritualizing in the West." *Ritual Studies* 9 (1995): 109–36.

Novak, David. "'Be Fruitful and Multiply': Issues Relating to Birth in Judaism." In *Celebration and Renewal: Rites of Passage in Judaism,* edited by Rela M. Geffen, 12–31. Philadelphia: Jewish Publication Society, 5753/1993.

————. *Jewish Social Ethics.* New York: Oxford University Press, 1992.

————. "Natural Law, Halakhah, and the Covenant." In *Jewish Social Ethics,* edited by David Novak, 22–44. New York: Oxford University Press, 1992.

Orenstein, Debra, ed. *Lifecycles: Jewish Women on Life Passages and Personal Milestones.* Woodstock, Vt.: Jewish Lights Publishing, 1994.

Orenstein, Peggy. "Mourning My Miscarriage." *New York Times Magazine,* 21 April 2002.

Ortner, Sherry B. "Is Female to Male as Nature is to Culture?" In *Woman, Culture, and Society,* edited by Michelle Z. Rosaldo and Louise Lamphere, 67–88. Stanford, Calif.: Stanford University Press: 1974.

Ozick, Cynthia. "Notes Toward Finding the Right Question." In *On Being a Jewish Feminist,* edited by Susannah Heschel, 120–51. New York: Schocken Books, 1983.

Ozment, Steven. "Re-inventing Family Life." *Christian History* 12, no. 3 (1993): 22–26.

Pagels, Elaine. *Adam, Eve, and the Serpent.* New York: Columbia University Press, 1988.

Pardes, Ilana. *Countertraditions in the Bible: A Feminist Approach.* Cambridge: Harvard University Press, 1992.

Parent, Marc. "A Dad at the Final Frontier." *New York Times,* 16 June 2001.

Payne, Karen, ed. *Between Ourselves: Letters Between Mothers and Daughters, 1750–1982.* Boston: Houghton-Mifflin, 1983.

Peli, Pinchas, ed. *Besod Hayahid vehayahad* (in Hebrew). Jerusalem: Orot, 1976.

Perry, M. E., ed. *Handbook of Sexology, Vol. 7: Childhood and Adolescent Sexology.* New York: Elsievier Science Publishers B.V. Biomedical Division, 1991.

Piaget, Jean. *The Moral Judgment of the Child.* New York: Free Press, 1954.

Pinker, Steven. *The Blank Slate: The Denial of Human Nature.* New York: Viking/Penguin, 2002.

Pirkei de Rabbi Eliezer. [notes of David Luria] Jerusalem, 1972.

Plaskow, Judith. *Standing Again at Sinai*. San Francisco: Harper & Row, 1990.

Plaut, W. Gunther. *The Growth of Reform Judaism: American and European Sources until 1948*. New York: World Union for Progressive Judaism, 1965.

———. *The Rise of Reform Judaism*. New York: World Union for Progressive Judaism, 1963.

Pogrebin, Letty Cottin. *Deborah, Golda, and Me: Being Female and Jewish in America*. New York: Crown Publishers, 1991.

Polaski, Donald. "On Taming Tamar: Amram's Rhetoric and Women's Roles in Pseudo-Philo's *Liberantiquitatum Biblicarum 9*." *Journal for the Study of the Pseudepigrapha* 13 (1995): 79–99.

Polish, David, ed. *Maaglei tsedek: Rabbi's Manual*. Annotated by W. Gunther Plaut. New York: Central Conference of American Rabbis, 1988.

Pollack, Miriam. "Circumcision: A Jewish Feminist Perspective." In *Jewish Women Speak Out: Expanding the Boundaries of Psychology*, edited by Kayla Weiner and Arinna Moon, 171–85. Seattle: Canopy Press, 1995.

Pomeroy, Sarah B., ed. *Women's History and Ancient History*. Chapel Hill: University of North Carolina Press, 1991.

Pool, David de Sola, ed. *Siddur* [Sephardi], 3d ed. New York: Behrman House, 1972.

Rank, Perry Raphael, and Gordon M. Freeman, eds. *Moreh Derekh: The Rabbinical Assembly Rabbi's Manual*. New York: The Rabbinical Assembly, 1998.

Rapoport, Chaim. "Why Women are Exempt from Positive Time-bound Commandments: Is There a Torah-true View?" *Le'ela*, no. 50 (December 2000): 53–64.

Rapoport, Nessa. "Family Matters: A Feminist Looks at Motherhood." *Hadassah Magazine* 76, no. 1 (1994).

———. *A Woman's Book of Grieving*. New York: William Morrow, 1994.

———. "The Woman Who Lost Her Names." In *The Women Who Lost her Names: Selected Writings by American Jewish Women.*, edited by Julia Wolf Mazow, 135–45. San Francisco: Harper & Row, 1980.

Ravitsky, Aviezer. "*Hadash Min Ha-Torah?* Modern versus Traditionalist Orientations in Contemporary Orthodoxy." In *Engaging Modernity: Rabbinic Leaders and the Challenge of the Twentieth Century*, edited by Moshe Z. Sokol, 35–56. Northvale, N.J.: Jason Aronson, 1997.

Rawls, John. *Political Liberalism*. New York: Columbia University Press, 1993.

Reed, Donald Collins. "Some Observations About How Moral Psychologists have Construed Autonomy." Paper presented at the conference of the Association for Moral Education, Vancouver, British Columbia, Canada, 2 October 2001.

Reguer, Sara. "Kaddish from the 'Wrong' Side of the Mehitzah." In *On Being a Jewish Feminist*, edited by Susannah Heschel, 177–81. New York: Schocken Books, 1983.

Reich, Tova. "My Mother, My Muse." *New York Times Magazine*, 6 November 1988, 30–31.

Reimers, Paula. "Feminism, Judaism and God the Mother." *Conservative Judaism* 46 (1993): 24–29.

Reinhartz, Adele. *"Why Ask My Name?": Anonymity and Identity in Biblical Narrative*. New York: Oxford University Press, 1998.

Review of *The Judaic Law of Baptism: Tractate Miqvaot in the Mishnah and Tosefta, a*

Form Analytical Translation and Commentary and a Legal and Religious History, by Jacob Neusner. *Shofar* 15, no. 4 (summer 1997).

Roetzel, Calvin. *The Letters of Paul: Conversations in Context.* Louisville, Ky.: Westminster/John Knox, 1991.

Roiphe, Anne. *Fruitful: A Real Mother in the Modern World.* Boston: Houghton Mifflin, 1996.

Rosaldo, Michelle Z. "Women, Culture, and Society: A Theoretical Overview." In *Woman, Culture, and Society,* edited by Michelle Z. Rosaldo and Louise Lamphere, 17–42. Stanford, Calif.: Stanford University Press, 1974.

Rosaldo, Michelle Z., and Louise Lamphere, eds. *Woman, Culture, and Society.* Stanford, Calif.: Stanford University Press, 1974.

Rosen, Jeffrey. "The New Look of Liberalism on the Court." *New York Times Magazine,* 5 October 1997.

Rosenstein, Harriet. "The Fraychie Story." In *The Woman Who Lost Her Names: Selected Writings by American Jewish Women,* edited by Julia Wolf Mazow, 38–48. San Francisco: Harper & Row, 1980.

Rosenthal, David S. *The Joyful Mother of Children.* New York: Feldheim, 1988.

Rosner, Fred. "Contraception in Jewish Law." In *Jewish Bioethics,* edited by Fred Rosner and J. David Bleich, 105–16. Hoboken, N.J.: Ktav Publishing, 2000.

Rosner, Fred, and J. David Bleich, eds. *Jewish Bioethics.* Hoboken, N.J.: Ktav Publishing, 2000.

Ross, Tamar. "Can the Demand for Change in the Status of Women be Halakhically Legitimated?" *Judaism* 42 (1993): 478–91.

———. "Modern Orthodoxy and the Challenge of Feminism." In *Jews and Gender: The Challenge to Hierarchy,* edited by Jonathan Frankel, 3–38. New York: Oxford University Press, 2000.

Rotenberg, M. "The Daughter Who Recited Kaddish." *Ha Doar* 54, no. 20, 21 March 1975.

Roth, Cecil. *Dona Gracia of the House of Nasi.* Philadelphia: Jewish Publication Society, 1977.

Roth, Joel. *The Halakhic Process: A Systematic Analysis.* New York: Jewish Theological Seminary, 1986.

Rubin, Nissan. "Coping with the Value of the *Pidyon haben* Payment in Rabbinic Literature—An Example of a Social Change Process." *Jewish History* 10, no. 1 (spring 1996): 39–62.

Rudavsky, T. M., ed. *Gender and Judaism: The Transformation of Tradition.* New York: New York University Press, 1995.

Ruddick, Sara. *Maternal Thinking: Toward a Politics of Peace.* New York: Ballantine, 1989.

Ruether, Rosemary. "Home and Work: Women's Roles and the Transformation of Values." In *Perspectives on Marriage: A Reader,* edited by Kieran Scott and Michael Warren, 285–96. New York: Oxford University Press, 1993.

———. *Sexism and God-talk: Towards a Feminist Theology.* Boston: Beacon, 1984.

Sacks, Karen. "Engels Revisited: Women, the Organization of Production, and Private Property." In *Woman, Culture, and Society,* edited by Michelle Z. Rosaldo and Louise Lamphere, 207–23. Stanford, Calif.: Stanford University Press, 1974.

Safrai, Chana, and Micah D. Halpern, eds. *Jewish Legal Writings by Women.* Jerusalem: Urim Publications, 1995.

Samuel, Jacob ben. "Responsa Beit Yaacov." In *Evolving Halakhah: A Progressive Approach to Traditional Jewish Law,* edited by Moshe Zemer. Woodstock, Vt.: Jewish Lights, 1999.

Sanday, Peggy. "Female Status in the Public Domain." In *Woman, Culture, and Society,* edited by Michelle Z. Rosaldo and Louise Lamphere, 189–206. Stanford, Calif.: Stanford University Press, 1974.

Sarna, Jonathan D. "Mixed Seating in the American Synagogue." In *The American Synagogue: A Sanctuary Transformed,* edited by Jack Wertheimer. New York: Cambridge University Press, 1987.

Satlow, Micahel L. *Jewish Marriage in Antiquity.* Princeton, N.J.: Princeton University Press, 2001.

———. *Tasting the Dish: Rabbinic Rhetorics of Sexuality.* Atlanta: Scholars Press, 1995.

———. "'Try to be a Man': The Rabbinic Construction of Masculinity." *Harvard Theological Review* 89 (1996): 19–40.

Scarf, Maggie. *Intimate Partners: Patterns in Love and Marriage.* New York: Random House, 1987.

———. *Unfinished Business: Pressure Points in the Lives of Women.* New York: Ballantine, 1981.

Schachter, Hershel. "Go Out in the Footsteps of the Sheep" (in Hebrew). *Bet Yitshak* 17 (1984–1985): 118–34.

———. "Halachic Aspects of Family Planning." In *Halacha and Contemporary Society,* edited by Alfred S. Cohen, 3–30. New York: Ktav Publishing, Rabbi Jacob Joseph School, 1984.

Scherman, Nosson, and Meir Zlotowitz, eds. *Siddur Ahavat Shalom: The Complete Artscroll Siddur.* New York: Mesorah Publications, 1984.

Schiffren, Lisa. "Lifestyles of the Rich and Infertile." *Commentary* 114, no. 1 (July–August 2002): 52–56.

Scholem, Gershom. *Kabbalah.* New York: Quadrangle/New York Times Book Co., 1974.

———. *The Messianic Idea in Judaism: And Other Essays on Jewish Spirituality.* New York: Schocken Books, 1971.

———. "Revelation and Tradition as Religious Categories in Judaism." In *The Messianic Idea in Judaism: And Other Essays on Jewish Spirituality,* 282–303. New York: Schocken Books, 1971.

Scott, Joan Wallach. *Gender and the Politics of History.* New York: Columbia University Press, 1999.

Scott, Kieran, and Michael Warren, eds. *Perspectives on Marriage: A Reader.* New York: Oxford University Press, 1993.

Seeman, Don. "The Silence of Rayna Batya." *The Torah U-Madda Journal* 6 (1995–1996): 91–128.

Seligman, Ruth. "On Being 70: Women Ponder the Meaning of Turning Seventy Years Old." *Na'Amat Women* 12:5 (1997).

Seltzer, Robert M., ed. *Judaism: A People and Its History.* New York: Macmillan Press, 1989.

Seltzer, Robert M., and Norman J. Cohen, eds. *The Americanization of the Jew*. New York: New York University Press, 1995.

Sered, Susan S. *What Makes Women Sick: Maternity, Modesty, and Militarism in Israeli Society*. Hanover, N.H.: Brandeis University Press and University Press of New England, 2000.

———. "Women and Religious Change in Israel: Rebellion or Revolution?" *Sociology of Religion* 58 (1997): 1–24.

———. *Women as Ritual Experts: The Religious Lives of Elderly Jewish Women in Jerusalem*. New York: Oxford University Press, 1992.

Shalom, Benjamin Ish. Review of *Rav Avraham Itzhak HaCohen Kook: Between Rationalism and Mysticism*, by Rochelle L. Millen. *Association of Jewish Studies* 12, no.1 (1996), 104–12.

Shalom, Benjamin Ish, and Shalom Rosenberg, eds. *The World of Rav Kook's Thought*. Jerusalem: Avi Chai, 1991.

Sharfstein, Asher. *Tikkun La Koreim* (in Hebrew). New York: Ktav Publishing, 1946, reprinted 1969.

Shulman, Nisson E. *Jewish Answers to Medical Ethics Questions: Questions and Answers from the Medical Ethics Department of the Office of the Chief Rabbi of Great Britain*. Northvale, N.J.: Jason Aronson, 1998.

———. "Sexuality and Reproduction." In *Jewish Answers to Medical Ethics Questions: Questions and Answers from the Medical Ethics Department of the Office of the Chief Rabbi of Great Britain,* edited by Nisson E. Shulman, 41–114. Northvale, N.J.: Jason Aronson, 1998.

Shweder, Richard A., Nancy C. Much, Manamohan Mahapatra, and Lawrence Park. "The 'Big Three' of Morality (Autonomy, Community, Diversity) and the 'Big Three' Explanations of Suffering." In *Morality and Health,* edited by Allan M. Brandt and Paul Rozin, section 2. Florence, Ky.: Routledge, 1997.

Siegel, Seymour, ed. *Conservative Judaism and Jewish Law*. New York: The Rabbinical Assembly, 1977.

Silberstein, Laurence J., and Robert Cohn, eds. *The Other in Jewish Thought and History: Construction of Jewish Culture and Identity*. New York: New York University Press, 1994.

Silverman, Charles. *A Certain People: American Jews and Their Lives Today*. New York: Summit Books, 1985.

Silverman, Morris, ed. *Passover Haggadah*. Hartford, Conn.: Prayer Book Press, 1966.

Sklare, Marshall. *Conservative Judaism: An American Religious Movement*. New York: Schocken Books, 1972.

Smith, William. 1890. *Dictionary of Greek and Roman Antiquities*. 2d ed. Aperture, 1977.

Sobel, Zvi, and Benjamin Beit-Hallahoomi, eds. *Tradition, Innovation, and Conflict: Jewishness and Judaism in Contemporary Israel*. Albany: State University of New York Press, 1991.

Sokol, Moshe Z. "Personal Authority and Religious Authority." in *Rabbinic Authority and Personal Autonomy,* edited by Moshe Z. Sokol, 169–216. Northvale, N.J.: Jason Aronson, 1992.

———, ed. *Engaging Modernity: Rabbinic Leaders and the Challenge of the Twentieth Century*. Northvale, N.J.: Jason Aronson, 1997.

———. *Rabbinic Authority and Personal Autonomy*. Northvale, N.J.: Jason Aronson, 1992.

Soloveitchik, Aaron. *Od Yisrael Yosef Beni Chai* (in Hebrew). Chicago: Yeshivat Brisk, 1993.

Soloveitchik, Joseph B. "Catharsis." *Tradition* 17, no.2 (spring 1978): 38–54.

———. "The Community." *Tradition* 117, no. 2 (spring 1979): 7–24.

———. *Halakhic Man*. Translated by Lawrence Kaplan. Philadelphia, Pa.: Jewish Publication Society, 1983.

———. "Kol Dodi Dofek" (in Hebrew). In *Besod Hayahid Veha Yahad,* edited by Pinchas Peli, 331–400. Jerusalem: Orot, 1976.

———. "The Lonely Man of Faith." *Tradition* 7, no. 2 (summer 1965): 1–69.

———. "Majesty and Humility." *Tradition* 17, no. 2 (spring 1978): 25–37.

Song of Songs Rabbah (in Hebrew). Jerusalem: Levi Epstein Publishing, 1960.

Soskice, Janet Martin. "Can a Feminist Call God 'Father'?" In *Women's Voices: Essays in Contemporary Feminist Theology,* edited by Theresa Elwes, 15–30. London: Marshall Pickering/Harper Collins, 1992.

Sperber, Daniel. *The Customs of Israel* (in Hebrew). Jerusalem: Mossad Harav Kook, 1990.

Spiegel, Marcia Cohn. "Spirituality for Survival: Jewish Women Healing Themselves." *Journal of Feminist Studies in Religion* 12 (1996): 121–37.

Spitz, Elie. "'Through Her I Too Shall Bear a Child': Birth Surrogates in Jewish Law." *Journal of Religious Ethics* 24 (1996): 65–97.

Stefansky, Chaim, ed. *The Carlebach Haggadah*. New York: Urim Publications, 2001.

Steinsaltz, Adin. *The Talmud: A Reference Guide*. New York: Random House, 1989.

Stern, Chaim, Donna Berman, Edward Graham, and H. Leonard Poller, eds. *On the Doorposts of Your House*. New York: Central Conference of American Rabbis, 1994.

Stern, Sacha. *Jewish Identity in Early Rabbinic Writings*. New York: E. J. Brill, 1994.

Stolper, Pinchas. *Jewish Alternatives in Love, Dating, and Marriage*. New York: Orthodox Union and University Press of America, 1967.

Stout, Jeffrey. *The Flight from Authority*. Notre Dame, Mich.: University of Notre Dame Press, 1981.

Strassfeld, Michael, and Sharon Strassfeld. *The Second Jewish Catalog: Sources and Resources*. Philadelphia, Pa.: Jewish Publication Society, 1976.

Tannen, Deborah. *Gender and Discourse*. New York: Oxford University Press, 1994.

Taubes, Zvi, ed. *Otzar Ha-geonim*. Jerusalem: Mosad Ha-Rav Kook, 1966.

Tavris, Carol. *The Mismeasure of Woman*. New York: Simon and Schuster, 1992.

Tikkun Lakoreim (in Hebrew). New York: Ktav Publishing, 1969.

Tirosh-Rothchild, Hava. "'Dare to Know': Feminism and the Discipline of Jewish Philosophy." In *Feminist Perspectives on Jewish Studies,* edited by Lynn Davidman and Shelly Tenebaum, 85–120. New Haven, Ct.: Yale University Press, 1994.

Todd, Mary. *Authority Vested: A Story of Identity and Change in the Lutheran Church–Missouri Synod*. Grand Rapids, Mich.: W. B. Eerdmans, 2000.

Trible, Phyllis. *God and the Rhetoric of Sexuality*. Philadelphia: Fortress Press, 1978.

Twersky, Mayer. "Halakhic Values and Halakhic Decisions: Rav Soloveitchik's Pesak Regarding Women's Prayer Groups." *Tradition* 32, no. 3 (spring 1998), 5–18.

———. "Torah Perspectives on Women's Issues." *Jewish Action* 57, no. 4 (summer 1997): 24–29.

Umansky, Ellen. "Piety, Persuasion, and Friendship: Female Jewish Leadership in Modern Times." In *Embodied Love: Sensuality and Relationship as Feminist Values,* edited by Paula M. Cooey, 190–206. San Francisco: Harper & Row, 1987.

Uziel, Ben-Zion Meir Hai. *Mispetei Uziel* (in Hebrew). Levitski: Tel Aviv, 1935–1940.

Valler, Shulamit. *Women and Womanhood in the Stories of Babylonian Talmud.* Tel Aviv: Kibbutz Hameuchad, 1993.

Viorst, Judith. *Imperfect Control.* New York: Fireside/Simon & Schuster, 1999.

Wahrman, Shlomo Halevi. *She'erit Yosef.* Vol. 2. New York: Balsham, 1981.

Walsh, Mary Williams. "So Where Are the Corporate Husbands?" *New York Times,* Money and Business Section, 24 June 2001.

Waldenberg, Eliezer. *Tzitz Eliezer* (in Hebrew). Jerusalem: Eliezer Waldenberg, 1961–1998.

Wasserfall, Rahel R., ed. *Women and Water: Menstruation in Jewish Life and Law.* Hanover, N.H.: University Press of New England, 1999.

Wegner, Judith Romney. *Chattel or Person? The Status of Women in the Mishnah.* New York: Oxford University Press, 1988.

Weinberg, Yehiel Jacob. *Responsa Seridei Esh* (in Hebrew). Jerusalem: The Committee for Publication of Rabbi Weinberg's Writings, 1999.

Weinberg, Sydney Stahl. *The World of Our Mothers: The Lives of Jewish Immigrant Women.* Chapel Hill: The University of North Carolina Press, 1988.

Weiner, Kayla, and Arinna Moon, eds. *Jewish Women Speak Out: Expanding the Boundaries of Psychology.* Seattle: Canopy Press, 1995.

Weissman, Deborah. "Bais Yaacov: A Historical Model for Jewish Feminists." In *The Jewish Woman: New Perspectives,* edited by Elizabeth Koltun, 139–148. New York: Schocken Books, 1976.

Wertheimer, Jack, ed. *The American Synagogue: A Sanctuary Transformed.* New York: Cambridge University Press, 1987.

———. *Conservative Synagogues and Their Members.* New York: Jewish Theological Seminary, 1996.

Wieselthier, Leon. *Kaddish.* New York: A. Knopf, 1998.

Williams, Juanita H. *Psychology of Women: Behavior in a Biosocial Context.* 3d ed. New York: W. W. Norton, 1987.

Wilson, Josephine. *Biological Foundations of Human Behavior.* Pacific Grove, Calif.: Wadsworth, 2002.

Wittelson, Sandra, and Doreen Kimura. "Sex Differences in the Brain." *Scientific American* 267 (September 1992): 118–25.

Wolf, Naomi. *Misconceptions: Truth, Lies, and the Unexpected on the Journey to Motherhood.* New York: Doubleday, 2001.

Wolowelsky, Joel B. Letter to the Editor. *HaDarom* 57 (5748/1988): 157–58.

———. "A Quiet Berakha ['. . . Who Has Not Made Me a Woman'; Others Say]." *Tradition* 29 (1995): 61–68.

———. "Women and Kaddish." *Judaism* 44, no. 3 (summer 1995): 282–90.

———. "Women, Jewish Law and Modernity: New Opportunities in a Post-Feminist Age." *Emunah* (spring/summer 1997).

"Women Leadership Project Launched." *Forward,* 2 Nov. 2001.

Wurzburger, Walter. "Confronting the Challenge of the Value of Modernity." *Torah U'mada Journal* I (1989): 104–12.

Yezierska, Anzia. *Bread Givers.* New York: Persea Books, 1925.

Yosef, Ovadia. *Yabia omer* (in Hebrew). Jerusalem: Porat Yosef, 1963–1995.

———. *Yehaveh daat* (in Hebrew). Jerusalem: Makhon Ovadia, 1976–77.

Zaidman, Nurit. "Variations of Jewish Feminism: The Traditional, Modern, and Postmodern Approaches." *Modern Judaism* 16 (1996): 47–65.

Zakovitch, Yair. "The Woman's Rights in the Biblical Law of Divorce." *Jewish Law Annual* 14 (1981): 28–46.

Zeiger, Robin B. "Reflections on Infertility." In *Jewish Women Speak Out: Expanding the Boundaries of Psychology,* edited by Kayla Weiner and Arinna Moon, 77–98. Seattle: Canopy Press, 1995.

Zemer, Moshe, ed. *Evolving Halakhah: A Progressive Approach to Traditional Jewish Law.* Woodstock, Vt.: Jewish Lights, 1999.

Zevin, Shlomo Josef, ed. *Encyclopedia Talmudit* (in Hebrew). Jerusalem: Mosad Harav Kook, 1952.

Zinsser, Judith P. *History and Feminism: A Glass Half Full.* New York: Twayne Publishing, 1993.

Zivotofsky, Ari Z., and Naomi T. S. Zivotofsky. "What's Right with Women and Zimun." *Judaism* 42, no. 4 (fall 1993).

Zohar, Noam. "Women, Men and Religious Status: Deciphering a Chapter in Mishnah." In *Approaches to Ancient Judaism,* Vol. 5, edited by Herbert W. Basser and Simcha Fishbein, 33–54. Atlanta: Scholars Press, 1993.

Zohar, Zvi. "Traditional Flexibility and Modern Strictness: Two Halakhic Positions on Women's Suffrage." In *Sephardi and Middle Eastern Jewries,* edited by Harvey E. Goldberg, 119–33. Bloomington: Indiana University Press, 1996.

Zornberg, Avivah Gottleib. *Genesis: The Beginning of Desire.* Philadelphia, Pa.: Jewish Publication Society, 1995.

Index

Abortion and threat of barrenness, 59

Abraham, God's covenant with, 74–75

Abstinence, sexual, 40, 177n22

Adler, Rachel, 164

Adoption, 18, 186n13

Agency, women's traditional lack of, 50–51

Agricultural societies, overlap of public/private spheres in, 103–4

Akiva, Rabbi, 115, 116–17

America, gender role influences on Jewish immigrants, 7

Angel, R. Marc, 96

Aquinas, St. Thomas, 182n122

Arama, Isaac, 26–27, 59

Augustine, Saint, 78, 206–7n156

Authority and types of autonomy, 106–8, 182–83n137

Autonomy and community: autonomous ethical thinking vs. rabbinic mandate, 42, 43; and birth ritual for daughters, 106–8, 182–83n137; and contraception, 46–54, 57; and gender roles, 10–11; integration for women, 164–65; and kaddish by women, 124, 155–59; tensions in Reform Judaism, 143; women's autonomy in birth choice, 57, 68

Babylonian Talmud: on childbirth, 16–17, 24; circumcision and covenantal membership, 74; dates for composition of, 197n7; and kaddish origin, 114–15; male compliance with mitzvot as superior in value, 190n17; and sexual quality of woman's voice, 128–29; women's participation in funerals, 144, 145; and women's rights in public sphere, 170n32; women's sexuality vs. men's, 175–76nn37–38

Bachrach, R. Yair, 114, 118–20, 122, 123–24, 134–35

Bais Yaacov, 118

Baptism vs. circumcision, 78

Bat Mitzvah, Orthodox problems with, 113

Beauvoir, Simone de, 16, 71, 173n2

Be'er Heitev, 120

Benisch, Pearl, 118

Bereavement rituals for infant deaths, 67–68. See also *Kaddish* (mourning observance)

Berman, Saul J., 128

Biblical society: overlap of public/private spheres in, 103–4; and patrilineal descent, 75

Biblical text: call to social justice, 102; circumcision and covenantal membership, 73, 74; and companionship purpose of marriage, 40, 174–75n26; and female personhood beyond motherhood, 26–27; inclusiveness on gender roles, 19, 20–22, 23; lack of sexual essentialism in, 44; as superseding rabbinic literature, 200n49; universal ethical principles, 175n31; and wasting of seed prohibition, 30, 177n9; water immersion ceremonies, 84

Bioethics, Jewish, 177n15

Biology vs. culture: and gender roles, 2, 4, 16, 101; and male power over procreation, 21; and women's connection to nature, 9. See also Essentialist view of sex

Birnbaum *siddur* (prayerbook), 97–98

Birth: and essentialist view of gender roles, 44, 58–59; immigrant fatalism about, 63; male envy of, 46; women's autonomy in, 57; and women's private sphere, 44, 45, 182n124; and women's role in Jewish culture, 15–25, 192–93n60; women's status as bound to, 50–51. See also Fertility; Procreation; *Simhat bat* (birth ritual for daughters)

Birth control. *See* Contraception
Birth suppression vs. birth control, 41
Blair, R. Moshe Leib, 122, 123, 124,
 125–26, 134
Bokser, R. Ben Zion, 36–37
Book of Splendor, The, 144
Borowitz, Eugene B., 42–43
Bread Givers (Yezierska), 7
Bris Milah, 76
Brit banot (Covenant of Daughters). See
 Simhat bat (birth ritual for daughters)
Brit milah (covenant of circumcision),
 73–81, 82, 96, 101, 191n37
Buchwald, R. Ephraim, 151
Burial practices, 146–47, 206n153

Candle lighting, Shabbat, and women's
 religious obligations, 16
Cardin, Rabbi, 67
Care, ethics of, 107
Careers: and health effects of delays in
 childbearing, 37; need for integration
 with family life, 58, 61, 69, 104;
 women's vs. men's in Jewish commu-
 nity, 51
Caro, R. Joseph, 144, 145
Central Conference of American Rabbis,
 67
Challah and women's religious obliga-
 tions, 16
Chavot Yair (Bachrach), 114
Childbirth, women's right to, 24. *See also*
 Birth
Children: as carriers of culture, 56–57;
 and parental stresses, 63; responsibility
 for kaddish, 116, 117; sacred purpose
 of, 71. *See also* Procreation; *Simhat
 bat* (birth ritual for daughters)
Chodorow, Nancy, 52
Choosing a Sex Ethic: A Jewish Inquiry
 (Borowitz), 43
Christianity: vs. Judaism in Kantian phi-
 losophy, 48–49; opposition to circum-
 cision, 78
Circumcision, 73–81, 82, 96, 101,
 191n37

Cohabitation aspect of marriage. *See*
 Companionship aspect of marriage
Cohen, R. J. Simcha, 127–28
Cohen, Shaye, 77–79, 80
Commandments for all humans, 175n31.
 See also *Mitzvot;* Obligations,
 religious
Community: importance in Judaism,
 205–6n149; importance of family
 structure to, 57, 59, 63; origins of Jewish concept, 46–47; public prayer as
 connection to, 117; public vs. domestic, 7, 47; role of kaddish in, 114; sub-
 mersion of women's identity in, 156;
 and variations on autonomy, 106–7;
 women's role in, 10, 51, 158, 185n1.
 See also Autonomy and community;
 Individualism vs. collectivism
Companionship aspect of marriage: biblical source for, 40, 174–75n26; importance of, 27, 40, 185n5; and permission for contraceptive use, 31; and rule
 against abstinence, 177n22; and sexual
 activity without possibility of procreation, 39
Condoms and wasting of seed prohibition, 32
Conservative Judaism: birth rituals for
 daughters, 98–99; on contraception,
 36–38; feminism and democracy in,
 164–65; funeral practices, 143–47; and
 infertility, 65, 66, 67; on kaddish by
 women, 133–39; women in public
 sphere, 152–54
Conservative Judaism: The New Century
 (Sklare), 138
Context. *See* Historical context
Continuity of culture, gender roles in,
 55–57, 72, 116
Contraception: autonomy and community, 46–54, 57; as common in Jewish
 community, 63; Conservative perspectives, 36–38; and identity beyond
 motherhood, 26–27; and infertility, 64;
 Orthodox perspectives, 33–35; public
 and private spheres, 44–46; rabbinic

rulings on, 27–33; Reform perspectives, 37, 38–43; and women's exemption from procreation mitzvah, 24; and women's historical social status, 23
Covenantal membership for women, 73–81, 100–101
Covenant of Blood: Circumcision and Gender in Rabbinic Judaism (Hoffman), 75–76
Cultural issues: ancient vs. industrialized gender roles, 44–45, 103–4; and circumcision, 77; continuity of culture, 55–57, 72, 116; Jewishness as ethnically based vs. faith based, 78; and male as agent of procreation, 20–21; men vs. women as carriers of Jewish culture, 52, 101, 192–93n60; and origin of gender differences, 2–4, 16, 101; outside influences on Jewish culture, 1; overvaluation of public sphere, 45–46; and simhat bat ceremonies, 81–82; and transcendence of nature, 9. *See also* Patriarchy; Status, social
Custom vs. law: and birth rituals for girls, 84; in Conservative Judaism, 136–38; custom as superseding law, 132; and funerals, 145, 146; and gender roles, 105–6, 127, 153; and kaddish, 116, 126; Orthodox fears of change, 134–35, 154

Dangers to life: and childbirth obligation, 16, 18, 23; and contraceptive use, 27, 28, 29, 31–32, 36, 40, 57; and Rosner on contraception, 34
Daughters, birth rituals for. See *Simhat bat* (birth ritual for daughters)
Death rituals. See *Kaddish* (mourning observance)
Democratic principles and Judaism, 105, 163–65
Diaphragm, rabbinic literature on use of, 34–35
Diasporic vs. Israeli fertility rates, 59–60
Dinnerstein, Dorothy, 52
Divorce, 1, 24, 185n1

Eastern Europe, and women as successful business owners, 6–7
Economic power: and contraceptive use, 34, 36–37; and men's lack of domestic participation, 51; and tradition of women's independence, 6–7, 162–63; and women's historical social status, 23, 44–45
Education and postponement of childbearing, 63
Efrat program, 58–59
Egalitarianism in gender relations: and birth rituals for daughters, 85; in Conservative Judaism, 153; equal rights vs. equal participation, 104–5; vs. equity, 105–6; justice of, 19; and nurturing as valid for men and women, 157; in Reform Judaism, 154–55, 158–59
Eger, R. Akiva, 31–32
Eilberg-Schwartz, Howard, 75
Emotional disorders and contraception justification, 34–35
Epistemic autonomy, 49
Equity vs. egalitarianism, 105–6
Ervah (sexual incitement), woman's voice as, 128–31, 171n48
Essentialist view of sex: and birth role of women, 44, 58–59; diminishment of, 86; insupportability of, 162–63; and male as conquerer, 21–22; and male vs. female sex drives, 23–24; and Orthodox Judaism, 132, 151; and public/private gender roles, 148–50; and rabbinic literature, 8, 101
Ethic of virtue and religious vs. humanistic personal choice, 50. *See also* Morality
Ethnicity, Jewishness as, 78, 82–83, 113
Evil and sin, cause-and-effect relationship of, 16
Ezrat Nashim, 84

Family: feminism as threat to structure, 61–62, 102–3; gender transformation of attitudes, 52–53; importance in Jewish community, 57, 59, 63; need for